OMNIBUS

JIM CORBETT

SANAGE
PUBLISHING HOUSE

Paperback: 978-811900721-9
Hardcover: 978-811900722-6
eBook: 978-811900734-9

Printed by: Manipal Technologies Limited, Manipal

Sanage Publishing House LLP
Mumbai, India

sanagepublishing@gmail.com

Edward James Corbett CIE VD (25 July 1875 – 19 April 1955) was a British hunter, tracker, naturalist, and author who hunted a number of man-eating tigers and leopards in India. He held the rank of colonel in the British Indian Army and was frequently called upon by the Government of the United Provinces of Agra and Oudh, now the Indian states of Uttar Pradesh and Uttarakhand, to kill man-eating tigers and leopards that were preying on people in the nearby villages of the Kumaon-Garhwal Regions.

He authored **Man-Eaters of Kumaon**, Jungle Lore, and other books recounting his hunts and experiences, which enjoyed critical acclaim and commercial success. He became an avid photographer and spoke out for the need to protect India's wildlife from extermination.

CONTENTS

MAN EATERS OF KUMAON

THE MAN-EATING LEOPARD OF RUDRAPRAYAG

MY INDIA

Man Eaters of Kumaon

THE CHAMPAWAT MAN-EATER

I

I was shooting with Eddie Knowles in Malani when I first heard of the tiger which later received official recognition as the 'Champawat man-eater'.

Eddie, who will long be remembered in this province as a sportsman par excellence and the possessor of an inexhaustible fund of shikar yarns, was one of those few, and very fortunate, individuals who possess the best of everything in life. His rifle was without equal in accuracy and striking power and while one of his brothers was the best gunshot in India, another brother was the best tennis player in the Indian Army. When, therefore, Eddie informed me that his brother-in law, the best *shikari* in the world, had been deputed by the Government to shoot the Champawat man-eater, it was safe to assume that a very definite period has been put to the animal's activities.

The tiger, however, for some inexplicable reason, did not die, and was causing the Government a great deal of anxiety when I visited Nainital four years later. Rewards were offered, special *shikaris* employed, and parties of Gurkhas sent out from the depot in Almora. Yet, in spite of these measures, the toll of the human victims continued to mount alarmingly.

The tigress, for such the animal turned out to be, had arrived in Kumaon as a full-fledged man-eater, from Nepal, from whence she had been driven out by a body of armed Nepalese after she had killed two hundred human beings and during the four years, she had been operating in Kumaon had added two hundred and thirty-four to this number.

This is how matters stood, when shortly after my arrival in Nainital I received a visit from Berthoud. Berthoud, who was Deputy Commissioner of the Nainital at that time, and who after his tragic death now lies buried in an obscure grave in Haldwani, was a man who was loved and respected by all who knew him, and it is not surprising therefore that when he told me of the trouble that man- eater was giving the people of his district, and the anxiety it was causing him, he took my promise with him that I would start for Champawat immediately on receipt of news of the next human kill.

Two conditions I made, however: one that the Government rewards be cancelled, and the other, special *shikaris*, and regulars from Almora, be withdrawn. My reasons for making these conditions need no explanation for I am sure all sportsmen share my aversion to being classed as a reward hunter and are as anxious as I am to avoid the risk of being accidentally shot. These conditions were agreed to, and a week later Berthoud paid me an early morning visit and informed me that news had been brought in during the night by runners that a woman had been killed by the man-eater at Pali, a village between Dabidhura and Dhunaghat.

In anticipation of start at short notice, I had engaged six men to carry my camp kit, and leaving after breakfast, we did a march the first day seventeen miles to Dhari. Breakfasting at Mornaula next morning, we spent the night at Dabidhura, and arrived at Pali the following evening, five days after the woman had been killed.

The people of the village, numbering some fifty men, women and children, were in the state of abject terror, and though the sun was still up when I arrived, I found the entire population inside their homes behind locked doors, and it was not until my men had made a fire in the courtyard and I was sitting down to a cup of tea that a door here and there was cautiously opened, and the frightened inmates emerged.

I was informed that for five days no one had gone beyond their own doorsteps, the insanitary condition of the courtyard testified to the truth of this statement that food was running short, and that the people would starve if the tiger was not killed or driven away.

That the tiger was still in the vicinity was apparent. For three nights it had been heard calling on the road, distant a hundred yards from the houses, and that very day it had been seen on the cultivated land at the lower end of the village.

The Headman of the village very willingly placed a room at my disposal, but as there were eight of us to share it, and the only door it possessed opened on to the insanitary courtyard, I elected to spend the night in the open.

After a scratch meal which had to do duty for dinner, I saw my men safely shut into the room and myself took up a position on the side of the road, with my back to the tree. The villagers said the tiger was in the habit of perambulating along this road and as the moon was at full, I thought there was a chance of getting a shot provided I saw it first.

I had spent many nights in the jungle looking for game, but this was the first time I had ever spent a night looking for a man-eater. The length of road immediately in front of me was brilliantly lit by the moon, but to the right and left the overhanging trees cast dark shadows, and when the night wind agitated the branches and the shadow moved, I saw a dozen tigers advancing on me and bitterly regretted the impulse that had induced me to place myself at the man-eater's mercy. I was too frightened to carry out my self-imposed task, and with teeth chattering, as much from fear as from cold, I sat out the long night. As the grey dawn was lighting up the snowy range which I was facing, I rested my head on my drawn-up knees and it was in this position my men an hour later found me, fast asleep of the tiger I had neither heard nor seen anything.

Back in the village I tried to get the men, who I could see were very surprised I had survived the night to take me to the places where the people of the village had from time to time been killed but this they were unwilling to do. From the courtyard they pointed out the direction in which the kills had taken place; the last kill, the one that had brought me to the spot I was told, had taken place round the shoulder of the hill to the west village. The women and girls, some twenty in number, who had been out collecting oak leaves for the cattle when the unfortunate woman had been killed, were eager to give me details of the occurrence. It appeared that the party had set out two hours before midday and after going half a mile, had climbed into trees to cut leaves. The victim and two other women had selected a tree growing on the edge of a ravine, which I subsequently found was about four feet deep and ten to twelve feet wide. Having cut all the leaves she needed, the woman was climbing down from the tree when the tiger, who had approached unseen, stood up on its hind legs and caught her by the foot. Her hold was torn from the branch she was letting herself down by, and, pulling her into the ravine, the tiger released her foot and while she was struggling to rise, caught her by the throat. After killing her it sprang up the side of the ravine and disappeared with her into some heavy undergrowth.

All this had taken place a few feet from the two women on the tree and had been witnessed by the entire party. As soon as the tiger and its victim were out of sight, the terror-stricken women and girls ran back to the village. The men had just come in for their midday meal and, when all were assembled and armed with drums, metal cooking-pots anything intact that would produce a noise, the rescue party set off, the men leading and the women bringing up the rear.

Arrived at the ravine in which the woman had been killed, the very important question of 'what next?' was being debated when the tiger interrupted the proceedings by emitting a loud roar from the bushes thirty yards away. As one man, the party turned and fled helter-skelter back to the village. When breath had been regained, accusations were made against one another of having been the first to run and cause the stampede. Words ran high until it was suggested that if no one was afraid and all were as brave as they claimed to be, why not go back, and rescue the woman without loss of more time? The suggestion was adopted, and three times the party got as far as the ravine. On the third occasion the one man who was armed with a gun fired it off and brought the tiger roaring out of the bushes; after this the attempted rescue was very wisely abandoned. On my asking the gun man why he had not discharged his piece into the bushes instead of up into the air, he said the tiger was already greatly enraged and that if by any mischance he had hit it, it would undoubtedly have killed him.

For three hours that morning I walked round the village looking for tracks and hoping, and at the same time dreading, to meet the tiger. At one place in the dark heavily wooded ravine, while I was striking some bushes, a covey of *kalege* pheasants fluttered screaming out of them and I thought my heart had stopped beating for good.

My men had cleared a spot under a walnut tree for my meals, and after breakfast the Headman of the village asked me to mount guard while the wheat crop was being cut. He said that if the crop was not harvested in my presence, it would not be harvested at all, for the people were too frightened to leave their homes. Half an hour later the entire population of the village, assisted by men, were hard at work while I stood on guard with a loaded rifle. By evening the crop from five large fields had been garnered, leaving only two small patches close to the houses, which the Headman said he would have no difficulty in dealing with the next day.

The sanitary condition of the village had been much improved, and a second room for my exclusive use was placed at my disposal and that night, with thorn bushes securely wedged in the doorway to admit ventilation and exclude the man-eater, I made up for the sleep I had lost the previous night.

My presence was beginning to put new heart into the people, and they were moving about more freely, but I had not yet gained their confidence sufficiently to renew my request of being shown round the jungle, to which I attached some importance. These people knew every foot of the ground for miles round, and could, if they wished, show me where I was most likely to find the tiger, or in any case, where I could see its pugmarks. That the man-eater was a tiger was an established fact, but it was not known whether the animal was young or old, a male or a female, and this information, which I believed would help me to get in touch with it, I could only ascertain by examining its pugmarks.

After an early tea that morning, I announced that I wanted meat for my men and asked the villagers if they could direct me to where I could shoot a *ghooral* (mountain goat). The village was situated on the top of a long ridge running east and west; and just below the road on which I had spent the night the hill fell steeply away to the north in a series of grassy slopes; on these slopes I was told *ghooral* were plentiful, and several men volunteered to show me over the ground. I was careful not to show my pleasure at this offer and, selecting three men, I set out, telling the Headman that if I found the *ghooral* as plentiful as he said they were, I would shoot two for the village in addition to shooting one for my men.

Crossing the road, we went down a very steep ridge, keeping a sharp look out to right and left, but saw nothing. Half a mile down the hill the ravines converged, and from their junction was a good view of the rocky and grass-covered slope to the right. I had been sitting for some minutes, scanning the slope, with my back to a solitary pine which grew at this spot, when a movement high up on the hill caught my eye. When the movement was repeated, I saw it was a ghooral flapping its ears; the animal was standing in grass and only its head was visible. The men had not seen the movement, and as the head was now stationary and blended in with its surroundings it was not possible to point it out to them. Giving them a general idea of the animals' positions, I made them sit down and watch while I took a shot. I was armed with an old Martini Henry rifle, a weapon that atoned for its vicious kick by being dead accurate up to any range. The distance was as near 200 yards as made no matter and lying down and resting the rifles on a convenient pine root, I took careful aim and fired.

The smoke from the black powder cartridge obscured my view and the men said nothing had happened and that I had probably fired at the rock, or a bunch of dead leaves. Retaining my position, I reloaded the rifle and presently saw the grass, a little below where I had fired, moving and the hind quarters of the *ghooral* appeared. When the whole animal was free of the grass it started to roll over and over, gaining momentum as it came down the steep hill. When it was halfway down it disappeared into heavy grass and disturbed two *ghooral* that had been lying up there. Sneezing their alarm call, the two animals dashed out of the grass and went bounding up the hill. The range was shorter now and adjusting the leaf sight, I waited until the bigger of the two slowed down and put a bullet through its back, and as the other one turned and made off diagonally across the hill, I shot it through the shoulder.

On occasions one is privileged to accomplish the seemingly impossible. Lying in an uncomfortable position and shooting up to an angle of sixty degrees at a range of 200 yards at the small white mark on the *ghooral's* throat, there did not appear to be one chance in a million of the shot coming off and yet the heavy lead bullet driven by black powder had not been deflected by a hair's breadth and had gone true to its mark, killing the animal instantaneously. Again, on the steep hillside which was broken up by small ravines and jutting rocks, the dead animal had slipped and rolled straight to the spot where its two companions were lying up; and before it had cleared the patches of grass the two companions in their turn were slipping and rolling down the hill. As the three dead animals landed in the ravine in front of us it was amusing to observe the surprise and delight of the men who never before had seen a rifle in action. All thought of the man-eater was for the time being forgotten as they scrambled down into the ravine to retrieve the bag.

The expedition was a great success in more ways than one for in addition to providing a ration of meat for everyone, it gained the confidence of the entire village. Shikar yarns, as everyone knows, never lose anything in repetition, and while the *ghooral* were being skinned and divided up, the three men who had accompanied me gave full rein to their imagination, and from where I sat in the open, having breakfast, I could hear the exclamations of the assembled crowd when they were told that the *ghooral* had been shot at a range of over a mile, and that the magic bullets used had not only killed the animals like that but had also drawn them to the *sahib's* feet.

After the midday meal the Headman asked me where I wanted to go, and how many men I wished to take with me. From the eager throng of men who pressed round I selected two of my late companions, and with them to guide me set off to visit the scene of the last human tragedy.

The people of our hills are Hindus and cremate their dead, and when one of their number had been carried off by a man-eater it is incumbent on the relatives to recover some portion of the body for cremation even if it be only a few splinters of bone. In the case of this woman the cremation ceremony was yet to be performed, and as we started out, the relatives requested us to bring back any portion of the body we might find.

From early boyhood I have made a hobby of reading and interpreting jungle signs. In the present case I had the account of the eyewitnesses who were present when the woman was killed but eyewitnesses are not always reliable, whereas jungle signs are a true record of all that has transpired. On arrival at the spot a glance at the ground showed me that the tiger could only have approached the tree one way, without being seen, and that was up the ravine. Entering the ravine, a hundred yards below the tree, and working up, I found the pugmarks of the tiger in some fine earth that had shifted down between two big rocks; these pugmarks showed the animal to be a tigress, a little past her prime. Further up the ravine, and some ten yards from the tree, the tigress had lain down behind a rock, presumably to wait for the woman to climb down from the tree. The victim had been the first to cut all the leaves she needed, and as she was letting herself down by a branch some two inches in diameter the tigress had crept forward and, standing up on her hind legs, had caught the woman by the foot and pulled her down into the ravine. The branch showed the desperation with which the unfortunate woman had clung to it, for adhering to the rough oak bark where the branch and eventually the leaves, had slipped through her grasp were strands of skin which had been torn from the palms of her hands and fingers. Where the tigress had killed the woman there were signs of a struggle and a big patch of dried blood; from here the blood trail, now dry but distinctly visible, led across the ravine and up the opposite bank. Following the blood trail from where it left the ravine, we found the places in the bushes where the tigress had eaten her kill.

It is a popular belief that man-eaters do not eat the head, hands, and feet of the human victims. This is incorrect. Man-eaters, if not disturbed, eat everything including the blood-soaked clothes, as I found on one occasion; however, that is another story and will be told some other time.

On present occasion we found the woman's clothes and a few pieces of bone which we wrapped up in the clean cloth we had brought for the purpose. Pitifully little as these remains were, they would suffice for the cremation ceremony which would ensure the ashes of the high-caste woman reaching Mother Ganges.

After tea I visited the scene of yet another tragedy. Separated from the main village by the public road was a small holding of a few acres. The owner of this holding had built himself a hut on the hillside just above the road. The man's wife, and the mother of his two children, a boy and a girl aged four and six respectively, was the younger of two sisters. These two sisters were out cutting grass one day on the hill above the hut when the tigress suddenly appeared and carried off the elder sister. For a hundred yards the younger woman ran after the tigress to let her sister go and take her instead. This incredible act of heroism was witnessed by the people in the main village. After carrying the dead woman for a hundred yards the tigress put her down and turned on her pursuer. With a loud roar it sprang at the brave woman who, turning, raced down the hillside, across the road and into the village, evidently with the intention of telling the people what they, unknown to her, had already witnessed. The woman's incoherent noises were at the time attributed to loss of breath, fear and excitement and it was not until the rescue party that had set out with all speed had returned, unsuccessful, that it was found the woman had lost her power of speech. I was told this tale in the village and when I climbed the path to the two-roomed hut where the woman was engaged in washing clothes,' she had then been dumbed for twelve months.

Except for a strained look in her eyes the dumb woman appeared to be quite normal and, when I stopped to speak to her and tell her I had come to try and shoot the tiger that had killed her sister, she put her hands together and stooping down touched my feet, making me feel a wretched impostor. True, I had come with the avowed object of shooting the man-eater, but with an animal that had the reputation of never killing twice in the same locality, never returning to a kill, and whose domain extended over an area of many hundred square miles, the chance of my accomplishing my object was about as good as finding a needle in two haystacks.

Plans in plenty I had made way back in Nainital one I had already tried, and wild horses would not induce me to try it again, and the others, now that I was on the ground, were just as unattractive. Further there was no one I could ask for advice for this was the first man-eater that had ever been known in Kumaon and yet something would have to be done. So, for the next three days I wandered through the jungle from sunrise to sunset, visiting all the places for miles round where the villagers told me there was a chance of seeing the tigress.

I would like to interrupt my tale here for a few minutes to refute a rumour current throughout the hills that on this and on several subsequent occasions, I assumed the dress of a hill woman and, going into the jungle, attracted the man-eaters to myself and killed them with either a sickle or an axe. All I have ever done in the matter of alteration of dress has been to borrow a sari and with it draped round me cut grass, or climbed into trees and cut leaves, and in no case has the ruse proved successful; though on two occasions to my knowledge man-eaters have stalked the tree I was on, taking cover, on one occasion behind a rock and on the other behind a fallen tree and giving me no opportunity of shooting them.

To continue. As the tigress now appeared to have left this locality I decided, much to the regret of the people of Pali, to move to Champawat fifteen miles due east of Pali. Making an early start, I breakfasted at Dhunaghat and completed the journey to Champawat by sunset. The roads in this area were considered very unsafe, and men only moved from village to village or to the bazaars in large parties. After leaving Dhunaghat, my party of eight was added to by men from villages adjoining the road, and we arrived at Champawat thirty strong. Some of the men who joined me had been in a party of twenty men who had visited Champawat two months earlier, and they told me the following very pitiful story.

'The road for a few miles on this side of Champawat runs along the south face of the hill, parallel to, and about fifty yards above the valley. Two months ago, a party of twenty of us men were on our way to the bazaar at Champawat, and as we were going along this length of the road at about midday, we were startled by hearing the agonized cries of a human being coming from the valley below. Huddled together on the edge of the road we cowered in fright as these cries drew nearer and nearer, and presently into view came a tiger, carrying a naked woman. The woman's hair was trailing on the ground on one side of the tiger, and her feet on the other, the tiger was holding her by the small of the back and she was beating her chest and calling alternately on God and man to help her. Fifty yards from, and in clear view of us, the tiger passed with its burden, and when the cries had died away in the distance we continued on our way.'

'And you twenty men did nothing?'

'No, *sahib*, we did nothing for we were afraid, and what can men do when they are afraid? And further, even if we had been able to rescue the woman without angering the tiger and bringing misfortune on ourselves, it would have availed the woman nothing, for she was covered with blood and would of a surety have died of her wounds.'

I subsequently learned that the victim belonged to a village near Champawat and that she had been carried off by the tiger while collecting dry sticks. Her companions had run back to the village and raised an alarm, and just as a rescue party was starting, the twenty frightened men arrived. As these men knew the direction in which the tiger had gone with its victim, they joined the party and can best carry on the story.

'We were fifty or sixty strong when we set out to rescue the woman, and several of the party were armed with guns. A furlong from where the sticks collected by the woman were lying, and from where she had been carried off, we found her torn clothes. Thereafter the men started beating their drums and firing off their guns and, in this way, we proceeded for more than a mile right up to the head of the valley, where we found the woman, who was little more than a girl, lying dead on a great slab of rock. Beyond licking off all the blood and making her body clean the tiger had not touched her and there being no woman in our party, we men averted our faces as we wrapped her body in the loincloths which one and another gave, for she looked as she lay on her back as one who sleeps and would waken in shame when touched.'

With experiences such as these to tell and retell through the long night watches behind fast-shut doors, it is little wonder that the character and outlook on life of people living year after year in a man-eater country should change, and that one coming from the outside should feel that he had stepped right into a world of stark realities and the rule of the tooth and claw, which forced man in the reign of the saber-toothed tiger to shelter in dark caverns. I was young and unexperienced in those far-off Champawat days but even so, the conviction I came to after a brief sojourn in that stricken land, that there is no more terrible thing than to live and have one's been under the shadow of a man-eater, has been strengthened by thirty-two years' subsequent experience.

The Tahsildar of Champawat, to whom I had been given letters of introduction, paid me a visit that night at the Dak Bungalow where I was putting up, and suggested I should move next day to a bungalow a few miles away, in the vicinity of which many human beings had been killed.

Early next morning, accompanied by the Tahsildar, I set out for the bungalow; and while I was having breakfast on the verandah two men arrived with news that a cow had been killed by a tiger in a village ten miles away. The Tahsildar excused himself to attend to some urgent work at Champawat and said he would return to the bungalow in the evening and stay the night with me. My guides were good walkers, and as the track went downhill most of the way we covered the ten miles in record time. Arrived at the village I was taken to a cattle-shed in which I found a week-old calf, killed and partly eaten by a leopard. Not having the time or the inclination to shoot the leopard I rewarded my guides and retraced my steps to the bungalow. Here I found the Tahsildar had not returned, and as there was still an hour or more of daylight left, I went out with the chowkidar of the bungalow to look at a place where he informed me a tiger was in the habit of drinking; this place I found to be the head of the spring which supplied the garden with irrigation water. In the soft earth round the spring were tiger pugmarks several days old, but these tracks were quite different from the pugmarks I had seen, and carefully examined in the ravine in which the woman from Pali village had been killed.

On returning to the bungalow, I found the Tahsildar was back, and as we sat on the verandah, I told him of my day's experience. Expressing regret at my having had to go so far on a wild-goose chase, he rose, saying that as he had a long way to go, he must start at once. This announcement caused me no little surprise, for twice that day he had said he would stay the night with me. It was not the question of his staying the night that concerned me, but the risk he was taking; however, he was deaf to all my arguments and, as he stepped off the verandah into the dark night, with only one man following him carrying a smoky lantern which gave a mere glimmer of light, to do a walk of four miles in a locality in which men only moved in a target, parties in daylight, I took off my hat to a very brave man. Having watched him out of sight I turned and entered the bungalow.

I have a tale to tell of that bungalow, but I will not tell it here, for this is a book of jungle stories, and tales 'beyond the laws of nature' do not consort well with such stories.

II

I spent the following morning in going round the very extensive fruit orchard and tea garden and in having a bath at the spring, and at about midday the Tahsildar, much to my relief, returned safely from Champawat.

I was standing talking to him while looking down a long sloping hill with a village surrounded by cultivated land in the distance, when I saw a man leave the village and start up the hill in our direction. As the man drew nearer, I saw he was alternately running and walking, and was quite evidently the bearer of important news. Telling the Tahsildar I would return in a few minutes, I set off at a run down the hill, and when the man saw me coming, he sat down to take a breath. As soon as I was near enough to hear him, he called out, 'Come quickly, *sahib*, the man-eater had just killed a girl.' 'Sit still,' I called back and turning, ran up to the bungalow. I passed the news on to the Tahsildar while I was getting a rifle and some cartridges and asked him to follow me down to the village.

'The man who had come for me was one of those exasperating individuals whose legs and tongue cannot function at the same time. When he opened his mouth he stopped dead, and when he started to run, his mouth closed, so telling him to shut his mouth and lead the way, we ran in silence down the hill.

At the village an excited crowd of men, women and children awaited us and as usually happens on these occasions, all started to talk at the same time. One man was vainly trying to quieten the babel. I led him aside and asked him to tell me what had happened. Pointing to some scattered oak trees on a gentle slope a furlong or so from the village, he said a dozen people were collecting dry sticks under the trees when a tiger suddenly appeared and caught one of their number, a girl sixteen or seventeen years of age. The rest of the parties had run back to the village, and as it was known that I was staying at the bungalow, a man had immediately been dispatched to inform me.

The wife of the man I was speaking to had been of the party, and she now pointed out the tree, on the shoulder of the hill, under which the girl had been taken. None of the party had looked back to see if the tiger was carrying away its victim and, if so, in which direction it had gone. Instructing the crowd not to make a noise, and to remain in the village until I returned, I set off in the direction of the tree. The ground here was quite open, and it was difficult to conceive how an animal the size of the tiger could have approached twelve people unseen, its presence not detected, until attention had been attracted by the choking sound made by the girl.

The spot where the girl had been killed was marked by a pool of blood and near it, in vivid contrast to the crimson pool, was a broken necklace of brightly coloured blue beads which the girl had been wearing. From this spot the track led up and round the shoulder of the hill.

The track of the tigress was clearly visible. On one side of it were great splashes of blood where the girl's head had hung down, and on the other side the trail of her feet. Half a mile up the hill I found the girl's sari, and on the brow of the hill her skirt. Once again, the tigress was carrying a naked woman, but mercifully on this occasion her burden was dead.

On the brow of the hill the track led through a thicket of blackthorn, on the thorns of which long strands of the girl's raven-black hair had caught. Beyond this was a bed of nettles through which the tigress had gone, and I was looking for a way round this obstruction when I heard footsteps behind me. Turning round I saw a man armed with a rifle coming towards me. I asked him why he followed me when I had left instructions at the village that no one was to leave it. He said the Tahsildar had instructed him to accompany me, and that he was afraid to disobey orders. As he appeared determined to carry out his orders, and to argue the point would have meant the loss of valuable time, I told him to remove the heavy pair of boots he was wearing and, when he had hidden them under bush, I advised him to keep close to me, and to keep a sharp lookout behind.

I was wearing a very thin pair of stockings, shorts, and a pair of rubber-soled shoes, and as there appeared to be no way round the nettles I followed the tigress through them much to my discomfort.

Beyond the nettles the blood trail turned sharply to the left, and went straight down the very steep hill, which was densely clothed with bracken and ringals (Hill Bamboos). A hundred yards down, the blood trail led into a narrow and very steep watercourse, down which the tigress had gone with some difficulty, as could be seen from the dislodged stones and earth. I followed this watercourse for five or six hundred yards, my companion getting more and more agitated the further we went. A dozen times he caught my atm and whispered in a voice full of tears that he could hear the tiger, either on one side or the other, or behind us. Halfway down the hill we came on a great pinnacle of rock some thirty feet high, and as the man had by now had all the man-eater hunting, he could stand, I told him to climb the rock and remain on it until I returned. Very gladly he went up, and when he straddled the top and signaled to me that he was all right I continued on down the watercourse, which after skirting round the rock, went straight down for a hundred yards to where it met a deep ravine coming down from the left. At. the junction was a small pool and as I approached it, I saw patches of blood on my side of water.

The tigress had carried the girl straight down on this spot, and my approach had disturbed her at her meal. Splinters of bone were scattered round the deep pugmarks into which discoloured water was slowly seeping, and at the edge of the pool was an object which had puzzled me as I came down the watercourse, and which I now found was part of a human leg. In all the subsequent years I have hunted man-eaters, I have not seen anything as pitiful as that young comely leg bitten off a little below the knee as clean as though severed by the stroke of an axe out of which the warm blood was trickling.

While looking at the leg I had forgotten all about the tigress until I suddenly felt that I was in great danger. Hurriedly grounding the butt of the rifle, I put two fingers on the triggers raising my head as I did so and saw a little earth from the fifteen-foot bank in front of me, come rolling down the steep side and plop into the pool. I was new to this game of man-eater hunting, or I should not have exposed myself to an attack in the way I had done. My prompt action in pointing the rifle upwards had possibly saved my life and in stopping her spring or in turning to get away, the tigress had dislodged the earth from the top of the bank.

The bank was too steep for scrambling, and the only way of getting up was to take it at a run. Going up the watercourse a short distance I sprinted down, took the pool in my stride, and got far enough up the other side to grasp a bush and pull myself on to the bank. A bed of Strobilanthes, the bent stalks of which were slowly regaining their upright position, showed where, and how recently, the tigress had passed, and a little further on under an overhanging rock I found where she had left her kill when she came to have a look at me.

Her tracks now, as she carried away the girl led into the wilderness of rocks, some acres in extent, where the going was both difficult and dangerous. The cracks and chasms between the rocks were masked with ferns and blackberry vines, and a false step, which might easily have resulted in a broken limb, would have been fatal. Progress under these conditions was of necessity slow, and the tigress was taking advantage of it to continue her meal. A dozen times I found where she had rested and after each of these rests the blood trail became more distinct.

This was her four hundred and thirty-sixth human kill and she was quite accustomed to being disturbed at her meals by rescue parties but this, I think, was the first time she had been followed up so persistently and she now began to show her resentment by growling. To appreciate a tiger's growl to the full it is necessary to be situated as I then was rocks, all round with dense vegetation between, and the imperative necessity of testing each footstep to avoid falling headlong into unseen chasms and caves.

I cannot expect you who read this at your fireside to appreciate my feelings at the time. The sound of the growling and the expectation of an attack terrified me at the same time as it gave me hope. If the tigress lost her temper sufficiently to launch an attack, it would not only give me an opportunity of accomplishing the object for which I had come, but it would enable me to get even with her for all the pain and suffering she had caused.

The growling, however, was only a gesture, and when she found that instead of shooing me of it was bringing me faster on her heels, she abandoned it.

I had now been on her track for over four hours. Though I had repeatedly seen the undergrowth moving I had not seen so much as a hair of her hide, and a glance at the shadows climbing up the opposite hillside warned me it was time to retrace my steps if I was to reach the village before dark.

The late owner of the severed leg was a Hindu, and some portion of her would be needed for the cremation, so as I passed the pool, I dug a hole in the bank and buried the leg where it would be safe from the tigress and could be found when wanted.

My companion on the rock was very relieved to see me. My long absence, and the growling he had heard, had convinced him that the tigress had secured another kill and his difficulty, as he quite frankly admitted, was how he was going to get back to the village alone.

I thought when we were climbing down the watercourse that I knew of no more dangerous proceeding than walking in front of the nervous man carrying a loaded gun, but I changed my opinion when on walking behind him he slipped and fell, and I saw where the muzzle of his gun, a converted 450 without a safety catch was pointing. Since that day 'except when accompanied by Ibbotson, I have made it a hard and fast rule to go alone when hunting man-eaters for if one's companion is unarmed it is difficult to protect him, and if he is armed, it is even more difficult to protect oneself.

Arrived at the crest of the hill, where the man had hidden his boots, I sat down to have a smoke and think out my plans for the morrow.

The tigress would finish what was left of the kill during the night and would certainly lie among the rocks the next day.

On the ground she was on there was very little hope of my being able to stalk her, and if I disturbed her without getting a shot, she would probably leave the locality and I should lose touch with her.

A beat therefore was the only thing to do, provided I could raise sufficient men.

I was sitting on the south edge of the great Amphitheatre of hills, without a habitation of any kind in sight. A stream entering from the west had fretted its way down, cutting a deep valley right across the Amphitheatre. To the east the stream had struck solid rock and turning north had left the Amphitheatre by a narrow gorge.

The hill in front of me, rising to a height of some two thousand feet, was clothed in short grass with a pine tree dotted here and there, and the hill to the east was too precipitous for anything but a *ghooral* to negotiate. If I could collect sufficient men to man the entire length of the ridge from the stream to the precipitous hill, and get them to stir up the tigress, her most natural line of retreat would be through the narrow gorge.

Admittedly a very difficult beat, for the steep hillside facing north, on which I had left the tigress, was densely wooded and roughly three-quarters of a mile long and half-a-mile wide; however, if I could get the beaters to carry out instructions, there was a reasonable chance of my getting a shot.

The Tahsildar was waiting for me at the village. I explained the position to him and asked him to take immediate steps to collect as many men as he could, and to meet me at the tree where the girl had been killed at ten o'clock the following morning. Promising to do his best, he left for Champawat, while I climbed the hill to the bungalow.

I was up at the crack of dawn next morning, and after a substantial meal told my men to pack up and wait for me at Champawat and went down to have another look at the ground I intended beating. I could find nothing wrong with the plans I had made, and an hour before my time I was at the spot where I had asked the Tahsildar to meet me.

That he would have a hard time in collecting the men I had no doubt, for the fear of the man-eater had sunk deep into the countryside and more than mild persuasion would be needed to make the men leave the shelter of their homes. At ten o'clock the Tahsildar and one man turned up and thereafter the men came in twos, and threes and tens, until by midday two hundred and ninety-eight had collected.

The Tahsildar had let it be known that he would turn a blind eye towards all unlicensed firearms, and further that he would provide ammunition where required; and the weapons that were produced that day would have stocked a museum.

When the men were assembled and had received the ammunition they needed, I took them to the brow of the hill where the girl's skirt was lying, and pointing to a pine tree on the opposite hill that had been struck by lightning and stripped of bark, I told them to line themselves up along the ridge and, when they saw me wave a handkerchief from under the pine, those of them who were armed were to fire off their pieces, while the others beat drums, shouted, and rolled down rocks, and that no one was on any account to leave the ridge until I returned and personally collected him. When I was assured that all presents had heard and understood my instructions, I set off with the Tahsildar, who said he would be safer with me than with the beaters whose guns would probably burst and cause many causalities.

Making a wide detour I crossed the upper end of the valley; gained the opposite hill and made my way down to the blasted pine. From here the hill went steeply down and Tahsildar, who had on a thin pair of patent leather shoes, said it was impossible for him to go any further. While he was removing his inadequate footgear to ease his blisters, the men on the ridge, thinking I had forgotten to give the prearranged signal, fired off their guns and set up a great shout. I was still a hundred and fifty yards from the gorge, and that I did not break my neck a dozen times in covering this distance was due to my having been brought up on the hills and being in consequence as surefooted as a goat.

As I ran down the hill, I noticed that there was a patch of green grass near the mouth of the gorge, and as there was no time to look round for a better place, I sat down in the grass, with my back to the hill down which I had just come. The grass was about two feet high and hid half my body and if I kept perfectly still there was a good chance of my not being seen. Facing me was the hill that was being beaten, and the gorge that I hoped the tigress would make for was behind my left shoulder.

Pandemonium had broken loose on the ridge. Added to the fusillade of guns was the wild beating of drums and the shouting of hundreds of men, and when the din was at its worst, I caught sight of the tigress bounding down a grassy slope between two ravines to my right front, and about three hundred yards away. She had only gone a short distance when Tahsildar from his position under the pine let off both barrels of his shotgun. On hearing the shot's, the tigress whipped round and went straight back the way she had come and as she disappeared into thick cover, I threw up my rifle and sent a despairing bullet after her.

The men on the ridge, hearing the three shots, not unnaturally concluded that the tigress had been killed. They emptied all their guns and gave a final yell, and I was holding my breath and listening for the screams that would herald the tigress's arrival on the ridge, when she suddenly broke cover to my left front and, taking the stream at a bound, came straight for the gorge. The 500 modified cordite rifle, sighted at sea level, shot at this altitude, and when the tigress stopped dead, I thought the bullet had gone over her back, and that she had pulled up on finding her retreat cut off; as a matter of fact, I had hit her all right, but a little far back. Lowering her head, she half turned towards me, giving me a beautiful shot at the point of her shoulder at a range of less than thirty yards. She flinched at this second shot but continued, with her ears laid flat and bared teeth, to stand her ground, while I sat with rifle to shoulder trying to think what it would be best for me to do when she charged, for the rifle was empty and I had no more cartridges. Three cartridges were all that I had brought with me, for I never thought I should get a chance of firing more than two shots, and the third cartridge was for an emergency.

Fortunately, the wounded animal most unaccountably decided against a charge. Very slowly she turned, crossed the stream to her right, climbed over some fallen rocks, and found a narrow ledge that went diagonally up and across the face of the precipitous hill to where there was a great flat projecting rock. Where this rock joined the cliff, a small bush had found roothold and going up to it the tigress started to strip its branches. Throwing caution to the winds I shouted to the Tahsildar to bring me his gun. A long reply was shouted back, the only word which I caught was 'feet'. Laying down my rifle I took the hill at a run, grabbed the gun out of Tahsildar's hands and raced back.

As I approached the stream the tigress left the bush and came out on the protecting rock towards me. When I was within twenty feet of her, I raised the gun and found to my horror that there was a gap of about three-eighths of an inch between the barrels and the breechblock. The gun had not burst when both barrels had been tired, and would probably not burst now, but there was danger of being blinded by a blow back.

However, the risk would have to be taken, and, aligning the great blob of a bead that did duty as a sight on the tigress's open mouth, I tired. Maybe I bobbed, or maybe the gun was not capable of throwing the cylindrical bullet accurately for twenty feet; anyway, the missile missed the tigress's mouth and struck her on the right paw, from where I removed it later with my fingernails. Fortunately, she was at her last gasp, and the tap on the foot was sufficient to make her lurch forward. She came to rest with her head projecting over the side of the rock.

From the moment the tigress had broken cover in her attempt to get through the gorge I had forgotten the beaters, until I was suddenly reminded of their existence by hearing a shout, from a short distance up the hill, of 'There it is on the rock! Pull it down and let us hack it to bits.' I could not believe my ears when I heard 'hack it to bits', and yet I had heard a right, for others now had caught sight of the tigress and from all over the hillside the shout was being repeated.

The ledge by which the wounded animal had gained the projecting rock was fortunately on the opposite side from the beaters and was just wide enough to permit my shuffling along it sideways. As I reached the rock and stepped over the tigress hoping devoutly, she was dead for I had not had time to carry out the usual test of pelting her with stones the men emerged from the forest and came running across the open, brandishing guns, axes, rusty swords, and spears.

At the rock, which was twelve to fourteen feet in height, their advance was checked, for the outer face had been worn smooth by the stream when in space and afforded no foothold even for their bare toes. The rage of the crowd on seeing their dread enemy was quite understandable, for there was not a man among them who had not suffered at her hands. One man, who appeared demented and was acting as ringleader, was shouting over and over again as he ran to and from brandishing a sword, 'This is the shaitan[1] that killed my wife and my two sons.' As happens with crowds, the excitement died down as suddenly as it had flared up, and to the credit of the man who had lost his wife and sons be it said that he was the first to lay down his weapon. He came near to the rock and said, 'We were mad, sahib, when we saw our enemy, but the madness has now passed, and we ask you and the Tahsildar sahib to forgive us.' Extracting the unspent cartridge, I laid the gun across the tigress and hung it down by my hands

1 Devil

and was assisted to the ground. When I showed the men how I had gained the rock, the dead animal was very gently lowered and carried to an open spot, where all could crowd round and look at her.

When the tigress had stood on the rock looking down at me, I had noticed that there was something wrong with her mouth and on examining her now, I found that the upper and lower canine teeth on the right side of her mouth were broken, the upper one in half, and the lower one right down to the bone. This permanent injury to her teeth, the result of a gunshot wound had prevented her from killing her natural prey and had been the cause of her becoming a man-eater.

The men begged me not to skin the tigress there and asked me to let them have her until nightfall to carry through their villages, saying that if their womenfolk and children did not see her with their own eyes, they would not believe that their dreaded enemy was dead.

Two saplings were now cut and laid one on either side of the tigress, and with *pugrees*, waistbands and loincloths she was carefully and very securely lashed to them. When all was ready the saplings were manned and we moved to the foot of the precipitous hill; the men preferred to take the tigress up this hill, on the far side of which their villages lay, to going up the densely wooded hill which they had just beaten. Two human ropes were made by the simple expedient of the man behind taking a firm grip of the waistband or other portion of clothing of the man in front of him. When it was considered that the ropes were long and strong enough to stand the strain, they attached themselves to the saplings and with men on either side to hold the feet of the bearers and give them a foothold, the procession moved up the hill, looking for all the world like an army of ants carrying a beetle up the face of a wall. Behind the main army was a second and a smaller one, the Tahsildar being carried up. Had the ropes broken at any stage of that thousand-foot climb, the casualties would have been appalling, but the rope did not break. The men gained the crest of the hill and" set off eastwards, singing on their triumphal march, while the Tahsildar and I turned west and made for Champawat.

Our way lay along the ridge and once again I stood among the blackthorn bushes on the thorns of which long tresses of the girl's hair had caught, and for the last time looked down into the Amphitheatre which had been the scene of our recent exploit.

On the way down the hill the beaters had found the head of the unfortunate girl, and a thin column of smoke rising straight up into the still air from the mouth of the gorge showed where the relations were performing the last rites of the Champawat man-eater's last victim on the very spot on which the man-eater had been shot.

After dinner, while I was standing in the courtyard of the tahsil, I saw a long procession of pine torches winding its way down the opposite hillside, and presently the chanting of a hill song by a great concourse of men was borne up on the still night air. An hour later, the tigress was laid down at my feet.

It was difficult to skin the animal with so many people crowding round and to curtail the job I cut the head and paws from the trunk and left them adhering to the skin, to be dealt with later. A police guard was then mounted over the carcass, and next day, when all the people of the countryside were assembled, the trunk, legs, and tail of the tigress were cut up into small pieces and distributed. These pieces of flesh and bone were required for the lockets which hill children wear around their necks; and the addition of a piece of tiger to the other potent charms is credited with giving the wearer courage, as well as immunity from the attacks of wild animals. The fingers of the girl which the tigress had swallowed whole were sent to me in spirits by the Tahsildar and were buried by me in the Nainital lake close to the Nandadevi temples.

While I had been skinning the tigress the Tahsildar and his staff, assisted by the Headmen and greybeards of the surrounding villages and merchants of the Champawat bazzar, had been busy drawing up a programme for a great feast and dance for the morrow, at which I was to preside. Round about midnight, when the last of the great throng of men had left with shouts of delight at being able to use roads and village paths that the man-eater had closed for four years, I had a final smoke with the Tahsildar, and telling him that I could not stay any longer and that he would have to take my place at the festivities, my men and I set off on our seventy-five mile journey, with two days in hand to do it in.

At sunrise I left my men and, with the tigress's skin strapped to the saddle of my horse, rode on ahead to put in a few hours in cleaning the skin at Dabidhura, where I intended spending the night. When passing the hut on the hill at Pali it occurred to me that it would be some little satisfaction to the dumb woman to know that her sister had been avenged, so leaving the horse to browse, he had been bred near the snowline and could eat anything from oak trees to nettles. I climbed the hill to the hut and spread out the skin with the head supported on a stone facing the door. The children of the house had been round-eyed spectators of these proceedings and, hearing me talking to them, their mother, who was inside cooking, came to the door.

I am not going to hazard any theories about shock and counter shock, for I know nothing of these matters. All I know is that this woman, who was alleged to have been dumb a twelvemonth and who four days previously had made no attempt to answer any questions, was now running backwards and forwards from the hut to the road calling to her husband and the people in the village to come quickly and see what the *sahib* had brought. This sudden return of speech appeared greatly to mystify the children, who could not take their eyes off their mother's face.

I rested in the village while a dish of tea was being prepared for me and told the people who thronged round how the man-eater had been killed. An hour later I continued my journey and for half a mile along my way I could hear the shouts of goodwill of the men of Pali.

I had a very thrilling encounter with a leopard the following morning, which I only mention because it delayed my start from Dabidhura and put an extra strain on my small mount and myself. Fortunately, the little pony was as strong on his legs as he was tough inside, and by holding his tail on the upgrades, riding him on the flat and running behind him on the downgrades, we covered the forty-five miles to Nainital between 9 a.m. and 6 p.m.

At a durbar held in Nainital a few months later Sir John Hewett, Lieutenant-Governor of the United Provinces, presented the Tahsildar of Champawat with a gun and the man who accompanied me when I was looking for the girl with a beautiful hunting-knife, for the help they had given me. Both weapons were suitably engraved and will be handed down as heirlooms in the respective families.

ROBIN

I never saw either of his parents. The Knight of the Broom, I purchased him from said he was a spaniel, that his name was Pincha and that his father was a 'keen gun dog'. This is all I can tell you about his pedigree.

I did not want a pup, and it was quite by accident that I happened to be with a friend when the litter of seven was decanted from a very filthy basket for her inspection. Pincha was the smallest and the thinnest of the litter, and it was quite evident that he had reached the last ditch in his tight for survival. Leaving his little less miserable brothers and sisters, he walked once round me, and then curled himself up between my big feet. When I picked him up and put him inside my coat, it was a bitterly cold morning, he tried to show his gratitude by licking my face and I tried to show him I was not aware of his appalling stench.

He was rising for three months then, and I bought him for fifteen rupees. He is rising thirteen years now and all the gold in India would not buy him.

When I got him home and he had made his first acquaintance with a square meal, warm water, and soap, we scrapped his kennel name of Pincha, and rechristened him Robin, in memory of a faithful old collie who had saved my young brother aged four and myself, aged six, from the attack of an infuriated she-bear.

Robin responded to regular meals as parched land does to rain, and after he had been with us for a few weeks, acting on the principle that a boy's and a pup's training cannot be started too early, I took him out one morning, intending to get a little away from him and fire a shot or two to get him used to the sound of gunfire.

At the lower end of our estate there are some dense thorn bushes, and while I was skirting round them a peafowl got up, and forgetting all about Robin, who was following at heel, I brought the bird fluttering down. It landed in the thorn bushes and Robin dashed in after it. The bushes were too thick and thorny for me to enter them, so I ran round to the far side where beyond the bushes was open ground, and beyond that again heavy tree and grass jungle which I knew the wounded bird would make for. The open ground was flooded with morning sunlight and if I had been armed with a movie camera, I should have had an opportunity of securing a unique picture. The peafowl, an old hen, with neck feathers stuck out at right angles, and one wing broken, was making for the tree jungle, while Robin with stern to the ground, was hanging on to her tail and being dragged along. Running forward, I very foolishly caught the bird by the neck and lifted it clear of the ground, whereon it promptly lashed out with both legs, and sent Robin heels-over-head. In a second he was up and, on his feet, again and when I laid the dead bird down, he danced round it, making little dabs alternately at its head and tail. The lesson was over for that morning, and as we returned home it would have been difficult to say which of us was the prouder Robin, at bringing home his first bird, or I, at having picked a winner out of a filthy basket. The shooting season was now drawing to a close, and for the next few days Robin was not given anything larger than quail, cloves, and an occasional partridge to retrieve.

We spent the summer on the hills, and on our annual migration to the foothills in November at the end of a long fifteen-mile march as we turned a sharp corner, one of a big troop of *langurs (Entellus* monkeys) jumped off the hillside and crossed the road a few inches in front of Robin's nose. Disregarding my whistle, Robin dashed down the khudside after the langur, which promptly sought safety in a tree. The ground was open with a few trees here and there, and after going steeply down for thirty or forty yards flattened out for a few yards, before going sharply down into the valley below. On the right-hand side of this flat ground there were a few bushes, with a deep channel scoured out by rainwater running through them. Robin had hardly entered these bushes when he was out again, and with ears laid back and tail tucked in was running for dear life, with an enormous leopard bounding after him and gaining on him at every bound. I was unarmed and all the assistance I could render was to 'Ho' and 'Har' at the full extent of my lungs. The men carrying M.'s *dandy* joined in lustily, the pandemonium reaching its climax when the hundred or more *langurs* added their alarm calls in varying keys. For twenty-five or thirty yards the desperate and unequal race continued, and just as the leopard was within reach of Robin, it unaccountably swerved and disappeared into the valley, while Robin circled round a shoulder of the hill and rejoined us on the road. Two very useful lessons Robin learned from his hairbreadth escape, which he never in his afterlife forgot. First, that it was dangerous to chase *langurs*, and second that the alarm call of a *langur* denoted the presence of a leopard.

Robin resumed his training where it had been interrupted in spring, but it soon became apparent that his early neglect and starvation had affected his heart, for he fainted now after the least exertion.

There is nothing more disappointing for a gun dog than to be left at home when his master goes out, and as bird-shooting was now taboo for Robin, I started taking him with me when I went out after big game. He took to this new form of sport as readily as a duck takes to water, and from then on has accompanied me whenever I have been out with a rifle.

The method we employ is to go out early in the morning, pick up the tracks of a leopard or tiger, and follow them. When the pugmarks can be seen, I do the tracking, and when the animal we are after takes to the jungle, Robin does the tracking. In this way we have on occasions followed an animal for miles before coming up with it.

When shooting on foot, it is very much easier to kill an animal outright than when shooting down on it from a machan, or from the back of an elephant. For one thing, when wounded animals have to be followed up on foot, chance shots are not indulged in, and for another, the vital parts are more accessible when shooting on the same level as the animal than when shooting down on it. However, even after exercising the greatest care over the shot, I have sometimes only wounded leopards and tigers, who have rampaged round before being quietened by a second or third shot, and only once during all the years that we have shot together has Robin left me in a tight corner. When he rejoined me after his brief absence that day, we decided that the incident was closed and would never be referred to again, but we are older now and possibly less sensitive, anyway Robin who has exceeded the canine equivalent of three score years and ten and who lies at my feet as I write on a bed, he will never again leave has with a smile from his wise brown eyes and a wag of his small stump of a tail given me permission to go ahead and tell you the story.

We did not see the leopard until it stepped clear of the thick undergrowth and came to a stand, looked back over its left shoulder.

He was an outsized male with a beautiful dark glossy coat, the rosettes on his skin standing out like clear-cut designs on a rich velvet ground. I had an unhurried shot with an accurate rifle at his right shoulder, at the shot range of fifteen yards. By how little I missed his heart makes no matter, and while the bullet was kicking up the dust fifty yards away, he was high in the air and turning a somersault, landed in the thick undergrowth he had a minute before left. For twenty, forty, fifty yards we heard him crashing through the cover, and then the sound ceased as abruptly as it had begun. This sudden cessation of sound could be accounted for in two ways: either the leopard had collapsed and died in his tracks, or fifty yards away he had reached open ground.

We had walked far that day; the sun was near setting, and we were still four miles from home. This part of the jungle was not frequented by man,' and there was not one chance in a million of anyone passing that way by night, and last, and the best reason of all for leaving the leopard, M. was unarmed, and could neither be left alone nor taken along to follow up the wounded animal, so we turned to the north and made for home. There was no need for me to mark the spot, for I had walked through these jungles by day and often by night for nearly half a century and could have found my way blindfolded to any part of them.

Night had only just given place today the following morning when Robin, who had not been with us the previous evening and I arrived at the spot I had fired from. Very warily Robin, who was leading, examined the ground where the leopard had stood, and then raising his head and sniffing the air, he advanced to the edge of the undergrowth where the leopard, in falling, had left great splashes of blood. There was no need for me to examine the blood to determine the position of the wound, for at the short range I had fired at I had seen the bullet strike, and the spurt of dust on the far side was proof that the bullet had gone right through the leopard's body.

It might be necessary later on to follow up the blood trail, but just at present a little rest after our four-mile walk in the dark would do no harm and might on the other hand prove of great value to us. The sun was near rising, and at that early hour of the morning all the jungle folk were on the move, and it would be advisable to hear what they had to say on the subject of the wounded animal before going further.

Under a nearby tree, I found a dry spot to which the saturating dew had not penetrated, and with Robin stretched out at my feet, had finished my cigarette when a chital hind and then a second and a third, started calling some sixty yards to our left front. Robin sat up and slowly turning his head looked at me, and, on catching my eye, as slowly turned back in the direction of the calling deer. He had travelled far along the road of experience since the day he had first heard the alarm call of a langur and he knew now, as did every bird and animal within hearing that the chital were warning the jungle folk of the presence of a leopard.

From the manner in which the *chital* were calling it was evident that the leopard was in full view of them. A little more patience and they would tell us if he was alive. They had been calling for about five minutes when suddenly, and all together, they called once and again, and then settled down to their regular call; the leopard was alive and had moved and was now quiet again. All that we needed to know now was the position of the leopard and this information we could get by stalking the *chital*.

Moving down-wind for fifty yards we entered the thick undergrowth and started to stalk the deer not a difficult task for Robin can move through any jungle as silently as a cat, and long practice has taught me where to place my feet. The *chital* were not visible until we were within a few feet of them. They were standing in the open and looking towards the north in the exact direction, as far as I was able to judge, in which the crashing sound of the evening before had ceased.

Up to this point, the chital had been of great help to us; they had told us the leopard was lying out in the open and that it was alive, and they had now given us the direction. It had taken us the best part of an hour to acquire this information, and if the *chital* now caught sight of us and warned the jungle folk of our presence, they would in one second undo the good they had so far done. I was debating whether it would be better to retrace our steps and work down below the calling deer and try to get a shot from behind them or move them from our vicinity by giving the call of a leopard, when one of the hinds turned her head and looked straight into my face. Next second, with a cry of 'Ware man', they dashed away at top speed. I had only about five yards to cover to reach the open ground, but quick as I was the leopard was quicker, and I was only in time to see his hind quarters and tail disappearing behind some bushes. The *chital* had very effectively spoilt my chance of a shot, and the leopard would now have to be located and marked down all over again, this time by Robin.

I stood on the open ground for some minutes, to give the leopard time to settle down and the scent he had left in his passage to blow past us, and then took Robin due west across the track of the wind, which was blowing from the north. We had gone about sixty or seventy yards when Robin, who was leading, stopped, and turned to face into the wind. Robin is mute in the jungles and has wonderful control over his nerves. There is one nerve, however, running down the back of his hind legs, which he cannot control when he is looking at a leopard, or when the scent of a leopard is warm and strong. This nerve was now twitching and agitating the long hair on the upper part of his hind legs.

A very violent cyclonic storm had struck this part of the forest the previous summer, uprooting a number of trees; it was towards one of these fallen trees, forty yards from where we were standing, that Robin was now looking the branches were towards us and on either side of the trunk there were light bushes and a few scattered tufts of short grass.

At any other time, Robin and I would have made straight for our quarry but on this occasion a little extra caution was advisable. Not only were we dealing with an animal who when wounded knows no fear, but in addition we were dealing with a leopard who had had fifteen hours in which to nurse his grievance against man, and who could in consequence be counted on to have all his fighting instincts thoroughly aroused.

When leaving home that morning I had picked up the .275 rifle I had used the previous evening. A good rifle to carry when miles have to be covered, but not the weapon one would select to deal with a wounded leopard; so instead of a direct approach, I picked a line that would take us fifteen yards from, and parallel to, the fallen tree. Step by step, Robin leading, we moved along this line, and had passed the branches and were opposite the trunk when Robin stopped.

Taking the direction from him, I presently saw what had attracted his attention the tip of the leopard's tail slowly raised, and as slowly lowered the warning a leopard invariably gives before charging. Pivoting to the right on my heels, I had just got the rifle to my shoulder when the leopard burst through the intervening bushes and sprang at us. My bullet, fired more with the object of deflecting him than with any hope of killing or even hitting him, passed under his belly and went through the fleshy part of his left thigh. The crack of the rifle, more than the wound, had the effect of deflecting the leopard sufficiently to make him pass my right shoulder without touching me and before I could get in another shot, he disappeared into the bushes beyond.

Robin had not moved from my feet, and together we now examined the ground the leopard had passed over. Blood, we found in plenty but whether it had come from the old wounds torn open by the leopard's violent exertions, or from my recent shot, it was impossible to say. Anyway, it made no difference to Robin who without a moment's hesitation took up the trail. After going through some very heavy cover, we came on knee-high undergrowth and had proceeded about a couple of hundred yards when I saw the leopard get up in front of us, and before I could get the rifle to bear on him, he disappeared under a lantana bush. This bush with its branches resting on the ground was as big as a cottage tent, and in addition to affording the leopard ideal cover gave him all the advantages for launching his next attack.

Robin and I had come very well out of our morning's adventure, and it would have been foolish now, armed as I was to pursue the leopard further so without more ado we turned about and made for home.

Next morning, we were back on the ground. From a very early hour Robin had been agitating to make a start, and, ignoring all the interesting smells the jungle holds in the morning, would have made me do the four miles at a run had that been possible.

I had armed myself with a 450/400 and was in consequence feeling much happier than I had done the previous day. When we were several hundred yards from the lantana bush, I made Robin slow down and advance cautiously, for it is never safe to assume that wounded animal Will be found where it has been left hours previously, as. the following regrettable incident shows.

A sportsman of my acquaintance wounded a tiger one afternoon and followed the blood trail for several miles along a valley. Next morning, accompanied by a number of men, one of whom was carrying his empty rifle and leading the way, he set out intending to take up the tracking where he had left off. His way led over the previous day's blood trail, and while still a mile from the spot where the tiger had been left, the leading man, who incidentally was the local shikari, walked on to the wounded tiger and was killed. The rest of the party escaped some by climbing trees and others by showing a clean pair of heels.

I had marked the exact position of the lantana bush, and now took Robin along a line that would pass a few yards on the lee side of it. Robin knew all that was worth knowing about this method of locating the position of an animal by cutting across the wind, and we had only gone a short distance, and were still a hundred yards from the bush, when he stopped, turned, and faced into the wind, and communicated to me that he could smell the leopard. As on the previous day, he was facing a fallen tree which was lying along the edge of, and parallel to, the thick undergrowth through which we had followed the leopard to the lantana bush after he had charged us. On our side of the tree the ground was open, but on the far side there was a dense growth of waist-high basonta bushes. Having signaled to Robin to carry on along our original line, we went past the lantana bush, in which he showed no interest, to a channel washed out by rainwater. Here, removing my coat, I filled it with as many stones as the stitches would hold and with this improvised sack slung over my shoulder returned to the open ground near the tree.

Resuming my coat, and holding the rifle ready for instant use, I took up a position fifteen yards from the tree and started throwing the stones, first on to the tree and then into the bushes on the far side of it with the object of making the leopard assuming he was still alive charge on to the open ground where I could deal with him. When all my ammunition was exhausted, I coughed, clapped my hands, and shouted, and neither during the bombardment nor after it did the leopard move or make any sound to indicate that he was alive.

I should now have been justified in walking straight up to the tree and looking on the far side of it but remembering an old jungle saying, 'It is never safe to assume that a leopard is dead until it he has been skinned', I set out to circle round the tree, intending to reduce the size of the circle until I could see right under the branches and along the whole length of the trunk. I made the radius of the first circle about twenty-five yards and had gone two-thirds of the way round when Robin stopped. As I looked down to see what had attracted his attention, there was a succession of deep-throated, angry grunts, and the leopard made straight for us. All I could see was the undergrowth being violently agitated in a direct line towards us, and I only just had time to swing half right and bring the rifle up, when the head and shoulders of the leopard appeared out of the bushes a few feet away.

The leopard's spring and my shot were simultaneous and sidestepping to the left and leaning back as far as I could. I fired the second barrel from my hip into his side as he passed me.

When a wounded animal, be he leopard or tiger, makes a headlong charge and fails to contact he invariably carries on and does not return to the attack until he is again disturbed.

I had side-stepped to the left to avoid crushing Robin and when I looked down for him now, he was nowhere to be seen. For the first time in all the years we had hunted together we had parted company in a tight corner, and he was now probably trying to find his way home, with very little chance of being able to avoid the many dangers that lay before him in the intervening four miles of jungle. Added to the natural dangers he would have to face in the jungle with which, owing to its remoteness from home, he was not familiar, was the weak condition of his heart. And it was therefore with very great misgivings that I turned about to go in search of him; as I did so, F caught sight of his head projecting from behind a tree trunk at the edge of a small clearing only a hundred yards away. When I raised my hand and beckoned, he disappeared into the undergrowth, but a little later, with drooped eyes and drooping ears, he crept silently to my feet. Laying down the rifle I picked him up in my arms and, for the second time in his life, he licked my face telling me as he did so, with little throaty sounds, how glad he was to find me unhurt, and how terribly ashamed he was of himself for having parted company from me.

Our reactions to the sudden and quite unexpected danger that had confronted us were typical of how a canine and a human being act in an emergency, when the danger that threatens is heard, and not seen. In

Robin's case it had impelled him to seek safety in a silent and rapid retreat, whereas in my case it had the effect of gluing my feet to the ground and making retreat rapid or otherwise impossible.

When I had satisfied Robin that he was not to blame for our temporary separation, and his small body had stopped trembling, I put him down and together we walked up to where the leopard, who had put up such a game fight, and had so nearly won the last round, was lying dead.

I have told you the story, and while I have been telling it, Robin the biggest-hearted and the most faithful friend man ever had, has gone to the Happy Hunting Grounds, where I know I shall find him waiting for me.

THE CHOWGARH TIGERS

I

The map of Eastern Kumaon that hangs on the wall before me is marked with a number of crosses, and below each cross is a date. These crosses indicate the locality, and the date, of the officially recorded human victims of the man-eating tiger of Chowgarh. There are sixty-four crosses on the map. I do not claim this as being a correct tally, for the map was posted up by me for two years and during this period all kills were not reported to me; further, victims who were only mauled, and who died subsequently, have not been awarded a cross and a date.

HUMAN BEINGS KILLED BY THE CHOWGARH MAN-EATER

Village	Number
THALI	1
DEBGURA	1
BARHON	2
CHAMOLI	6
KAHOR	1
AM	2
DALKANIA	7
LOHAR	8
AGHAURA	2
PAHARPANI	1
PADAMPURI	2

Village	Number
TANDA	1
NESORIYA	1
I HANGAON	1
KABRAGAON	1
KALAAGAR	8
RIKHAKOT	1
MATELA	3
KUNDAL	3
BABYAR	1
KHANSIUN	1
GARGARI	1
HAIRAKHAN	2
UKHALDHUNGA	1
PAKHARI	1
DUNGARI	2
GALNI	3
TOTAL	64

ANNUAL TOTALS

1926	15 KILLED
1927	9 KILLED
1928	14 KILLED
1929	17 KILLED
1930	9 KILLED
TOTAL	64

The first cross is dated 15 December 1925 and the last, 21 March 1930. The distance between the extreme crosses, north to south, is fifty miles, and east to west, thirty miles, an area of 1,500 square miles of mountain and vale where the snow lies deep during winter, and the valleys are scorching hot in summer. Over this area the Chowgarh tiger had established a reign of terror. Villages of varying size, some with a population of hundred or more, and others with only a small family or two, are scattered throughout the area. Footpaths, beaten hard by bare feet, connect the villages. Some of these paths pass through thick forests, and when a man-eater renders their passage dangerous, inter-village communication is carried on by shouting. Standing on a commanding point, maybe a big rock or the roof of a house, a man cooees to attract the attention of the people in a neighbouring village and when the cooee is answered, the message is shouted across in a high-pitched voice. From village to village the message is tossed and is broadcast throughout large areas in an incredibly short space of time.

It was at a District Conference in February 1929 that I found myself committed to having a try for this tiger. There were at that time three man-eaters in the Kumaon division, and as the Chowgarh tiger had done most damage I promised to go in pursuit of it first.

The map with the crosses and date, furnished to me by the Government, showed that the man-eater was most active in the villages on the north and east face of the Kala Agar ridge. This ridge, some forty miles in length, rises to a height of 8,500 feet and is thickly wooded along the crest. A forest road runs along the north face of the ridge, in some places passing for miles through dense forest of oak and rhododendron, and in others forming a boundary between the forest and cultivated lands. In one place the road forms a loop, and in this loop is situated the Kala Agar Forest Bungalow. This Bungalow was my objective, and after a four days' march, culminating in a stiff climb of 4,000 feet, I arrived at it one evening in April 1929. The last human victim in this area was a young man of twenty-two, who had been killed while out grazing cattle, and while I was having breakfast, the morning after my arrival, the grandmother of the young man came to see me.

She informed me that the man-eater had without any provocation, killed the only relative she had in the world. After giving me her grandson's history from the day he was born and extolling his virtues, she pressed me to accept her three milch buffaloes to use as a bait for the tiger, saying that if I killed the tiger with the help of her buffaloes, she would have the satisfaction of feeling that she had assisted in avenging her grandson. These full-grown animals were of no use to me but knowing that refusal to accept them would give offence, I thanked the old lady and assured her I would draw on her for bait as soon as I had used up the four young male buffaloes, I had brought with me from Nainital. The Headmen of the nearby villages had now assembled, and from them I learned that the tiger had last been seen ten days previously in a village twenty miles away, on the eastern slope of the ridge, where it had killed and eaten a man and his wife.

A trail ten days old was not worth following up, and alter a long discussion with the Headmen, I decided to make for Dalkania village on the eastern side of the ridge. Dalkania is ten miles from Kala Agar and about the same distance from the village where the man and his wife had been killed.

From the number of crosses Dalkania and the villages adjoining it had earned, it appeared that the tiger had its headquarters in the vicinity of these villages.

After breakfast next morning I left Kala Agar and followed the forest road, which I informed would take me to the end of the ridge, where I should have to leave the road and take a path two miles downhill to Dalkania. This road, running right to the end of the ridge through dense forest was very little used and examining it for tracks as I went along, I arrived at the point where the path took off at about 2 p.m. Here I met a number of men from Dalkania. They had heard via the cooee method of communication, of my intention of camping at their village and had come up to the ridge to inform me that the tiger had that morning attacked a party of women, while they had been cutting their crops in a village ten miles to the north of Dalkania.

The men carrying my camp equipment had done eight miles and were quite willing to carry on but on learning from the villagers that the path of this village ten miles away was very rough and ran through dense forest, I decided to send my men with the villagers to Dalkania and visit the scene of the tiger's attack alone. My servant immediately set about preparing a substantial meal for me, and at 3 p.m., having fortified myself, I set out on my ten-mile walk. Ten miles under favourable conditions is a comfortable two and a half hours' walk, but here the conditions were anything but favourable. The trace running along the east face of the hill wound in and out through deep ravines and was bordered alternately by rocks, dense undergrowth, and trees and when every obstruction capable of concealing sudden death in the form of a hungry man-eater, had to be approached with caution, progress was of necessity slow. I was still several miles from my objective when the declining day warned me it was time to call a halt.

In any other area, sleeping under the stars on a bed of dry leaves would have ensured a restful night, but here, to sleep on the ground would have been to court death in a very unpleasant form. Long practice in selecting a suitable tree, and the ability to dispose myself comfortably in it, has made sleeping up aloft a simple matter. On this occasion I selected an oak tree and with the rifle tied securely to a branch, had been asleep for some hours when I was awakened by the rustling of several animals under the tree. The sound moved on, and presently I heard the scraping of claws on bark and realized that a family of bears were climbing some *karphal* (Karphal is found on our hills at an elevation of 6,000 feet. The tree grows to a height of about forty feet and produces a small red and very sweet berry, which is greatly fancied by both human beings and bears.) trees I had noticed growing a little way down the hill side. Bears are very quarrelsome when feeding and sleeping was impossible until they had eaten their fill and moved on.

The sun had been up a couple of hours when I arrived at the village, which consisted of two huts, and a cattle-shed in a clearing of five acres surrounded by forest. The small community was in a state of terror and was overjoyed to see me. The wheatfield, a few yards from the huts, where the tiger, with belly to ground, had been detected only just in time, stalking the three women cutting the crop, was eagerly pointed out to me. The "man who had seen the tiger, and given the alarm, told me that the tiger had retreated into the jungle, where it had been joined by a second tiger and that the two animals had gone down the hill side into the valley below. The occupants of the two huts had no sleep, for the tigers, baulked of their prey, had called at short intervals throughout the night and had only ceased calling a little before my arrival. This statement, that there were two tigers, confirmed the reports I had already received that the man-eater was accompanied by a full-grown cub.

Our hill folks are very hospitable, and when the villagers learned that I spent the night in the jungle, and that my camp was at Dalkania, they offered to prepare a meal for me. This I knew would strain the resources of the small community, so I asked for a dish of tea, but as there was no tea in the village. I was given a drink of fresh milk sweetened to excess with jaggery, a very satisfying and not unpleasant drink when one gets used to it. At the request of my hosts, I mounted guard while the remaining portion of the wheat crop was cut and at midday, taking the good wishes of the people with me, I went down into the valley in the direction in which the tigers had been heard calling.

The valley, starting from the watershed of the three rivers Ladhya, Nandhour and Eastern Goula, runs south-west for twenty miles and is densely wooded. Tracking was impossible and my only hope of seeing the tigers was to attract them to myself or helped by the jungle folk to stalk them.

To those of you who may be inclined to indulge in the sport of man- eater hunting on foot, it will be of interest to know that the birds and animals of the jungle, and the four winds of heaven, play a very important part in this form of sport. This is not the place to give the name of the jungle folk on whose alarm calls the sportsman depends, to a great extent, for his safety and knowledge of his quarry's movements for in a country in which a walk up or downhill of three or four miles might mean a difference in altitude of as much as a thousand feet, the variation in fauna, in a well-stocked area, is considerable. The wind, however, at all altitudes, remains a constant factor and a few words relevant to its importance in connexion with man-eater hunting on foot will not be out of place.

Tigers do not know that human beings have no sense of smell, and when a tiger becomes a man-eater, it treats human beings exactly as it treats wild animals, that is, it approaches its victims up-wind, or lies up in wait for them down-wind.

The significance of this will be apparent when it is realized that while the sportsman is trying to spot the tiger, the tiger is in all probability trying to stalk the sportsman or is lying up in wait for him. This contest, owing to the tiger's height, colouring and ability to move without making a sound, would be very unequal were it not for the wind-factor operating in favour of the sportsman.

In all cases where killing is done by stalking or stealth, the victim is approached from behind. This being so, it would be suicidal for the sportsman to enter the dense jungle in which he had every reason to believe a man-eater was lurking, unless he was capable of making full use of the currents of air. For example, assuming that the sportsman has to proceed, owing to the nature of the ground, in the direction from which the wind is blowing, the danger would lie behind him, where he would be least able to deal with it, but by frequently tracking across the wind he could keep the danger alternately to right and left of him. In print this scheme may not appear very attractive but in practice it works; and, short of walking backwards, I do not know of a better or safer method of going up-wind through dense cover in which a hungry man-eater is lurking.

By evening I had reached the upper end of the valley, without having seen the tigers and without having received any indication from a bird or animal of their presence in the jungle. The only habitation then in sight was a cattle-shed, high up on the north side of the valley.

I was careful in the selection of a tree on this second night and was rewarded by an undisturbed night's rest. Not long after dark the tigers called and a few minutes later two shots from a muzzle-loader came echoing down the valley, followed by a lot of shouting from the graziers at the cattle station. Thereafter the night was silent.

By the afternoon of the following day, I had explored every bit of the valley, and I was making my way up a grassy slope intent on rejoining my men at Dalkania when I heard a long drawn out cooee from the direction of the cattle-shed. The cooee was repeated once and again, and on my sending back an answering call I saw a man climb on a projecting rock, and from this vantage point he shouted across the valley to ask if I was the *sahib* who had come from Nainital to shoot the man-eater. On my telling him I was that *sahib*, he informed me that his cattle had stampeded out of a ravine on my side of the valley at about midday, and that when he counted them on arrival at the cattle-station he found that one, a white cow, was missing.

He suspected that the cow had been killed by the tigers he had heard calling the previous night, half a mile to the west of where I was standing. Thanking him for his information, I set off to investigate the ravine. I had gone but a short distance along the edge of the ravine when I came on the tracks of the stampeding cattle and following these tracks back, I had no difficulty in finding the spot where the cow had been killed. After killing the cow, the tigers had taken it down the steep hillside into the ravine. An approach along the drag was not advisable, so going down into the valley I made a wide detour and approached the spot where I expected the kill to be from the other side of the ravine. This side of the ravine was less steep than the side down which the kill had been taken and was deep in young bracken ideal ground for stalking over. Step by step, and as silently as a shadow, I made my way through the bracken, which reached above my waist and when I was some thirty yards from the bed of the ravine a movement in front of me caught my eye. A white leg was suddenly thrust up into the air and violently agitated, and the next moment there was a deep-throated growl, the tigers were on the kill and were having a difference of opinion over some toothful morsel.

For several minutes I stood perfectly still; the leg continued to be agitated, but the growl was not repeated. A nearer approach was not advisable, for even if I succeeded in covering the thirty yards without being seen, and managed to kill one of the tigers, the other, as likely as not, would blunder into me, and the ground I was on would give me no chance of defending myself. Twenty yards to my left front, and about the same distance from the tigers, there was an outcrop of rock, some ten to fifteen feet high. If I could reach this rock without being seen, I would in all probability get an easy shot at the tigers. Dropping on hands and knees, and pushing the rifle before me, I crawled through the bracken to the shelter of the rocks, paused a minute to regain my breath and make quite sure the rifle was loaded, and then climbed the rock. When my eyes were level with the top, I looked over and saw the two tigers.

One was eating at the hind quarters of the cow, while the other was lying nearby licking its paws. Both tigers appeared to be about the same size, but the one that was licking its paws was several shades lighter than the other; and concluding that her light colouring was due to age and that she was the old man-eater, I aligned the sights very carefully on her, and fired. At my shot she reared up and fell backwards, while the other bounded down the ravine and was out of sight before I could press the second trigger. The tiger I had shot did not move again, and after pelting it with stones to make sure it was dead, I approached and met with a great disappointment: for a glance at close quarters showed me I had make a mistake and shot the cub, a mistake that during the ensuing twelve months cost the district fifteen lives and incidentally nearly cost me my own life.

Disappointment was to a certain extent mitigated by the thought that this young tigress, even if she had not actually killed any human beings herself, had probably assisted her old mother to kill (this assumption I later found to be correct), and in any case, having been nurtured on human flesh she could save my feelings be classified as a potential man-eater.

Skinning a tiger with assistance on open ground and with the requisite appliances is an easy job, but here the job was anything but easy, for I was alone, surrounded by thick cover and my only appliance was a penknife and though there was no actual danger to be apprehended from the man-eater for tigers never kill in excess of their requirements, there was the uneasy feeling in the back of my mind that the tiger had returned and was watching my every movement.

The sun was near setting before the arduous task was completed, and as I should have spent yet another night in the jungles I decided to remain where I was. The tigress was a very old animal, as I could see from her pugmarks, and having lived all her life in a district in which there are nearly as many firearms as men to use them, had nothing to learn about men and their ways. Even so, there was just a chance that she might return to the kill some time during the night and remain in the vicinity until light came in the morning.

My selection of a tree was of necessity limited and the one I spent that night in proved, by morning, to be the most uncomfortable tree I have ever spent twelve hours in. The tigress called at intervals throughout the night, and as morning drew near the calling became fainter and fainter, and eventually died away on the ridge above me.

Cramped, and stiff, and hungry, I had been without food for sixty hours and with my clothes clinging to me, it had rained for an hour during the night. I descended from the tree when objects were clearly visible, and, after tying the tiger's skin up in a coat, set off for Dalkania.

I have never weighed a tiger's skin when green, and if the skin, plus the head and paws, which I carried for fifteen miles that day weighed 40 pounds at the start, I would have taken my oath it weighed 200 pounds before I reached my destination.

In a courtyard, flagged with great slabs of blue slate, and common to a dozen houses, I found my men in conference with a hundred or more villagers. My approach, along a yard-wide lane between two houses, had not been observed, and the welcome I received when, bedraggled and covered with blood, I staggered into the circle of squatting men will live in my memory as long as memory lasts.

My 40-lb. tent had been pitched in a field of stubble a hundred yards from the village, and I had hardly reached it before tea was laid out for me on a table improvised out of a couple of suitcases and borrowed from the village. I was told later by the villagers that my men, who had been with me for years and had accompanied me on several similar expeditions, refusing to believe that the man-eater had claimed me as a victim, had kept a kettle on the boil night and day in anticipation of my return, and, further, had stoutly opposed the Headmen of Dalkania and the adjoining villages sending a report to Almora and Naini Tal that I was missing.

A hot bath, taken of necessity in the open and in full view of the village, I was too dirty and too tired to care who saw me was followed by an ample dinner, and I was thinking of turning in for the night when a flash of lightning succeeded by a loud peal of thunder heralded the approach of a storm. Tent-pegs are of little use in a field, so long stakes were hurriedly procured and securely driven into the ground, and to these stakes the tent-ropes were tied. For further safety all the available ropes in camp were crisscrossed over the tent and lashed to the stakes. The storm of wind and rain lasted an hour and was one of the worst the little tent had ever weathered. Several of the guy-ropes were torn from the canvas, but the stakes and crisscross ropes held. Most of my things were soaked through, and a little stream several inches deep was running from end to end of the tent; my bed, however, was comparatively dry, and by 10 o'clock my men were safely lodged behind locked doors in the house the villagers had placed at their disposal, while I, with a loaded rifle for company, settled down to a sleep which lasted for twelve hours.

The following day was occupied in drying my kit and in cleaning and pegging out the tiger's skin. While these operations were in progress, the villagers, who had taken a holiday from their field work, crowded round to hear my experiences and to tell me theirs. Every man present had lost one or more relatives and several bore tooth and claw marks, inflicted by the man-eater, which they will carry to their graves. My regret at having lost an opportunity of killing the man-eater was not endorsed by the assembled men.

True, there had originally been only one man-eater but of recent months, rescue parties who had gone out to recover the remains of human victims had found two tigers on the kill and only a fortnight previously a man and his wife had been killed simultaneously, which was proof sufficient for them that both tigers were established man-eaters.

My tent was on a spur of the hill and commanded an extensive view. Immediately below me was the valley of the Nandhour river, with a hill, devoid of any cultivation, rising to a height of 9,000 feet on the far side. As I sat on the edge of the terraced fields that evening with a pair of good binoculars in my hand and the Government map spread out beside me, the villagers pointed out the exact positions where twenty human beings had been killed during the past three years. These kills were more or less evenly distributed over an area of forty square miles.

The forests in this area were open to grazing, and on the cattle-paths leading to them I decided to tie up my four young buffaloes.

During the following ten days no news was received of the tigress, and I spent the time visiting the buffaloes in the morning, searching the forests in the day, and tying out the buffaloes in the evening. On the eleventh day my hopes were raised by the report that a cow had been killed on a ravine on the hill above my tent. A visit to the kill, however, satisfied me the cow had been killed by an old leopard, whose pugmarks I had repeatedly seen. The villagers complained that the leopard had for several years been taking a heavy toll of their cattle and goats, so I decided to sit up for him. A shallow cave close to the dead cow gave me the cover I needed. I had not been long in the cave when I caught sight of the leopard coming down the opposite side of the ravine, and I was raising my rifle for a shot when I heard a very agitated voice from the direction of the village calling to me.

There could be but one reason for this urgent call, and grabbing up my hat I dashed out of the cave, much to the consternation of the leopard, who first flattened himself out on the ground, and then with an angry woof went bounding back the way he had come, while I scrambled up my side of the ravine and arriving at the top, shouted to the man that I was coming and set off at top speed to join him.

The man had run all the way uphill from the village, and when he regained his breath, he informed me that a woman had just been killed by the man-eater, about half a mile on the far side of the village. As we ran down the hillside, I saw a crowd of people collected in the courtyard already alluded to. Once again, my approach through the narrow lane was not observed, and looking over the heads of the assembled men, I saw a girl sitting on the ground.

The upper part of her clothing had been torn off her young body, and with head thrown back and hands resting on the ground behind to support her, she sat without sound or movement, other than the heaving up and down of her breast, in the hollow of which the blood, that was flowing down her face and neck, was collecting in a sticky congealed mass.

My presence was soon detected, and a way made for me to approach the girl. While I was examining her wounds, a score of people, all talking at the same time, informed me that the attack on the girl had been made on comparatively open ground in full view of a number of people including the girl's husband; that alarmed at their combined shouts the tiger had left the girl and gone off in the direction of the forest; that leaving the girl for dead where she had fallen, her companions had run back to the village to inform me; that subsequently the girl had regained consciousness and returned to the village; that she would without doubt die of her injuries in a few minutes; and that they would then carry her back to the scene of the attack, and I could sit up over the corpse and shoot the tiger.

While this information was being imparted to me the girl's eyes never left my face and followed my every movement with the liquid pleading gaze of a wounded and frightened animal. Room to move unhampered, quiet to collect my wits, and clean air for the girl to breathe were necessary and I am afraid the methods I employed to gain them were not as gentle as they might have been. When the last of the men had left in a hurry, I set the women, who up to now had remained in the background, to warming water and to tearing my shirt, which was comparatively clean and dry, into bandages, while one girl, who appeared to be on the point of getting hysterics, was bundled off to scour the village for a pair of scissors. The water and bandages were ready before the girl I had sent for the scissors returned with the only pair, she said, the village could produce. They had been found in the house of a tailor, long since dead, and had been used by the widow for digging up potatoes. The rusty blades, some eight inches long, could not be made to meet at any point, and after a vein attempt, I decided to leave the thick coils of blood-caked hair alone.

The major wounds consisted of two claw cuts, one starting between the eyes and extending right over the head and down to the nape of the neck, leaving the scalp hanging in two halves, and the other, starting near the first, running across the forehead up to the right ear. In addition to these ugly gaping wounds there were a number of deep scratches on the right breast, right shoulder, and neck and one deep cut on the back of the right hand, evidently inflicted when the girl had put up her hand in a vain attempt to shield her head. A doctor friend whom I had once taken out tiger-shooting on foot had, on our return after an exciting morning, presented me with a two-ounce bottle of yellow fluid which he advised me to carry whenever I went out shooting. I had carried the bottle in the inner pocket of my shooting jacket for over a year and a portion of the fluid had evaporated; but the bottle was still three-parts full, and after I had washed the girl's head and body. I knocked the neck off the bottle and poured the contents, to the last drop, into the wounds. This done I bandaged the head, to try to keep the scalp in position, and then picked up the girl and carried her to her home, a single room combining living quarters, a kitchen and a nursery with the women following behind.

Slung from a rafter near the door was an open basket, the occupant of which was now clamouring to be fed. This was a complication with which I could not deal, so I left the solution of it to the assembled women. Ten days later, when on the eve of my departure I visited the girl for the last time, I found her sitting on the doorstep of her home with the baby asleep in her lap.

Her wounds, except for a sore at the nape of her neck where the tiger's claws had sunk deepest into the flesh, were all healed, and when parting her great wealth of raven-black hair to show me where the scalp had made a perfect join, she said, with a smile, that she was very glad her young sister had quite by mistake borrowed the wrong pair of scissors from the tailor's widow (for a shorn head here is the sign of widowhood). If these lines should ever be read by my friend, the doctor, I should like him to know that the little bottle of yellow fluid he so thoughtfully provided for me, saved the life of a very brave young mother.

While I had been attending to the girl my men had procured a goat. Following back the blood trail made by the girl I found the spot where the attack had taken place and tying the goat to a bush I climbed into a stunted oak, the only tree in the vicinity and prepared for an all-night vigil. Sleep, even in snatches, was not possible because my seat was only a few feet from the ground, and the tigress was still without her dinner.

However, I neither saw nor heard anything throughout the night. On examining the ground in the morning, I had not had time to do this the previous evening, I found that the tigress, after attacking the girl, had gone up the valley for half a mile to where a cattle track crossed the Nandhour river. This track it had followed for two miles to its junction with the forest road on the ridge above Dalkania. Here on the hard ground, I lost the tracks.

For two days the people in all the surrounding villages kept as close to their habitations as the want of sanitary conveniences permitted, and then on the third day news was brought to me by tour runners that the man-eater had claimed a victim at Lohali, a village five miles to the south of Dalkania. The runners stated that the distance by the forest road was ten miles but only five by a short cut by which they proposed taking me back. My preparations were soon made, and a little after midday I set off with my four guides.

A very stiff climb of two miles brought us to the crest of the long ridge south of Dalkania and in view of the valley three miles below; where the 'kill' was reported to have taken place. My guides could give me no particulars. They lived in a small village a mile on the near side of Lohali and at 10 a.m. a message had come to them in the manner already described that a woman of Lohali had been killed by the man-eater and they were instructed to convey this information to me at Dalkania.

The top of the hill on which we were standing was bare of trees, and while I regained my breath and had a smoke, my companions pointed out the landmarks. Close to where we were resting, and under the shelter of a great rock, there was a small, ruined hut, with a circular thorn enclosure nearby. Questioned about this hut, the men told me the following story. Four years previously a Bhutia (a man from across the border), who had all the winter been sending packages of gur, salt, and other commodities from the bazaars at the foothills into the interior of the district, had built the hut with the object of resting and fattening his flock of goats through the summer and rains, and getting them fit for the next winter's work. After a few weeks the goats wandered down the hill and damaged my informants' crops, and when they came up to lodge a protest, they found the hut empty, and the fierce sheepdog these men invariably keep with them to guard their camps at night, chained to an iron stake and dead. Foul play was suspected, and the next day men were collected from adjoining villages and a search organized. Pointing to an oak tree scored by lightning and distant some four hundred yards, my informants said that under it the remains of the man, his skull and a few splinters of bone and his clothes had been found. This was the Chowgarh man-eater's first human victim.

There was no way of descending the precipitous hill from where we were sitting, and the men informed me we should have to proceed half a mile along the ridge to where we should find a very steep and rough track which would take us straight down, past their village, to Lohali, which we could see in the valley below. We had covered about half the distance we had to go along the ridge, when all at once and without being able to ascribe any reason for it, I felt we were being followed. Arguing with myself against this feeling was of no avail; there was only one man-eater in all this area, and she had procured a kill three miles away which she was not likely to leave. However, the uneasy feeling persisted, and as we were now at the widest part of the grassy ridge, I made the men sit down, instructing them not to move until I returned and myself set out on a tour of investigation. Retracing my steps to where we had first come out on the ridge, I entered the jungle and carefully worked round the open ground and back to where the men were sitting. No alarm call of animal or bird indicated that a tiger was anywhere in the vicinity, but from there on I made the four men walk in front of me, while I brought up the rear, with thumb on safety catch and a constant lookout behind.

When we arrived at the little village my companions had started from, they asked for permission to leave me. I was very glad of this request, for I had a mile of dense scrub jungle to go through, and though the feeling that I was being followed had long since left me, I felt safer and more comfortable with only my own life to guard. A little below the outlying terraced fields, and where the dense scrub started, there was a crystal-clear spring of water, from which the village drew its water supply. Here in the soft wet ground, I found the fresh pugmarks of the man-eater.

These pugmarks, coming from the direction of the village I was making for, coupled with the uneasy feeling I had experienced on the ridge above, convinced me that something had gone wrong with the 'kill' and that my quest would be fruitless. As I emerged from the scrub jungle, I came in view of Lohali, which consisted of five or six small houses. Near the door of one of these houses a group of people were gathered.

My approach over the steep open ground and narrow terraced fields was observed, and a few men detached themselves from the group near the door and advanced to meet me. One of the numbers, on old man, bent down to touch my feet, and with tears streaming down his cheeks implored me to save the life of his daughter. His story was as short as it was tragic. His daughter, who was a widow and the only relative he had in the world, had gone out at about ten o'clock to collect dry sticks with which to cook their midday meal. A small stream flows through the valley and on the far side of the stream from the village the hill goes steeply up. On the lower slope of this hill there are a few terraced fields. At the edge of the lowest field, and distant about 150 yards from the home, the woman had started to collect sticks. A little later, some women who were washing their clothes in the stream heard a scream, and on looking up saw the woman and a tiger disappearing together into the dense thorn bushes, which extended from the edge of the field right down to the stream. Dashing back to the village, the women raised an alarm. The frightened villagers made no attempt at a rescue, and a message for help was shouted to a village higher up the valley, from where it was tossed back to the village from which the four men had set out to find me. Half an hour after the message had been sent, the wounded woman crawled home. Her story was that she had seen the tiger just as it was about to spring on her and as there was no time to run, she had jumped down the almost perpendicular hillside and while she was in the air the tiger had caught her and they had gone clown the hill together. She remembered nothing further until she regained consciousness and found herself near the stream; and being unable to call for help, she had crawled back to the village on her hands and knees.

We had reached the door of the house while this tale was being told. Making the people stand back from the door, the only opening in the four walls of the room. I drew the bloodstained sheet off the woman, whose pitiful condition I am not going to attempt to describe. Had I been a qualified doctor, armed with modern appliances, instead of just a mere man with a little permanganate of potash in his pocket, I do not think it would have been possible to have saved the woman's life; for the deep tooth and claw wounds in her face, neck and other parts of her body had, in that hot unventilated room, already turned septic. Mercifully she was only semi-conscious. The old father had followed me into the room and more for his satisfaction than for any good I thought it would do, I washed the caked blood from the woman's head and body and cleaned out the wounds as best I could with my handkerchief and a strong solution of permanganate.

It was now too late to think of returning to my camp, and a place would have to be found in which to pass the night. A little way up the stream and not far from where the women had been washing their clothes, there was a giant pipal tree, with a foot-high masonry platform round it used by the villagers for religious ceremonies.

I undressed on the platform and bathed in the stream; and when the wind had carried out the functions of a towel, dressed again, put my back to the tree and, laying the loaded rifle by my side, prepared to see the night out. Admittedly it was an unsuitable place in which to spend the night, but any plate was preferable to the village, and that dark room, with its hot fetid atmosphere and swarm of buzzing flies, where a woman in torment fought desperately for breath.

During the night the wailing of women announced that the sufferer's troubles were over, and when I passed through the village at daybreak, preparations for the funeral were well advanced.

From the experience of this unfortunate woman, and that of the girl at Dalkania, it was now evident that the old tigress had depended, to a very great extent, on her cub to kill the human beings she attacked. Usually only one out of every hundred people attacked by man-eating tigers' escapes but in the case of this man-eater it was apparent that more people would be mauled than killed outright, and as the nearest hospital was fifty miles away, when I returned to Nainital I appealed to Government to send a supply of disinfectants and dressings to all the headmen of villages in the area in which the man-eater was operating. On my subsequent visit I was glad to learn that the request had been complied with, and that the disinfectants had saved the lives of a number of people.

I stayed at Dalkania for another week and announced on a Saturday that I would leave for home the following Monday. I had now been in the man-eater's domain for close to a month, and the constant strain of sleeping in an open tent, and of walking endless miles during the day with the prospect of every step being the last, was beginning to tell on my nerves. The villagers received my announcement with consternation, and only desisted from trying to make me change my decision when I promised them, I would return at the first opportunity.

After breakfast on Sunday morning the Headman of Dalkania paid me a visit and requested me to shoot them some game before I left. The request was gladly acceded to, and half an hour later, accompanied by four villagers and one of my own men, and armed with a 275 rifle and a clip of cartridges, I set off for the hill on the far side of the Nandhour river, on the upper slopes of which I had, from my camp, frequently seen *ghooral* feeding.

One of the villagers accompanying me was a tall gaunt man with a terribly disfigured face. He had been a constant visitor to my camp and finding in me a good listener had told and retold his encounter with the man-eater so often that I could, without effort, repeat the whole story in my sleep. The encounter took place four years previously and is best told in his own words.

'Do you see that pine tree, *sahib*, at the bottom of the grassy slope on the shoulder of the hill? Yes, the pine tree with a big white rock to the east of it. Well, it was at the upper edge of the grassy slope that the man-eater attacked me. The grassy slope is as perpendicular as the wall of a house, and none but a hillman could find foothold on it. My son, who was eight years of age at the time, and I had cut grass on that slope on the day of my misfortune, carrying the grass up in armfuls to the belt of trees where the ground is level.

'I was stooping down at the very edge of the slope, tying the grass into a big bundle, when the tiger sprang at me and buried its teeth, one under my right eye, one in my chin and the other two here at the back of my neck. The tiger's mouth struck me with a great blow, and I fell over on my back, while the tiger lay on top of me chest to chest, with its stomach between my legs. When falling backwards I had flung out my arms and my right hand had come in contact with an oak sapling. As my fingers grasped the sapling, an

idea came to me. My legs were free, and if I could draw them up and insert my feet under and against the tiger's belly, I might be able to push the tiger off, and run away. The pain, as the tiger crushed all the bones on the right side of my face, was terrible; but I did not lose consciousness, for you see, *sahib*, at that time I was a young man, and in all the hills there was no one to compare with me in strength. Very slowly, so as not to anger the tiger, I drew my legs up on either side of it, and gently inserted my bare feet against its belly. Then placing my left hand against its chest and pushing and kicking upwards with all my might, I lifted the tiger right off the ground and, we are being on the very edge of the perpendicular hillside, the tiger went crashing down and belike would have taken me with him, had my hold on the sapling not been a good one.

'My son had been too frightened to run away, and when the tiger had gone, I took his loincloth from him and wrapped it round my head and holding his hand I walked back to the village. Arrived at my home I told my wife to call all my friends together, for I wished to see their faces before I died. When my friends were assembled and saw my condition, they wanted to put me on a charpoy and carry me fifty miles to the Almora hospital, but this I would not consent to; for my suffering was great and being sure that my time had come I wanted to die where I had been born, and where I had lived all my life. Water was brought, for I was thirsty, and my head was on fire, but when it was poured into my mouth, it all flowed out through the holes in my neck. Thereafter, for a period beyond measure, there was great confusion in my mind, and much pain in my head and in my neck, and while I waited and longed for death to end my sufferings, my wounds healed of themselves, and I became well.

'And now, *sahib*, I am as you see me, old and thin, and with white hair, and a face that no man can look on without repulsion. My enemy lives and continues to claim victims but do not be deceived into thinking it is a tiger, for it is no tiger but an evil spirit, who, when it craves-for human flesh and blood, takes on for a little while the semblance of a tiger. But they say you are a *sadhu, sahib*, and the spirits that guard *sadhus* are more powerful than this evil spirit, as is proved by the fact that you spent three days and three nights alone in the jungle and came out, as your men said you would alive and unhurt.'

Looking at the great frame of the man, it was easy to picture him as having been a veritable giant. And a giant in strength he must have been, for no man, unless he had been endowed with strength far above the average, could have lifted the tigress into the air, torn its hold from the side of his head, carrying away, as it did, half his face with it, and hurled it down the precipitous hill.

My gaunt friend constituted himself our guide, and with a beautifully polished axe, with a long tapering handle, over his shoulder, led us by devious steep paths to the valley below. Fording the Nandhour river, we crossed several wide terraced fields, now out of cultivation for fear of the man-eater and on reaching the foot of the hill started, what proved to be a very stiff climb, through forest, to the grass slopes above. Gaunt my friend may have been, but he lacked nothing in wind, and tough as I was it was only by calling frequent halts to admire the view that I was able to keep up with him.

Emerging from the tree forest, we went diagonally across the grassy slope, in the direction of a rock cliff that extended upwards for a thousand feet or more. It was on this cliff, sprinkled over with tufts of short grass, that I had seen *ghooral* feeding from my tent. We had covered a few hundred yards when one of these small mountain goats started up out of a ravine, and at my shot crumpled up and slipped back out of sight. Alarmed by the report of the rifles, another *ghooral*, that had evidently been lying asleep at the foot of the cliff, sprang to his feet and went up the rock face, as only he or his big brother the tahr could have done. As he climbed upwards, I lay down and, putting the sight to 200 yards, waited for him to stop. This he presently did, coming out on a projecting rock to look down on us. At my shot he staggered, regained his footing, and very slowly continued his climb. At the second shot he fell, hung for a second or two on a narrow ledge, and then fell through space to the grassy slope from whence he had started. Striking the ground, he rolled over and over, passing within a hundred yards of us, and eventually came to rest on a cattle track a hundred and fifty yards below.

I have only once, in all the three years I have been shooting, witnessed a similar sight to the one we saw during the next few minutes, and on that occasion the marauder was a leopard.

The *ghooral* had hardly come to rest when a big Himalayan bear came lumbering out of a ravine on the side of the grassy slope and, with never a pause or backward look, came at a fast trot along the cattle track. On reaching the dead goat he sat down and took it into his lap, and as he started nosing the goat, I fired. Maybe I hurried over my shot or allowed too much for refraction, anyway the bullet went low and struck the bear in the stomach instead of in the chest. To the six of us who were intently watching, it appeared that the bear took the smack of the bullet as an assault from the *ghooral*, for, rearing up, he flung the animal from him and came galloping along the track, emitting angry grunts. As he passed a hundred yards below us, I fired my fifth and last cartridge, the bullet, as I found later, going through the fleshy part of his hind quarters.

While the man retrieved the two *ghooral* I descended to examine the blood trail. The blood on the track showed the bear to be hard hit, but even so there was danger in following it up with an empty rifle, for bears are bad tempered at the best of times and are very ugly customers to deal with when wounded.

When the men rejoined me a short council of war was held. Camp was three and a half miles away, and as it was now 2 p.m. it would not be possible to fetch more ammunition, track down and kill the bear, and get back home by dark so it was unanimously decided that we should follow up the wounded animal and try to finish it off with stones and the axe.

The hill was steep and fairly tree of undergrowth, and by keeping above the bear there was a sporting chance of our being able to accomplish our task without serious mishap. We accordingly set off, I lead the way, followed by three men, the rear being brought up by two men each with a ghooral strapped to his back. Arrived at the spot where I had fired my last shot, additional blood on the track greatly encouraged us. Two hundred •'yards further on, the blood trail led down into a deep ravine. Here we divided up our force, two men crossing to the far side, the owner of the axe and I remaining on the near side, with the men carrying the *ghooral* following in our rear. On the word being given we started to advance down the hill. In the bed of the ravine, and fifty feet below us, was a dense patch of stunted bamboo, and when a stone was thrown into this thicket, the bear got up with a scream of rage; and six men, putting their best foot foremost, went straight up the hill. I was not trained to this form of exercise, and on looking back to see if the bear was gaining on us, I saw, much to my relief, that he was going as hard downhill as we were going uphill. A shout to my companions, a rapid change of direction, and we were off in a full cry and rapidly gaining on our quarry. A few well-aimed shots had been registered, followed by delighted shouts from the marksmen, and angry grunts from the bear, when at a sharp bend in the ravine, which necessitated a cautious advance, we lost touch with the bear. To have followed the blood trail would have been easy but here the ravine was full of big rocks, behind any of which the bear might have been lurking, so while the encumbered men sat down for a rest, a cast was made on either side of the ravine. While my companion went forward to look down into the ravine, I went to the right to prospect a rocky cliff that went sheer down for some two hundred feet. Holding on to a tree for support, I leaned over and saw the bear lying on a narrow ledge forty feet immediately below me. I picked up a stone, about thirty pounds in weight, and, again advancing to the edge and in imminent danger of going over myself, I raised the stone above my head with both hands and hurled it.

The stone struck the ledge a few inches from the bear's head, and scrambling to his feet he disappeared from sight, to reappear a minute later on the side of the hill. Once again, the hunt was on. The ground was here more open and less encumbered with rocks, and the four of us who were running light had no difficulty in keeping up with him. For a mile or more we ran him at top speed, until we eventually cleared the forest and emerged on to the terraced fields.

Rainwater had cut several deep and narrow channels across the fields, and in one of these channels the bear took cover.

The man with the distorted face was the only armed member of the party and he was unanimously elected executioner. Nothing loth, he cautiously approached the bear and, swinging his beautifully polished axe aloft, brought the square head down on the bear's skull. The result was as alarming as it was unexpected. The axe-head rebounded off the bear's skull as though it had been struck on a block of rubber, and with a scream of rage the animal reared up on his hind legs. Fortunately, he did not follow up his advantage, for we were bunched together and in trying to run got in each other's way.

The bear did not appear to like this open ground, and after going a short way down the channel again took cover. It was now my turn with the axe. The bear, however, having once been struck, resented my approach, and it was only after a great deal of manoeuvring that I eventually got within striking distance. It has been my ambition when a boy to be a lumber- man in Canada, and I had attained sufficient proficiency with an axe to split a matchstick. I had no fear, therefore, as the owner had, of the axe glancing of and getting damaged on the stones, and the moment I got within reach I buried the entire blade in the bear's skull.

Himalayan bearskins are very greatly prized by our hill folk, and the owner of the axe was a very proud and envied man when I told him he could have the skin in addition to a double share of the *ghooral* meat. Leaving the men, whose numbers were being rapidly augmented by new arrivals from the village to skin and divide up the bag, I climbed up to the village and paid, as already related, a last visit to the injured girl. The day had been a strenuous one, and if the man-eater had paid me a visit that night she would have 'caught me napping'.

On the road I had taken when coming to Dalkania there was several long stiff climbs up treeless hills, and when I mentioned the discomforts of this road to the villagers, they had suggested that I should go back via Haira Khan. This route would necessitate only one climb to the ridge above the village, from where it was downhill all the way to Ranibagh, whence I could complete the journey to Nainital by car.

I had warned my men overnight to prepare for an early start, and a little before sunrise, leaving them to pack up and follow me, I said good- bye to my friends at Dalkania, and started on the two- mile climb to the forest road on the ridge above. The footpath I took was not the one by which my men, and later I, had arrived to Dalkania but was one the villagers used when going to, and returning from, the bazaars in the foothills.

The path wound in and out of deep ravines, through thick oak and pine forests and dense undergrowth. There had been no news of the tigress for a week. This absence of news made me all the more careful, and an hour after leaving camp I arrived without mishap at an open glade near the top of the hill, within a hundred yards of the forest road.

The glade was pear-shaped, roughly a hundred yards long and fifty yards wide, with a stagnant pool of rainwater in the centre of it. Sambhar and other game used this pool as a drinking place and to wallow and, curious to see the tracks round it, I left the path, which skirted the left-hand side of the glade and passed close under a cliff of rock which extended up to the road. As I approached the pool, I saw the pugmarks of the tigress in the soft earth at the edge of the water. She had approached the pool from the same direction as I had and evidently disturbed by me, had crossed the water, and gone into the dense tree and scrub jungle on the right-hand side of the glade. A great chance was lost, for had I kept as careful a lookout in front as I had behind, I should have seen her before she saw me. However, though I had missed a chance, the advantages were now all on my side and distinctly in my favour.

The tigress had seen me, or she would not have crossed the pool and hurried for shelter, as her tracks showed she had done. Having seen me she had also seen that I was alone, and watching me from cover as she undoubtedly was, she would assume I was going to the pool to drink as she had done. My movements up to this point had been quite natural, and if I could continue to make her think I was unaware of her presence, she would possibly give me a second chance. Stooping down and keeping a very sharp lookout from under my hat, I coughed several times, splashed the water about, and then, moving very slowly and gathering dry sticks on the way, I went to the foot of the steep rock. Here I built a small fire, and resting my back against the rock, lit a cigarette. By the time the cigarette had been smoked the fire had burnt out. I then lay down and pillowing my head on my left arm placed the rifle on the ground with my finger on the trigger.

The rock above me was too steep for any animal to find a foothold on. I had therefore only my front to guard, and as the heavy cover nowhere approached within less than twenty yards of my position, I was quite safe. I had all this time neither seen nor heard anything; nevertheless, I was convinced that the tigress was watching me. The rim of my hat, while effectually shading my eyes, did not obstruct my vision and inch by inch I scanned every bit of the jungle within my range of view. There was not a breath of wind blowing and not a leaf or a blade of grass stirred. My men, whom I had instructed to keep close together and sing from the time they left camp until they joined me on the forest road, were not due for an hour and a half, and during this time it was more than likely that the tigress would break cover and try to stalk, or rush, me.

There are occasions when time draws, and others when it files. My left arm, on which my head was pillowed, had long since ceased to prick and had gone dead but even so the singing of the men in the valley below reached me-all too soon. The voices grew louder and presently I caught sight of the men as they rounded a sharp bend. It was possibly at this bend that the tigress had seen me as she turned round to retrace her steps after having her drink. Another failure and the last chance on this trip gone.

After my men had rested, we climbed up to the road, and set off on what proved to be a very long twenty- mile march to the Forest Rest House at Haira Khan. After going a couple of hundred yards over open ground, the road entered very thick forest, and here I made the men walk in front while I brought up the rear. We had gone about two miles in this order, when on turning a corner, I saw a man sitting on the road, herding buffaloes. It was now time to call a halt for breakfast, so I asked the man where we could get the water. He pointed down the hill straight in front of him and said there was a spring down there from which his village, which was just round the shoulder of the hill, drew its water supply. There was, however, no necessity for us to go down the hill for water, for if we continued a little further, we would find a good spring on the road.

His village was at the upper end of the valley in which the women of Lohali had been killed the previous week, and he told me that nothing had been heard of the man-eater since and added that the animal was possibly now at the other end of the district. I disabused his mind on this point by telling him about the fresh pugmarks I had seen at the pool and advised him very strongly to collect his buffaloes and return to the village. His buffaloes, some ten in number, were straggling up towards the road and he said he would leave as soon as they had grazed up to where he was sitting. Handing him a cigarette, I left him with a final warning. What occurred after I left was related to me by the man of the village, when I paid the district a second visit some months later.

When the man eventually got home that day he told the assembled villagers of our meeting, and my warning and said that after he had watched me go round a bend in the road a hundred yards away; he started to light the cigarette I had given him. A wind was blowing, and to protect the flame of the match he bend forward, and while in this position he was seized from behind by the right shoulder and pulled backwards. His first thought was of the party who had just left him, but unfortunately, his cry for help was not heard by them. Help, however, was near at hand, for as soon as the buffaloes heard his cry, mingled with the growl of the tigress, they charged on to the road and drove the tigress off. His shoulder and arms were broken, and with great difficulty he managed to climb on the back of one of his brave rescuers, and followed by the rest of the herd, reached his home. The villagers tied up his wounds as best they could and carried him thirty miles, non-stop to the Haldwani hospital, where he died shortly after admission.

When Atropos who snips the threads of life misses one thread, she cuts another, and we who do not know why one thread is missed and another cut, call it Fate, Kismet, or what we will.

For a month I had lived in an open tent, a hundred yards from the nearest human being, and from dawn to dusk had wandered through the jungles, and on several occasions had disguised myself as a woman and cut grass in places where no local inhabitant dared to go. During this period the man-eater had quite possibly, missed many opportunities of adding me to her bag and now; when making a final effort, she had quite by chance encountered this unfortunate man and claimed him as a victim.

II

The following February I returned to Dalkania. A number of human beings had been killed, and many more wounded, over a wide area since my departure from the district the previous summer and as the whereabouts of the tigress was not known and the chances in one place were as good as in another, I decided to return and camp on the ground with which I was now familiar.

On my arrival at Dalkania I was told that a cow had been killed the previous evening, on the hill on which the bear hunt had taken place. The men who had been herding the cattle at the time were positive that the animal they had seen killing the cow was a tiger. The kill was lying near some bushes at the edge of a deserted field and was clearly visible from the spot where my tent was being put up. Vultures were circling over the kill and looking through my field glasses I saw several of these birds perched on a tree, to the left of the kill. From the fact that the kill was lying out in the open, and the vultures had not descended on it, I concluded (a) that the cow had been killed by a leopard, and (b) that the leopard was lying up close to the kill.

The ground below the field on which the cow was lying was very steep and overgrown with dense brushwood. The man-eater was still at large and an approach over this ground was therefore inadvisable.

To the right was a grassy slope, but the ground here was too open to admit my approaching the kill without being seen. A deep heavily wooded ravine, starting from near the crest of the hill, ran right down to the Nandhour river, passing within a short distance of the kill. The tree on which the vultures were perched was growing on the edge of this ravine. I decided on this ravine as my line of approach. While I had been planning out the stalk with the assistance of the villagers, who knew every foot of the ground, my men had prepared tea for me. The day was now on the decline but by going hard I should just have time to visit the kill and return to camp before nightfall.

Before setting off I instructed my men to be on the lookout. If, after hearing a shot, they saw me on the open ground near the kill, three or four of them were immediately to leave camp, and, keeping to the open ground, to join me. On the other hand, if I did not fire and failed to return by morning, a search party was to be organized.

The ravine was overgrown with raspberry bushes and strewn with great rocks, and as the wind was blowing downhill, my progress was slow. After a stiff climb I eventually reached the tree on which the vultures were perched, only to find that the kill was not visible from this spot. The deserted field, which through my field glasses had appeared to be quite straight, I found to be crescent-shaped, ten yards across at its widest part and tapering to a point at both ends. The outer edge was bordered with dense undergrowth, and the hill fell steeply away from the inner edge. Only two-thirds of the field was visible from where I was standing, and in order to see the remaining one-third, on which the kill was lying, it would be necessary either to make a wide detour and approach from the far side or climb the tree on which the vultures were perched.

I decided on the latter course. The cow, as far as I could judge, was about twenty yards from the tree, and it was quite possible that the animal that had killed her was even less than that distance from me. To climb the tree without disturbing the killer would have been an impossible feat, and would not have been attempted had it not been for the vultures. There were by now some twenty of these birds on the tree and their number was being added to by new arrivals, and as the accommodation on the upper branches was limited there was much flapping of wings and quarrelling. The tree was leaning outwards away from the hill, and about ten feet from the ground a great limb projected out over the steep hillside. Hampered with the rifle, I had great difficulty in reaching this limb. Waiting until a fresh quarrel had broken out among the vultures, I stepped out along the branch, a difficult balancing feat where a slip or false step would have resulted in a fall of a hundred or more feet on to the rocks below reached a fork and sat down.

The kill, from which only a few pounds of flesh had been eaten, was now in full view. I had been in position about ten minutes, and was finding my perch none too comfortable, when two vultures, who had been circling round and were uncertain of their reception on the tree, alighted on the field a short distance from the cow. They had hardly come to rest when they were on the wing again, and at the same moment the bushes on my side of the kill were gently agitated and out into the open stepped a fine male leopard.

Those who have never seen a leopard under favourable conditions in his natural surroundings can have no conception of the grace of movement, and beauty of colouring, of this the most graceful and the most beautiful of all animals in our Indian jungles. Nor are his attractions limited to outward appearances, for, pound for pound, his strength is second to none and in courage he lacks nothing. To class such an animal as Vermin, as is done in some parts of India, is a crime which only those could perpetrate whose knowledge of the leopard is limited to the miserable, underfed, and mangy specimens seen in captivity.

But beautiful as the specimen was that stood before me, his life was forfeit, for he had taken to cattle killing, and I had promised the people of Dalkania and other villages on my last visit that I would rid them of this their minor enemy, if opportunity offered. The opportunity had now come, and I do not think the leopard heard the shot that killed him.

Of the many incomprehensible things, one meets with in life, the hardest to assign any reason for is the way in which misfortune dogs an individual, or a family, take as an example the case of the owner of the cow over which I had shot the leopard. He was a boy, eight years of age and an only child. Two years previously his mother, while out cutting grass for the cow, had been killed and eaten by the man-eater and twelve months later his father had suffered a like fate. The few pots and pans the family possessed had been sold to pay off the small debt left by the father, and the son started life as the owner of one cow; and this particular cow the leopard had selected, out of a herd of two or three hundred head of village cattle and killed. (I am afraid my attempt to repair a heartbreak was not very successful in this case, for though the new cow, a red one, was an animal of parts, it did not make up to the boy for the loss of his lifelong white companion.)

My young buffaloes had been well cared for by the man in whose charge I had left them, and the day after my arrival I started tying them out, though I had little hope of the tigress accepting them as bait.

Five miles down the Nandhour valley nestles a little village at the foot of a great cliff of rock, some thousand or more feet high. The man-eater had, during the past few months, killed four people on the outskirts of this village. Shortly after I shot the leopard, a deputation came from this village to request me to move my camp from Dalkania to a site that had been selected for me near their village. I was told that the tiger had -frequently been seen on the cliff above the village and that it appeared to have its home in one of the many caves in the cliff face. That very morning, I was informed, some women out cutting grass had seen the tiger, and the villagers were now in a state of terror, and too frightened to leave their homes. Promising the deputation, I would do all I could to help them, I made a very early start next morning, climbed the hill opposite the village, and scanned the cliff for an hour or more through my field glasses. I then crossed the valley, and by way of a very deep ravine climbed the cliff above the village, here the going was very difficult and not at all to my liking, for added to the danger of a fall, which would have resulted in a broken neck, was the danger of an attack on ground on which it would be impossible to defend oneself

By 2 p.m. I had seen as much of the rock cliff as I shall ever want to see again and was making my way up the valley towards my camp and breakfast, when on looking back before starting the stiff climb to Dalkania, I saw two men running towards me from the direction in which I had just come. On joining me the men informed me that a tiger had just killed a bullock in the deep ravine up which I had gone earlier in the day. Telling one of the men to go on up to my camp and instruct my servant to send tea and some food, I turned round and, accompanied by the other man, retraced my steps down the valley.

The ravine where the bullock had been killed was about two hundred feet deep and one hundred feet wide. As we approached it, I saw a number of vultures rising, and when we arrived at the kill, I found the vultures had cleaned it out, leaving only the skin and bones. The spot where the remains of the. bullock were lying was only a hundred yards from the village but there was no way up the steep bank, so my guide took me a quarter of a mile down the ravine, to where a cattle track crossed it. This track, after gaining the high ground, would go in and out through dense scrub jungle before it finally fetched up at the village. On arrival at the village, I told the Headman that the vultures had ruined the kill and asked him to provide me with a young buffalo and a short length of stout rope; while these were being procured, two of my men arrived from Dalkania with the food I had sent for.

The sun was near setting when I re-entered the ravine, followed by several men leading a vigorous young male buffalo which the Headman had purchased for me from an adjoining village. Fifty yards from where the bullock had been killed, one end of a pine tree washed down from the hill above had been buried deep in the bed of the ravine. After tying the buffalo very securely to the exposed end of the pine, the men returned to the village. There were no trees in the vicinity, and the only possible place for a sit-up was a narrow ledge on the village side of the ravine. With great difficulty I climbed to this lodge, which was about two feet wide by five feet long, and twenty foot above the bed of the ravine. From a little below the ledge the rock shelved inwards, forming a deep recess that was not visible from the ledge. The lodge canted downwards at an uncomfortable angle, and when I had taken my seat on it, I had my back towards the direction from which I expected the tiger to come, while the tethered buffalo was to my left front, and distant about thirty yards from me.

The sun had set when the buffalo, who had been lying down, scrambled to his feet, and faced up the ravine, and a moment later a stone came rolling down. It would not have been possible for me to have fired in the direction from which the sound had come, so to avoid detection I sat perfectly still. After some time, the buffalo gradually turned to the left until he was facing in my direction. This showed that whatever he was frightened of, and I could see he was frightened was in the recess below me. Presently the head of a tiger appeared directly under me. A headshot at a tiger is only justified in an emergency, and any movement on my part might have betrayed my presence. For a long minute or two the head remained perfectly still, and then, with a quick dash forward and one great bound, the tiger was on the buffalo. The buffalo, as I have stated, was facing the tiger, and to avoid a frontal attack with the possibility of injury from the buffalo's horns, the tiger's dash carried him to the left of the buffalo, and he made his attack at right angles. There was no fumbling for tooth-hold, no struggle, and no sound beyond the impact of the two heavy bodies, after which the buffalo lay quite still with the tiger lying partly over it and holding it by the throat. It is generally believed that tigers kill by delivering a smashing blow on the neck. This is incorrect. Tigers kill with their teeth.

The right side of the tiger was towards me and, taking careful aim with the .275 I had armed myself with when leaving camp that morning, I fired. Relinquishing its hold on the buffalo, the tiger, without making a sound, turned, and bounded off up the ravine and out of sight. Clearly a miss, for which I was unable to assign any reason. If the tiger had not seen me or the flash of the rifle there was a possibility that it would return so recharging the rifle, I sat on.

The buffalo, after the tiger left him, lay without movement and the conviction grew on me that I had shot him instead of the tiger. Ten, fifteen minutes had dragged by, when the tiger's head for a second time appeared from the recess below me. Again, there was a long pause, and then, very slowly, the tiger emerged, walked up to the buffalo, and stood looking down at it. With the whole length of the back as a target I was going to make no mistake the second time. Very carefully the sights were aligned, and the trigger slowly pressed; but instead of the tiger falling dead as I expected it to, it sprang to the left and went tearing up a little ravine, dislodging stones as it went up the steep hillside.

Two shots fired in comparatively good light at a range of thirty yards and heard by anxious villagers for miles round; and all I should have to show for them would be, certainly one, and quite possibly two, bullet holes in a dead buffalo. Clearly my eyesight was failing, or in climbing the rock I had knocked the foresight out or alignment. But on focusing my eyes on small objects I found there was nothing wrong with my eyesight and a glance along the barrel showed that the sights were all right, so the only reason I could assign for having missed the tiger twice was bad shooting.

There was no chance of the tiger returning a third time and even if it did return, there was nothing to be gained by risking the possibility of only wounding it in bad light when I had not been able to kill it while the light had been comparatively good. Under those circumstances there was no object in my remaining any longer on the ledge.

My clothes were still damp from my exertions earlier in the day, a cold wind was blowing and promised to get colder, my shorts were of thin khaki and the rock was hard and cold, and a hot cup of tea awaited me in the village. Good as these reasons were, there was a better and a more convincing reason for my remaining where I was the man-eater. It was now quite dark. A quarter-of-mile walk, along a boulder-strewn ravine and a winding path through dense undergrowth lay between me and the village. Beyond the suspicions of the villagers that the tiger they had seen the previous day and that I had quite evidently just fired at, was the man-eater, I had no definite knowledge of the man-eater's whereabouts; and though at that moment she might have been fifty miles away, she might also have been watching me from a distance of fifty yards, so, uncomfortable as my perch was, prudence dictated that I should remain where I was. As the long hours dragged by, the conviction grew on me that man-eater shooting, by night, was not a pastime that appealed to me and that if this animal could not be shot during daylight hours she would have to be left to die of old age. This conviction was strengthened when, cold and stiff, I started to climb down as soon as there was sufficient light to shoot by and slipping on the dew-drenched rock completed the descent with my feet in the air. Fortunately, I landed on a bed of sand, without doing myself or the rifle any injury.

Early as it was, I found the village astir, and I was quickly in the middle of a small crowd. In reply to the eager questions from all sides, I was only able to say that I had been firing at an imaginary tiger with blank ammunition.

A pot of tea drunk while sitting near a roaring fire did much to restore warmth to my inner and outer man, and then, accompanied by most of the men and all the boys of the village, I went to where a rock jutted out over the ravine and directly above my overnight exploit. To the assembled throng I explained how the tiger had appeared from the recess under me and had bounded on to the buffalo, and how after I fired it had dashed off in that direction and as I pointed up the ravine there was an excited shout of 'Look, *sahib*, there's the tiger lying dead!' My eyes were strained with an all-night vigil but even after looking away and back again there was no denying the fact the tiger was lying there, dead. To the very natural question of why I had fired a second shot after a period of twenty or thirty minutes, I said that the tiger had appeared a second time from exactly the same place, and that I had fired at it while it was standing near the buffalo and that it had gone up that side ravine and there were renewed shouts, in which the women and girls who had now come up joined, of 'Look, *sahib*, there is another tiger lying dead!' Both tigers appeared to be about the same size, and both were lying sixty yards from where I had fired.

Questioned on the subject of this second tiger, the villagers said that when the four human beings had been killed, and also on the previous day when the bullock had been killed, only one tiger had been seen. The mating season for tigers is an elastic one extending from November to April and the man-eater, if either of the two tigers lying within view was the man-eater had evidently provided herself with a mate.

A way into the ravine, down the steep rock face, was found some two hundred yards below where I had sat up, and, followed by the entire population of the village, I went past the dead buffalo to where the first tiger was lying. As I approached it hopes rose high, for she was an old tigress, Handing the rifle to the nearest man I got down on my knees to examine her feet. On that day when the tigress had tried to stalk the women cutting wheat, she had left some beautiful pugmarks on the edge of the field. They were the first pugmarks I had seen of the man-eater, and I had examined them very carefully. They showed the tigress to be a very old animal, whose feet had splayed out with age. The pads of the forefeet were heavily rutted, one deep rut running right across the pad of-the right forefoot, and the toes were elongated to a length I had never before Seen in a tiger. With these distinctive feet it would have been easy to pick the man-eater out of a hundred dead tigers. The animal before me was, I found to my great regret, not the man-eater. When I conveyed this information to the assembled throng of people there was a murmur of strong dissent from all sides. It was asserted that I myself, on my previous visit, had declared the man-eater to be an old tigress, and such an animal I had now shot a few yards from where, only a short time previously, four of their number had been killed. Against this convincing evidence, of what value was the evidence of the feet, for the feet of all tigers were alike!

The second tiger could, under the circumstances, only be a male, and while I made preparations to skin the tigress, I sent a party of men to fetch him. The side ravine was steep and narrow, and after a great deal of shouting and laughter the second tiger, a fine male was laid down alongside the tigress.

The skinning of those two tigers that had been dead fourteen hours, with the sun beating down on my back and an ever-growing crowd pressing round, was one of the most unpleasant tasks I have ever undertaken. By early afternoon the job was completed and with the skins neatly tied up for my men to carry I was ready to start on my five-mile walk back to camp.

During the morning Headmen and others had come in from adjoining villages and before leaving I assured them that the Chowgarh man-eater was not dead and warned them that the slackening of precautions would give the tigress the opportunity she was waiting for. Had my warning been heeded, the man-eater would not have claimed as many victims as she did during the succeeding months.

There was no further news of the man-eater, and after a stay of a few weeks at Dalkania, I left to keep an appointment with the district officials in the terai.

III

In March 1950, Vivian, our District Commissioner, was touring through the man-eater's domain and on the 22nd of the month I received an urgent request from him to go to Kala Agar, where he said he would await my arrival. It is roughly fifty miles from Nainital to Kala Agar and two days after receipt of Vivian's letter I arrived in time for breakfast at the Kala Agar Forest Bungalow, where he and Mrs. Vivian were staying.

Over breakfast the Vivians told me they had arrived at the bungalow on the afternoon of 21st, and while they were having tea on the verandah, one of six women who were cutting grass in the compound of the bungalow had been killed and carried off by the man-eater. Rifles were hurriedly seized and accompanied by some of his staff, Vivian followed up the 'drag' and found the dead woman tucked away under a bush at the foot of an oak tree. On examining the ground later, I found that on the approach of Vivian's party the tigress had gone off down the hill, and throughout the subsequent proceedings had remained in a thicket of raspberry bushes, fifty yards from the kill. A *machan* was put up in the oak tree for Vivian, and two others in trees near the forest road which passed thirty yards above the kill, for members of his staff. The *machans* were occupied as soon as they were ready and the party sat up the whole night, without, however, seeing anything of the tigress.

Next morning the body of the woman was removed for cremation, and a young buffalo was tied up on the forest road about half a mile from the bungalow and killed by the tigress the same night. The following evening the Vivians sat up over the buffalo. There was no moon, and just as daylight was fading out and nearby objects becoming indistinct, they first heard, and then saw an animal coming up to the kill, which in the uncertain light they mistook for a bear; but for this unfortunate mistake their very sporting effort would have resulted in their bagging the man-eater for both the Vivian's are good rifle shots.

On the 25th The Vivians left Kala Agar, and during the course of the day my four buffaloes arrived from Dalkania. As the tigress now appeared to be inclined to accept this form of bait, I tied them up at intervals of a few hundred yards along the forest road. For three nights in succession the tigress passed within a few feet of the buffaloes without touching them, but on the fourth night the buffalo nearest the bungalow was killed. On examining the kill in the morning, I was disappointed to find that the buffalo had been killed by a pair of leopards I had heard calling the previous night above the bungalow. I did not like the idea of firing in this locality, for fear of driving away the tigress, but it was quite evident that if I did not shoot the leopards they would kill my three remaining buffaloes, so I stalked them while they were sunning themselves on some big rocks above the kill and shot both of them.

The forest road from the Kala Agar Bungalow runs for several miles' due west through very beautiful forests of pine, oak, and rhododendron, and in this forest, there is compared with the rest of Kumaon, quite a lot of game in the way of *sambhar, kakar* (barking deer), and *pig*, in addition to "I great wealth of bird life. On two occasions I suspected the tigress of having killed *sambhar* in this forest and though on both occasions I found the bloodstained spot where the animal had been killed, I failed to find either of the kills. For the next fourteen days I spent all the daylight hours either on the forest road, on which no one but myself ever set foot, or in the jungle, and only twice during that period did I get near the tigress. On the first occasion I had been down to visit an isolated village, on the south face of Kala Agar ridge, that had been abandoned the previous year owing to the depredations of the man-eater and on the way back had taken a cattle track that went over the ridge and down the far side to the forest road, when, approaching a pile of rocks, I suddenly felt there was danger ahead. The distance from the ridge to the forest road was roughly three hundred yards. The track, after leaving the ridge, went steeply down for a few yards and then turned to the right and ran diagonally across the hill for a hundred yards; the pile of rocks was about midway on the right-hand side of this length of the track. Beyond the rocks a hairpin bend carried the track to the left and a hundred yards further on, another sharp bend took it down to its junction with the forest road.

I had been along this track many times, and this was the first occasion on which I hesitated to pass the rocks. To avoid them I should either have had to go several hundred yards through dense undergrowth or make a wide detour round and above them; the former would have subjected me to very great danger, and there was no time for the latter, for the sun was near setting and I had still two miles to go. So, whether I liked it or not, there was nothing for it but to face the rocks. The wind was blowing up the hills, so I was able to ignore the thick cover on the left of the track and concentrate all my attention on the rocks to my right. A hundred feet would see me clear of the danger zone, and this distance I covered foot by foot, walking sideways with my face to the rocks and the rifle to my shoulder; a strange mode of progression, had there been any to see it.

Thirty yards beyond the rocks was an open glade, starting from the right-hand side of the track and extending up the hill for fifty or sixty yards, and screened from the rocks by a fringe of bushes. In this glade a *kakar* was grazing. I saw her before she saw me and watched her out of the corner of my eye. On catching sight of me she threw up her head, and as I was not looking in her direction and was moving slowly on, she stood stuck still, as these animals have a habit of doing when they are under the impression that they have not been seen. On arrival at the hairpin bend I looked over my shoulder and saw that the *kakar* had lowered her head and was once more cropping the grass.

I had walked a short distance along the track after passing the bend when the *kakar* went dashing up the hill, barking hysterically. In a few quick strides I was back at the bend and was just in time to see a movement in the bushes on the lower side of the track. That the *kakar* had seen the tigress was quite evident, and the only place where she could have seen her was on the track. The movement I had seen might have been caused by the passage of a bird, on the other hand it might have been caused by the tigress; anyway, a little investigation was necessary before proceeding further on my way.

A trickle of water seeping out from under the rocks had damped the red clay of which the track was composed, making an ideal surface for the impression of tracks. In this damp clay I had left footprints, and over these footprints I now found the splayed-out pugmarks of the tigress where she had jumped down from the rocks and followed me, until the *kakar* had seen her and given its alarm call, whereupon the tigress had left the track and entered the bushes where I had seen the movement. The tigress was undoubtedly familiar with every foot of the ground, and not having had an opportunity of killing me at the rocks and her chance of bagging me at the first hairpin bend having been spoilt by the *kakar*, she was probably now making her way through the dense under-growth to try to intercept me at the second bend.

Further progress along the track was now not advisable so I followed the *kakar* up the glade, and turning to the left worked my way down, over open ground, to the forest road below. Had there been sufficient daylight I believe I could, that evening, have turned the tables on the tigress, for the conditions, after she left the shelter of the rocks, were all in my favour. I knew the ground as well as she did, and while she had no reason to suspect my intention towards her, I had the advantage of knowing, very clearly, her intentions towards me. However, though the conditions were in my favour, I was unable to take advantage of them owing to the lateness of the evening.

I have made mention elsewhere of the sense that warns us of impending danger and will not labour the subject further beyond stating that this sense is a very real one and that I do not know and therefore cannot explain what brings it into operation. On this occasion I had neither heard nor seen the tigress, nor had I received any indication from bird or beast of her presence and yet I knew, without any shadow of doubt, that she was lying up for me among the rocks. I had been out for many hours that day and had covered many miles of jungle with unflagging caution, but without one moments unease, and then, on cresting the ridge, and coming in sight of the rocks, I knew they held danger for me, and this knowledge was confirmed a few minutes later by the *kakars* warning call to the jungle folk, and by my finding the man-eater's pugmarks superimposed on my footprints.

IV

To those of my readers who have had the patience to accompany me so far in my narrative, I should like to give a clear and a detailed account of my first and last meeting with the tigress.

The meeting took place in the early afternoon of the 11th of April 1930, nineteen days after my arrival at Kala Agar.

I had gone out that day at 2 p.m. with the intention of tying up my three buffaloes at selected places along the forest road, when at a point a mile from the bungalow; where the road crosses a ridge and goes from the north to the west face of the Kala Agar range, I came on a large party of men who had been out collecting firewood. In the party was an old man who, pointing down the hill to a thicket of young oak trees some five hundred yards from where we were standing, said it was in that thicket where the man-eater, a month previously, had killed his only son, a lad eighteen years of age. I had not heard the father's version of the killing of his son, so, while we sat on the edge of the road smoking, he told his story, pointing out the spot where the lad had been killed, and where all that was left of him had been found the following day. The old man blamed the twenty-five men who had been out collecting firewood on that day for the death of his son, saying, very bitterly, that they had run away and left him to be killed by the tiger. Some of the men sitting near me had been in that party of twenty-five and they hotly repudiated responsibility for the lad's death, accusing him of having been responsible for the stampede by screaming out that he had heard the tiger growling and telling everyone to run for their lives. This did not satisfy the old man. He shook his head and said, 'you are grown men and he was only a boy, and you ran away and left him to be killed.' I was sorry for having asked the questions that had led to this heated discussion and more to placate the old man than for any good it would do, I said I would tie up one of my buffaloes near the spot where he said his son had been killed. So, handing two of the buffaloes over to the party to take back to the bungalow, I set off followed by two of my men leading the remaining buffalo.

A footpath, taking off close to where we had been sitting, went down the hill to the valley below and zigzagged up the opposite pine-clad slope to join the forest road two miles further on. The path passed close to an open patch of ground which bordered the oak thicket in which the lad had been killed. On this patch of ground, which was about thirty yards square, there was a solitary pine sapling. This I cut down. I tied the buffalo to the stump, set one man to cutting a supply of grass for it, and sent the other man, Madho Singh, who served in the Garhwalis during the Great War and is now serving in the United Provinces Civil Pioneer Force, up an oak tree with instructions to strike a dry branch with the head of his axe and call at the top of his voice as hill people do when cutting leaves for their cattle. I then took up a position on a rock, about four feet high, on the lower edge of the open ground. Beyond the rock the hill fell steeply away to the valley below and was densely clothed with Tree, and scrub jungle.

The man on the ground had made several trips with the grass he had cut and Madho Singh on the tree was alternately shouting and singing lustily, while I stood on the rock smoking, with the rifle in the hollow of my left arm, when, all at once, I became aware that the man-eater had arrived. Beckoning urgently to the man on the ground to come to me, I whistled to attract Madho Singh's attention and signaled to him to remain quiet. The ground on three sides was comparatively open. Madho Singh on the tree was to my left front, the man cutting grass had been in front of me, while the buffalo now showing signs of uneasiness was to my right front. In this area the tigress could not have approached without my seeing her and as she had approached, there was only one place where she could now be and that was behind and immediately below me.

When taking up my position I had noticed that the further side of the rock was steep and smooth, that it extended down the hill for eight or ten feet, and that the lower portion of it was masked by thick undergrowth and young pine saplings. It would have been a little difficult, but quite possible, for the tigress to have climbed the rock, and I relied for my safety on hearing her in the undergrowth should she make the attempt.

I have no doubt that the tigress, attracted, as I had intended, She should be, by the noise Madho Singh was making, had come to the rock, and that it was while she was looking up at me and planning her next move that I had become aware of her presence. My change of front coupled with the silence of the men, may have made her suspicious; anyway, after a lapse of a few minutes, I heard a dry twig snap a little way down the hill; thereafter the feeling of unease left me, and the tension relaxed. An opportunity lost; but there was still a very good chance of my getting a shot, for she would undoubtedly return before long, and when she found us gone would probably content herself with killing the buffalo. There were still four or five hours of daylight, and by crossing the valley and going up the opposite slope I should be able to overlook the whole of the hillside on which the buffalo was tethered. The shot, if I did get one, would be a long one of from two to three hundred yards, but the .275 rifle I was carrying was accurate, and even if I only wounded the tigress, I should have a blood trail to tallow, which would be better than feeling about for her in hundreds of square miles of jungle, as I had been doing these many months.

The men were a difficulty. To have sent them back to the bungalow alone would have been nothing short of murder, so of necessity I kept them with me.

Tying the buffalo to the stump in such a manner as to make it impossible for the tigress to carry it away, I left the open ground and rejoined the path to carry out the plan I had outlined of trying to get a shot from the opposite hill.

About a hundred yards along the path, I came to a ravine. On the far side of this the path entered very heavy undergrowth, and as it was inadvisable to go into thick cover with two men following me, I decided to take to the ravine, follow it down to its junction with the valley, work up the valley and pick up the path on the far side of the undergrowth.

The ravine was about ten yards wide and four or five feet deep, and as I stepped down into it a nightjar fluttered off a rock on which I had put my hand. On looking at the spot from which the bird had risen, I saw two eggs. These eggs, straw-colored, with rich brown markings, were of a most unusual shape, one being long and very pointed, while the other was as round as a marble and as my collection lacked night jar egg's I decided to add this odd clutch to it. I had no receptacle of any kind in which to carry the eggs, so cupping my left hand I placed the eggs in it and packed them round with a little moss.

As I went down the ravine the banks became higher, and sixty yards from where I had entered it, I came on a deep drop of some twelve to

^ fourteen feet. The water that rushes down all these hill ravines in the * rains had worn the rock as smooth as glass, and as it was too steep to offer a foothold, I handed the rifle to the men and, sitting on the edge, proceeded to slide down. My feet had hardly touched the sandy bottom when the two men, with a flying leap, landed one on either side of me and thrusting the rifle into my hand asked in a very agitated manner if I had heard the tiger. As a matter of fact, I had heard nothing possibly due to the scraping of my clothes on the rocks and when questioned, the men said that what they had heard was a deep-throated growl from somewhere close at hand, but exactly from which direction the sound had come, they were unable to say. Tigers do not betray their presence by growling when looking for their dinner and the only, and very unsatisfactory, explanation I can offer is that the tigress followed us after we left the open ground, and on seeing that we were going down the ravine had gone ahead and taken up a position where the ravine narrowed to half its width and that when she was on the point of springing out on me, I had disappeared out of sight down the slide and she had involuntarily given vent to her disappointment with a low growl. Not a satisfactory reason, unless one assumes without any reason that she had selected me for her dinner, and therefore had no interest in the two men.

Where the three of us now stood in a bunch we had the smooth steep rock behind us, to our right a wall of rock slightly leaning over the ravine and fifteen feet high, and to our left a tumbled bank of big rocks thirty or forty feet high. The sandy bed of the ravine, on which we were standing, was roughly forty feet long and ten feet wide. At the lower end of this sandy bed a great pine tree had fallen across, damming the ravine, and the collection of the sand was due to this dam. The wall of overhanging rock came to an end twelve or fifteen feet from the fallen tree, and as I approached the end of the rock, my feet making no sound on the sand, I very fortunately noticed that the sandy bed continued round to the back of the rock.

This rock about which I have said so much I can best describe as a giant school slate, two feet thick as its lower end and standing up, not quite perpendicularly on one of its long sides.

As I stepped clear of the giant slate, I looked behind me over my right shoulder and looked straight into the tigress's face.

I would like you to have a clear picture of the situation.

The sandy bed behind the rock was quite flat. To the right of it was the smooth slate fifteen feet high and leaning slightly outwards, to the left of it was a scoured-out steep bank also some fifteen feet high overhung by a dense tangle of thorn bushes, while at the far end was a slide similar to, but a little higher than, the one I had glissaded down. The sandy bed, enclosed by these three natural walls, was about twenty feet long and half as wide, and lying on it, with her forepaws stretched out and her hind legs well tucked under her, was the tigress. Her head, which was raised a few inches off her paws, was eight feet (measured later) from me, and on her face was a smile, similar to that one sees on the face of a dog welcoming his master's home after a long absence.

Two thoughts flashed through my mind, one, that it was up to me to make the first move, and the other, that the move would have to be made in such a manner as not to alarm the tigress or make her nervous.

The rifle was in my right hand held diagonally across my chest, with the safety catch off, and in order to get it to bear on the tigress the muzzle would have to be swung round three-quarters of a circle.

The movement of swinging round the rifle, with one hand began very slowly and hardly perceptibly, and when a quarter of a circle had been made, the stock came in contact with my right side. It was now necessary to extend my arm, and as the stock cleared my side, the swing continued very slowly. My arm was now at full stretch and the weight of the rifle was beginning to tell. Only a little further now for the muzzle to go and the tigress, who had not once taken her eyes off mine, was still looking up at me with the pleased expression still on her face.

How long it took the rifle to make the three-quarter circle, I am not in a position to say. To me, looking into the tigress's eyes and unable therefore to follow the movement of the barrel, it appeared that my arm was paralyzed, and that the swing would never be completed. However, the movement was completed at last, and as soon as the rifle was pointing at the tigress's body, I pressed the trigger.

I heard the report, exaggerated in that restricted space, and felt the jar of the recoil and but for these tangible proofs that the rifle had gone off, I might, for all the immediate result the shot produced, have been in the grip of one of those awful nightmares in which triggers are vainly pulled of rifles that refused to be discharged at the critical moment.

For a perceptible fraction of time the tigress remained perfectly still, and then, very slowly, her head sank on to her outstretched paws, while at the same time a jet of blood issued from the bullet-hole. The bullet had injured her spine and shattered the upper portion of her heart.

The two men who were following a few yards behind me and who were separated from the tigress by the thickness of the rock came to a halt when they saw me stop and turn my head. They knew instinctively that I had seen the tigress and judged from my behaviour that she was close at hand and Madho Singh said afterwards that he wanted to call out and tell me to drop the eggs and get both hands on the rifle. When I had fired my shot and lowered the point of the rifle on to my toes, Madho Singh at a sign, came forward to relieve me of it, for very suddenly my legs appeared to be unable to support me, so I made for the fallen tree and sat down. Even before looking at the pads of her feet, I knew it was the Chowgarh tigress I had sent to the Happy Hunting Grounds, and that the shears that had assisted her to cut the threads of sixty-four human lives, the people of the district put the number at twice that figure had, while the game was in her hands, turned, and cut the thread of her own life.

Three things, each of which would appear to you to have been to my disadvantage, were actually in my favour. These were (a) the eggs in my left hand (b) the light rifle I was carrying, and (c) the tiger being a man-eater. If I had not had the eggs in my hand, I should have had both hands on the rifle, and when I looked back and saw the tiger at such close quarters. I should instinctively have tried to swing round to face her, and the spring that was arrested by my lack of movement would inevitably have been launched. Again, if the rifle had not been a light one it would not have been possible for me to have moved it in the way it was imperative I should move it, and then discharge it at the full extent of my arm and lastly, if the tiger had been just an ordinary tiger, and not a man-eater, it would, on finding itself cornered have made for the opening and wiped me out of the way and to be wiped out of the way by a tiger usually has fatal results.

While the men made a detour and went up the hill to free the buffalo and secure the rope, which was needed for another and more pleasant purpose, I climbed over the rocks and went up the ravine to restore the eggs to their rightful owner. I plead guilty of being as superstitious as my brother sportsmen. For three long periods, extending over a whole year, I had tried and tried hard to get a shot at the tigress, and had failed; and now within a few minutes of having picked the eggs my luck had changed.

The eggs, which all this time had remain safely in the hollow of my left hand, were still warm when I replaced them in the little depression in the rock that did duty as a nest, when I again passed that way half an hour later, they had vanished under the brooding mother whose colouring so exactly matched the mottled rock that it was difficult for me, who knew the exact spot where the nest was situated, to distinguish her from her surroundings.

The buffalo, who after months of care was now so tame that it followed like a dog, came scrambling down the hill in the wake of the men, nosed the tigress and lay down on the sand to chew the cud of contentment, while we lashed the tigress to the stout pole the men had cut.

I had tried to get Madho Singh to return to the bungalow for help, but this he would not hear of doing. With no one would he and his companion share the honour of carrying in the man-eater, and if I would lend a hand, the task, he said, with frequent halts for rest, would not be too difficult. We were three hefty men, two accustomed from childhood to carry heavy loads and all three hardened by a life of exposure but even so, the task we set ourselves was a herculean one.

The path down which we had come was too narrow and too winding for the long pole to which the tigress was lashed, so, with frequent halts to regain breath and readjust pads to prevent the pole biting too deep into shoulder muscles, we went straight up the hill through a tangle of raspberry and briar bushes, on the thorns of which we left a portion of our clothing and an amount of skin which made bathing for many days a painful operation.

The sun was still shining on the surrounding hills when three disheveled and very happy men, followed by a buffalo, carried the tigress to the Kala Agar Forest Bungalow, and from that evening to this day no human being has been killed or wounded over the hundreds of square miles of mountain and vale over which the Chowgarh tigress, for a period of five years, held sway.

I have added one more cross and date to the map of Eastern Kumaon that hangs on the wall before me, the cross and the date the man-eater earned. The cross is two miles west of Kala Agar, and the date under it is II April 1930.

The tigress's claws were broken, and bushed out, and one of her canine teeth was broken, and her front teeth were worn down to the bone. It was these defects that had made her a man-eater and were the cause of her not being able to kill outright and by her own efforts, a large proportion of the human beings she had attacked since the day she had been deprived of the assistance of the cub I had on my first visit shot by mistake.

THE BACHELOR OF POWALGARH

I

Three miles from our winter home, and in the heart of the forest, there is an open glade some four hundred yards long and half as wide, grassed with emerald- green and surrounded by big trees interlaced with cane creepers. It was in this glade, which for beauty has no equal, that I first saw the tiger who was known throughout the United Provinces as 'The Bachelor of Powalgarh', who from 1920 to 1930 was the most sought-after big-game trophy in the province.

The sun had just risen one winter's morning when I crested the high ground overlooking the glade. On the far side, a score of red jungle fowl were scratching among the dead leaves bordering a crystal-clear stream, and scattered over the emerald-green grass, now sparkling with dew, fifty or more *chital* were feeding. Sitting on a tree stump and smoking, I had been looking at this scene for some time when the hind nearest to me raised her head, turned in my direction and called and a moment later the Bachelor stepped into the open, from the thick bushes below me. For a long minute he stood with head held high surveying the scene and then with slow unhurried steps started to cross the glade. In his rich winter coat, which the newly risen sun was lighting up, he was a magnificent sight as, with head turning now to the right and now to the left, he walked down the wide lane the deer had made for him. At the stream he lay down and quenched his thirst, then sprang across and as he entered the dense tree jungle beyond, called three times in acknowledgement of the homage the jungle folk had paid him for from the time he had entered the glade every *chital* had called, every jungle fowl had cackled and every one of a troupe of monkeys on the trees had chattered.

The Bachelor was far afield that morning, for his home was in a ravine six miles away. Living in an area in which the majority of tigers are bagged with the aid of elephants, he had chosen his home wisely. The ravine, running into the foothills, was half a mile long, with steep hills on either side rising to a height of a thousand feet. At the upper end of the ravine there was a waterfall some twenty feet high, and at the lower end, where the water had cut through red clay, it narrowed to four feet. Any sportsman therefore who wished to try conclusions with the Bachelor, while he was at home, would of a necessity have to do so on foot. It was this secure retreat and Government rules prohibiting night shooting that had enabled the Bachelor to retain possession of his much sought-after skin.

In spite of the many and repeated attempts that had been made to bag him with the aid of buffalo bait, the Bachelor had never been fired at, though on two occasions, to my knowledge, he had only escaped death by the skin of his teeth. On the first occasion, after a perfect beat, a guy rope by which the *machan* was suspended interfered with the movement of Fred Anderson's rifle at the critical moment, and the second occasion the Bachelor arrived at the *machan* before the beat started and found Huish Edye filling his pipe. On both these occasions he had been viewed at a range of only a few feet, and while Anderson described him as being as big as a Shetland pony, Edye said he was as big as a donkey.

The winter following these and other unsuccessful attempts, I took Wyndham, our Commissioner, who knows more about tigers than any other man in India, to a fire track skirting the upper end of the ravine in which the Bachelor lived, to show him the fresh pugmarks of the tiger which I had found on the fire track that morning. Wyndham was accompanied by two of his most experienced *shikaris*, and after the three of them had carefully measured and examined the pugmarks, Wyndham said that in his opinion the tiger was ten feet between pegs, and while one *shikari* said he was 10´5" over curves, the other said he was 10'6" or a little more. All three agreed that they had never seen the pugmarks of a bigger tiger.

In 1930 the Forest Department started extensive fallings in the area surrounding the bachelor's home and annoyed at the disturbance he changed his quarters, this I learnt from two sportsmen who had taken out a shooting pass with the object of hunting down the tiger. Shooting passes are only issued for fifteen days of each month, and throughout that winter, shooting party after shooting party failed to make contact with the tiger.

Towards the end of the winter an old dak runner, who passes our gate every morning and evening on his seven-mile run through the forest to a hill village, came to me one evening and reported that on his way out that morning he had seen the biggest pugmarks of a tiger that he had seen during the thirty years of his service. The tiger, he said, had come from the west and after proceeding along the road for two hundred yards had gone east, taking a path that started from near an almond tree. This tree was about two miles from our home and was a well-known landmark. The path the tiger had taken runs through very heavy jungle for half a mile before crossing a wide watercourse, and then joins a cattle track which skirts the foot of the hills before entering a deep and well-wooded valley, a favourite haunt of tigers.

Early next morning, with Robin at my heels, I set out to prospect, my objective being the point where the cattle track entered the valley, for at this point the tracks of all the animals entering or leaving the valley are to be found. From the time we started Robin appeared to know that we had a special job at hand, and he paid not the least attention to the jungle fowl we disturbed, the *kakar* that let us get quite close to it, and the two *sambhar* that stood and belled at us. Where the cattle track entered the valley, the ground was hard and stony, and when we reached this spot Robin put down his head and very carefully smelt the stones, and on receiving a signal from me to carry on he turned and started down the track, keeping a yard ahead of me; I could tell from his behaviour that he was on the scent of a tiger and that the scent was hot. A hundred yards further down, where the track flattens out and run along the foot of the hill, the ground is soft; here I saw the pugmarks of a tiger and a glance at them satisfied me we were on the heels of the Bachelor and that he was only a minute or two ahead of us.

Beyond the soft ground the track runs for three hundred yards over stones, before going steeply down on to an open plain. If the tiger kept to the track, we should probably see him on this open ground. We had gone another fifty yards when Robin stopped and, after running his nose up and down a blade of grass on the left of the track, turned and entered the grass which was here about two feet high. On the far side of the grass there was a patch of clerodendron, about forty yards wide. This plant grows in dense patches to a height of five feet and has widely spread leaves and a big head of flowers not unlike horse-chestnut. It is greatly fancied by tigers, *sambhar*, and *pigs* because of the shade it gives. When Robin reached the clerodendron he stopped and backed towards me, thus telling me that he could not see into the bushes ahead and wished to be carried. Lifting him up, I put his hind legs into my left-hand pocket, and when he had hooked his forefeet over my left arm, he was safe and secure, and I had both hands free for the rifle. On these occasions Robin was always in deadly earnest and no matter what he saw, or how our quarry behaved before or after fired at, he never moved and spoilt my shot, or impeded my view. Proceeding very slowly, we had gone halfway through the clerodendron when I saw the bushes directly in front of us swaying. Waiting until the tiger had cleared the bushes. I went forward expecting to see him in the more or less open jungle, but he was nowhere in sight, and when I put Robin down, he turned to the left and indicated that the tiger had gone into a deep and narrow ravine nearby. This ravine ran to the foot of an isolated hill on which there were caves frequented by tigers, and as I was not armed to deal with a tiger at close quarters, and further, as it was time for breakfast, Robin and I turned and made for home.

After breakfast I returned alone, armed with heavy .450 rifle, and as I approached the hill, which in the days of long ago had been used by the local inhabitants as a rallying point against the Gurkha invaders, I heard the boom of a big buffalo bell, and a man shouting. These sounds were coming from the top of the hills, which is flat, and about half an acre in extent, so I climbed up and saw a man on a tree, striking a dead branch with the head of his axe and shouting, while at the foot of the tree a number of buffaloes were collected. When he saw me, the man called out, saying I had just arrived in time to save him and his buffaloes from a *shaitan* of a tiger, the size of a camel, that had been threatening them for hours. From his story I gathered that he had arrived on the hill shortly after Robin and I had left for home and that as he started to cut bamboo leaves for his buffaloes, he saw a tiger coming towards him. He shouted to drive the tiger away, as he had done on many previous occasions with other tigers, but instead of going away this one had started to growl. He took to his heels, followed by his buffaloes, and climbed up the nearest tree. The tiger, paying no heed to his shouts, had then set to pacing round and round, while the buffaloes kept their heads towards it. Probably the tiger had heard me coming, for it had left only a moment before I had arrived. The man was an old friend, who before his quarrel with the Headman of his village had done a considerable amount of poaching in these jungles with the Headman's gun. He now begged me to conduct both himself and his cattle safely out of the jungle so telling him to lead on, I followed behind to see that there were no stragglers. At first the buffaloes were disinclined to break up their close formation, but after a little persuasion we got them to start, and we had gone halfway across the open plain I have alluded to when the tiger called in the jungle to our right. The man quickened his pace, and I urged on the buffaloes, for a mile of very thick jungle lay between us and the wide, open watercourse beyond which lay my friend's village and safety for his buffaloes.

I have earned the reputation of being keener on photographing animals than on killing them and before I left my friend, he begged me to put aside photography for this once, and kill the tiger, which he said was big enough to eat a buffalo a day; and ruin him in twenty-five days. I promised to do my best and turned to retrace my steps to the open plain, to meet with an experience every detail of which has burnt itself deep into my memory.

On reaching the plane I sat down to wait for the tiger to disclose his whereabouts, or for the jungle folk to tell me where he was. It was then about 3 p.m., and as the sun was warm and comforting, I put my head down on my drawn-up knees and had been dozing, a few minutes when I was awakened by the tiger calling; thereafter he continued to call at short intervals.

Between the plain and the hills there is a belt, some half a mile wide of the densest scrub jungle for a hundred miles round, and I located the tiger as being on the hills on the far side of the scrub about three-quarters of a mile from me and from the way he was calling it was evident he was in search of a mate.

Starting from the upper left-hand corner of the plain and close to where I was sitting, an old cart track, used some years previously for extracting timber, ran in an almost direct line to where the tiger was calling. This track would take me in the direction of the calling animal, but on the hills was high grass, and without Robin to help me there would be little chance of my seeing him. So instead of my going to look for the tiger, I decided he should come and look for me. I was too far away for him to hear me, so I sprinted up the cart track for a few hundred yards, laid down my rifle, climbed to the top of a high tree and called three times. I was immediately answered by the tiger. After climbing down, I ran back, calling as I went, and arrived on the plain without having found a suitable place in which to sit and await the tiger. Something would have to be done and done in a hurry; for the tiger was rapidly coming nearer, so, after rejecting a little hollow which I found to be full of black stinking water, I lay down flat in the open, twenty yards from where the track entered the scrub. From this point I had a clear view up the track for fifty yards, to where a bush leaning over it impeded my further view. If the tiger came down the track, as I expected him to, I decided to fire at him as soon as he cleared the obstruction.

After opening the rifle to make quite sure it was loaded, I threw off the safety catch, and with elbows comfortably resting on the soft ground waited for the tiger to appear. I had not called since I came out on the plain, so to give him directions I now gave a low call, which he immediately answered from a distance of a hundred yards. If he came on at his usual pace, I judged he would clear the obstruction in thirty seconds. I counted this number very slowly, and went on counting up to eighty, when out of the corner of my eye I saw a movement to my right front, where the bushes approached within ten yards of me. Turning my eyes in that direction I saw a great head projecting above the bushes, which here were four feet high. The tiger was only a foot or two inside the bushes, but all I could see of him was his head. As I very slowly swung the point of the rifle round and ran my eyes along the sights, I noticed that his head was not quite square on to me, and as I was firing up and he was looking down, I aimed an inch below his right eye, pressed the trigger and for the next half-hour nearly died of fright.

Instead of dropping dead as I expected him to, the tiger went straight up into the air above the bushes for his full length, falling backwards on to a tree a foot thick which had been blown down in a storm and was still green. With unbelievable fury he attacked this tree and tore it to bits, emitting as he did so roar upon roar, and what was even worse, a dreadful blood-curdling sound as though he was savaging his worst enemy. The branches of the tree tossed about as though struck by a tornado, while the bushes on my side shook and bulged out and every moment, I expected to have him on top of me, for he had been looking at me when I fired and knew where I was.

Too frightened even to recharge the rifle for fear the slight movement and sound should attract the attention of the tiger, I lay and sweated for half an hour with my finger on the left trigger. At last, the branches of the tree and the bushes ceased waving about, and the roaring became less frequent, and eventually, to my great relief, ceased. For another half-hour I lay perfectly still, with arms cramped by the weight of the heavy rifle, and then started to pull myself backwards with my toes. After progressing for thirty yards in this manner I got to my feet and crouching low, made for the welcome shelter of the nearest tree. Here I remained for some minutes and as all was now silent, I turned and made for home.

II

Next morning, I returned accompanied by one of my men, an expert tree-climber. I had noticed the previous evening that there was a tree growing on the edge of the open ground, and about forty yards from where the tiger had fallen. We approached this tree very cautiously, and I stood behind it while the man climbed to the top. After a long and careful scrutiny, he looked down and shook his head, and when he re-joined me on the ground, he told me that the bushes over a big area had been flattened down, but that the tiger was not in sight.

I sent him back to his perch on the tree with instructions to keep a sharp lookout and warn me if he saw any movement in the bushes and went forward to have a look at the spot where the tiger had raged. He had enraged to some purpose, for in addition to tearing branches and great strips of wood off the tree, he had torn up several bushes by the roots, and bitten down others. Blood in profusion was sprinkled everywhere, and on the ground were two congealed pools, near one of which was lying a bit of bone two inches square, which I found on examination to be part of the tiger's skull.

No blood trail led away from this spot and this, combined with the two pools of blood, was proof that the tiger was still here when I left and that the precautions, I had taken the previous evening had been very necessary, for when I started on my 'getaway' I was only ten yards from the most dangerous animal in the world, a freshly wounded tiger. On circling round the spot, I found a small smear of blood here and there on leaves that had brushed against his face. Noting that those indications of the tiger's passage led in a direct line to a giant *semul* tree (Bombax malabaricum, the Silk Cotton Tree) two hundred yards away, I went back and climbed the tree my man was on in order to get a bird's-eye view of the ground I should have to go over, for I had a very uneasy feeling that I should find him alive: a tiger shot in the head can live for days and can even recover from the wound. True, this tiger had a bit of his skull missing, and as I had never dealt with an animal in his condition before, I did not know whether he was likely to live for a few hours or days or live on to die of old age. For this reason, I decided to treat him as an ordinary wounded tiger, and not to take any avoidable risks when following him up.

From my elevated position on the tree, I saw that, a little to the left of the line to the *semul* tree, there were two trees, the nearer one thirty yards from where the blood was, and the other fifty yards further on. Leaving my man on the tree, I climbed down, picked up my rifle and a shotgun and bag of a hundred cartridges, and very cautiously approached the nearer tree and climbed up it to a height of thirty feet, pulling the rifle and gun, which I had tied to one end of a strong cord, up after me. After fixing the rifle in a fork of the tree where it would be handy if needed, I started to spray the bushes with small shots, yard by yard up to the tooth of the second tree. I did this with the object of locating the tiger, assuming he was alive and, in that area, for a wounded tiger, on hearing a shot fired close to him, or on being struck by a pellet, will either growl or charge. Receiving no indication of the tiger's presence I went to the second tree and sprayed the bushes to within a few yards of the *semul* tree, firing the last shot at the tree itself. After this last shot I thought I heard a low growl, but it was not repeated, and I put it down to my imagination. My bag of cartridges was now empty, so after recovering my man I called it a day and went home.

When I returned next morning, I found my friend the buffalo man feeding his buffaloes on the plain. He appeared to be very-much relieved to see me, and the reason for this I learnt later. The grass was still wet with dew, but we found a dry spot and there sat- down to have a smoke and relate our experiences. My friend, as I have already told you, had done a lot of poaching, and having spent all his life in tiger-infested jungles tending his buffaloes, or shooting, his jungle knowledge was considerable.

After I had left him that day at the wide, open watercourse, he had crossed to the far side and had sat down to listen for sounds coming from the direction in which I had gone. He had heard two tigers calling; he had heard my shot followed by the continuous roaring of a tiger, and very naturally concluded I had wounded one of the tigers and that it had killed me. On his return next morning to the same spot, he had been greatly mystified by hearing a hundred shots fired, and this morning, not being able to contain his curiosity any longer, he had come to see what had happened. Attracted by the smell of blood, his buffaloes had shown him where the tiger had fallen, and he had seen the patches of dry blood and had found the bit of bone. No animal in his opinion could possibly live for more than a few hours after having a bit of its skull blown away and so sure was, he that the tiger was dead that he offered to take his buffaloes into the jungle and find it for me. I had heard of this method of recovering tigers with the help of buffaloes but had never tried it myself, and after my friend had agreed to accept compensation for any damage to his cattle, I accepted his offer.

Rounding up the buffaloes, twenty-five in number, and keeping to the line I had sprinkled with shot the previous day, we made for the *semul* tree, followed by the buffaloes. Our progress was slow, for not only had us to move the chin-high bushes with our hands to see where to put our feet, but we also had frequently to check a very natural tendency on the part of the buffaloes to stray. As we approached the *semul* tree, where the bushes were lighter, I saw a little hollow filled with dead leaves that had been pressed flat and on which were several patches of blood, some dry, others in the process of congealing, and one quite fresh; and when I put my hand to the ground, I found it was warm. Incredible as it may appear, the tiger had lain in this hollow the previous day while I had expended a hundred cartridges and had only moved off when he saw us and the buffaloes approaching. The buffaloes had now found the blood and were pawing up the ground and snorting, and as the prospect of being caught between a charging tiger and angry buffaloes did not appeal to me, I took hold of my friend's arm, turned him round and made for the open plain, followed by the buffaloes. When we were back on safe ground, I told the man to go home and said I would return next day and deal with the tiger alone.

The path through the jungles that I had taken each day when coming from and going home ran for some distance over soft ground, and on this soft ground, on this fourth day, I saw the pugmarks of a big male tiger. By following these pugmarks, I found the tiger had entered the dense brushwood a hundred yards to the right of the semul tree. Here was an unexpected complication, for if I now saw a tiger in this jungle I should not know unless I got a very close look at it whether it was the wounded or the unwounded one. However, this contingency would have to be dealt with when met and in the meantime worrying would not help, so I entered the bushes and made for the hollow at the foot of the semul tree.

There was no blood trail to follow so I zigzagged through the bushes, into which it was impossible to see further than a few inches, for an hour or more, until I came to a ten-foot-wide dry watercourse. Before stepping down into this watercourse I looked up at it and saw the left hind leg and tail of a tiger. The tiger was standing perfectly still with its body and head hidden by a tree, and only this one leg visible. I raised the rifle to my shoulder, and then lowered it. To have broken the leg would have been easy, for the tiger was only ten yards away, and it would have been the right thing to do if its owner was the wounded animal but there were two tigers in this area, and to have broken the leg of the wrong one would have doubled my difficulties, which were already considerable. Presently the leg was withdrawn, and I heard the tiger moving away, and going to the spot where he had been standing, I found a few drops of blood, too late now to regret not having broken that leg.

A quarter of a mile further on there was a little stream and it was possible that the tiger, now recovering from his wound, was making for this stream. With the object of intercepting him or failing that, waiting for him at the water, I took a game path which I knew went to the stream and had proceeded along it for some distance when a *sambhar* belled to my left, and went dashing off through the jungle. It was evident now that I was abreast of the tiger, and I had only taken a few more steps when I heard the loud crack of a dry stick breaking as though some heavy animal had fallen on it, the sound had come from a distance of fifty yards and from the exact spot where the *sambhar* had belled. The *sambhar* had in unmistakable tones warned the jungle folk of the presence of a tiger, and the stick therefore could only have been broken by the same animal so getting down on my hands and knees I started to crawl in the direction from which the sound had come.

The bushes here were from six to eight feet high, with dense foliage on the upper branches and very few leaves on the stems, so that I could see through them for a distance of ten to fifteen feet. I had covered thirty yards, hoping fervently that if the tiger charged, he would come from in front (for in no other direction could I have fired), when I caught sight of something red on which the sun, drifting through the upper leaves, was shining; it might only be a bunch of dead leaves; on the other hand, it might be the tiger. I could get a better view of this object from two yards to the right, so lowering my head until my chin touched the ground. I crawled this distance with my belly to ground and on raising my head saw the tiger in front of me. He was crouching down looking at me, with the sun shining on his left shoulder, and on receiving my two bullets he rolled over on his side without making a sound.

As I stood over him and ran my eyes over his magnificent proportions, it was not necessary to examine the pads of his feet to know that before me lay the Bachelor of Powalgarh.

The entry of the bullet fired four days previously was hidden by a wrinkle of skin, and at the back of his head was a big hole which, surprisingly, was perfectly clean and healthy.

The report of my rifle was, I knew, being listened for so I hurried home to relieve anxiety and while I related the last chapter of the hunt and drank a pot of tea, my men were collecting.

Accompanied by my sister and Robin and a carrying party of twenty men, I returned to where the tiger was lying, and before he was roped to a pole my sister and I measured him from nose to tip of tail, and from tip of tail to nose. At home we measured him again to make quite sure we had made no mistake the first time. These measurements are valueless, for there were no independent witnesses present to certify them. They are, however, interesting as showing the accuracy with which experienced woodsmen can judge the length of a tiger from his pugmarks. Wyndham, you will remember, said the tiger was ten feet between pegs, which would give roughly 10'6" over curves; and while one *shikari* said was 10'5.09" over curves, the other said he was 10'6" or a little more. Shot seven years after these estimates were made, my sister and I measured the tiger as being 10'7" over curves.

I have told the story at some length, as I feel sure that those who hunted the tiger between 1920 and 1930 will be interested to know how the Bachelor of Powalgarh met his end.

THE MOHAN MAN-EATER

I

Eighteen miles from our summer home in the Himalayas there is a long ridge running east and west, some 9,000 feet in height. On the upper slopes of the eastern end of this ridge, there is a luxuriant growth of oat grass; below this grass the hill falls steeply away in a series of rock cliffs to the Kosi river below.

One day a party of women and girls from the village on the north face of the ridge were cutting the oat grass, when a tiger suddenly appeared in their midst. In the stampede that followed, an elderly woman lost her footing, rolled down the steep slope and disappeared over the cliff. The tiger, evidently alarmed by the screams of the women, vanished as mysteriously as it had appeared, and when the women had reassembled and recovered from their fright, they went down the grassy slope and, looking over the cliff, saw their companion lying on a narrow ledge some distance below them.

The woman said she was badly injured it was found later that she had broken a leg and fractured several ribs and that she could not move. Ways and means of a rescue were discussed, and it was finally decided that it was a job for men; and as no one appeared to be willing to remain at the spot, they informed the injured woman that they were going back to the village for help. The woman begged not to be left alone, however and at her entreaty a girl, sixteen years of age, volunteered to stay with her. So, while the rest of the party set off for the village, the girl made her way down to the right, where a rift in the cliff enabled her to get a foothold on the ledge.

This ledge only extended halfway across the face of the cliff and ended, a few yards from where the woman was lying, in a shallow depression. Fearing that she might fall off the ledge and be killed on the rocks hundreds of feet below; the woman asked the girl to move her to this depression, and this difficult and dangerous feat the girl successfully accomplished. There was only room for one in the depression, so that the girl squatted, as only an Indian can squat, on the ledge facing the woman.

The village was four miles away, and once, and once again, the two on the ledge speculated as to the length of time it would take their companions to get back to the village; what men they were likely to find in the village at that time of day; how long it would take to explain what had happened, and finally, how long it would take the rescue party to arrive.

Conversation had been carried on in whispers for fear that the tiger might be lurking in the vicinity and hear them and then, suddenly, the woman gave a gasp and the girl, seeing the look of horror on her face and the direction in which she was looking, turned her head and over her shoulder saw the tiger, stepping out of the rift in the cliff on to the ledge.

Few of us, I imagine, have escaped that worst of all nightmares in which, while our limbs and vocal cords are paralyzed with fear, some terrible beast in a monstrous form approach to destroy us; the nightmare from which, sweating fear in every pore, we waken with a cry of thankfulness to Heaven that it was only a dream. There was no such happy awakening from the nightmare of that unfortunate girl, and little imagination was needed to picture the scene. A rock cliff with a narrow ledge running partly across it and ending in a little depression in which an injured woman is lying; a young girl frozen with terror, squatting on the ledge, and a tiger slowly creeping towards her; retreat in every direction cut off, and no help at hand.

Mothi Singh, an old friend of mine, was in the village visiting a sick daughter when the women arrived, and he headed the rescue party. When this party went down the grassy slope and looked over the cliff, they saw the woman lying in a swoon and on the ledge, they saw splashes of blood.

The injured woman was carried back to the village, and when she had been revived and had told her story, Mothi Singh set out on his eighteen-mile walk to me. He was an old man well over sixty, but he scouted the suggestion that he was tired and needed a rest, so we set off together to make investigations. But there was nothing that I could do, for twenty-four hours had elapsed and all that the tiger had left of the brave young girl, who had volunteered to stay with her injured companion, were a few bits of bone and her torn and bloodstained clothes.

This was the first human being killed by the tiger which later received recognition in the Government records as 'The Mohan Man-eater'.

After killing the girl, the tiger went down the Kosi valley for the winter, killing on its way among other people, two men of the Public Works Department, and the daughter-in-law of our member of the Legislative Council. As summer approached, it returned to the scene of its first kill, and for several years thereafter its beat extended up and down the Kosi valley from Kakrighat to Gargia, a distance of roughly forty miles until it finally took up its quarters on the hill above Mohan, in the vicinity of a village called Kartkanoula.

At the District Conference, to which reference has been made in a previous story, the three man-eating tigers operating at that time in the Kumaon Division were classed, as follows, in their order of importance:

1st—Chowgarh, Nainital District.

2nd—Mohan, Almora District.

3rd—Kanda, Garhwal District.

After the Chowgarh tiger had been accounted for, I was reminded by Baines, Deputy Commissioner, Almora, that only a part of my promise made at the conference had been fulfilled and that the Mohan tiger was next on the list. The tiger, he stated, was becoming more active and a greater menace every day and had during the previous week killed three human beings, residents of Kartkanoula village. It was to this village Baines now suggested I should go.

While I had been engaged with the Chowgarh tiger, Baines had persuaded some sportsmen to go to Kartkanoula but though they had sat up over human and animal kills, they had failed to make contact with the man-eater and had returned to their depot at Ranikhet. Baines informed me I should now have the ground to myself, a very necessary precaution, for nerves wear thin when hunting man-eaters, and accidents are apt to result when two or more parties are hunting the same animal.

II

It was on a blistering hot day in May that I, my two servants, and the six Garhwalis I had brought with me from Naini Tal alighted from the I p.m. train at Ramnagar and set off on our twenty-four-mile foot journey to Kartkanoula. Our first stage was only seven miles, but it was evening before we arrived at Gargia. I had left home in a hurry on receiving Baines' letter and had not had time to ask for permission to occupy the Gargia Forest Bungalow, so I slept out in the open.

On the far side of the Kosi river at Gargia there is a cliff several hundred feet high, and while I was trying to get sleep, I heard what I thought were stones falling off the cliff on the rocks below. The sound was exactly the same as would be made by bringing two stones violently together. After some time, this sound worried me, as sounds would on a hot night and as the moon was up and the light good enough to avoid stepping on snakes, I left my camp bed and set out to make investigations. I found that the sound was being made by a colony of frogs in a marsh by the side of the road. I have heard land, water and tree frogs making strange sounds in different parts of the world, but I have never heard anything so strange as the sound made by the frogs at Gargia in the month of May.

After a very early start next morning, we did the twelve miles to Mohan before the sun got hot and while my men were cooking their food and my servants were preparing my breakfast, the chowkidar of the bungalow, two Forest Guards and several men from the Mohan bazaar, entertained me with stories of the man-eater, the most recent of which concerned the exploits of a fisherman who had been fishing in the Kosi river. One of the Forest Guards claimed to be the proud hero of this exploit and he described very graphically how he had been out one day with the fisherman and, on turning a bend in the river, they had come face to face with the man-eater; and how the fisherman had thrown away his rod and had grabbed the rifle off his, the Forest Guard's shoulder and how they had run for their lives with the tiger close on their heels. 'Did you look back?' I asked. '*No, sahib*! said he, pitying my ignorance. 'How could a man who was running for his life from a man-eater look back?'; and how the fisherman, who was leading by a head, in a thick patch of grass had fallen over a sleeping bear, after which there had been great confusion and shouting and everyone, including the bear, had run in different directions and the fisherman had got lost; and how after a long time the fisherman had eventually found his way back to the bungalow and had said a lot to him, the Forest Guard on the subject of having run away with his rifle and left him empty-handed to deal with a man-eating tiger and an angry bear. The Forest Guard ended up his recital by saying that the fisherman had left Mohan the following day saying that he had hurt his leg when he fell over the bear, and that anyway there were no fish to be caught in the Kosi river.

By midday we were ready to continue our journey and with many warnings from the small crowd that had collected to see us off, to keep a sharp lookout for the man-eater while going through the dense forest that lay ahead of us, we set out on our four-thousand-foot climb to Kartkanoula.

Our progress was slow, for my men were carrying heavy loads and the track was excessively steep, and the heat terrific. There had been some trouble in the upper villages a short time previously, necessitating the dispatch from Nainital of a small police force, and I had been advised to take everything I needed for myself and my men with me, as owing to the unsettled conditions it would not be possible to get any stores locally. This was the reason for the heavy loads my men were carrying.

After many halts we reached the edge of the cultivated land in the late afternoon and as there was now no further danger to be apprehended for my men from the man-eater, I left them and set out alone for the Foresters' Hut which is visible from Mohan, and which had been pointed out to me by the Forest Guards as the best place for my stay while at Kartkanoula.

The hut is on the ridge of the high hill overlooking Mohan, and as I approached it along the level stretch of road running across the face of the hill, in turning a corner in a ravine where there is some dense undergrowth, I came upon a woman filling an earthenware pitcher from a little trickle of water flowing down a wooden trough. Apprehending that my approach on rubber-soled shoes would frighten her, I coughed to attract her attention, noticed that she started violently as I did so, and a few yards beyond her, stopped to light a cigarette. A minute or two later I asked, without turning my head, if it was safe for anyone to be in this lonely spot, and after a little hesitation the woman answered that it was not safe, but that water had to be fetched and as there was no one in the home to accompany her, she had come alone. Was there no man? Yes, there was a man, but he was in the fields ploughing, and in any case, it was the duty of women to fetch water. How long would it take to fill the pitcher? Only a little longer. The woman had got over her fright and shyness and I was now subjected to a close cross-examination. Was I a policeman? No. Was I a Forest Officer? No. Then who was I? Just a man. Why had I come? To try and help the people of Kartkanoula. In what way? By shooting the man-eater. Where had I heard about the man-eater? Why had I come alone? Where were my men? How many were there? How long would I stay? And so on.

The pitcher was not declared full until the woman had satisfied her curiosity and as she walked behind me, she pointed to one of several ridges running down the south face of the hill and pointing out a big tree growing on a grassy slope said that three days previously the man-eater had killed a woman under it; this tree I noted, with interest, was only two or three hundred yards from my objective the Foresters' Hut. We had now come to a footpath running up the hill and as she took it, the woman said the village from which she had come was just round the shoulder of the hill and added that she was now quite safe.

Those of you who know the women of India will realize that I had accomplished a lot, especially when it is remembered that there had recently been trouble in this area with the police. So far from alarming the woman and thereby earning the hostility of the entire countryside, I had, by standing by while she filled her pitcher and answering a few questions, gained a friend who would in the shortest time possible acquaint the whole population of the village with my arrival; that I was not an officer of any kind, and that the sole purpose of my visit was to try to rid them of the man-eater.

III

The Foresters' Hut was on a little knoll some twenty yards to the left of the road, and as the door was only fastened with a chain, I opened it and walked inside. The room was about ten feet square and quite clean but had a mouldy disused smell; I learnt later that the hut had not been occupied since the advent of the man-eater in that area eighteen months previously. On either side of the main room there were two narrow slips of rooms, one used as a kitchen and the other as a fuel store. The hut would make a nice safe shelter for my men and having opened the back door to let a current of air blow through the room, I went outside and selected a spot between the hut and the road for my 40-lb tent. There was no furniture of any kind in the hut, so I sat down on a rock near the road to await the arrival of my men.

The ridge at this point was about fifty yards wide, and as the hut was on the south edge of the ridge and the village on the north face of the hill, the latter was not visible from the former. I had been sitting on the rock for about ten minutes when a head appeared over the crest from the direction of the village, followed by a second and a third. My friend, the water carrier had not been slow in informing the village of my arrival.

When strangers meet in India and wish to glean information on any particular subject from each other, it is customary to refrain from broaching the subject that has brought them together whether accidentally or of set purpose until the very last moment and to fill up the interval by finding out everything concerning each other's domestic and private affairs as for instance, whether married and if so, the number and sex of children and their ages; if not married, why not occupation and amount of pay and so on. Questions that would in any other part of the world earn one a thick ear, are in India and especially in our hills asked so artlessly and universally that no one who has lived among the people dreams of taking offence at them.

In my conversation with the woman, I had answered many of the set questions, and the ones of a domestic nature which it is not permissible for a woman to ask of a man, were being put to me when my men arrived. They had filled a kettle at the little spring, and in an incredibly short time dry sticks were collected, a fire lit, the kettle boiled, and tea and biscuits produced. As I opened a tin of condensed milk, I heard the men asking my servant's why condensed milk was being used instead of fresh milk and receiving the answer that there was no fresh milk; and further that, as it had been apprehended that owing to some previous trouble in this area no fresh milk would be available, a large supply of tinned milk had been brought. The men appeared to be very distressed on hearing this and after a whispered conversation one of them, who I learnt later was the Headman of Kartkanoula, addressed me and said it was an insult to them to have brought tinned milk, when all the resources of the village were at my disposal. I admitted my mistake, which I said was due to my being a stranger to that locality and told the Headman that if he had any milk to spare, I would gladly purchase a small quantity for my daily requirement, but that beyond the milk, I wanted for nothing.

My loads had now been unstrapped, while more men had arrived from the village, and when I told my servants where I wanted them to pitch my tent there was a horrified exclamation from the assembled villagers. Live in a tent indeed! Was I ignorant of the fact that there was a man-eating tiger in this area and that it used this road regularly every night? If I doubted their word, let me come and see the claw marks on the doors of the houses where the road ran through the upper end of the village. Moreover, if the tiger did not eat me in the tent, it would certainly eat my men in the hut, if I was not there to protect them. This last statement made my men prick up their ears and add their entreaties to the advice of the villagers, so eventually I agreed to stay in the main room, while my two servants occupied the kitchen, and the six Garhwalis the fuel store.

The subject of the man-eater having been introduced; it was now possible for me to pursue it without admitting that it was the one subject I had wished to introduce from the moment the first man had put his head over the ridge. The path leading down to the tree where the tiger had claimed its last victim was pointed out to me and the time of day and the circumstances under which the woman had been killed, explained. The road along which the tiger came every night, I was informed, ran eastward to Baital Ghat with a branch down to Mohan, and westward to Chaknakl on the Ramganga river. The road going west, after running through the upper part of the village and through cultivated land for half a mile, turned south along the face of the hill, and on rejoining me ridge on which the hut was, followed the ridge right down to Chaknakl. This portion of the road between Kartkanoula and Chaknakl, some six miles long, was considered to be very dangerous, and had not been used since the advent of the man-eater; I subsequently found that after leaving the cultivated land, the road entered dense tree and scrub jungle, which extended right down to the river.

The main cultivation of Kartkanoula village is on the north face of the hill, and beyond this cultivated land there are several small ridges, with deep ravines between them. On the nearest of these ridges and distant about a thousand yards from the Foresters' Hut, there was a big pine tree. Near this tree, some ten days previously; the tiger had killed, partly eaten, and left a woman, and as the three sportsmen who were staying in a forest bungalow four miles away were unable to climb the pine tree, the villagers had put up three *machans* in three separate trees, at distances varying from one hundred to one hundred and fifty yards from the kill and the *machans* had been occupied by the sportsmen and their servants a little before sunset. There was a young moon at the time, and after it had set, the villagers heard a number of shots being fired, and when they questioned the servants next morning, the servants said they did not know what had been fired at for they themselves had not seen anything. Two days later a cow had been killed over which the sportsmen had sat and again, as on the previous occasion, shots had been fired after the moon had set. It is these admittedly sporting but unsuccessful attempt to bag man-eaters that makes them so wary and the more difficult to shoot the longer they live.

The villagers gave me one very interesting item of news in connexion with the tiger. They said they always knew when it had come into the village by the low moaning sound it made. On questioning them closely, I learnt that at times the sound was continuous as the tiger passed between the houses, while at other times the sound stopped for sometimes short and other times long periods.

From this information I concluded (a) that the tiger was suffering from a wound, (b) that the wound was of such a nature that the tiger only felt it when in motion, and that therefore, (c) the wound was in one of its legs. I was assured that the tiger had not been wounded by any local *shikari*{or by any of the sportsmen from Ranikhet who had sat up for it; however this was of little importance, for the tiger had been a man-eater for years, and the wound that I believed it was suffering from, might have been the original cause of its becoming a man-eater. A very interesting point and one that could only be cleared up by examining the tiger after it was dead.

The men were curious to know why I was so interested in the sound 'made by the tiger, and when I told them that it indicated the animal had a wound in one of its legs and that the wound had been caused either by a bullet or porcupine quills, they disagreed with my reasoning and said that on the occasions they had seen the tiger it appeared to be in sound condition and further that the ease with which it killed and carried off its victims was proof that it was not crippled in any way. However, what I told them was remembered and later earned me the reputation of being gifted with second sight.

IV

When passing through Ramnagar, I had asked the Tahsildar to purchase two young male buffaloes for me and to send them to Mohan, where my men would take them over.

I told the villagers I intended tying up one of the buffaloes near the tree where three days previously the woman had been killed and the other on the road to the Chaknakl and they said they could think of no better sites, but that they would talk the matter over among themselves and let me know in the morning if they had any other suggestions to make. Night was now drawing in, and before leaving the Headman promised to send word to all the adjoining villages in the morning to let them know of my arrival, the reason for my coming, and to impress on them the urgency of letting me know without loss of time of any kills, or attacks by the tiger in their areas.

The musty smell in the room had much decreased though it was still noticeable. However, I paid no attention to it, and after a bath and dinner put two stones against the doors, there being no other way of keeping them shut and being bone-tired after my day's exertions went to bed and to sleep. I am a light sleeper, and two or three hours later I awoke on hearing an animal moving about in the jungle. It came right up to the back door. Getting hold of a rifle and a torch, I moved the stone aside with my foot and heard an animal moving off as I opened the door, it might from the sound it was making have been the tiger, but it might also have been a leopard or a porcupine. However, the jungle was too thick for me to see what it was. Back in the room and with the stone once more in position, I noticed I had developed a sore throat, which I attributed to having sat in the wind after the hot walk up from Mohan but when my servant pushed the door open and brought in my early morning cup of tea, I found I was suffering from an attack of laryngitis, possibly due to my having slept in a long-disused hut, the roof of which was swarming with bats. My servant informed me that he and his companion had escaped infection, but that the six Garhwalis in the fuel store were all suffering from the same complaint as I was. My stock of medicine consisted of a two-ounce bottle of iodine and a few tablets of quinine and on rummaging in my gun-case I found a small paper pocket of permanganate which my sister had provided for me on a previous occasion. The packet was soaked through with gun oil, but the crystals were still soluble, and I put a liberal quantity of the crystals into a tin of hot water, together with some iodine. The resulting gargle was very potent, and while it blackened our teeth, it did much to relieve the soreness in our throats.

After an early breakfast I sent four men down to Mohan to bring up the two buffaloes, and myself set off to prospect the ground where the woman had been killed. From the directions I had received overnight, I had no difficulty in finding the spot where the tiger had attacked and killed the woman as she was tying the grass she had cut into the bundle. The grass, and the rope she was using, were lying just as they had been left, as were also two bundles of grass left by her companions when they had run off in fright to the village. The men had told me that the body of the woman had not been found, but from the fact that three perfectly good lengths of rope and the dead woman's sickle had been left in the jungle, I am inclined to think that no attempt had been made to find her.

The woman had been killed at the upper end of a small landslide, and the tiger had taken her down the slide and into a thick patch of undergrowth. Here the tiger had waited, possibly to give the women time to get out of sight and had then crossed the ridge visible from the hut, after which it had gone with its kill straight down the hill for a mile or more into dense tree and scrub jungle. The tracks were now four days old and there was nothing to be gained by following them further. I turned back to the hut.

The climb back to the ridge was a very steep one, and when I reached the hut at about mid-day, I found an array of pots and pans of various shapes and sizes on the verandah, all containing milk. In contrast to the famine of the day before, there was now abundance, sufficient milk in fact for me to have bathed in. My servants informed me they had protested to no effect and that each man had said, as he deposited his vessel on the verandah, that he would take good care that I used no more condensed milk while I remained in their midst.

I did not expect the man to return from Mohan with the buffaloes before nightfall, so after lunch I set out to have a look at the road to Chaknakl.

From the hut the hill sloped gradually upwards to a height of about five hundred feet and was roughly triangular in shape. The road, after running through cultivated land for half a mile, turned sharply to the left, went across a steep rocky hill until it regained the ridge, and then turned to the right and followed the ridge down to Chaknakl. The road was level for a short distance after coming out on the ridge and then went steeply down, the gradient in places being eased by hairpin bends.

I had the whole afternoon before me and examined about three miles of the road very carefully. When a tiger uses a road regularly it invariably leaves signs of its passage by making scratch marks on the side of the road. These scratch marks, made for the same purpose as similar marks made by domestic cats and all other members of the cat family, are of very great interest to the sportsman, for they provide him with the following very useful information: (I) whether the animal that has made the mark is a male or a female, (2) the direction in which it was travelling, (3) the length of time that has elapsed since it passed,

(4) the direction and approximate distance of its headquarters, (5) the nature of its kills, and finally (6) whether the animal has recently had a meal of human flesh. The value of this easily acquired information to one who is hunting a man-eater on strange ground will be easily understood. Tigers also leave their pugmarks on the roads they use, and these pugmarks can provide one with quite a lot of useful information, as for instance the direction and speed at which the animal was travelling, its sex and age, whether all four limbs are sound, and if not sound, which particular limb is defective.

The road I was on hand through long disuse got overgrown with short stiff grass and was therefore not, except in one or two damp places, a good medium on which to leave pugmarks. One of these damp places was within a few yards of where the road came out on the ridge, and just below this spot there was a green and very stagnant pool of water, a regular drinking place for *sambhar*.

I found several scratch marks just round the corner where the road turned to the left after leaving the cultivated ground, the most recent of which was three days old. Two hundred yards from these scratch marks the road for a third of its width ran under an overhanging rock. This rock was ten feet high and at the top of it there was a flat piece of ground two or three yards wide, which was only visible from the road when approaching the rock from the village side. On the ridge I found more scratch marks, but I did not find any pugmarks until I got to the first hairpin bend. Here, in cutting across the bend, the tiger had left its trace where it had jumped down on to the same soft earth. The tracks, which were a day old, were a little distorted, but even so it was possible to see that they had been made by a big, old, male tiger.

When one is moving in an area in which a man-eating tiger is operating, progress is of necessity very slow, for every obstruction in one's line of walk, be it a bush, a tree, a rock or an inequality in the ground capable of concealing death, has to be cautiously approached, while at the same time, if a wind is not blowing and there was no wind that evening a careful and constant lookout has to be maintained behind and on either side. Further, there was much of interest to be looked at, for it was the month of May, when orchids at this elevation 4,000 to 5,000 feet are at their best, and I have never seen a greater variety or a greater wealth of bloom than the forests on that hill had to show. The beautiful white butterfly orchids were in greatest profusion and every second tree of any size appeared to have decked itself out with them.

It was here that I first saw a bird that Prater of the Bombay Natural History Society later very kindly identified for me as the Mountain Crag Martin, a bird of a uniform ash colour, with a slight tinge of pink on its breast, and in size a little smaller than a Rosy Pastor. These birds had their broods with them, and while the young ones four to a brood sat in a row on a dry twig at the top of a high tree, the parent birds kept darting away often to a distance of two or three hundred yards to catch insects. The speed at which they flew was amazing and I am quite sure there is nothing in feathers in North India, not excluding our winter visitor the great Tibetan Swallow, that these Martins could not make rings round. Another thing about these birds that was very interesting was their wonderful eyesight. On occasion they would fly in a dead straight line for several hundred yards before turning and coming back. It was not possible, at the speed they were going, that they were chasing insects on these long flights, and as after each flight they invariably thrust some minute object into one of the gaping mouths, I believed they were able to see insects at a range at which they would not have been visible to the human eye through the most powerful field glasses.

Safeguarding my neck, looking out for tracks, enjoying nature generally and listening to all the jungle sounds, a sambhar a mile away down the hillside in the direction of Mohan was warning the jungle folk of the presence of a tiger, and a *kakar* and a langur on the road to Chaknakl were warning other jungle folk of the presence of a leopard time passed quickly, and I found myself back at the overhanging rock as the sun was setting. As I approached this rock, I marked it as being quite the most dangerous spot in all the ground I had so far gone over. A tiger lying on the grass-covered bit of ground above the rock would only have to wait until anyone going either up or down the road was under, or had passed it, to have them at his mercy, a very dangerous spot indeed and one that needed remembering.

When I got back to the hut, I found the two buffaloes had arrived, but it was too late to do anything with them that evening.

My servants had kept a fire going most of the day in the hut, the air of which was now sweet and clean, but even so I was not going to risk sleeping in a closed room again, so I made them cut two thorn bushes and wedge them firmly into the doorways before going to bed. There was no movement in the jungle near the back door that night and after a sound sleep, I woke in the morning with my throat very much better.

I spent most of the morning talking to the village people and listening to the tales they had to tell of the man-eater and the attempts that had been made to shoot it and after lunch I tied up one buffalo on the small ridge the tiger had crossed when carrying away the woman and the other at the hairpin bend where I had seen the pugmarks.

Next morning, I found both buffaloes sleeping peacefully after having eaten most of the big feed of grass I had provided them with. I had tied bells round the necks of both animals, and the absence of any sound from these bells as I approached each buffalo gave me two disappointments for, as I have said, I found both of them asleep. That evening I changed the position of the second buffalo from the hairpin bend to where the road came out on the ridge, close to the pool of stagnant water.

The methods most generally employed in tiger shooting can briefly be described as (a) sitting up, and (b) beating, and young male buffaloes are used as bait in both cases. The procedure followed is to select the area most convenient for a sit up, or for a beat, and to tie the bait out in the late evening using a rope which the bait cannot, but which the tiger can, break and when the bait is taken, to either sit up over the kill on a machan in a tree or beat the cover into which the kill has been taken.

In the present case neither of these methods was feasible. My throat, though very much better, was still sore and it would not have been possible for me to have sat up for any length of time without coughing, and a beat over that vast area of heavily wooded and broken ground would have been hopeless even if I had been able to muster a thousand men, so I decided to stalk the tiger and to this end carefully sited my two buffaloes and tied them to stout saplings with four one-inch-thick hemp ropes and left them out in the jungle for the whole twenty-four hours.

I now stalked the buffaloes in turn each morning as soon as there was sufficient light to shoot by and again in the evening, for tigers, be they man-eaters or not, kill as readily in the day as they do at night in areas in which they are not disturbed, and during the day, while I waited for news from the outlying villages, nursed my throat and rested, my six Garhwalis fed and watered the buffaloes.

On the fourth evening when I was returning at sunset after visiting the buffalo on the ridge, as I came round a bend in the road thirty yards from the overhanging rock, I suddenly, and for the first time since my arrival at Kartkanoula, felt I was in danger and that the danger that threatened me was on the rock in front of me. For five minutes I stood perfectly still with my eyes fixed on the upper edge of the rock, watching for movement. At that short range the flicker of an eyelid would have caught my eyes, but there was not even this small movement and after going forward ten paces, I again stood watching for several minutes. The fact that I had seen no movement did not in any way reassure me, the man-eater was on the rock of that I was sure, and the question was, what was I going to do about it? The hill, as I have already told you, was very steep, had great rocks jutting out of it, and was overgrown with long grass and tree and scrub jungle. Bad as the going was, had it been earlier in the day I would have gone back and worked round and above the tiger to try to get a shot at him, but with only half an hour of daylight left, and the best part of a mile still to go, it would have been madness to have left the road. So, slipping up the safety catch and putting the rifle to my shoulder, I started to pass the rock.

The road here was about eight feet wide and going to the extreme outer edge I started walking crab-fashion, feeling each step with my feet before putting my weight down to keep from stepping off into space. Progress was slow and difficult but as I drew level with the overhanging rock and then began to pass it, hope rose high that the tiger would remain where he was, until I reached that part of the road from which the flat bit of ground above the rock, on which he was lying, was visible. The tiger, however, having failed to catch me off my guard was taking no chances, and I had just got clear of the rock when I heard a low muttered growl above me, and a little later first a *kakar* went off barking to the right, and then two *sambhar* hinds started belling near the crest of the triangular hill.

The tiger had got away with a sound skin but for that matter, so had I, so there was no occasion for regrets, and from the place on the hill where the *sambhar* was, I felt sure he would hear the bell I had hung round the neck of the buffalo that was tied on the ridge near the stagnant pool.

When I reached the cultivated land, I found a group of men waiting for me. They had heard the *kakar* and *sambhar* and were very disappointed that I had not seen the tiger but cheered up when I told them I had great hopes for the morrow.

V

During the night a dust-storm came on, followed by heavy rain, and I found to my discomfort that the roof of the hut was very porous. However, I eventually found a spot where it was leaking less than in others, dragged my camp bed to it and continued my sleep. It was brilliantly clear morning when I awoke, the rain had washed the heat haze and dust out of the atmosphere and every leaf and blade of grass was glistering in the newly risen sun.

Hitherto I had visited the nearer buffalo first, but this morning I had an urge to reverse the daily procedure, and after instructing my men to wait until the sun was well up and then go to feed and water the nearer buffalo, I set off with high hopes down the Chaknakl road, having first cleaned and oiled my 450/400 rifle, a very efficient weapon and a good and faithful friend of many years' standing.

The overhanging rock that I had passed with such trouble the previous evening did not give me a moment's uneasiness now and after passing it I started looking for tracks, for the rain had softened the surface of the road. I saw nothing however until I came to the damp place on the road, which, as I have said, was on the near side of the ridge and close to the pool where the buffalo was tied. Here in the soft earth, I found the pugmarks of the tiger, made before the storm had come on and going in the direction of the ridge. Close to this spot there is a rock about three feet high, on the khud side of the road. On the previous occasions that I had stalked down the road, I had found that by standing on this rock I could look over a hump in the road and see the buffalo where it was tied forty yards away. When I now climbed on to the rock and slowly raised my head, I found that the buffalo had gone. This discovery was as disconcerting as it was inexplicable. To prevent the tiger from carrying the buffalo away to some distant part of the jungle, where the only method of getting a shot would have been by sitting up on the ground or in a tree, a hopeless proceeding with my throat in the condition it was in, I had used four thicknesses of strong one-inch-thick hemp rope and, even so the tiger had got away with the kill.

I was wearing the thinnest of rubber-soled shoes, and very silently I approached the sapling to which the buffalo had been tied and examined the ground. The buffalo had been killed before the storm but had been carried away after the rain had stopped, without any portion of it having been eaten. Three of the ropes I had twisted together had been gnawed through, and the fourth had been broken. Tigers do not usually gnaw through ropes however this one had done so and had carried off the kill down the hill facing Mohan. My plans had been badly upset but very fortunately the rain had come to my assistance. The thick carpet of dead leaves which the day before had been as dry as tinder were now wet and pliable, and provided I made no mistakes, the pains the tiger had been to in getting away with the kill might yet prove his undoing.

When entering a jungle in which rapid shooting might at any moment become necessary, I never feel happy until I have reassured myself that my rifle is loaded. To pull a trigger in an emergency and wake up in the Happy Hunting Grounds or elsewhere because one had omitted to load a weapon, would be one of those acts of carelessness for which no excuse could be found, so though I knew I had loaded my rifle before I came to the overhanging rock, I now opened it and extracted the cartridges. I changed one that was discoloured and dented, and after moving the safety catch up and down several times to make sure it was working smoothly, I have never carried a cocked weapon. I set off to follow the drag.

This word 'drag', when it is used to describe the mark left on the ground by a tiger when it is moving its kill from one place to another, is misleading, for a tiger when taking its kill any distance (I have seen a tiger carry a full-grown cow for four miles) does not drag it, it carries it and if the kill is too heavy to be carried, it is left. The drag is distinct or faint according to the size of the animal that is being carried and the manner in which it is being held. For instance, assuming the kill is a *sambhar*, and the tiger is holding it by the neck, the hind quarters will trail on the ground leaving a distinct drag mark. On the other hand, if the *sambhar* is being held by the middle of the back, there may be a faint drag mark, or there may be none at all.

In the present case the tiger was carrying the buffalo by the neck, and the hind quarters trailing on the ground were leaving a drag mark that was easy to follow. For a hundred yards the tiger went diagonally across 'the face of the hill until he came to a steep clay bank. In attempting to cross this bank he had slipped and relinquished his hold of the kill, which had rolled down the hill for thirty or forty yards until it had fetched up against a tree. On recovering the kill the tiger picked it up by the back, and from now on only one leg occasionally touched the ground, leaving a faint drag mark, which nevertheless, owing to the hillside being carpeted with bracken, was not very difficult to follow. In his fall the tiger had lost direction, and he now appeared to be undecided where to take the kill. First, he went a couple of hundred yards to the right, then a hundred yards straight down the hill through a dense patch of *ringals*. After forcing his way with considerable difficulty through the *ringals*, he turned to the left and went diagonally across the hill for a few hundred yards until he came to a great rock, to the right of which he skirted. This rock was flush with the ground on the approach side and rising gently for twenty feet, appeared to project out over a hollow or dell of considerable extent. If there was a cave or recess under the projection, it would be a very likely place for the tiger to have taken his kill to, so leaving the drag I stepped on to the rock and moved forward very slowly, examining every yard of ground below and on either side of me, as it came into view. On reaching the end of the projection and looking over, I was disappointed to find that the hill came up steeply to meet the rock and that there was no cave or recess under it as I had expected there would be.

As the point of the rock offered a good view of the dell and of the surrounding jungle and was comparatively safe from an attack from the man-eater I sat down and as I did so, I caught sight of a red and white object in a dense patch of short undergrowth, forty or fifty yards directly below me. When one is looking for a tiger in a dense jungle, everything red that catches the eye is immediately taken for the tiger, and here, not only could I see the red of the tiger, but I could also see his stripes. For a long minute I watched the object intently, and then, as the face you are told to look for in a freak picture suddenly resolves itself, I saw that the object I was looking at was the kill, and not the tiger; the red was blood where he had recently been eating, and the stripes were the ribs from which he had torn away the skin. I was thankful for having held my fire for that long minute, for in a somewhat similar case a friend of mine ruined his chance of bagging a very fine tiger by putting two bullets into a kill over which he had intended sitting, fortunately he was a good shot and the two men whom he had sent out in advance to find the kill and put up a machan over it and who were, at the time he fired, standing near the kill screened by a bush, escaped injury.

When a tiger that has not been disturbed leaves his kill out in the open, it can be assumed that he is lying up close at hand to guard the kill from vultures and other scavengers and the fact that I could not see the tiger did not mean that he was not lying somewhere close by in the dense undergrowth.

Tigers are troubled by flies and do not lie long in one position, so I decided to remain where I was and watch for movement, but hardly had I come to this decision, when I felt an irritation in my throat. I had not quite recovered from my attack of laryngitis and the irritation grew rapidly worse until it became imperative for me to cough. The usual methods one employs on these occasions, whether in church or the jungle, such as holding the breath and swallowing hard, gave no relief until it became a case of cough, or burst and in desperation I tried to relieve my throat by giving the alarm call of the *langur*. Sounds are difficult to translate into words and for those of you who are not acquainted with our jungles I would try to describe this alarm call, which can be heard for half a mile, as khok, khok, khok, repeated again and again at short intervals and ending up with khokorror. All *langurs* do not call at tigers, but the ones in our hills certainly do, and as this tiger had probably heard the call every day of his life, it was the one sound I could make to which he would not pay the slightest attention. My rendering of the call in this emergency did not sound very convincing but it had the desired effect of removing the irritation from my throat.

For half an hour thereafter, I continued to sit on the rock, watching for movement and listening for news from the jungle folk, and when I had satisfied myself that the tiger was not anywhere within my range of vision, I got off the rock and moving with the utmost caution, went down to the kill.

VI

I regret I am not able to tell you what weight of flesh a full-grown tiger can consume at a meal, but you will have some idea of his capacity when I tell you he can eat a *sambhar* in two days, and a buffalo in three, leaving possibly a small snack for the fourth day.

The buffalo I had tied up was not full-grown, but he was by no means a small animal, and the tiger had eaten approximately half of him. With a meal of that dimension inside of him I felt sure he had not gone far, and as the ground was still wet and would remain so for another hour or two, I decided to find out in what direction he had gone, and if possible, stalk him.

There was a confusion of tracks near the kill but by going round in widening circles I found the tracks the tiger had made when leaving. Soft- footed animals are a little more difficult to track than hard-footed ones, yet after long years of experience tracking needs as little effort as a gun dog exerts when following a scent. As silently and as slowly as a shadow I took up the track, knowing that the tiger would be close at hand. When I had gone a hundred yards I came on a flat bit of ground, twenty feet square and carpeted with that variety of short soft grass that has highly scented roots on this grass the tiger had lain, the imprint of his body being clearly visible.

As I was looking at the imprint and guessing at the size of the animal that had made it, I saw some of the blades of grass that had been crushed down, spring erect. This indicated that the tiger had been gone only a minute or so.

You will have some idea of the layout when I tell you that the tiger had brought the kill down from the north, and on leaving it had gone west, and that the rock on which I had sat, the kill, and the spot where I was now standing, formed the points of a triangle, one side of which was forty yards and the other two sides a hundred yards long.

My first thought on seeing the grass spring erect was that the tiger had seen me and moved off, but this I soon found was not likely, for neither the rock nor the kill was visible from the grass plot, and that he had not seen me and moved after I had taken up his track, I was quite certain. Why then had he left his comfortable bed and gone away? The sun shining on the back of my neck provided the answer. It was now nine o'clock of an unpleasantly hot May morning, and a glance at the sun and the treetops over which it had come showed that it had been shining on the grass for ten minutes. The tiger had evidently found it too hot and gone away a few minutes before my arrival to look for a shady spot.

I have told you that the grass plot was twenty feet square. On the far side to that from which I had approached, there was a fallen tree, lying north and south. This tree was about four feet in diameter, and as it was lying along the edge of the grass plot in the middle of which I was standing, it was ten feet away from me. The root end of the tree was resting on the hillside, which here went up steeply and was overgrown with brushwood, and the branch end (which had been snapped off when the tree had fallen) was projecting out over the hillside. Beyond the tree the hill appeared to be more or less perpendicular and running across the face of it was a narrow ledge of rock, which disappeared into the dense jungle thirty yards further on.

If my surmise, that the sun had been the cause of the tiger changing his position, was correct, there was no more suitable place than the lee of the tree for him to have taken shelter in and the only way of satisfying myself on this point was to walk up to the tree and look over. Here a picture seen long years ago in Punch flashed into memory. The picture was of a lone sportsman who had gone out to hunt lions and who on glancing up, on to the rock he was passing, looked straight into the grinning face of the most enormous lion in Africa. Underneath the picture was written, 'When you go out looking for a lion, be quite sure that you want to see him'. True, there would be this small difference, that whereas my friend in Africa looked up into the lion's face, I would look down into the tiger's otherwise the two cases assuming that the tiger was on the far side of the tree would be very similar.

Slipping my feet forward an inch at a time on the soft grass, I now started to approach the tree, and had covered about half the distance that separated me from it when I caught sight of a black and yellow object about three inches long on the rocky ledge, which I now saw was a well-used game path. For a long minute I stared at this motionless object, until I was convinced that it was the tip of the tiger's tail. If the tail was pointing away from me the head must obviously be towards me, and as the ledge was only some two feet wide, the tiger could only be crouching down and waiting to spring the moment my head appeared over the bole of the tree. The tip of the tail was twenty feet from me and allowing eight feet for the tiger's length while crouching, his head would be twelve feet away. But I should have to approach much nearer before I should be able to see enough of his body to get in a crippling shot, and a crippling shot it would have to be if I wanted to leave on my feet. And now, for the first time in my life, I regretted my habit of carrying an un-cocked rifle. The safety catch of my 450/400 makes a very distinct click when thrown off, and to make any sound now would either bring the tiger right on top of me or send him straight down the steep hillside without any possibility of my getting in a shot.

Inch by inch I again started to creep forward, until the whole of the tail, and after it the hind quarters, came into view. When I saw the hind quarters, I could have shouted with delight for they showed that the tiger was not crouching and ready to spring but was lying down. As there was' only room for his body on the two-foot-wide ledge, he had stretched his hind legs out and was resting them on the upper branches of an oak sapling growing up the face of the almost perpendicular hillside. Another foot forward and his belly came into view, and from the regular way in which it was heaving up and down I knew that he was asleep. Less slowly now I moved forward, until his shoulder, and then his whole length, was exposed to my view. The back of his head was resting on the edge of the grass plot, which extended for three or four feet beyond the fallen tree; his eyes were fast shut, and his nose was pointing to heaven.

Aligning the sights of the rifle on his forehead I pressed the trigger and, while maintaining a steady pressure on it, pushed up the safety catch. I had no idea how this reversal of the usual method of discharging a rifle would work, but it did work; and when the heavy bullet at that short range crashed into his forehead not so much as a quiver went through his body. His tail remained stretched straight out; his hind legs continued to rest on the upper branches of the sapling; and his nose still pointed to heaven. Nor did his position change in the slightest when I sent a second, and quite unnecessary, bullet to follow the first. The only change noticeable was that his stomach had stopped heaving up and down, and that blood was trickling down his forehead from two surprisingly small holes.

I do not know how the close proximity of a tiger reacts on others, but me it always leaves with a breathless feeling due possibly as much to fear as to excitement and a desire for a little rest. I sat down on the fallen tree and lit the cigarette I had denied myself from the day my throat had got bad and allowed my thoughts to wander. Any task well accomplished gives satisfaction, and the one just completed was no exception. The reason for my presence at that spot was the destruction of the man-eater and from the time I had left the road two hours previously right up to the moment I pushed up the safety catch, everything including the langur call had worked smoothly and without a single fault. In this there was great satisfaction, the kind of satisfaction I imagine an author must feel when he writes FINIS to the plot that, stage by stage, has unfolded itself just as he desired it to. In my case, however, the finish had not been satisfactory, for I had killed the animal, that was lying five feet from me, in his sleep.

My personal feelings in the matter are, I knew of little interest to others, but it occurs to me that possibly you also might think it was not cricket, and in that case, I should like to put the arguments before you that I used on myself, in the hope that you will find them more satisfactory than I did. These arguments were (a) the tiger was a man-eater that was better dead than alive (b) therefore it made no difference whether he was awake or asleep when killed, and (c) that had I walked away when I saw his belly heaving up and down. I should have been morally responsible for the deaths of all the human beings he killed thereafter. All good and sound arguments, you will admit, for my having acted as I did; but the regret remains that through fear of the consequences to myself, or fear of losing the only chance I might ever get, or possibly a combination of the two, I did not awaken the sleeping animal and give him a sporting chance.

The tiger was dead, and if my trophy was to be saved from falling into the valley below and ruined, it was advisable to get him off the ledge with as little delay as possible. Leaning the rifle, for which I had no further use, against the fallen tree, I climbed up to the road and once round the corner near the cultivated land, I cupped my hands and sent a cooee echoing over the hills and valleys. I had no occasion to repeat the call, for my men had heard my two shots when returning from attending to the first buffalo and had run back to the hut to collect as many villagers as were within calling distance. Now, on hearing my cooee, the whole crowd came helter-skelter down the road to meet me.

When stout ropes and an axe had been procured, I took the crowd back with me, and after I had secured the ropes round the tiger, willing hands half carried and half dragged him off the ledge and over the fallen tree, on to the plot of grass. Here I would have skinned him, but the villagers begged me not to do so, saying that the women and children of Kartkanoula and the adjoining villages would be very disappointed if they were not given an opportunity of seeing the tiger with their own eyes and satisfying themselves that the man-eater, in fear of whom they had lived for so many years, and who had established a reign of terror over the whole district, was really and truly dead.

While a couple of saplings to assist in carrying the tiger back to the hut were being felled, I saw some of the men passing their hands over the tiger's limbs, and knew they were satisfying themselves that their assertion that the tiger had not been suffering from any old, or crippling, wounds was correct. At the hut the tiger was placed in the shade of a wide-spreading tree and the villagers informed that it was at their disposal up to two o'clock longer I could not give them, for it was a very hot day and there was fear of the hair slipping, and the skin being ruined.

I myself had not looked closely at the tiger, but at 2 p.m., when I laid him on his back to start the skinning, I noticed that most of the hair from the inner side of his left foreleg was missing, and that there were a number of small punctures in the skin, from which yellow fluid was exuding. I did not draw attention to these punctures, and left the skinning of the leg, which was considerably thinner than the right leg, to the last. When the skin had been removed from the rest of the animal, I made a long cut from the chest to the pad of the festering left leg, and as I removed the skin, drew out of the flesh, one after another, porcupine quills which the men standing round eagerly seized as souvenirs; the longest of these quills was about five inches, and their total number was between twenty- five and thirty. The flesh under the skin, from the tiger's chest to the pad of his foot, was soapy, and of a dark yellow colour cause enough to have made the poor beast moan when he walked and quite sufficient reason for his having become and having remained a man-eater, for porcupine quills do not dissolve no matter how long they are embedded in flesh.

I have extracted, possibly, a couple of hundred porcupine quills from the man-eating tigers I have shot. Many of these quills have been over nine inches in length and as thick as pencils. The majority were embedded in hard muscles, a few were wedged firmly between bones, and all were broken off short under the skin.

Unquestionably the tigers acquired the quills when killing porcupines for food, but the question arises to which I regret I am unable to give any satisfactory answer, why animals with the intelligence and the agility of tigers should have been so careless as to drive quills deep into themselves or so slow in their movements as to permit porcupines whose only method of defending themselves is walking backwards to do so and further, why the quills should have been broken off short for porcupine quills are not brittle.

Leopards are just as partial to porcupines as our hill tigers are, but they do not get quills stuck in them, for they kill porcupines as I have seen by catching them by the head and why tigers do not employ the same safe and obvious method of killing as leopards employ and so avoid injury to themselves is a mystery to me.

And now I have done telling you the story of the second of the three man-eating tigers mentioned at that District Conference of long ago and, when opportunity offers, I will tell you how the third tiger, the Kanda man-eater, died.

THE FISH OF MY DREAMS

Fishing for *mahseer* in a well-stocked submontane river is, in my opinion, the most fascinating of all field sports. Our environments, even though we may not be continuously conscious of them, nevertheless play a very important part in the sum total of our enjoyment of any form of outdoor sport. I am convinced that the killing of the fish of one's dreams in uncongenial surroundings would afford an angler as little pleasure as the winning of the Davis Cup would to a tennis player if the contest were staged in the Sahara.

The river I have recently been fishing in flows, for some forty miles of its length, through a beautifully wooded valley, well stocked with game and teeming with bird life. I had the curiosity to count the various kinds of animals and birds seen in one day, and by the evening of that day my count *showed, among animals, sambbar, chital, kakar, ghooral, pig, langur* and red monkeys and among birds seventy-five varieties including peafowl, red jungle fowl, *kalege* pheasants, black partridge, and bush quail.

In addition to these I saw a school of five otter in the river, several small muggers and a python. The python was lying on the surface of a big still pool, with only the top of its flat head and eyes projecting above the gin-clear water. The subject was one I had long wished to photograph and in order to do this it was necessary to cross the river above the pool and climb the opposite hillside; but fortunately, I had been seen by those projecting eyes and as I cautiously stepped backwards, the reptile, which appeared to be about eighteen feet long, submerged, to retire to its subterranean home among the piled-up boulders at the head of the pool.

In some places the valley through which the river flows is so narrow that a stone can be tossed with ease from one side to the other and other places it widens out to a mile or more. In these open spaces grow amaltas with their two-feet-long sprays of golden bloom, *karaunda* and box bushes with their white star-shaped flowers. The combined scent from these flowers fills the air, throbbing with the spring songs of a multitude of birds with the most delicate and pleasing of perfumes. In these surroundings angling for *mahseer* might well be described as the sport fit for kings. My object in visiting this sportsman's paradise was not, however, to kill *mahseer*, but to try to secure a daylight picture of a tiger, and it was only when light conditions were unfavourable that I laid aside my movie camera for a rod.

I had been out from dawn one day, trying, hour after hour, to get a picture of a tigress and her two cubs. The tigress was a young animal, nervous as all young mothers are and as often as I stalked her, she retired with the cubs into heavy cover. There is a limit to the disturbance a tigress, be she young or old, will suffer when accompanied by cubs and when the limit on this occasion had been reached, I altered my tactics and tried sitting up in trees over open glades and lying-in high grass near a stagnant pool in which she and her family were accustomed to drink but with no better success.

When the declining sun was beginning to cast shadows over the open places I was watching, I gave up the attempt and added the day to the several hundred days I had already spent in trying to get a picture of a tiger in its natural surroundings. The two men I had brought from camp had passed the day in the shade of a tree on the far side of the river. I instructed them to return to camp by way of the forest track, and, exchanging my camera for a rod, set off along the river, intent on catching a fish for my dinner.

The fashion in rods and tackle has altered, in recent years, as much as the fashion in ladies' dress. Gone, one often wonders where, are the 18-foot greenheart rods with their unbreakable accompaniments and gone the muscles to wield them and their place has been taken by light one-handed fly rods.

I was armed with an Il-foot tournament trout rod, a reel containing 50 yards of casting line and 200 yards of fine silk backing, a medium gut cast, and a one-inch home-made brass spoon.

When one has unlimited undisturbed water to fish one is apt to be over-critical. A pool is discarded because the approach to it is over rough ground, or a run is rejected because of a suspected snag. On this occasion, half a mile had been traversed before a final selection was made a welter of white-water cascading over rocks at the head of a deep oily run 80 yards long and at tin-end of the run a deep still pool 200 yards long and 70 yards wide. Here was the place to catch the fish for my dinner.

Standing just clear of the white water I flicked the spoon into the run, pulling a few yards of line off the reel as I did so, and as I raised the rod to allow the line to run through the rings the spoon was taken by a fish, near the bank and close to where I was standing. By great good luck the remaining portion of the slack line tightened on the drum of the reel and did not foul the butt of the rod or handle of the reel, as so often happens.

In a flash the fish was off downstream, the good well-oiled reel singing a paean of joy as the line was stripped off it. The 50 yards of casting line followed by 100 yards of backing were gone, leaving in their passage burned furrows in the fingers of my left hand, when all at once the mad rush ceased as abruptly as it had begun, and the line went dead.

The speculations one makes on these occasions chased each other through my mind, accompanied by a little strong language to ease my feelings. The hold had been good without question. The cast, made up a few days previously from short lengths of gut procured from the Pilot Gut Coy, had been carefully tied and tested. Suspicion Centred on the split ring, possibly cracked on a stone on some previous occasion, it had now given way.

Sixty yards of the line are back on the reel, when the slack line is seen to curve to the left, and a moment later is cutting a strong furrow upstream, the fish is still on and is heading for the white water. Established here, pulling alternately from upstream, at right angles and downstream fails to dislodge him. Time drags on and the conviction grows that the fish has gone, leaving the line hung up on a snag. Once again and just as hope is being abandoned the line goes slack and then tightens a moment later, as the fish for the second time goes madly downstream.

And now he appears to have made up his mind to leave this reach of the river for the rapids below the pool. In one strong steady run he reaches the tail of the pool. Here, where the water fans out and shallows, he hesitates, and finally returns to the pool. A little later he shows on the surface for the first time and if not for the fact that the taut line runs direct from the point of the rod to the indistinctly seen object on the far side of the pool, it would be impossible to believe that the owner of that great triangular fin, projecting five inches out of the water, had taken a fly spoon a yard or two from my feet.

Back in the depths of the pool, he was drawn inch by inch into slack water. To land a big fish single-handed on a trout rod is not an easy accomplishment. Four times he was stranded with a portion of his great shoulders out of water and four times at my very cautious approach he lashed out, and, returning to the pool, had to be fought back inch by inch. At the fifth attempt, with the butt of the rod held at the crook of my thumb and reversed, rings upwards to avoid the handle of the reel coming into contact with him, he permits me to place one hand and then the other against his sides and very gently propel him through the shallow water up on to dry land.

A fish I had set out to catch, and a fish I had caught, but he would take no part in my dinner that night, for between me and camp lay three and a half miles of rough ground, half of which would have to be covered in the dark.

When sending away my II-lb camera, I had retained the cotton cord I use for drawing it up after me when I sit in trees. One end of this cord was passed through the gills of the fish and out at his mouth, and securely tied in a loop. The other end was made fast to the branch of a tree. When the cord was paid out the fish lay snugly against a great slab of rock, in comparatively still water. Otter were the only danger and to scare them off I made a flag of my handkerchief, and fixed the end of the improvised flagstaff in the bed of the river a little below the fish. The sun was gilding the mountain tops next morning when I was back at the pool and found the fish lying just where I had left it the previous evening. Having unfastened the cord from the branch, I wound it round my hand as I descended the slab of rock towards the fish. Alarmed at my approach, or feeling the vibration of the cord, the fish suddenly galvanized into life, and with a mighty splash dashed upstream. Caught at a disadvantage, I had no time to brace my feet on the sloping and slippery rock but was jerked headlong into the pool.

I have a great distaste for going over my depth in these submontane rivers for the thought of being encircled by a hungry python is very repugnant to me, and I am glad there were no witnesses to the manner in which I floundered out of that pool. I had just scrambled out on the far side with the fish still attached to my right hand, when the men I had instructed to follow me arrived. Handing the fish over to them to take down to our camp on the bank of the river, I went on ahead to change and get my camera ready.

I had no means of weighing the fish and at a rough guess both the men and I put it at 50 lb.

The weight of the fish is immaterial, for weights are soon forgotten. Not so forgotten are the surroundings in which the sport is indulged in. The steel blue of the fern-fringed pool where the water rests a little before cascading over rock and shingle to draw breath again in another pool more beautiful than the one just left, the flash of the gaily coloured kingfisher as he breaks the surface of the water, shedding a shower of diamonds from his wings as he rises with a chirp of delight, a silver minnow held firmly in his vermilion bill, the belling of the *sambhar* and the clear tuneful call of the *chital* apprising the jungle folk that the tiger, whose pugmarks show wet on the sand where a few minutes before he crossed the river, is out in search of his dinner. These are things that will not be forgotten and will live in my memory, the lodestone to draw me back to that beautiful valley, as yet unspoiled by the hand of man.

THE KANDA MAN-EATER

However little faith we have in the superstitions we share with others thirteen at a table, the passing of wine at dinner, walking under a ladder and so on our own private superstitions, though a source of amusement to our friends, are very real to us.

I do not know if sportsmen are more superstitious than the rest of mankind, but I do know that they take their superstitions very seriously. One of my friends invariably takes five cartridges, never more and never less, when he goes out after big game, and another as invariably takes seven cartridges. Another, who incidentally was the best-known big-game sportsman in northern India, never started the winter shooting season without first killing a *mahseer*. My own private superstition concerns snakes. When after man-eaters I have a deep-rooted conviction, that, however much I may try, all my efforts will be unavailing until I have first killed a snake.

During the hottest days of one May, I had from dawn to dark climbed innumerable miles up and down incredibly steep hills, and through thick thorn bushes that had left my hands and knees a mass of ugly scratches, in search of a very wary man-eater. I returned on that fifteenth evening, dog-tired to the two-roomed Forest Bungalow I was staying at to find a deputation of villagers waiting for me with the very welcome news that the man-eater, a tiger had been seen that day on the outskirts of their village. It was too late to do anything that night, so the deputation were provided with lanterns and sent home with strict injunctions that no one was to leave the village the following day.

The village was situated at the extreme end of the ridge on which the bungalow was, and because of its isolated position and the thick forest that surrounded it, had suffered more from the depredations of the tiger than any other village in the district. The most recent victims were two women and a man.

I had made one complete circle of the village the following morning and had done the greater part of a second circle, a quarter of a mile below the first, when after negotiating a difficult scree of shale I came upon a little nullah made by the rush of rainwater down the steep hillside. A glance up and down the nullah satisfied me that the tiger was not in it, and then a movement just in front of me, and about twenty-five feet Away; caught my eye. At this spot there was a small pool of water the size of a bathtub and on the far side of it was a snake that had evidently been drinking. The lifting of the snake's head had caught my eye and it was not until the head had been raised some two or three feet from the ground and the hood expanded that I realized it was a hamadryad. It was the most beautiful snake I had ever seen. The throat, as it faced me, was a deep orange red shading to golden yellow where the body met the ground. The back, olive green was banded by ivory-coloured chevrons and some four feet of its length from the tip of its tail upwards was shiny black, with white chevrons. In length the snake was between thirteen and fourteen feet.

One hears many tales about hamadryads, their aggressiveness when disturbed, and the speed at which they can travel. If, as it seemed about to do, the snake attacked, up or down hill I should be at a disadvantage but across the shale scree I felt that I could hold my own. A shot at the expanded hood, the size of a small plate, would have ended the tension but the rifle in my hands was a heavy one and I had no intention of disturbing the tiger that had showed up after so many days of weary waiting and toil. After an interminably long minute, during which time the only movement was the flicking in and out of a long and quivering forked tongue, the snake closed his hood, lowered his head to the ground and, turning, made off up the opposite slope. Without taking my eyes off him I groped with my hand on the hillside and picked up a stone that filled my hand as comfortably as a cricket ball. The snake had just reached a sharp ridge of hard clay when the stone, launched with the utmost energy I was capable of, struck it on the back of the head. The blow would have killed any other snake outright but the only, and very alarming, effect it had on the hamadryad was to make it whip round and come straight towards me. A second and a larger stone fortunately caught it on the neck when it had covered half the distance between us, and after that the rest was easy. With a great feeling of satisfaction, I completed the second circle round the village, and through it proved as fruitless as the first, I was elated at having killed the snake. Now, for the first time in many days, I had a feeling that my search for the man-eater would be successful.

The following day I again searched the forest surrounding the village, and towards evening found the fresh pugmarks of the tiger at the edge of a ploughed field overlooking the village. The occupants of the village, numbering about a hundred, were by now thoroughly alarmed, and leaving them with the assurance that I would return early next day I set out on my lonely four-mile walk back to the Forest Bungalow.

To walk with safety through forests or along deserted roads in an area in which a man-eater is operating, calls for the utmost caution and the strict observance of many rules. It is only when the hunter has repeatedly been the hunted that the senses can be attuned to the required pitch, and those rules be strictly adhered to, the breaking of which would provide the man-eater with an easy victim.

The reader may ask, 'Why a lonely walk?', when I probably had men to spare with me in camp. My answer to this very natural question would be: first, because one is apt to get careless and rely too much on one's companions, and second, because in a mix-up with a tiger one has a better chance when one is alone.

The next morning, as I approached the village, I saw an eager throng of men waiting for me, and when within earshot I was greeted with the gratifying news that a buffalo had been killed during the night. The animal had been killed in the village, and after being dragged some distance along the ridge had been taken down into a narrow, deep, and very heavily wooded valley on the north face of the hill.

A very careful reconnaissance from a projecting rock on the ridge satisfied me that an approach down the steep hill, along the line of the drag, would not be advisable, and that the only thing to do was to make a wide detour, enter the valley from the lower end and work up to the spot where I expected to find the kill.

This manoeuvre was successfully accomplished and by midday I had arrived at the spot marked from above where the valley flattened out for a hundred yards before going straight up three hundred yards to the ridge above. It was at the upper end of this flat bit of ground that I expected to find the kill and with luck, the tiger. The long and difficult climb up the valley through dense thickets of thorn bush and stunted bamboo had brought out a bath of sweat, and as it was not advisable to take on a job where quick firing might be necessary with sweaty hands, I sat down for a much-needed rest and for a smoke.

The ground in front of me was strewn with large smooth boulders among which a tiny stream meandered, forming wherever possible small crystal-clear pools. Shod with the thinnest of rubber-soled shoes, the going over these boulders was ideal for my purpose, and when I had cooled and dried. I set off to stalk the kill in the hope of finding the tiger lying asleep near it. When three-quarters of the ground had been covered I caught sight of the kill tucked away under a bank of ferns and about twenty-five yards away from where the hill went steeply up to the ridge. The tiger was not in sight and very cautiously drawing level with the kill I took up my position on a flat boulder to scan every inch of ground visible.

The premonition of impending danger is too well known and established a fact to need any comment. For three or four minutes I had stood perfectly still with no thought of danger and then all at once I became aware that the tiger was looking at me at a very short range. The same sense that had conveyed the feeling of impending danger to me had evidently operated in the same way on the tiger and awakened him from his sleep. To my left front were some dense bushes, growing on a bit of flat ground. On these bushes, distant fifteen to twenty feet from me, and about the same distance from the kill, my interest centred. Presently the bushes were gently stirred and the next second I caught sight of the tiger going at full speed up the steep hillside. Before I could get the rifle to bear on him, he disappeared behind a creeper-covered tree and it was not until he had covered about sixty yards that I again saw him, as he was springing up the face of a rock. At my shot he fell backwards and came roaring down the hill, bringing an avalanche of stones with him. A broken back, I concluded and just as I was wondering how best to deal with him when he should arrive all of a heap at my feet, the roaring ceased and the next minute, as much to my relief as to my disappointment, I saw him going full out, and apparently unwounded, across the side of the hill. The momentary glimpses I caught of him offered no shot worth taking, and with a crash through some dry bamboos he disappeared round the shoulder of the hill into the next valley.

I subsequently found that my bullet, fired at an angle of seventy-five degrees, had hit the tiger on the left elbow and chipped out a section from that bone which some cynical humorist has named the 'funny bone'. Carrying on, the bullet had struck the rock and, splashing back had delivered a smashing blow on the point of the jaw. Neither wound, however painful it may have been, was fatal and the only result of my following up the very light blood trail into the next valley was to be growled at from a dense thorn thicket, to enter which would have been suicidal.

My shot had been heard in the village and an expectant crowd were waiting for me on the ridge. They were even more disappointed, if that were possible, than I was at the failure of my carefully planned and as carefully executed stalk.

On visiting the kill the following morning, I was very pleased and not a little surprised to find that the tiger had returned to it during the night and taken a light meal. The only way now of getting a second shot was to sit up over the kill and here a difficulty presented itself. There were no suitable trees within convenient distance of the kill, and the very unpleasant experience I had on a former occasion had effectively cured me of sitting at night on the ground for a man-eater. While still undecided where to sit I heard the tiger call, some distance down the valley up which I had climbed the previous day. The calling of the tiger offered me a very welcome chance of shooting it in the most pleasant way it is possible of bringing one of these animals to bag. The conditions under which a tiger can be called up are (a) when rampaging through the forest in search of a mate and (b) when rampaging, wounded. It goes without saying that the sportsman must be able to call sufficiently well to deceive the tiger, and that the call must come from a spot to which the tiger will quite naturally come, a dense thicket, or a patch of heavy grass and that the sportsman must be prepared to take his shot at a very close range. I am quite certain that many sportsmen will be skeptical of a statement I have made that a lightly wounded tiger will come to a call. I would ask all such to reserve their judgement until they have tried to experiment for themselves. On the present occasion, however, though the tiger answered me, call for call, for upwards of an hour, he refused to come any nearer, and I attributed my failure to the fact that I was calling from the spot where the previous day the tiger had met with an unfortunate experience.

The tree I finally selected was growing on the very edge of a perpendicular bank and had a convenient branch about eight feet from the ground. When sitting on this branch I should be thirty feet from, and directly above, the boulder-strewn ravine up which I expected the tiger to come. The question of the tree settled, I returned to the ridge where I had instructed my men to meet me with breakfast.

By four o'clock in the evening I was comfortably seated on the branch and prepared for a long and hard sit-up. Before leaving my men, I had instructed them to cooee to me from the ridge at sunrise next morning. If I answered with the call of a leopard they were to sit tight, but if they received no answer, they were to form two parties with as many villagers as they could collect and come down on either side of the valley, shouting and throwing stones.

I have acquired the habit of sleeping in any position on a tree, and as I was tired the evening did not pass unpleasantly. As the setting sun was gilding the hilltops above me, I was roused to full consciousness by the alarm call of a *langur*. I soon located the monkey, sitting in a tree-top on the far side of the valley, and as it was looking in my direction, I concluded it had mistaken me for a leopard. The alarm call was repeated at short intervals and finally ceased as darkness came on.

Hour after hour I strained my eyes and ears and was suddenly startled by a stone rolling down the hillside and striking my tree. The stone was followed by the stealthy padding of a heavy, soft-footed animal, unmistakably the tiger. At first, I comforted myself with the thought that his coming in this direction, instead of up the valley, was accidental, but this thought was soon dispelled when he started to emit low deep growls from immediately behind me. Quite evidently, he had come into the valley while I was having breakfast and taking up a position on the hill, where the monkey had later seen him, had watched me climbing into the tree. Here was a situation I had not counted on and one that needed careful handling. The branch that had provided a comfortable seat while daylight lasted, admitted of little change of position in the dark. I could, of course, have fired off my rifle into the air but the terrible results I have seen following an attempt to drive away a tiger at very close quarters by discharging a gun dissuaded me from taking this action. Further, even if the tiger had not attacked, the discharge of the rifle (a 450/400) so near him would probably have made him leave the locality and all my toil would have gone for nothing.

I knew the tiger would not spring for that would have carried him straight down a drop of thirty feet on to the rocks below. But there was no need for him to spring, for by standing on his hind legs he could easily reach me. Lifting the rifle off my lap and reversing it, I pushed the barrel between my left arm and side, depressing the muzzle and slipping up the safety catch as I did so. This movement was greeted by a deeper growl than any that had preceded it. If the tiger now reached up for me, he would in all probability come in contact with the rifle, round the triggers of which my fingers were crooked, and even if I failed to kill him the confusion following on my shot would give me a sporting chance of climbing higher into the tree. Time dragged by on leaden feet, and, eventually, tiring of prowling about the hillside and growling, the tiger sprang across a little ravine on my left and a few minutes later I heard the welcome sound of a bone being cracked at the kill. At last, I was able to relax in my uncomfortable position and the only sounds I heard for the rest of the night came from the direction of the kill.

The sun had been up, but a few minutes and the valley was still in deep shadow when my men cooeed from the ridge and almost immediately afterwards I caught sight of the tiger making off at a fast canter up, and across, the hill on my left. In the uncertain light and with my nightlong-strained eyes the shot was a very difficult one, but I took it, and had the satisfaction of seeing the bullet going home. Turning with a great roar, he came straight for my tree, and as he was in the act of springing the second bullet, with great good fortune, crashed into his chest. Diverted in his spring by the impact of the heavy bullet, the tiger struck the tree just short of me, and ricochetting off it went headlong into the valley below, where his fall was broken by one of the small pools already alluded to. He foundered out of the water, leaving it dyed red with his blood and went lumbering down the valley and out of sight.

Fifteen hours on the hard branch had cramped every muscle in my body and it was not until I had swarmed down the tree, staining my clothes in the great gouts of blood the tiger had left on it and had massaged my stiff limbs, that I was able to follow him. He had gone but a short distance and I found him lying dead at the foot of a rock in another pool of water.

Contrary to my orders the men, collected on the ridge, hearing my shot and the tigers roar followed by a second shot, came in a body down the hill. Arrived at the bloodstained tree, at the foot of which my soft hat was lying, they not unnaturally concluded I had been carried off by the tiger. Hearing their shouts of alarm, I called out to them and again with a gasp of dismay when they saw my bloodstained clothes. Reassured that I was not injured and that the blood on my clothes was not mine, a moment later they were crowding round the tiger. A stout sapling was soon cut and lashed to him with creepers, and the tiger, with no little difficulty and a great deal of shouting, was carried up the steep hill to the village.

In remote areas in which long-established man-eaters are operating, many gallant acts of heroism are performed, which the local inhabitants accept as everyday occurrences, and the outside world has no means of hearing about. I should like to put on record one such act concerning the Kanda man-eater's last human victim. I arrived on the scene shortly after the occurrence, and from details supplied by the villagers and from a careful examination of the ground, which had not been disturbed in the interval; I am able to present you with a story which I believe to be correct in every detail.

In the village near which I shot the Kanda man-eater lived an elderly man and his only son. The father had served in the army during the 1914-18 war and it was his ambition to get his son enlisted in the Royal Garhwal Rifles, not as simple a job in the piping days of peace, when vacancies were few and applicants many as it is today. Shortly after the lad's eighteenth birthday a party of men passed through the village on their way to the bazaar at Lansdowne. The lad joined this party and immediately on arrival at Lansdowne presented himself at the Recruiting Office. As his father had taught him to salute with military precision and how to conduct himself in the presence of a Recruiting Officer, he was accepted without any hesitation and after enrolment was given leave to deposit his few personal possessions at home before starting his army training.

He arrived back home at about midday, after an absence of five days and was told by the friends who thronged round him to hear his news that his father was away ploughing their small holding at the extreme end of the village and would not return before nightfall. (The field that was being ploughed was the same one on which I had seen the pugmarks of the man-eater the day I killed the hamadryad.)

One of the lad's jobs had been to provide fodder for their cattle, and after he had partaken of the midday meal in a neighbour's house, he set out with a party of twenty men to collect leaves.

The village, as I have told you, is situated on a ridge, and is surrounded by forests. Two women had already been killed by the man-eater while cutting grass in these forests, and for several months the cattle had been kept alive on leaves cut from the trees surrounding the village. Each day the men had to go further afield to get their requirements, and on this particular day the party of twenty-one, after crossing the cultivated land, went for a quarter of a mile down a very steep rocky hill to the head of the valley which runs east for eight miles, through dense forest, to where it meets the Ramganga river opposite the Dhikala Forest Bungalow.

COPY OF PETITION
SENT TO THE AUTHOR BY THE PEOPLE OF GARHWAL

The Promise mentioned on Page 125, was made after receiving this petition

From

The Public of Patty Painaun,

Bungi and Bickla Badalpur District Garhwal

To

Captain J.E. Carbitt, Esq., I.A.R.O.,

Kaladhungi,

Distt. Nainital

Respected Sir,

We all the public (of the above 3 Patties) most humbly and respectfully beg to lay the following few lines for your kind consideration and doing needful.

That in this vicinity a tiger has turned out man-eater since December last. Up to this date he has killed 5 men and wounded 2. So, we the public are in a great distress. By the fear of this tiger, we cannot watch our wheat crop at night so the deer's have nearly ruined it. We cannot go in the forest for fodder grass, nor we can enter our cattle in the forest to graze so many of our cattle are to the. Under the circumstances we are nearly to be ruined. The Forest Officials are doing every possible arrangement to kill this tiger but there is no hope of any success. 2 *shikari* gentlemen also tried to shoot it but unfortunately, they could not get it. Our kind District Magistrate has notified Rs. 150 rewards for killing this tiger, so everyone is trying to kill it but no success. We have heard that your kind self-have killed many man-eater tigers and leopards. For this you have earned a good name specially in Kumaon revenue Division. The famous man-eater leopard of Nagpur has been shot by you. This it, the voice of all the public here that this tiger also will be killed only by you. So, we the public venture to request that you very kindly take trouble to come to this place and shoot this tiger (our enemy) and save the public from this calamity. For this act of kindness, we the public will be highly obliged and will pray for your long life and prosperity. Hope you will surely consider our condition and take trouble to come here for saving us from this calamity. The route to this place is as follows Ramnagar to Sultan, Sultan to Lahachaur, Lahachaur to Kanda. If your honour kindly informs us the date of your arrival at Ramnagar we will send our men and cart to Ramnagar to meet you and accompany you.

We beg to remain Sir
Your most sincerely

Dated Jharat
The 18th February 1933

Signed Govind Singh Negi
Headman Village Jharat

followed by 40 signatures and 4 thumb impressions of inhabitants of Painaun, Bungi and Bickla Badalpur Patties.

Address

The Govind Singh Negi

Village Jharat Patty

Painaun P.O.

Badialgaon Disc, Garhwal, U.P

At the head of the valley the ground is more or less flat and overgrown with big trees. Here the men separated, each climbing into a tree of his choice, and after cutting the quantity of leaves required, they tied them into bundles with rope brought for the purpose and returned to the village in twos and threes.

Either when the party of men were coming down the hill, talking at the top of their voices to keep up their courage and scare away the man-eater or when they were on the trees shouting to each other, the tiger, who was lying up in a dense patch of cover half a mile down the valley, heard them. Leaving the cover, in which it had four days previously killed and eaten a *sambhar* hind, the tiger crossed a stream and by way of a cattle track that runs the entire length of the valley hurried up in the direction of the men. (The speed at which a tiger has travelled over any ground on which he has left signs of his passage can be easily determined from the relative position of his fore and hind pugmarks.)

The lad of my story had selected a Bauhinia tree from which to cut leaves for his cattle. This tree was about twenty yards above the cattle track, and the upper branches were leaning out over a small ravine in which there were two rocks. From a bend in the cattle track the tiger saw the lad on the tree, and after lying down and watching him for some time it left the track and concealed itself behind a fallen silk cotton tree some thirty yards from the ravine. When the lad had cut all the leaves he needed, he descended from the tree and collected them in a heap, preparatory to tying them into a bundle. While doing this on the open flat ground he was comparatively safe but unfortunately, he had noticed that two of the branches he had cut had fallen into the ravine between the two big rocks, and he sealed his fate by stepping down into the ravine to recover them. As soon as he was out of sight the tiger left the shelter of the fallen tree and crept forward to the edge of the ravine, and as the lad was stooping down to pick up the branches, it sprang on him and killed him. Whether the killing took place while the other men were still on the trees, or after they had left, it was not possible for me to determine.

The father of the lad returned to the village at sunset and was greeted with the very gratifying news that his son had been accepted for the army, and that he had returned from Lansdowne on short leave. Asking where the lad was, he was told that he had gone out earlier in the day to get fodder, and surprise was expressed that the father had not found him at home. After bedding down the bullocks the father went from house to house to find his son. All the men who had been out that day were questioned in turn, and all had the same tale to tell that they had separated at the head of the valley, and no one could remember having seen the lad after that.

Crossing the terraced cultivated land the father went to the edge of the steep hill, and called, and called again, to his son but received no answer.

Night was by now setting in. The man returned to his home and lit a small smoke-dimmed lantern and as he passed through the village, he horrified his neighbours by telling them, in reply to their questions, that he was going to look for his son. He was asked if he had forgotten the man-eater and answered that it was because of the man-eater that he was so anxious to find his son, for it was possible he had fallen off a tree and injured himself and, for fear of attracting the man-eater, had not answered to his call.

He did not ask anyone to accompany him, and no one offered to do so, and for the whole of that night he searched up and down that valley in which no one had dared to set foot since the advent of the man-eater. Four times during the night, as I saw from his footprints when going along the cattle track, he had passed within ten feet of where the tiger was lying eating his son.

Weary and heartsick he climbed a little way up the rocky hill as light was coming and sat down for a rest. From this raised position he could see into the ravine. At sunrise he saw a glint of blood on the two big rocks and hurrying down to the spot he found all that the tiger had left of his son. These remains he collected and took back to his home and when a suitable shroud had been procured, his friends helped him to carry the remains to the burning ghat on the banks of the Mandal river.

I do not think it would be correct to assume that acts such as these are performed by individuals who lack imagination and who therefore do not realize the grave risks they run. The people of our hills, in addition to being very sensitive to their environments, are very superstitious, and every hilltop, valley, and gorge is credited with possessing a spirit in one form or another, all of the evil and malignant kind most to be feared during the hours of darkness. A man brought up in these surroundings, and menaced for over a year by a man-eater, who, unarmed and alone, from sunset to sunrise, could walk through dense forests which his imagination peopled with evil spirits, and in which he had every reason to believe a man-eater was lurking, was in my opinion possessed of a quality and a degree of courage that is given to few. All the more do I give him credit for his act of heroism for not being conscious that he had done anything unusual, or worthy of notice. When at my request he sat down near the man-eater to enable me to take a photograph he looked up at me and said in a quiet and collected voice, 'I am content now, *sahib*, for you have avenged my son.'

This was the last of the three man-eaters that I had promised the District Officials of Kumaon and later the people of Garhwal, that I would do my best to rid them of.

THE PIPAL PANI TIGER

Beyond the fact that he was born in a ravine running deep into the foothills and was one of a family of three, I know nothing of his early history.

He was about a year old when, attracted by the calling of a *chital* hind early one November morning, I found his pugmarks in the sandy bed of the little stream known locally as Pipal Pani. I thought at first that he had strayed from his mother's care, but, as week succeeded week and his single tracks showed on the game paths of the forest, I came to the conclusion that the near approach of the breeding season was an all-sufficient reason for his being alone. Jealously guarded one day, protected at the cost of the parent life if necessary, and set adrift the next, is the lot of all jungle folk, nature's method of preventing inbreeding.

The winter he lived on peafowl, *kakar*, small *pig* and an occasional *chital* hind, making his home in a prostrate giant of the forest felled for no apparent reason and hollowed out by times and porcupines. Here he brought most of his kills, basking, when the days were cold, on the smooth bole of the tree, where many a leopard had basked before him.

It was not until January was well advanced that I saw the cub at close quarters. I was out one evening without any definite object on view, when I saw a crow rise from the ground and wipe its beak as it lit on the branch of tree. Crows, vultures, and magpies always interest me in the jungle, and many are the kills I have found both in India and in Africa with the help of these birds. On the present occasion the crow led me to the scene of an overnight tragedy. A *chital* had been killed and partly eaten and, attracted to the spot probably as I had been, a party of men passing along the road, distant some fifty yards, had cut up and removed the remains. All that was left of the *chital* were a few splinters of bone and a little congealed blood off which the crow had lately made his meal. The absence of thick cover and the proximity of the road convinced me that the animal responsible for the kill had not witnessed the removal and that it would return in due course, so I decided to sit up and make myself as comfortable in a plum tree as the thorns permitted.

I make no apology to you, my reader, if you differ with me on the ethics of the much-debated subject of sitting up over kills. Some of my most pleasant shikar memories centre round the hour or two before sunset that I have spent in tree over a natural kill, ranging from the time when, armed with a muzzle-loader whipped round with brass wire to prevent the cracked barrel from bursting, I sat over a *langur* killed by a leopard, to a few days ago, when with the most modern rifle across my knees, I watched A tigress and her two full-grown cubs eat up the *sambhar* stag they had killed and counted myself no poorer for not having secured a trophy.

True, on the present occasion there is no kill below me, but for the reason given, that will not affect any chance of shot, scent to interest the jungle folk there is in plenty in the blood-soaked ground, as witness the old grey-whiskered boar who has been quietly rooting along for the past ten minutes, and who suddenly stiffens to attention as he comes into the line of the blood-tainted wind. His snout held high and worked as only a *pig* can work that member, tells him more than I was able to glean from the ground which showed no tracks, his method of approach, a short excursion to the right and back into the wind and then a short to the left and again back into the wind, each manoeuvre bringing him a few yards nearer, indicates the *chital* was killed by a tiger. Making sure once and again that nothing worth eating has been left, he finally trots off and disappears from view.

Two *chital*, both with horns in velvet, now appear and from the fact that they are coming down-wind and making straight for the blood-soaked spot, it is evident they were witnesses to the overnight tragedy. Alternately snuffing the ground or standing rigid with every muscle tensed for instant flight, they satisfy their curiosity and return the way they came.

Curiosity is not a human monopoly: many an animal's life is cut short by indulging in it. A dog leaves the verandah to bark at a shadow, a deer leaves the herd to investigate a tuft of grass that no wind agitated, and the waiting leopard is provided with a meal.

The sun is nearing the winter line when a movement to the right front attracts attention. An animal has crossed an opening between two bushes at the far end of a wedge of scrub that terminates thirty yards from my tree. Presently the bushes at my end part, and out into the open, with never a look to right or left, steps the cub. Straight up to the spot where his kills had been he goes, his look of expectancy giving place to one of disappointment as he realizes that his *chital*, killed, possibly, after hours of patient stalking, is gone. The splinters of bone and congealed blood are rejected and his interest centres on a tree stump lately used as a butcher's block to which some shreds of flesh are adhering. I was not the only one who carried firearms in these jungles and if the cub was to grow into a tiger, it was necessary he should be taught the danger of carelessly approaching killers in daylight. A scatter-gun and dust-shot would have served my purpose better, but the rifle will have to do this time and as he raises his head to smell the stump, my bullet crashes into the hard wood an inch from his nose. Only once in the years that followed did the cub forget that lesson.

The following winter I saw him several times. His ears did not look so big now and he had changed his baby hair for a coat of rich tawny red with well-defined stripes. The hollow tree had been given up to its rightful owners, a pair of leopards, new quarter found in a thick belt of scrub skirting the foothills and young *sambhar* added to his menu.

On my annual descent from the hills next winter, the familiar pugmarks no longer showed on the game paths and at the drinking places and for several week's I thought the cub had abandoned his old haunts and gone further afield. Then one morning his absence was explained for, side by side with his tracks, were the smaller and more elongated tracks of the mate he had gone to find. I only once saw the tiger, for the cub was a tiger now, together. I had been out before dawn to try to bag a sarao that lived in the foothills and returning along a fire track my attention was arrested by a vulture, perched on the dead limb of a Sal tree.

The bird had his back towards me and was facing a short stretch of scrub with dense jungle beyond. Dew was still heavy on the ground, and without a sound I reached the tree and peered round. One antler of a dead *sambhar*, for no living deer would lie in that position, projected above the low bushes. A convenient moss-covered rock afforded my rubber-shod feet silent and safe hold and as I drew myself erect the *sambhar* came into full view. The hind quarters had been eaten away and, lying on either side of the kill, were the pair, the tiger being on the far side with only his hind legs showing. Both tigers were asleep. Ten feet straight in front, to avoid a dead branch, and thirty feet to the left would give me a shot at the tiger's neck but in planning the stalk I had forgotten the silent spectator. Where I stood, I was invisible to him but before the ten feet had been covered. I came into view and alarmed at my near proximity, he flapped off his perch, omitting as he did so to notice a thin creeper dependent from a branch above him against which he collided and came ignominiously to ground. The tigress was up and away in an instant, clearing at a bound the kill and her mate, the tiger not being slow to follow; a possible shot, but too risky with thick jungle ahead where a wounded animal would have all the advantages. To those who have never tried it, I can recommend the stalking of leopards and tigers on their lolls as a most pleasant form of sport. Great care should however be taken over the shot, for if the animal is not killed outright or anchored, trouble is bound to follow.

A week later the tiger resumed his bachelor existence. A change had now come over his nature. Hitherto he had not objected to my visiting his kills but, after his mate left, at the first drag I followed up I was given very clearly to understand that no liberties would in future be permitted. The angry growl of a tiger at close quarters than which there is no more terrifying sound in the jungles, has to be heard to be appreciated.

Early in March the tiger killed his first full-grown buffalo. I was near the foothills one evening when the agonized bellowing of a buffalo, mingled with the angry roar of a tiger, rang through the forest. I located the sound as coming from a ravine about six hundred yards away. The going was bad, mostly over loose rocks and through thorn bushes and when I crawled up a steep bluff commanding a view of the ravine the buffalo's struggles were over, and the tiger nowhere to be seen. For an hour I lay with finger on trigger without seeing anything of the tiger. At dawn next morning I again crawled up the bluff, to find the buffalo lying just as I had left her. The soft ground, torn up by hoof and claw, testified to the desperate nature of the struggle and it was not until the buffalo had been hamstrung that the tiger had finally succeeded in pulling her down, in a fight which had lasted from ten to fifteen minutes. The tiger's tracks led across the ravine and, on following them up, I found a long smear of blood on a rock and a hundred yards further on, another smear on a fallen tree. The wound inflicted by the buffalo's horns was in the tiger's head and sufficiently severe to make the tiger lose all interest in the kill, for he never returned to it.

Three years later the tiger, disregarding the lesson received when a cub (his excuse may have been that it was the close season for tigers), incautiously returned to a kill, over which a zamindar and some of his tenants were sitting at night, and received a bullet in the shoulder which fractured the bone. No attempt was made to follow him up and thirty-six hours later, his shoulder covered with a swarm of flies, he limped through the compound of the Inspection Bungalow, crossed a bridge flanked on the far side by a double row of tenanted houses, the occupants of which stood at their doors to watch him pass, entered the gate of a walled-in compound, and took possession of a vacant go down. Twenty-four hours later, possibly alarmed by the number of people who had collected from neighbouring villages to see him, he left the compound the way he had entered it, passed our gate, and made his way to the lower end of our village. A bullock belonging to one of our tenants had died the previous night and had been dragged into some bushes at the edge of the village, this the tiger found and here he remained a few days, quenching his thirst at an irrigation furrow.

When we came down from the hills two months later the tiger was preying on small animals (calves, sheep, goats, etc.) that he was able to catch on the outskirts of the village. By March his wound had healed, leaving his right foot turned inwards. Returning to the forest where he had been wounded, he levied heavy toll on the village cattle, taking, for safety's sake, but one meal off each and in this way killing five times as many as he would ordinarily have done. The zamindar who had wounded him and who had a herd of some four hundred head of cows and buffaloes was the chief sufferer.

In the succeeding years he gained as much in size as in reputation, and many were the attempts made by sportsmen and others to bag him.

One November evening, a villager, armed with a single-barrel muzzle¬loading gun, set out to try to bag a *pig*, selecting for his ground *machan* an isolated bush growing in a twenty-yard-wide rowkah (dry watercourse) running down the centre of some broken ground. This ground was rectangular, flanked on the long sides by cultivated land and on the short sides by a road, and by a ten-foot canal that formed the boundary between our cultivation and the forest. In front of the man was a four-foot-high bank with a cattle track running along the upper edge; behind him a patch of dense scrub. At 8 p.m. an animal appeared on the track and taking what aim he could, he fired. On receiving that shot the animal fell off the bank and passed within a few feet of the man, grunting as it entered the scrub behind. Casting aside his blanket, the man ran to his hut two hundred yards away. Neighbours soon collected and, on hearing the man's account, came to the conclusion that a *pig* had been hard hit. It would be a pity, they said, to leave the *pig* for hyenas and jackals to eat, so a lantern was lit and as a party of six bold spirits set out to retrieve the bag, one of my tenants (who declined to join the expedition and who confessed to me later that he had no stomach for looking for wounded pig in dense scrub in the dark) suggested that the gun should be loaded and taken.

His suggestion was accepted and, as a liberal charge of powder was being rammed home, the wooden ramrod jammed and broke inside the barrel. A trivial accident which undoubtedly saved the lives of six men. The broken rod was eventually and after great trouble extracted, the gun loaded, and the party set off.

Arrived at the spot where the animal had entered the bushes, a careful search was made and, on blood being found, every effort to find the '*pig*' was made; it was not until the whole area had been combed out that the quest for that night was finally abandoned. Early next morning the search was resumed, with the addition of my informant of weak stomach, who was a better woodsman than his companions and who, examining the ground under a bush where there was a lot of blood, collected and brought some bloodstained hairs to me which I recognized as tiger's hairs. A brother sportsman was with me for the day and together we went to have a look at the ground.

The reconstruction of jungle events from signs on the ground has always held great interest for me. True, one's deductions are sometimes wrong, but they are also sometimes right. In the present instance I was right in placing the wound in the inner forearm of the right foreleg but was wrong in assuming the leg had been broken and that the tiger was a young animal and a stranger to the locality.

There was no blood beyond the point where the hairs had been found and, as tracking on the hard ground was impossible, I crossed the canal to where the cattle track ran through a bed of sand. Here from the pugmarks, I found that the wounded animal was not a young tiger as I had assumed but my old friend the Pipal Pani tiger who, when taking a short cut through the village, had in the dark been mistaken for a *pig*.

Once before when badly wounded he had passed through the settlement without harming man or beast, but he was older now, and if driven by pain and hunger might do considerable damage. A disconcerting prospect, for the locality was thickly populated and I was due to leave within the week, to keep an engagement that could not be put off.

For three days I searched every bit of the jungle between the canal and the foothills, an area of about four-square miles, without finding any trace of the tiger. On the fourth afternoon, as I was setting out to continue the search, I met an old woman and her son hurriedly leaving the jungle. From them I learnt that the tiger was calling near the foothills and that all the cattle in the jungle had stampeded. When out with a rifle I invariably go alone, it is safer in a mix-up and one can get through the jungle more silently. However, I stretched a point on this occasion and let the boy accompany me since he was very keen on showing me where he had heard the tiger.

Arrived at the foothills, the boy pointed to a dense bit of cover, bounded on the far side by the fire-track to which I have already referred, and on the near side by the Pipal Pani stream. Running parallel to and about a hundred yards from the stream was a shallow depression some twenty feet wide, more, or less open on my side and fringed with bushes on the side nearer the stream. A well-used path crossed the depression at right angles. Twenty yards from the path, and on the open side of the depression, was a small tree. If the tiger came down the path, he would in all likelihood stand for a shot on clearing the bushes. Here I decided to take my stand and, putting the boy into the tree with his feet on a level with my head and instructing him to signal with his toes if from his raised position he saw the tiger before I did, I put my back to the tree and called.

You, who have spent as many years in the jungle as I have, need no description of the call of a tigress in search of a mate and to you less fortunate ones I can only say that the call to acquire which necessitates close observation and the liberal use of throat salve, cannot be described in words.

To my great relief, for I had crawled through the jungle for three days with finger on trigger, I was immediately answered from a distance of about five hundred yards, and for half an hour thereafter it may have been less and certainly appeared more, the call was tossed back and forth. On the one side the urgent summons of the king and on the other, the subdued and coaxing answer of his handmaiden. Twice the boy signalled but I had as yet seen nothing of the tiger, and it was not until the setting sun was flooding the forest with golden light that he suddenly appeared, coming down the path at a fast walk with never a pause as he cleared the bushes. When halfway across the depression, and just as I was raising the rifle, he turned to the right and came straight towards me.

This manoeuvre, unforeseen when selecting my stand, brought him nearer than I had intended he should come and, moreover, presented me with a head shot which at that short range I was not prepared to take. Resorting to an old device, learned long years ago and successfully used on similar occasions, the tiger was brought to a stand without being alarmed. With one paw poised, he slowly raised his head, exposing as he did so his chest and throat. After the impact of the heavy bullet, he struggled to his feet and tore blindly through the forest, coming down with a crash within a few yards of where, attracted by the calling of a *chital* hind one November morning, I had first seen his pugmarks.

It was only then that I found he had been shot under a misapprehension for the wound which I feared might make him dangerous, proved on examination to be almost healed and caused by a pellet of lead having severed a small vein in his right forearm.

Pleasure at having secured a magnificent trophy, he measured 10´3" over curves and his winter coat was in perfect condition was not unmixed with regret for never again would the jungle folk and I listen with bated breath to his deep-throated call resounding through the foothills, and never again would his familiar pugmarks show on the game paths that he and I had trodden for fifteen years.

THE THAK MAN-EATER

I

Peace had reigned in the Ladhya valley for many months when in September 1938 a report was received in Naini Tal that a girl, twelve years of age, had been killed by a tiger at Kot Kindri village. The report which reached me through Donald Stewart of the Forest Department gave no details and it was not until I visited the village some weeks later that I was able to get particulars of the tragedy. It appeared that, about noon one day, this girl was picking up windfalls from a mango tree close to and in full view of the village, when a tiger suddenly appeared. Before the men working nearby were able to render any assistance, it carried her off. No attempt was made to follow up the tiger, and as all signs of drag and blood trail had been obliterated and washed away long before I arrived on the scene, I was unable to find the place where the tiger had taken the body.

Kot Kindri is about four miles south-west of Chuka, and three miles due west of Thak. It was in the valley between Kot Kindri and Thak that the Chuka man-eater had been shot the previous April.

During the summer of 1938 the Forest Department had marked all the trees in this area for felling, and it was feared that if the man-eater was not accounted for before November, when the felling of the forest was due to start the contractors would not be able to secure labour and would repudiate their contracts. It was in this connexion that Donald Stewart had written to me shortly after the girl had been killed but when in compliance with his request, I promised to go to Kot Kindri, I must confess that it was more in the interests of the local inhabitants than in the interest of the contractors that I gave my promise.

My most direct route to Kot Kindri was to go by rail to Tanakpur, and from there by foot via Kaldhunga and Chuka. This route however though it would save me a hundred miles of walking, would necessitate my passing through the deadliest malaria belt in northern India, and to avoid it I decided to go through the hills to Mornaula and from there along the abandoned Sherring road to its termination of the ridge above Kot Kindri.

While my preparations for this long trek were still under way a second report reached Naini Tal of a kill at Sem, a small village on the left bank of the Ladhya and distant about half a mile from Chuka.

The victim on this occasion was an elderly woman, the mother of the Headman of Sem. This unfortunate woman had been killed while cutting brushwood on a steep bank between two terraced fields. She had started work at the further end of the fifty-yard-long bank and had cut the brushwood to within a yard of her hut when the tiger sprang on her from the field above. So sudden and unexpected was the attack that the woman only had time to scream once before the tiger killed her and taking her up the twelve-foot-high bank crossed the upper field and disappeared with her into the dense jungle beyond. Her son, a lad some twenty years of age, was at the time working in a paddy field a few yards away and witnessed the whole occurrence but was too frightened to try to render any assistance. In response to the lad's urgent summons the Patwari arrived at Sem two days later, accompanied by eighty men he had collected. Following up in the direction the tiger had gone, he found the woman's clothes and a few small bits of bone. This kill had taken place at 2 p.m. on a bright sunny day, and the tiger had eaten its victim only sixty yards from the hut where it had killed her.

On receipt of this second report, Ibbotson, Deputy Commissioner of the three Districts of Almora, Naini Tal and Garhwal, and I held a council of war, the upshot of which was that Ibbotson, who was on the point of setting out to settle a land dispute at Askot on the border of Tibet, changed his tour programme and, instead of going via Bagashwar, decided to accompany me to Sem, and from there go on to Askot.

The route I had selected entailed a considerable amount of hill climbing so we eventually decided to go up the Nandhour valley, cross the watershed between the Nandhour and Ladhya and follow the latter river down to Sem. The Ibbotsons accordingly left Nainital on 12th October and the following day I joined them at Chaurgallia.

Going up the Nandhour and fishing as we went, our best day's catch on light trout rods was a hundred and twenty fish, we arrived on the fifth day at Durga Pepal. Here we left the river and after a very stiff climb camped for the night on the watershed. Making an early start next morning we pitched our tents that night on the left bank of the Ladhya, twelve miles from Chalti.

The monsoon had given over early, which was very fortunate for us, for owing to the rock cliffs that run sheer down into the valley the river has to be crossed every quarter of a mile or so. At one of these fords my cook, who stands five feet in his boots, was washed away and only saved from a watery grave by the prompt assistance of the man who was carrying our lunch basket. On the tenth day after leaving Chaurgallia we made camp on a deserted field at Sem, two hundred yards from the hut where the woman had been killed and a hundred yards from the junction of the Ladhya and Sarda rivers.

Gill Waddell, of the Police, whom we met on our way down the Ladhya, had camped for several days at Sem and had tied out a buffalo that MacDonald of the Forest Department had very kindly placed at our disposal and though the tiger had visited Sem several times during Waddell's stay, it had not killed the buffalo.

The day following our arrival at Sem, while Ibbotson was interviewing Patwaris, Forest Guards, and Headmen of the surrounding villages, I went out to look for pugmarks. Between our camp and the junction, and also on both banks of the Ladhya, there were long stretches of sand. On this sand I found the tracks of a tigress, and of a young male tiger possibly one of the cubs, I had seen in April. The tigress had crossed and recrossed the Ladhya a number of times during the last few days, and the previous night had walked along the strip of sand in front of our tents. It was this tigress the villagers suspected of being the man-eater, and as she had visited Sem repeatedly since the day the Headman's mother had been killed, they were probably correct.

An examination of the pugmarks of the tigress showed her as being an average-sized animal, in the prime of life. Why she had become a man-eater would have to be determined later but one of the reasons might have been that she had assisted to eat the victims of the Chuka tiger when they were together the previous mating season and having acquired a taste for human flesh and no longer having a mate to provide her with it, had now turned a man-eater herself. This was only a surmise and proved later to be incorrect.

Before leaving Nainital I had written to the Tahsildar of Tanakpur and asked him to purchase four young male buffaloes for me, and to send them to Sem. One of these buffaloes died on the road, the other three arrived on the 24th, and we tied them out the same evening together with the one MacDonald had given us. Ongoing out to visit these animals next morning, I found the people of Chuka in a great state of excitement. The fields round the village had been recently ploughed, and the tigress the previous night had passed close to three families who were sleeping out on the fields with their cattle, fortunately in each case the cattle had seen the tigress and warned the sleepers of her approach. After leaving the cultivated land the tigress had gone up the track in the direction of Kot Kindri and had passed close to two of our buffaloes without touching either of them.

The Patwari, Forest Guards, and villagers had told us on our arrival at Sem that it would be a waste of time trying out our young buffaloes, as they were convinced the man-eater would not kill them. The reason they gave was that this method of trying to shoot the man-eater had been tried by others without success and that in any case if the tigress wanted to eat buffaloes there were many grazing in the jungles for her to choose from. In-spite of this advice however we continued to tie out our buffaloes and for the next two nights the tigress passed close to one or more of them, without touching them.

On the morning of the 27th, just as we were finishing breakfast, a party of men led by Tewari, the brother of the Headman of Thak, arrived in camp and reported that a man from their village was missing. They stated that this man had left the village at about noon the previous day, telling his wife before leaving that he was going to see that his cattle did not stray beyond the village boundary and as he had not returned, they feared he had been killed by the man-eater. Our preparations were soon made, and at ten o'clock the Ibbotsons and I set off for Thak, accompanied by Tewari and the men he had brought with him. The distance was only about two miles, but the climb was considerable and as we did not want to lose more time than we could possibly help, we arrived at the outskirts of the village out of breath, and in a lather of sweat.

As we approached the village over the scrub-covered flat bit of ground which I have reason to refer to later, we heard a woman crying. The wailing of an Indian woman mourning her dead is unmistakable, and on emerging from the jungle we came on the mourner, the wife of the missing man and some ten or fifteen men, who were waiting for us on the edge of the cultivated land. These people informed us that from their houses above they had seen some white object, which looked like part of the missing man's clothing, in a field overgrown with scrub thirty yards from where we were now standing. Ibbotson, Tewari, and I set off to investigate the white object, while Mrs. Ibbotson took the woman and the rest of the men up to the village.

The field, which had been out of cultivation for some years, was covered with a dense growth of scrub not unlike chrysanthemum, and it was not until we were standing right over the white object that Tewari recognized it as the loincloth of the missing man. Near it was the man's cap. A struggle had taken place at this spot, but there was no blood. The "absence of blood where the attack had taken place and for some considerable distance along the drag could be accounted for by the tigress having retained her first hold, for no blood would flow in such a case until the hold had been changed.

Thirty yards on the hill above us there was a clump of bushes roofed over with creepers. This spot would have to be looked at before following up the drag, for it was not advisable to have the tigress behind us. In the soft earth under the bushes, we found the pugmarks of the tigress and where she had lain before going forward to attack the man.

Returning to our starting point we agreed on the following plan of action. Our primary object was to try to stalk the tigress and shoot her on kill: to achieve this end I was to follow the trail and at the same time keep a lookout in front, with Tewari who was unarmed, a yard behind me keeping a sharp lookout to right and left, and Ibbotson a yard behind Tewari to safeguard us against an attack from the rear. In the event of either Ibbotson or I, seeing so much as a hair of the tigress, we were to risk a shot.

Cattle had grazed over this area the previous day, disturbing the ground, and as there was no blood and the only indication of the tigress's passage was an occasional turned-up leaf or crushed blade of grass, progress was slow, After carrying the man for two hundred yards the tigress had killed and left him. She had returned and carried him off several hours later, when the people of Thak had heard several *sambhar* calling in this direction. The reason why the tigress did not carry the man away after she had killed him was possibly because the cattle had witnessed the attack on him and had driven her away.

A big pool of blood had formed where the man had been lying and as the blood from the wound in his throat had stopped flowing by the time the tigress had picked him up again, and further, as she was now holding him by the small of the back, whereas she had previously held him by the neck, tracking became even more difficult. The tigress kept to the con tour of the hill and as the undergrowth here was very dense and visibility only extended to a few yards, our advance was slowed down. In two hours, we covered half a mile, and reached a ridge beyond which lay the valley in which, six months previously, we had tracked down and killed the Chuka man-eater. On this ridge was a great slab of rock, which sloped upwards and away from the direction in which we had come. The tigress's tracks went down to the right of the rock, and I felt sure she was lying up under the over-hanging portion of it or in the close vicinity.

Both Ibbotson and I had on light soled shoes Tewari was barefooted and we had reached the rock without making a sound. Signing to my two companions to stand still and keep a careful watch all round, I got a foothold on the rock, and inch by inch went forward. Beyond the rock was a short stretch of flat ground, and as more of this ground came into view, I felt certain my suspicion that the tigress was lying under the projection was correct. I had still a foot or two to go before I could look over, when I saw a movement to my left front. A golden rod that had been pressed down had sprung erect, and a second later there was a slight movement in the bushes beyond, and a monkey in a tree on the far side of the bushes started calling.

The tigress had chosen the spot for her after-dinner sleep with great care, but unfortunately for us she was not asleep and when she saw the top of my head, I had removed my hat appearing over the rock, she had risen and, taking a step sideways, had disappeared under a tangle of blackberry bushes. Had she been lying anywhere but where she was, she could not have got away, no matter how quickly she had moved, without my getting a shot at her. Our so carefully carried out stalk had failed at the very last moment and there was nothing to be done now but to find the kill and see if there was sufficient of it left for us to sit up over. To have followed her into the blackberry thicket would have been useless and would also have reduced our chances of getting a shot at her later.

The tigress had eaten her meal close to where she had been lying and as this spot was open to the sky and to the keen eyes of vultures, she had removed the kill to a place of safety where it would not be visible from the air. Tracking now was easy, for there was a blood trail to follow. The trail led over a ridge of great rocks and fifty yards beyond these rocks we found the kill.

I am not going to harrow your feelings by attempting to describe that poor torn and mangled thing; stripped of every stitch of clothing and atom of dignity, which only a few hours previously had been a man, the father of two children and the breadwinner of the wailing woman who was facing without any illusions, the fate of a widow of India. I have seen many similar sights, each more terrible than the one preceding it, in the thirty-two years I have been hunting man-eaters and, on each occasion, I have felt that it would have been better to have left the victim to the slayer than recover a mangled mass of flesh to be a nightmare ever after to those who saw it. And yet the cry of blood for blood, and the burning desire to rid a countryside of a menace than which there is none more terrible, is irresistible and then there is always the hope, no matter how absurd one knows it to be, that the victim by some miracle may still be alive and in need of succour.

The chance of shooting over a kill, an animal that has in all probability become a man-eater through a wound received over a kill, is very remote, and each succeeding failure, no matter what its cause, tends to make the animal more cautious, until it reaches a state when it either abandons its kill after one meal or approaches it as silently and as slowly as a shadow, scanning every leaf and twig with the certainty of discovering its would-be slayer, no matter how carefully he may be concealed or how silent and motionless he may be; a one-in-a-million chance of getting a shot, and yet, who is there among us who would not take it?

The thicket into which the tigress had retired was roughly forty yards square, and she could not leave it without the monkey seeing her and warning us, so we sat down back-to-back, to have a smoke and listen if the jungle had anything further to tell us while we considered our next move.

To make a *machan* it was necessary to return to the village, and during our absence the tigress was almost certain to carry away the kill. It had been difficult when she was carrying a whole human being to track her, but now, when her burden was considerably lighter and she had been disturbed, she would probably go for miles and we might never find her kill again, so it was necessary for one of us to remain on the spot, while the other two went back to the village for ropes.

Ibbotson, with his usual disregard for danger, elected to go back and while he and Tewari went down the hill to avoid the difficult ground we had recently come over, I stepped up on to a small tree close to the kill. Four feet above ground the tree divided in two and by leaning on one half and putting my feet against the other, I was able to maintain a precarious seat which was high enough off the ground to enable me to see the tigress if she approached the kill, and also high enough, if she had any designs on me to see her before she got to within striking distance.

Ibbotson had been gone fifteen or twenty minutes when I heard a rock tilt forward and then back. The rock was evidently very delicately poised and when the tigress had put her weight on it and felt it tilt forward, she had removed her foot and let the rock fall back into place. The sound had come from about twenty yards to my left front, the only direction in which it would have been possible for me to have fired without being knocked out of the tree.

Minutes passed, each pulling my hopes down a little lower from the heights to which they had soared, and then, when tension on my nerves and the weight of the heavy rifle were becoming unbearable, I heard a stick snap at the upper end of the thicket. Here was an example of how a tiger can move through the jungle. From the sound she had made I knew her exact position, had kept my eyes fixed on the spot and yet she had come, seen me, stayed some time watching me and then gone away without my having seen a leaf or a blade of grass move.

When tension on nerves is suddenly relaxed, cramped, and aching muscles call loudly for ease and though in this case it only meant the lowering of the rifle on to my knees to take the strain off my shoulders and arms, the movement, small though it was, sent a comforting feeling through the whole of my body. No further sound came from the tigress and an hour or two later I heard Ibbotson returning.

Of all the men I have been on shikar with, Ibbotson is by far and away the best, for not only has he the heart of a lion but he thinks of everything and with it all is the most unselfish man that carries a gun. He had gone to fetch a rope and he returned with rugs, cushions, more hot tea than even I could drink, and an ample lunch and while I sat on the windward side of the kill to refresh myself, Ibbotson put a man in a tree forty yards away to distract the tigress's attention and climbed into a tree overlooking the kill to make a rope *machan*.

When the *machan* was ready Ibbotson moved the kill a few feet, a very unpleasant job and tied it securely to the foot of a sapling to prevent the tigress carrying it away, for the moon was on the wane and the first two hours of the night at this heavily wooded spot would be pitch dark. After a final smoke I climbed on to the machan and when I had made myself comfortable Ibbotson recovered the man who was making a diversion and set off in the direction of Thak to pick up Mrs. Ibbotson and return to camp at Sem.

The retreating party were out of sight but were not yet out of sound when I heard a heavy body brushing against leaves, and at the same moment the monkey, which had been silent all this time and which I could now see sitting in a tree on the far side of the blackberry thicket, started calling. Here was more luck than I hoped for and our ruse of putting a man up a tree to cause a diversion appeared to be working as successfully as it had done on a previous occasion. A tense minute passed, a second, and a third, and then from the ridge where I had climbed on to the big slab of rock a *kakar* came dashing down towards me, barking hysterically. The tigress was not coming to the kill but had gone off after Ibbotson. I was now in a fever of anxiety, for it was quite evident that she had abandoned her kill and gone to try to secure another victim.

Before leaving, Ibbotson had promised to take every precaution but on hearing the *kakar* barking on my side of the ridge he would naturally assume the tigress was moving in the vicinity of the kill, and if he relaxed his precautions the tigress would get her chance. Ten very uneasy minutes for me passed, and then I heard a second *kakar* barking in the direction of Thak, the tigress was still following, but the ground there was more open, and there was less fear of her attacking the party. The danger to the Ibbotsons was, however not over by any means for they had to go through two miles of very heavy jungle to reach camp; and if they stayed at Thak until sundown listening for my shot, which I feared they would do and which as a matter of fact they did do, they would run a very grave risk on the way down. Ibbotson fortunately realized the danger and kept his party close together and though the tigress followed them the whole way, as her pugniarks the following morning showed they got back to camp safely.

The calling of *kakar* and *sambhar* enabled me to follow the movements of the tigress. An hour after sunset she was down at the bottom of the valley two miles away. She had the whole night before her, and though there was only one chance in a million of her returning to the kill I determined not to lose that chance. Wrapping a rug round me, for it was a bitterly cold night, I made myself comfortable in a position in which I could remain for hours without movement.

I had taken my seat on the *machan* at 4 p.m., and at 10 p.m. I heard two animals coming down the hill towards me. It was too dark under the trees to see them, but when they got to the lee of the kill, I knew they were porcupines. Rattling their quills and making the peculiar booming noise that only a porcupine can make, they approached the kill and, after walking round it several times, continued on their way. An hour later and when the moon had been up some time, I heard an animal in the valley below. It was moving from east to west and when it came into the wind blowing downhill from the kill it made a long pause, and then came cautiously up the hill. While it was still some distance away, I heard it snuffing the air, and knew it to be a bear. The smell of blood was attracting him but mingled with it was the less welcome smell of a human being and taking no chances he was very carefully stalking the kill. His nose, the keenest of any animals in the jungle had apprised him while he was still in the valley that the kill was the property of a tiger. This to a Himalayan hear who fears nothing and who will, as I have on several occasions seen, drive a tiger away from its kill, was no deterrent but what was and what was causing him uneasiness was the smell of a human being mingled with the smell of blood and tiger.

On reaching the flat ground the bear sat down on his haunches a few yards from the kill, and when he had satisfied himself that the hated human smell held no danger for him, he stood erect and turning his head sent a long-drawn-out cry, which I interpreted as a call to a mate, echoing down into the valley. Then without any further hesitation he walked boldly up to the kill, and as he nosed it, I aligned the sights of my rifle on him. I know of only one instance of a Himalayan bear eating a human being; on that occasion a woman cutting grass had fallen down a cliff and been killed and a bear finding the mangled body had carried it away and had eaten it. This bear, however, on whose shoulder my sights were aligned, appeared to draw the line at human flesh and after looking at and smelling the kill continued his interrupted course to the west. When the sounds of his retreat died away in the distance the jungle settled down to silence until interrupted, a little after sunrise, by Ibbotson's very welcome arrival.

With Ibbotson came the brother and other relatives of the dead man, who very reverently wrapped the remains in a clean white cloth and, lying it on a cradle made of two saplings and rope which Ibbotson provided, set off for the burning ghat on the banks of the Sarda, repeating under their breath as they went the Hindu hymn of praise '*Ram nam sat hai*' with its refrain, '*Satya bol gat hai*'.

Fourteen hours in the cold had not been without its effect on me but after partaking of the hot drink and food Ibbotson had brought, I felt none the worse for my long vigil.

II

After following the Ibbotsons down to Chuka on the evening of the 27th the tigress, sometime during the night, crossed the Ladhya in the scrub jungle at the back of our camp. Through this scrub ran a path that had been regularly used by the villagers of the Ladhya valley until the advent of the man-eater had rendered its passage unsafe. On the 28th the two mail-runners who carried Ibbotson's dak on its first stage to Tanakpur got delayed in camp and to save time took, or more correctly started to take, a short cut through this scrub. Very fortunately the leading man was on the alert and saw the tigress as she crept through the scrub and lay down near the path ahead of them.

Ibbotson and I had just got back from Thak when these two men dashed into camp and taking our rifles, we hurried off to investigate. We found the pugmarks of the tigress where she had come out on the path and followed the men for a short distance, but we did not see her though in one place where the scrub was very dense, we saw a movement and heard an animal moving off.

On the morning of the 29th, a party of men came down from Thak to report that one of their bullocks had not returned to the cattle-shed the previous night and on a search being made where it had last been seen a little blood had been found. At 2 p.m. the Ibbotsons and I were at this spot, and a glance at the ground satisfied us that the bullock had been killed and carried away by tiger. After a hasty lunch Ibbotson and I, with two men following carrying ropes for a *machan*, set out along the drag. It went diagonally across the face of the hill for a hundred yards and then straight down into the ravine in which I had fired at and missed the big tiger in April. A few hundred yards down this ravine the bullock, which was an enormous animal had got fixed between two rocks and not being able to move it, the tigress had eaten a meal off its hind quarters and left it.

The pugmarks of the tigress, owing to the great weight she was carrying, were splayed out and it was not possible to say whether she was the man-eater or not but as every tigress in this area was suspect, I decided to sit up over the kill. There was only one tree within reasonable distance of the kill, and as the men climbed into it to make a *machan* the tigress started calling in the valley below. Very hurriedly a few strands of rope were tied between two branches, and while Ibbotson stood on guard with his rifle, I climbed the tree and took my seat on what, during the next fourteen hours, proved to be the most uncomfortable as well as the most dangerous *machan* I have sat on. The tree was leaning away from the hill and from the three uneven strands of rope I was sitting on there was a drop of over a hundred feet into the rocky ravine below.

The tigress called several times as I was getting into the tree and continued to call at longer intervals late into the evening, and the last call coming from a ridge half a mile away. It was now quite evident that the tigress had been lying up close to the kill and had seen the men climbing into the tree. Knowing from past experience what this meant, she had duly expressed resentment at being disturbed and then gone away for though I sat on the three strands of rope until Ibbotson returned next morning I did not see or hear anything throughout the night.

Vultures were not likely to find the kill, for the ravine was deep and overshadowed by trees and as the bullock was large enough to provide tigress with several meals, we decided not to sit up over it again where it was now lying, hoping the tigress would remove it to a place more convenient and where we should have a better chance of getting a shot. In this however we were disappointed for the tigress did not again return to the kill.

Two nights later the buffalo we had tied out behind our camp at Sem was killed, and through a little want of observation on my part a great opportunity of bagging the man-eater was lost.

The men who brought in the news of this kill reported that the rope securing the animal had been broken, and that the kill had been carried away up the ravine at the lower end of which it had been tied. This was the same ravine in which MacDonald, and I had chased a tigress in April and as on that occasion she had taken her kill some distance up the ravine I now very foolishly concluded she had done the same with this kill.

After breakfast Ibbotson and I went out to find the kill and see what prospect there was for an evening sit-up.

The ravine in which the buffalo had been killed was about fifty yards wide and ran deep into the foothills. For two hundred yards the ravine was straight and then bent round to the left. Just beyond the bend, and on the left-hand side of it, there was a dense patch of young saplings backed by a hundred-foot ridge on which thick grass was growing. In the ravine, and close to the saplings, there was a small pool of water. I had been up the ravine several times in April and had failed to mark the patch of saplings as being a likely place for a tiger to lie up in and did not take the precautions I should have taken when rounding the bend, with the result that the tigress who was drinking at the pool saw us first. There was only one safe line of retreat for her, and she took it. This was straight up the steep hill, over the ridge and into the Sal forest beyond.

The hill was too steep for us to climb, so we continued on up the ravine to where a *sambhar* track crossed it and following this track, we gained the ridge. The tigress was now in a triangular patch of jungle bounded by the ridge, the Ladhya and a cliff down which no animal could go. The area was not large, and there were several deer in it which from time to time advised us of the position of the tigress, but unfortunately the ground was cut up by a number of deep and narrow rainwater channels in which we eventually lost touch with her.

We had not yet seen the kill, so we re-entered the ravine by the *sambhar* track and found the kill hidden among the saplings. These saplings were from six inches to a foot in girth, and were not strong enough to support a *machan*, so we had to abandon the idea of a *machan*. With the help of a crowbar a rock could possibly have been priced from the face of the hill and a place made in which to sit, but this was not advisable when dealing with a man-eater.

Reluctant to give up the chance of a shot we considered the possibility of concealing ourselves in the grass near the kill, in the hope that the tigress would return before dark and that we should see her before she saw us. There were two objections to this plan: (a) if we did not get a shot and the tigress saw us near her kill, she might abandon it as she had done her other two kills, and (b) between the kill and camp there was very heavy scrub jungle, and if we tried to go through this jungle in the dark the tigress would have us at her mercy. So very reluctantly we decided to leave the kill to the tigress for that night and hope for the best on the morrow.

On our return next morning we found that the tigress had carried away the kill. For three hundred yards she had gone up the bed of the ravine, stepping from rock to rock and leaving no drag marks.

At this spot, three hundred yards from where she had picked up the kill, we were at sea for though there were a number of tracks on a wet patch of ground, none of them had been made while she was carrying the kill. Eventually, after casting round in circles, we found where she had left the ravine and gone up the hill on the left.

This hill up which the tigress had taken her kill was overgrown with ferns and golden -rod and tracking was not difficult, but the going was, for the hill was very steep and in places a detour had to be made and the track picked up further on. After a stiff climb of a thousand feet, we came to a small plateau, bordered on the left by a cliff a mile wide. On the side of the plateau nearest the cliff the ground was seamed and cracked, and in these cracks a dense growth of sal, two to six feet in height, had sprung up. The tigress had taken her kill into this dense cover, and it was not until we actually trod on it that we were aware of its position.

As we stopped to look at all that remained of the buffalo there was a low growl to our right. With rifles raised we waited for a minute and then, hearing a movement in the undergrowth a little beyond where the growl had come from, we pushed our way through the young sal for ten yards and come on a small clearing, where the tigress had made herself a bed on some soft grass. On the far side of this grass the hill sloped upwards for twenty yards to another plateau, and it was from this slope that the sound we had heard had come. Proceeding up the slope as silently as possible we had just reached the flat ground, which was about fifty yards wide, when the tigress left the far side and went down into the ravine, disturbing some *kalege* pheasants and a *kakar* as she did so. To have followed her would have been useless, so we went back to the kill and, as there was still a good meal on it, we selected two trees to sit in, and returned to camp.

After an early lunch we went back to the kill and, hampered by our rifles, climbed with some difficulty into the trees we had selected. We sat up for five hours without seeing or hearing anything. At dusk we climbed down from our trees and stumbling over the cracked and uneven ground eventually reached the ravine when it was quite dark.

Both of us had an uneasy feeling that we were being followed, but by keeping close together we reached camp without incident at 9 p.m.

The Ibbotsons had now stayed at Sem as long as it was possible for them to do so, and early next morning they set out on their twelve days' walk to keep their appointment at Askot. Before leaving, Ibbotson extracted a promise from me that I would not follow up any kills alone, or further endanger my life by prolonging my stay at Sem for more than a day or two.

After the departure of the Ibbotsons and their fifty men, the camp, which was surrounded by dense scrub, was reduced to my two servants and myself, my coolies were living in a room in the Headman's house, so throughout the day I set all hands to collecting driftwood, of which there was an inexhaustible supply at the junction, to keep a fire going all night. The fire would not scare away the tigress, but it would enable us to see her if she prowled round our tents at night, and anyway the nights were setting in cold and there was ample excuse, if one were needed, for keeping a big fire going all night.

Towards evening, when my men were safely back in camp, I took a rifle and went up the Ladhya to see if the tigress had crossed the river. I found several tracks in the sand but no fresh ones and at dusk I returned, convinced that the tigress was still on our side of the river. An hour later, when it was quite dark, a kakar started barking close to our tents and barked persistently for half an hour.

My men had taken over the job of tying out the buffaloes, a task which Ibbotson's men had hitherto performed and next morning I accompanied them when they went out to bring in the buffaloes. Though we covered several miles, I did not find any trace of the tigress. After breakfast I took a rod and went down to the junction and had one of the best days' fishing, I have ever had. The junction was full of big fish, and though my light tackle was broken frequently, I killed sufficient *mahseer* to feed the camp.

Again, as on the previous evening, I crossed the Ladhya, with the intention of taking up a position on a rock overlooking the open ground on the right bank of the river and watching for the tigress to cross. As I got away from the roar of the water at the junction, I heard a *sambhar* and a monkey calling on the hill to my left, and as I neared the rock I came on the fresh tracks of the tigress. Following them back I found the stones still wet where she had forded the river. A few minutes' delay in camp to dry my fishing line and have a cup of tea cost a man his life, several thousand men weeks of anxiety and myself many days of strain, for though I stayed at Sem for another three days I did not get another chance of shooting the tigress.

On the morning of the 7th, as I was breaking camp and preparing to start on my twenty mile walk to Tanakpur, a big contingent of men from all the surrounding villages arrived and begged me not to leave them to the tender mercies of the man-eater. Giving them what advice, it was possible to give people situated as they were, I promised to return as soon as it was possible for me to do so.

I caught the train at Tanakpur, next morning and arrived back in Nainital on 9 November, having been away nearly a month.

III

I left Sem on the 7th of November and on the 12th the tigress killed a man at Thak. I received news of this kill through the Divisional Forest Officer, Haldwani, shortly after we had moved down to our winter home at the foot of the hills and by doing forced marches, I arrived at Chuka a little after sunrise on the 24th.

It had been my intention to breakfast at Chuka and then go on to Thak and make that village my headquarters, but the Headman of Thak, whom I found installed at Chuka, informed me that every man, woman and child had left Thak immediately after the man had been killed on the 12th, and added that if I carried out my intention of camping at Thak I might be able to safeguard my own life but it would not be possible to safeguard the lives of my men. This was quite reasonable, and while waiting for my men to arrive, the Headman helped me to select a site for my camp at Chuka where my men would be reasonably safe, and I should have some privacy from the thousands of men who were now arriving to fell the forest.

On receipt of the Divisional Forest Officers telegram acquainting me of the kill, I had telegraphed to the Tahsildar at Tanakpur to send three young male buffaloes to Chuka. My request had been promptly complied with and the three animals had arrived the previous evening.

After breakfast I took one of the buffaloes and set out for Thak, intending to tie it up on the spot where the man had been killed on the 12th. The Headman had given me a very graphic account of the events of that date, for he himself had nearly fallen a victim to the tigress. It appeared that towards the afternoon, accompanied by his granddaughter, a girl ten years of age, he had gone to dig up ginger tubers in field some sixty yards from his house. This field is about half an acre in extent and is surrounded on three sides by jungle and being on the slope of a fairly steep hill it is visible from the Headman's house. After the old man and his granddaughter had been at work for some time his wife, who was husking rice in the courtyard of the house, called out in a very agitated voice and asked him if he was deaf that he could not hear the pheasants and other birds that were chattering in the jungle above him. Fortunately for him, he acted promptly. Dropping his hoe, he grabbed the child's hand and together they ran back to the house, urged on by the woman who said she could now see a red animal in the bushes at the upper end of the field. Half an hour later the tigress killed a man who was lopping branches off a tree in a field three hundred yards from the Headman's house.

From the description I had received from the Headman I had no difficulty in locating the tree. It was a small, gnarled tree growing out of a three-foot-high bank between two terraced fields and had been lopped year after year for cattle fodder. The man who had been killed was standing on the trunk holding one branch and cutting another, when the tigress came up from behind, tore his hold from the branch and, after killing him, carried him away into the dense brushwood bordering the fields.

Thak village was a gift from the Chand Rajas, who ruled Kumaon for many hundreds of years before the Gurkha occupation, to the forefathers of the present owners in return for their services at the Purnagiri temples. (The promise made by the Chand Rajas that the lands of Thak and two other villages would remain rent-free for all time has been honoured by the British Government for a hundred years.) From a collection of grass huts the village has in the course of time grown into a very prosperous settlement with masonry houses roofed with slate tiles, for not only is the land very fertile but the revenue from the temples is considerable.

Like all other villages in Kumaon, Thak during its hundreds of years of existence has passed through many vicissitudes, but never before in its long history had it been deserted as it now was. On my previous visits I had found it a hive of industry, but when I went up to it this afternoon, taking the young buffalo with me, silence reigned over it. Every one of the hundred or more inhabitants had fled taking their livestock with them, the only animal I saw in the village was a cat, which gave me a warm welcome so hurried had the evacuation been that many of the doors of the houses had been left wide open. On every path in the village in the courtyards of the houses and in the dust before all the doors, I found the tigress's pugmarks. The open doorways were a menace, for the path as it wound through the village passed dose to them and in any of the houses the tigress might have been lurking.

On the hill thirty yards above the village were several cattle shelters, and in the vicinity of these shelter I saw more *kalege* pheasants, red jungle fowl, and white-capped babblers than I have ever before seen, and from the confiding way in which they permitted me to walk among them it is quite evident that the people of Thak have a religious prejudice against the taking of life.

From the terraced fields above the cattle shelters a bird's-eye view of the village is obtained and it was not difficult from the description the Headman had given me, to locate the tree where the tigress had secured her last victim. In the soft earth under the tree there were signs of a struggle and a few clots of dried blood. From here the tigress had carried her kill a hundred yards over a ploughed field, through a stout hedge and into the dense brushwood beyond.

The footprints from the village and back the way they had come, showed that the entire population of the village had visited the scene of the kill but from the tree to the hedge there was only one track, the track the tigress had made when carrying away her victim. No attempt had been made to follow her up and recover the body.

Scraping away a little earth from under the tree I exposed a root and to this root I tied my buffalo, bedding it down with a liberal supply of straw taken from a nearby haystack.

The village, which is on the north face of the hill, was now in shadow and if I was to get back to camp before dark it was time for me to make a start. Skirting round the village to avoid the menace of the open doorways, I joined the path below the houses.

This path after it leaves the village passes under a giant mango tree from the roots of which issues a cold spring of clear water. After running along a groove cut in a massive slab of rock, this water falls into a rough masonry trough, from where it spreads on to the surrounding ground, rendering it soft and slushy. I had drunk at the spring on my way up, leaving my footprints in this slushy ground, and on approaching the spring now for a second drink, I found the tigress's pugmarks superimposed on my footprints. After quenching her thirst the tigress had avoided the path and had gained the village by climbing a steep bank overgrown with strobilanthes and nettles and taking up a position in the shelter of one of the houses had possibly watched me while I was tying up the buffalo, expecting me to return the way I had gone; it was fortunate for me that I had noted the danger of passing those open doorways a second time and had taken the longer way round.

When coming up from Chuka I had taken every precaution to guard against a sudden attack, and it was well that I had done so, for I now found from her pugmarks that the tigress had followed me all the way up from my camp, and next morning when I went back to Thak, I found she had followed me from where I had joined the path below the houses, right down to the cultivated land at Chuka.

Reading with the illumination I had brought with me was not possible, so after dinner that night, while sitting near a fire which was as welcome for its warmth as it was for the feeling of security it gave me, I reviewed the whole situation and tried to think out some plan by which it would be possible to circumvent the tigress.

When leaving home on the 22nd I had promised that I would return in ten days and that this would be my last expedition after man-eaters. Years of exposure and strain and long absences from home, extending as in the case of the Chowgarh tigress and the Rudraprayag leopard to several months on end were beginning to tell as much on my constitution as on the nerves of those at home, and if by the 30th of November I had not succeeded in killing this man-eater, others would have to be found who were willing to take on the task.

It was now the night of the 24th, so I had six clear days before me. Judging from the behaviour of the tigress that evening, she appeared to be anxious to secure another human victim, and it should not therefore be difficult for me, in the time at my disposal to get in touch with her. There were several methods by which this could be accomplished, and each would be tried in turn. The method that offers the greatest chance of success of shooting a tiger in the hills is to sit up in a tree over a kill, and if during that night the tigress did not kill the buffalo I had tied up at Thak, I would the following night, and every night thereafter, tie up the other two buffaloes in places I had already selected, and failing to secure a human kill it was just possible that the tigress might kill one of my buffaloes, as she had done on a previous occasion when the Ibbotsons and I were camped at Sem in April. After making up the fire with logs that would burn all night, I turned in and went to sleep listening to a *kakar* barking in the scrub jungle behind my tent.

While breakfast was being prepared the following morning, I picked up a rifle and went out to look for tracks on the stretch of sand on the right bank of the river, between Chuka and Sem. The path after leaving the cultivated land, runs for a short distance through scrub jungle, and here I found the tracks of a big male leopard, possibly the same animal that had alarmed the *kakar* the previous night. A small male tiger had crossed and recrossed the Ladhya many times during the past week, and in the same period the man-eater had crossed only once, coming from the direction of Sem. A big bear had traversed the sand a little before my arrival, and when I got back to camp the timber contractors complained that while distributing work that morning, they had run into a bear which had taken up a very threatening attitude in consequence of which their labour had refused to work in the area in which the bear had been seen.

Several thousand men, the contractors put the figure at five thousand had now concentrated at Chuka and Kumaya Chak to fell and saw up the timber and carry it down to the motor road that was being constructed, and all the time this considerable labour force was working they shouted at the tops of their voices to keep up their courage. The noise in the valley resulting from axe and saw, the crashing of giant trees down the steep hillside, the breaking of rocks with sledgehammers and combined with it all the shouting of thousands of men can better be imagined than described. That there were many frequent alarms in this nervous community was only natural, and during the next few days I covered much ground and lost much valuable time in investigating false rumours of attacks and kills by the man-eater for the dread of the tigress was not confined to the Ladhya valley but extended right down the Sarda through Kaldhunga to the gorge an area of roughly fifty square miles in which an additional ten thousand men were working.

That a single animal should terrorize a labour force of these dimensions in addition to the residents of the surrounding villages and the hundreds of men who were bringing foodstuffs for the labourers or passing through the valley with hill produce in the way of oranges (purchasable at twelve annas a hundred), walnuts, and chillies to the market at Tanakpur is incredible and would be unbelievable were it not for the historical and nearly parallel, case of the man-eater of Tsavo, where a pair of lions, operating only at night held up work for long periods on the Uganda Railway.

To return to my story. Breakfast disposed of on the morning of the 25th, I took a second buffalo and set out for Thak. The path after leaving the cultivated land at Chuka, skirts along the foot of the hill for about half a mile before it divides. One arm goes straight up a ridge to Thak and the other, after continuing along the foot of the hill for another half-mile, zigzags up through Kumaya Chak to Kot Kindri.

At the divide I found the pugmarks of the tigress and followed them all the way back to Thak. The fact that she had come down the hill after me the previous evening was proof that she had not killed the buffalo. This, though very disappointing, was not at all unusual for tigers will on occasions visit an animal that is tied up for several nights in succession before they finally kill it, for tigers do not kill unless they are hungry.

Leaving the second buffalo at the mango tree, where there was an abundance of green grass, I skirted round the houses and found No. I buffalo sleeping peacefully after a big feed and a disturbed night. The tigress, coming from the direction of the village as her pugmarks showed, had approached to within a few feet of the buffalo, and had then gone back the way she had come. Taking the buffalo down to the spring I let it graze for an hour or two and then took it back and tied it up at the same spot where it had been the previous night.

The second buffalo I tied up fifty yards from the mango tree and at the spot where the wailing woman and villagers had met us the day the Ibbotsons and I had gone up to investigate the human kill. Here a ravine a few feet deep crossed the path, on one side of which there was a dry stump, and on the other an almond tree in which a *machan* could be made. I tied the second buffalo to the stump and bedded it down with sufficient hay to keep it going for several days. There was nothing more to be done at Thak, so I returned to camp and, taking the third buffalo, crossed the Ladhya and tied it up behind Sem, in the ravine where the tigress had killed one of our buffaloes in April.

At my request the Tahsildar of Tanakpur had selected three of the fattest young male buffaloes he could find. All three were now tied up in places frequented by the tigress, and as I set out to visit them on the morning of the 26th I had great hopes that one of them had been killed and that I should get an opportunity of shooting the tigress over it. Starting with the one across the Ladhya, I visited all in turn and found that the tigress had not touched any of them. Again, as on the previous morning, I found her tracks on that path leading to Thak, but on this occasion, there was a double set of pugmarks, one coming down and the other going back. On both her journeys the tigress had kept to the path and had passed within a few feet of the buffalo that was tied to the stump, fifty yards from the mango tree.

On my return to Chuka a deputation of Thak villagers led by the Headman came to my tent and requested me to accompany them to the village to enable them to replenish their supply of foodstuffs, so at midday, followed by the Headman and his tenants, and by four of my own men carrying ropes for a *machan* and food for me, I returned to Thak, and mounted guard while the men hurriedly collected the provisions they needed.

After watering and feeding the two buffaloes, I retied No. 2 to the stump and took No. 1 half a mile down the hill and tied it to a sapling on the side of the path. I then took the villagers back to Chuka and returned a few hundred yards up the hill for a scratch meal while my men were making the *machan*.

It was now quite evident that the tigress had no fancy for my fat buffaloes and as in three days I had seen her tracks five times on the path leading to Thak, I decided to sit up over the path and try to get a shot at her that way. To give me warning of the tigress's approach I tied a goat with a bell round its neck on the path, and at 4 p.m. I climbed into the tree. I told my men to return at 8 a.m. the following morning and began my watch.

At sunset a cold wind started blowing and while I was attempting to pull a coat over my shoulders the ropes on one side of the machan slipped, rendering my seat very uncomfortable. An hour later a storm came on, and though it did not rain for long it wet me to the skin, greatly adding to my discomfort. During the sixteen hours I sat in the tree I did not see or hear anything. The men turned up at 8 a.m. I returned to camp for a hot bath and a good meal and then accompanied by six of my men, set out for Thak.

The overnight rain had washed all the tracks off the path, and two hundred yards above the tree I had sat in I found the fresh pugmarks of the tigress, where she had come out of the jungle and gone up the path in the direction of Thak. Very cautiously I stalked the first buffalo, only to find it lying asleep on the path; the tigress had skirted round it, rejoined the path a few yards further on, and continued up the hill. Following on her tracks I approached the second buffalo and as I got near the place where it had been tied, two blue Himalayan magpies rose off the ground and went screaming down the hill.

The presence of these birds indicated (a) that the buffalo was dead, (b) that it had been partly eaten and not carried away and (c) that the tigress was not in the close vicinity.

On arrival at the stump to which it had been tied I saw that the buffalo had been dragged off the path and partly eaten, and on examining the animal I found that it had not been led by the tigress but that it had in all probability died of snake-bite (there were many hamadryads in the surrounding jungles) and that, finding it lying dead on the path, the tigress had eaten a meal of it and had then tried to drag it away. When she found she could not break the rope, she had partly covered the kill over with dry leaves and brushwood and continued on her way up to Thak.

Tigers as a rule are not carrion eaters but they do on occasions eat animals they themselves have not killed. For instance, on one occasion I left the carcass of a leopard on a fire track and, when I returned next morning to recover a knife I had forgotten, I found that a tiger had removed the carcass to a distance of a hundred yards and had eaten two-thirds of it.

On my way up from Chuka I had dismantled the *machan* I had sat on the previous night, and while two of my men climbed into the almond tree to make a seat for me, the tree was not big enough for a *machan* the other four went to the spring to fill a kettle and boil some water for tea. By 4 p.m. I had partaken of a light meal of biscuits and tea which would have to keep me going until the next day and refusing the men's request to be permitted to stay the night in one of the houses in Thak, I sent them back to camp. There was a certain amount of risk in doing this, but it was nothing compared to the risk they would run if they spent the night in Thak.

My seat on the tree consisted of several strands of rope tied between two upright branches, with a couple of strands lower down for my feet to rest on. When I had settled down comfortably, I pulled the branches round me and secured them in position with a thin cord, leaving a small opening to see and fire through. My 'hide' was soon tested, for shortly after the men had gone the two magpies returned, and attracted others, and nine of them fed on the kill until dusk. The presence of the birds enabled me to get some sleep, for they would have given me warning of the tigress's approach, and with their departure my all-night vigil started.

There was still sufficient daylight to shoot by when the moon, a day off the full, rose over the Nepal hills behind me and flooded the hillside with brilliant light. The rain of the previous night had cleared the atmosphere of dust and smoke and, after the moon had been up a few minutes, the light was so good that I was able to see a *sambhar* and her young one feeding in a field of wheat a hundred and fifty yards away.

The dead buffalo was directly in front and about twenty yards away, and the path along which I expected the tigress to come was two or three yards nearer, so I should have an easy shot at a range at which it would be impossible to miss the tigress provided she came and there was no reason why she should not do so.

The moon had been up two hours, and the *sambhar* had approached to within fifty yards of my tree, when a *kakar* started barking on the hill just above the village. The *kakar* had been barking for some minutes when suddenly a scream which I can only very inadequately describe as Ar-Ar-Arr' dying away on a long-drawn-out note, came from the direction of the village. So sudden and so unexpected had the scream been that I involuntarily stood up with the intention of slipping down from the tree and dashing up to the village, for the thought flashed through my mind that the man-eater was killing one of my men. Then in a second flash of thought I remembered I had counted them one by one as they had passed my tree, and that I had watched them out of sight on their way back to camp to see if they were obeying my instructions to keep close together.

The scream had been the despairing cry of a human being in mortal agony and reason questioned how such a sound could have come from a deserted village. It was not a thing of my imagination, for the *kakar* had heard it and had abruptly stopped barking and the *sambhar* had dashed away across the fields closely followed by her young one. Two days previously, when I had escorted the men to the village, I had remarked that they appeared to be very confident to leave their property behind doors that were not even shut or latched, and the Headman had answered that even if their village remained untenanted for years their property would be quite safe, for they were priests of Purnagiri and no one would dream of robbing them, he added that as long as the tigress lived she was a better guard of their property, if guard were needed than any hundred men could be, for no one in all that countryside would date to approach the village for any purpose, through the dense forests that surrounded it, unless escorted by me as they had been.

The screams were not repeated and as there appeared to be nothing that I could do I settled down again on my rope seat. At 10 p.m. a *kakar* that was feeding on the young wheat crop at the lower end of the fields dashed away barking and a minute later the tigress called twice. She had now left the village and was on the move, and even if she did not fancy having another meal off the buffalo there was every hope of her coming along the path which she had used twice every day for the past few days. With finger on trigger and eyes straining on the path I sat hour after hour until daylight succeeded moonlight, and when the sun had been up an hour, my men returned. Very thoughtfully they had brought a bundle of dry wood with them, and in a surprisingly short time I was sitting down to a hot cup of tea. The tigress may have been lurking in the bushes close to us, or she may have been miles away, for after she had called at 10 p.m. the jungles had been silent.

When I got back to camp, I found a number of men sitting near my tent. Some of these men had come to inquire what luck I had the previous night, and others had come to tell me that the tigress had called from midnight to a little before sunrise at the foot of the hill and that all the labourers engaged in the forests and on the new export road were too frightened to go to work. I had already heard about the tigress from my men, who had informed me that, together with the thousands of men who were camped round Chuka, they had sat up all night to keep big fires going.

Among the men collected near my tent was the Headman of Thak and when the others had gone, I questioned him about the kill at Thak on the 12th of the month when he so narrowly escaped falling a victim to the man-eater.

Once again the Headman told me in great detail how he had gone to his fields to dig ginger, taking his grandchild with him, and how on hearing his wife calling he had caught the child's hand and run back to the house, where his wife had said a word or two to him about not keeping his ears open and thereby endangering his own and the child's life and how a few minutes later the tigress had killed a man while he was cutting leaves off a tree in a field above his house.

All this part of the story I had heard before, and I now asked him if he had actually seen the tigress killing the man. His answer was no; and he added that the tree was not visible from where he had been standing. I then asked him how he knew the man had been killed, and he said, because he had heard him. In reply to further question's, he said the man had not called for help but had cried out and when asked if he had cried out once he said, 'No, three times', and then at my request he gave an imitation of the man's cry. It was the same but a very modified rendering as the screams I had heard the previous night.

I then told him what I had heard and asked him if it was possible for anyone to have arrived at the village accidentally and his answer was an emphatic negative. There were only two paths leading to Thak and every man, woman, and child in the village through which these two paths passed knew that Thak was deserted and the reason for its being so. It was known throughout the district that it was dangerous to go near Thak in daylight and it was therefore quite impossible for anyone to have been in the village at eight o'clock the previous night.

When asked if he could give any explanation for screams having come from a village in which there could not according to him have been any human beings, his answer was that he could not. And as I could do no better than the Headman it was best to assume that neither the *kakar*, the *sambhar*, nor I heard those very real screams, the screams of a human being in mortal agony.

IV

When all my visitors, including the Headman, had gone, and I was having breakfast, my servant informed me that the Headman of Sem had come to the camp the previous evening and had left word for me that his wife, while cutting grass near the hut where his mother had been killed, had come on a blood trail and that he would wait for me near the ford over the Ladhya in the morning. So, after breakfast I set out to investigate this trail.

While I was fording the river, I saw four men hurrying towards me, and as soon as I was on dry land, they told me that when they were coming down the hill above Sem they had heard a tiger calling across the valley on the hill between Chuka and Thak. The noise of the water had prevented my hearing the call. I told the men that I was on my way to Sem and would return to Chuka shortly and left them.

The Headman was waiting for me near his house, and his wife took me to where she had seen the blood trail the previous day. The trail, after continuing along a field for a short distance, crossed some big rocks, on one of which I found the hairs of a *kakar*. A little further on I found the pugmarks of a big male leopard, and while I was looking at them, I heard a tiger call. Telling my companions to sit down and remain quiet, I listened, in order to locate the tiger. Presently I heard the call again and thereafter it was repeated at intervals of about two minutes.

It was the tigress calling and I located her as being five hundred yards below Thak, and in the deep ravine which, starting from the spring under the mango tree, runs parallel to the path and crosses it at its junction with the Kumaya Chak path.

Telling the Headman that the leopard would have to wait to be shot at a more convenient time, I set off as hard as I could go for camp, picking up at the ford the four men who were waiting for my company to Chuka.

On reaching camp I found a crowd of men round my tent, most of them sawyers from Delhi, but including the petty contractors, agents, clerks, timekeepers, and gang men of the financier who had taken up the timber and road construction contracts in the Ladhya valley. These men had come to see me in connexion with my stay at Chuka. They informed me that many of the hillmen carrying timber and working on the road had left for their homes that morning and that if I left Chuka on 1st December, as they had heard I intended doing, the entire labour force, including themselves, would leave on the same day; for already they were too frightened to eat or sleep and no one would dare to remain in the valley after I had gone. It was then the morning of 29th November, and I told the men that I still had two days and two nights and that much could happen in that time, but that in any case it would not be possible for me to prolong my stay beyond the morning of the 1st.

The tigress had by now stopped calling, and when my servant had put together something for me to eat, I set out for Thak intending, if the tigress called again and I could locate her position, to try to stalk her; and if she did not call again, to sit up over the buffalo. I found her tracks on the path and saw where she had entered the ravine and though I stopped repeatedly on my way up to Thak and listened I did not hear her again. So, a little before sunset I ate the biscuits and drank the bottle of tea, I had brought with me and then climbed into the almond tree and took my seat on the few strands of rope that had to serve me as a *machan*. On this occasion the magpies were absent, so I was unable to get the hour or two's sleep the birds had enabled me to get the previous evening.

If a tiger fails to return to its kill the first night, it does not necessarily mean that the kill has been abandoned. I have on occasions seen a tiger returned on the tenth night and eat what could no longer be described as flesh. On the present occasion, however, I was not sitting over a kill, but over an animal that the tigress had found dead and off which she had made a small meal, and had she not been a man-eater, I would not have considered the chance of her returning the second night good enough to justify spending a whole night in a tree when she had not taken sufficient interest in the dead buffalo to return to it the first night. It was therefore with very little hope of getting a shot that I sat on the tree from sunset to sunrise, and though the time I spent was not as long as it had been the previous night, my discomfort was very much greater, for the ropes I was sitting on cut into me and a cold wind that started blowing shortly after moonrise and continued throughout the night chilled me to the bone. On this second night I heard no jungle or other sounds nor did the *sambhar* and her young one come out to feed on the fields. As daylight was succeeding moonlight, I thought I heard a tiger call in the distance but could not be sure of the sound or of its direction.

When I got back to camp my servant had a cup of tea and a hot bath ready for me, but before I could indulge in the latter my 40-lb. tent was not big enough for me to bathe in. I had to get rid of the excited throng of people who were clamouring to tell me their experiences of the night before. It appeared that shortly after moonrise the tigress had started calling close to Chuka, and after calling at intervals for a couple of hours had gone off in the direction of the labour camps at Kumaya Chak. The men in these camps hearing her coming started shouting to try to drive her away but so far from having this effect the shouting only infuriated her the more and she demonstrated in front of the camps until she had cowed the men into silence. Having accomplished this, she spent the rest of the night between the labour camps and Chuka, daring all and sundry to shout at her. Towards morning she had gone away in the direction of Thak and my informants were surprised and very disappointed that I had not met her.

This was my last day of man-eater hunting, and though I was badly in need of rest and sleep, I decided to spend what was left of it in one last attempt to get in touch with the tigress.

The people, not only of Chuka and Sem but of all the surrounding villages, and especially the men from Talla Des where some years previously I had shot three man-eaters, were very anxious that I should try sitting up over a live goat, for, said they, 'All hill tigers eat goats, and as you have had no luck with buffaloes, why not try a goat?' More to humour them than with any hope of getting a shot, I consented to spend this last day in sitting up over the two goats I had already purchased for this purpose.

I was convinced that no matter where the tigress wandered to at night her headquarters were at Thak, so at midday, taking the two goats and accompanied by four of my men, I set out for Thak.

The path from Chuka to Thak, as I have already mentioned, runs up a very steep ridge. A quarter of a mile on this side of Thak the path leaves the ridge and crosses a more or less flat bit of ground which extends right up to the mango tree. For its whole length across this flat ground the path passes through dense brushwood and is crossed by two narrow ravines which run east and join the main ravine. Midway between these two ravines, and a hundred yards from the tree I had sat in the previous two nights, there is a giant almond tree; this tree had been my objective when I left camp. The path passes right under the tree, and I thought that if I climbed halfway up not only should I be able to see the two goats, one of which I intended tying at the edge of the main ravine and the other at the foot of the hill to the right, but I should also be able to see the dead buffalo. As all three of these points were at some distance from the tree, I armed myself with an accurate .275 rifle, in addition to the 450/400 rifle which I took for an emergency.

I found the climb up from Chuka on this last day very trying, and I had just reached the spot where the path leaves the ridge for the flat ground, when the tigress called about a hundred and fifty yards to my left. The ground here was covered with dense undergrowth and trees interlaced with creepers, and was cut up by narrow and deep ravines, and strewn over with enormous boulders, a very unsuitable place in which to stalk a man-eater. However, before deciding on what action I should take it was necessary to know whether the tigress was lying down, as she very well might be, for it was then I p.m., or whether she was on the move and if so in what direction. So, making the men sit down behind me I listened and presently the call was repeated; she had moved some fifty yards, and appeared to be going up the main ravine in the direction of Thak.

This was very encouraging, for the tree I had selected to sit in was only fifty yards from the-ravine. After enjoining silence on the men and telling them to keep close behind me, we hurried along the path. We had about two hundred yards to go to reach the tree and had covered half the distance when, as we approached a spot where the path was bordered on both sides by dense brushwood, a covey of kalege pheasants rose out of the brushwood and went screaming away. I knelt down and covered the path for a few minutes, but as nothing happened, we went cautiously forward and reached the tree without further incident. As quickly and as silently as possible one goat was tied at the edge of the ravine, while the other was tied at the foot of" the hill to the right; then I took the men to the edge of the cultivated land and told them to stay in the upper verandah of the Headmans house until I fetched them and ran back to the tree. I climbed to a height of forty feet and pulled the rifle up after me with a cord I had brought for the purpose. Not only were the two goats visible from my seat, one at a range of seventy and the other at a range of sixty yards, but I could also see part of the buffalo, and as the .275 rifle was accurate, I felt sure I could kill the tigress if she showed up anywhere on the ground I was overlooking.

The two goats had lived together ever since I had purchased them on my previous visit and being separated now, were calling lustily to each other. Under normal conditions a goat can be heard at a distance of four yards, but here the conditions were not normal, for the goats were tied on the side of a hill down which a strong wind was blowing, and even if the tigress had moved after I had heard her, it was impossible for her not to hear them. If she was hungry, as I had every reason to believe she was, there was a very good chance of my getting a shot.

After I had been on the tree for ten minutes a kakar barked near the spot the pheasants has risen from. For a minute or two my hopes rose sky-high and then dropped back to earth for the kakar barked only three times and ended on a note of enquiry; evidently there was a snake in the scrub which neither he nor the pheasants liked the look of.

My seat was not comfortable, and the sun was pleasingly warm, so for the next three hours I remained in the tree without any discomfort. At 4 p.m. the sun went down behind the high hill above Thak and thereafter the wind became unbearably cold. For an hour I stood the discomfort, and then decided to give up, for the cold had brought on an attack of ague, and if the tigress came now, it would not be possible for me to hit her. I retied the cord to the rifle and let it down, climbed down myself and walked to the edge of the cultivated land to call up my men.

V

There are few people, I imagine, who have not experienced that feeling of depression that follows failure to accomplish anything they have set out to do. The road back to the camp after a strenuous day when the chukor (hill partridge) bag is full is only a step compared with the same road which one plods over, mile after weary mile, when the bag is empty and if this feeling of depression has ever assailed you at the end of a single day, and when the quarry has only been chukor, you will have some idea of the depth of my depression that evening when, after calling up my men and untying the goats, I set off on my two-mile walk to camp, for my effort had been not of a single day or my quarry a few birds nor did my failure concern only myself.

Excluding the time spent on the journeys from and to home, I had been on the heels of the man-eater from 23rd October to 7th November, and again from 24th to 30th November, and it is only those of you who have walked in fear of having the teeth of a tiger meet in your throat who will have any idea of the effect on one's nerves of days and weeks of such anticipation.

Then again, my quarry was a man-eater, and my failure to shoot it would very gravely affect anyone who was working in, or whose homes were in that area. Already work in the forests had been stopped, and the entire population of the largest village in the district had abandoned their homes. Bad as the conditions were, they would undoubtedly get worse if the man-eater was not killed, for the entire labour force could not afford to stop work indefinitely, nor could the population of surrounding villages afford to abandon their homes and their cultivation as the more prosperous people of Thak had been able to do.

The tigress had long since lost her natural fear of human beings as was abundantly evident from her having carried away a girl picking up mangoes in a field close to where several men were working, killing a woman near the door of her house, dragging a man off a tree in the heart of a village and the previous night, cowing a few thousand men into silence. And here was I, who knew full well what the presence of a man-eater meant to the permanent and to the temporary inhabitants and to all the people who passed through the district on their way to the markets at the foothills or the temples at Punagiri, plodding down to camp on what I had promised others would be my last day of man-eater hunting; reason enough for a depression of soul which I felt would remain with me for the rest of my days. Gladly at that movement would I have bartered the success that had attended thirty-two years of man-eater hunting for one unhurried shot at the tigress.

I have told you of some of the attempts I made during this period of seven days and nights to get a shot at the tigress, but these were by no means the only attempts I made. I knew that I was being watched and followed and every time I went through the two miles of jungle between my camp and Thak, I tried every trick I have learnt in a lifetime spent in the jungles to outwit the tigress. Bitter though my disappointment was, I felt that my failure was not in any way due to anything I had done or left undone.

VI

My men when they rejoined me said that, an hour after the *kakar* had barked, they had heard the tigress calling a long way off but were not sure of the direction. Quite evidently the tigress had as little interest in goats as she had in buffaloes but even so it was unusual for her to have moved at that time of day from a locality in which she was thoroughly at home, unless she had been attracted away by some sound which neither I nor my men had heard; however that may have been, it was quite evident that she had gone and as there was nothing further that I could do feet off on my weary tramp to camp.

The path, as I have already mentioned, joins the ridge that runs down to Chuka a quarter of a mile from Thak and when I now got to this spot where the ridge is only a few feet wide and from where a view is obtained of the two great ravines that run down to the Ladhya river, I heard the tigress call once and again across the valley on my left. She was a little above and to the left of Kumaya Chak, and a few hundred yards below the Kot Kindri ridge on which the men working in that area had built themselves grass shelters.

Here was an opportunity, admittedly forlorn and unquestionably desperate, of getting a shot, still it was an opportunity and the last I should ever have, and the question was, whether or not I was justified in taking it.

When I got down from the tree, I had one hour in which to get back to camp before dark. Calling up the men, hearing what they had to say, collecting the goats, and walking to the ridge had taken about thirty minutes, and judging from the position of the sun which was now casting a red glow on the peaks of the Nepal hills, I calculated I had roughly half an hour's daylight in hand. This time factor, or perhaps it would be more correct to say light factor, was all-important, for if I took the opportunity that it offered, on it would depend, the lives of five men.

The tigress was a mile away and the intervening ground was densely wooded, strewn over with great rocks, and cut up by a number of deep nullahs, but she could cover the distance well within the half-hour if she wanted to. The question I had to decide was, whether or not I should try to call her up. If I called and she heard me and came while it was still daylight and gave me a shot, all would be well, on the other hand, if she came and did not give me a shot some of us would not reach camp, for we had nearly two miles to go and the path the whole way ran through heavy jungle, and was bordered in some places by big rocks, and in others by dense brushwood. It was useless to consult the men, for none of them had ever been in a jungle before coming on this trip, so the decision would have to be mine.

I decided to try to call up the tigress.

Handing my rifle over to one of the men I waited until the tigress called again and, cupping my hands round my mouth and filling my lungs to their utmost limit, sent an answering call over the valley. Back came her call and thereafter, for several minutes, call answered call. She would come, had in fact already started, and if she arrived while there was light to shoot by, all the advantages would be on my side, for I had the selecting of the ground on which it would best suit me to meet her. November is the mating season for tigers and it' was evident that for the past forty-eight hours she had been rampaging through the jungles in search of a mate, and that now, on hearing what she thought was a tiger answering her mating call, she would lose no time in joining him.

Four hundred yards down the ridge the path runs for fifty yards across a flat bit of ground. At the far right-hand side of this flat ground the path skirts a big rock and then drops steeply and continues in a series of hairpin bends, down to the next bend. It was at this rock I decided to meet the tigress, and on my way to it I called several times to let her know I was changing my position, and also to keep in touch with her.

I want you now to have a clear picture of the ground in your mind, to enable you to follow the subsequent events. Imagine then a rectangular piece of ground forty yards wide and eighty yards long, ending in a more or less perpendicular rock face. The path coming down from Thak runs on to this ground at its short or south end and after continuing down the centre for twenty-five yards bends to the right and leaves the rectangle on its long or east side. At the point where the path leaves the flat ground there is a rock about four feet high. From a little beyond where the path bends to the right, a ridge of rock, three or four feet high, rises and extends to the north side of the rectangle, where the ground falls away in a perpendicular rock face. On the near or path side of this low ridge there is a dese line of bushes approaching to within ten feet of the four-foot-high rock I have mentioned. The rest of the rectangle is grown over with trees, scattered bushes, and short glasses.

It was my intention to lie on the path by the side of the rock and shoot the tigress as she approached me, but when I tried this position, I found it would not be possible for me to see her until she was within two or three yards and further, that she could get at me either round the rock or through the scattered bushes on my left without my seeing her at all. Projecting out of the rick, from the side opposite to that from which I expected the tigress to approach, there was a narrow ledge. By sitting sideways, I found I could get a little of my bottom on the ledge, and by putting my left hand flat on the top of the rounded rock and stretching out my right leg to its full extent and touching the ground with my toes, retain my position on it. The men and goats I placed immediately behind and ten to twelve feet below me.

The stage was now set for the reception of the tigress, who while these preparations were being made had approached to within three hundred yards. Sending out one final call to give her direction, I looked round to see if my men were all right.

The spectacle these men presented would under other circumstances have been ludicrous but was here tragic. Sitting in a tight little circle with the knees drawn up and their heads together, with the goats burrowing in under them, they had that look of intense expectancy on their screwed-up features that one sees on the faces of spectators waiting to hear a big gun go off. From the time we had first heard the tigress from the ridge, neither the men nor the goats had made a sound, beyond one suppressed cough. They were probably by now frozen with fear as well they might be and even if they were I take my hat off to those four men who had the courage to do what I, had I been in their shoes, would not have dreamt of doing. For seven days they had been hearing the most exaggerated and blood-curdling tales of this fearsome beast that had kept them awake the past two nights and now, while darkness was coming on and sitting unarmed in a position where they could see nothing, they were listening to the man-eater drawing nearer and nearer, greater courage and greater faith, it is not possible to conceive.

The fact that I could not hold my rifle, a D.B. 450/400, with my left hand (which I was using to retain my precarious seat on the ledge) was causing me some uneasiness, for apart from the fear of the rifle slipping on the rounded top of the rock, I had folded my handkerchief and placed the rifle on it to try to prevent this. I did know what would be the effect of the recoil of a high velocity rifle fired in this position. The rifle was pointing along the path, in which there was a hump, and it was my intention to fire into the tigress's face immediately once it appeared over this hump, which was twenty feet from the rock.

The tigress however did not keep to the con tour of the hill, which would have brought her out on the path a little beyond the hump but crossed a deep ravine and came straight towards where she had heard my last call, at an angle which I can best describe as one o'clock. This manoeuver put the low ridge of rock, over which I could not see, between us. She had located the direction of my last call with great accuracy but had misjudged the distance and not finding her prospective mate at the spot she had expected him to be, she was now working herself up into a perfect fury and you will have some idea of what the fury of a tigress in her condition can be when I tell you that not many miles from my home a tigress on one occasion closed a public road for a whole week, attacking everything that attempted to go along it, including a string of camels, until she was finally joined by a mate.

I know of no sound more liable to fret one's nerves than the calling of an unseen tiger at close range. What effect this appalling sound was having on my men I frightened to think and if they had gone screaming down the hill I should not have been at all surprised, for even though I had the heel of a good rifle to my shoulder and the stock against my cheek I felt like screaming myself.

But even more frightening than this continuous calling was the fading out of the light. Another few seconds, ten or fifteen at the most, and it would be too dark to see my sights, and we should then be at the mercy of a man-eater, plus a tigress wanting a mate. Something would have to be done and done in a hurry if we were not to be massacred and the only thing, I could think of was to call.

The tigress was now so close that I could hear the intake of her breath each time before she called, and as she again filled her lungs, I did the same with mine, and we called simultaneously. The effect was startlingly instantaneous. Without a second's hesitation she came tramping with quick steps through the dead leaves, over the low ridge and into the bushes a little to my right front and just as I was expecting her to walk right on top of me, she stopped and the next moment the full blast of her deep-throated call struck me in the face and would have carried the hat off my head had I been wearing one. A second's pause, then again quick steps, a glimpse of her as she passed between two bushes and then she stepped right out into the open, and, looking into my face, stopped dead.

By great and unexpected good luck, the half-dozen steps the tigress took to her right front carried her almost to the exact spot at which my rifle was pointing. Had she continued in the direction in which she was coming before her last call, my story if written would have had a different ending, for it would have been as impossible to slew the rifle on the rounded top of the rock as it would have been to lift and fire it with one hand.

Owing to the nearness of the tigress, and the fading light, all that I could see of her was her head. My first bullet caught her under the right eye and the second, fired more by accident than with intent, took her in the throat and she came to rest with her nose against the rock. The recoil from the right barrel loosened my hold on the rock and knocked me off the ledge, and the recoil from the left barrel, fired while I was in the air, brought the rifle up in violent contact with my jaw and sent me head over heels right on top of the men for, not knowing but what the tigress was going to land on them next, they caught me as I fell and saved me from injury and my rifle from being broken.

When I had freed myself from the tangle of the human and goat leg's I took the .275 rifle from the man who was holding it, rammed a clip of cartridges into the magazine and sent a stream of five bullets singing over the valley and across the valley and across the Sarda into Nepal. Two shots, to the thousands of men in the valley and in the surrounding villages who were anxiously listening for the sound of my rifle, might mean anything, but two shots followed by five more, spaced at regular intervals of five seconds, could only be interpreted as conveying one message, and that was that the man-eater was dead.

I had not spoken to my men from the time we had first heard the tigress from the ridge. On my telling them now that she was dead and that there was no longer any reason for us to be afraid, they did not appear to be able to take in what I was saying, so I told them to go up and have a look while I found and lit a cigarette. Very cautiously they climbed up to the rock, but went no further for, as I have told you, the tigress was touching the other side of it. Late in camp that night while sitting round a campfire, and relating their experiences to relays of eager listeners, their narrative invariably ended up with, 'and then the tiger whose roaring had turned our livers into water hit the *sahib* on the head and knocked him down on top of us, and if you don't believe us, go and look at his face'. A mirror is superfluous in camp and even if I had one it could not have made the swelling on my jaw, which put me on a milk diet for several days, look, as large and as painful as it felt.

By the time a sapling had been felled and the tigress lashed to it, lights were beginning to show in the Ladhya valley and in all the surrounding camps and villages. The four men were very anxious to have the honour of carrying the tigress to camp, but the task was beyond them, so I left them and set off for help.

In my three visits to Chuka during the past eight months I had been along this path many times by day and always with a loaded rifle in my hands and now I was stumbling down in the dark, unarmed, my only anxiety being to avoid a fall. If the greatest happiness one can experience is the sudden cessation of great pain, then the second greatest happiness is undoubtedly the sudden cessation of great fear. One short hour previously it would have taken wild elephants to have dragged from their homes and camps the men who now singing and shouting, were converging from every direction, singly and in groups, on the path leading to Thak. Some of the men of this rapidly growing crowd went up the path to help carry in the tigress, while other accompanied me on my way to camp, and would have carried me had I permitted them. Progress was slow, for frequent halts had to be made to allow each group of new arrivals to express their gratitude in their own particular way. This gave the party carrying the tigress time to catch us up, and we entered the village together. I will not attempt to describe the welcome my men and I received, or the scenes I witnessed at Chuka that night, for having lived the greater part of my life in the jungles I have not the ability to paint word-pictures.

A hayrick was dismantled, and the tigress laid on it, and an enormous bonfire made from driftwood close at hand to light up the scene and for warmth, for the night was dark and cold with a north wind blowing. Round about midnight my servant, assisted by the Headman of Thak and Kunwar Singh, near whose house I was camped, persuaded the crowd to return to their respective villages and labour camps, telling them they would have ample opportunity of feasting their eyes on the tigress the following day. Before leaving himself, the Headman of Thak told me he would send word in the morning to the people of Thak to return to their village. This he did, and two days later the entire population returned to their homes and have lived in peace ever since.

After my midnight dinner I sent for Kunwar Singh and told him that in order to reach home on the promised date I should have to start in a few hours and that he would have to explain to the people in the morning why I had gone. This he promised to do, and I then started to skin the tigress. Skinning tiger with a pocket-knife is a long job but it gives one an opportunity of examining the animal that one would otherwise not get, and in the case of man-eater enables one to ascertain, more or less accurately, the reason for the animal having become a man-eater.

The tigress was a comparatively young animal and in the perfect condition one would expect her to be at the beginning of the mating season. Her dark winter coat was without a blemish, and in spite of her having so persistently refused the meals I had provided for her she was encased in fat. She had two old gunshot wounds, neither of which showed on her skin. The one in her left shoulder, caused by several pellets of homemade buckshot, had become septic, and when healing the skin, over quite a large surface, had adhered permanently to the flesh. To what extent this wound had incapacitated her it would have been difficult to say, but it had evidently taken a very long time to heal and could quite reasonably have been the cause of her having become a man-eater. The second wound, which was in her right shoulder, had also been caused by a charge of buckshot, but had healed without becoming septic. These two wounds received over kills in the days before she had become a man-eater were quite sufficient reason for her not having returned to the human and other kills I had sat over.

After having skinned the tigress I bathed and dressed, and though my face was swollen and painful and I had twenty miles of rough going before me, I left Chuka walking on air, while the thousands of men in and around the valley were peacefully sleeping.

I have come to the end of the jungle stories I set out to tell you and I have also come near the end of my man-eater hunting career.

I have had a long spell and count myself fortunate in having walked out on my own feet and not been carried out on a cradle in the manner and condition of the man of Thak.

There have been occasions when life has hung by a thread and others when a light purse and disease resulting from exposure and strain have made the going difficult but for all these occasions I am amply rewarded if my hunting has resulted in saving one human life.

JUST TIGERS

I think that all sportsmen who have had the opportunity of indulging in the twin sports of shooting tigers with a camera and shooting them with a rifle will agree with me that the difference between these two forms of sport is as great, if not greater, than the taking of some trout on light tackle in a snow-fed mountain stream, and the killing of a fish on a fixed rod on the sunbaked bank of a tank.

Apart from the difference in cost between shooting with a camera and shooting with a rifle, and the beneficial effect it has on our rapidly decreasing stock of tigers, the taking of a good photograph gives far more pleasure to the sportsman than the acquisition of a trophy and further, while the photograph is of interest to all lovers of wildlife, the trophy is only of interest to the individual who acquired it. As an illustration, I would instance Fred Champion. Had Champion shot his tigers with a rifle instead of with a camera his trophies would long since have lost their hair and been consigned to the dustbin, whereas the records made by his camera are a constant source of pleasure to him and are of interest to sportsmen in all parts of the world.

It was looking at the photographs in Champion's book *With a Camera in Tiger-Land* that first gave me the idea of taking photographs of tigers. Champion's photographs were taken with a still camera by flashlight, and I decided to go one better and try to take tiger pictures with a cinecamera by daylight. The gift by a very generous friend of a Bell and Howell 16-mm camera put just the weapon I needed into my hands, and the 'Freedom of the Forests' which I enjoy enabled me to roam at large over a very wide field. For ten years I stalked through many hundreds of miles of tiger country, at times being seen off by tigers that resented my approaching their kills, and at other times being shooed out of the jungle by tigresses that objected to my going near their cubs. During this period, I learnt a little about the habits and ways of tigers and though I saw tigers on, possibly, two hundred occasions I did not succeed in getting one satisfactory picture. I exposed films on many occasions, but the results were disappointing owing either to overexposure, underexposure, obstruction of grass or leaves or cobwebs on the lens and in one case owing to the emulsion on the film having been melted while being processed.

Finally, in 1938 I decided to devote the whole winter to making one last effort to get a good picture. Having learnt by experience that it was not possible to get a haphazard picture of a tiger, my first consideration was to find a suitable site, and I eventually selected an open ravine fifty yards wide, with a tiny stream flowing down the centre of it and flanked on either side by dense tree and scrub jungle. To deaden the sound of my camera when taking pictures at close range I blocked the stream in several places, making miniature waterfalls a few inches high. I then cast round for my tigers, and having located seven, in three widely separated areas, started to draw them a few yards at a time to my jungle studio. This was a long and a difficult job, with many setbacks and disappointments, for the area in which I was operating is heavily shot over and it was only by keeping my tigers out of sight that I eventually got them to the exact spot where I wanted them. One of the tigers for some reason unknown to me left the day after her arrival, but not before I had taken a picture of her, the other six I kept together, and I exposed a thousand feet of film on them. Unfortunately, it was one of the wettest winters we have ever had, and several hundred feet of the film were ruined through moisture on the lens, underexposure, and packing of the film inside the camera due to hurried and careless threading. But, even so, I have got approximately six hundred feet of film of which I am inordinately proud, for it is a living record of six full grown tigers four males, two of which are over ten feet and two females, one of which is a white tigress filmed in daylight at ranges varying from ten to sixty feet.

The whole proceeding from start to finish took four and a half months, and during the countless hours I lay near the tiny stream and my miniature waterfalls, not one of the tigers ever saw me.

The stalking to within a few feet of six tigers in daylight would have been an impossible feat, so they were stalked in the very early hours of the morning, before night had gone and daylight come, the heavy winter dew making this possible and were filmed as light and opportunity offered.

The Man-Eating Leopard of Rudraprayag

THE PILGRIM ROAD

If you are a Hindu from the sun-scorched plains of India and you desire as all good Hindus do to perform the pilgrimage to the age- old shrines of Kedarnath and Badrinath, you must start on your pilgrimage from Hardwar and in order to acquire a full measure of the merits vouchsafed to you for the correct performance of the pilgrimage, you must walk every step of the way from Hardwar to Kedarnath and thence over the mountain track to Badrinath, barefoot.

Having purified yourself by immersion in the sacred Har-ki-pauri pool, done *darshan* at the many shrines and temples in Hardwar, and added your mite to their coffers, you must not omit to toss a coin within reach of the festering stumps which once were hands of the lepers who line the narrowest part of the pilgrim road above the sacred pool, for if you make this omission, they will call down curses on your head. What matter if these unfortunate ones have wealth beyond your dreams secreted in their filthy rags, or in the rock caves they call their homes? The curses of such as they were best avoided, and immunity will cost you but a few coppers.

You have now done all that custom and religion require of a good Hindu and are at liberty to start on your long and hard pilgrimage.

The first place of interest you will come to after leaving Hardwar is Rishikesh. Here you will make your first acquaintance with the Kalakamli Wallahas, so called because of the black blanket their founder wore and which many of his disciples still wear in the form of a habit or loose cloak bound round the middle with a cord of goat's hair and who are renowned throughout the land for their good deeds. I do not know if any of the other religious brotherhoods you will meet on your pilgrimage have any claim to renown, but I do know that the Kalakamli Wallahas have such a claim and justly so for, out of the offerings they receive at their many shrines and temples, they have built, and they maintain hospitals, dispensaries, and pilgrim shelters and they feed the poor and the needy.

With Rishikesh behind you, you will come next to Lachman *Jhula*, where the pilgrim road crosses from the right to the left bank of the Ganges on a suspension bridge. Here beware of the red monkeys who infest the bridge, for they are even more importunate than the lepers of Hardwar and if you omit to propitiate them with offerings of sweets or parched gram, your passage across the long and narrow bridge is likely to be both difficult and painful.

Three-day's journey up the left bank of the Ganges and you have reached the ancient capital of Garhwal Shreenagar an historic, religious, and trading centre of considerable importance and of great beauty, nestling in a wide, open valley surrounded by high mountains. It was here, in the year 1805, that the forebears of the Garhwali soldiers who have fought so gallantly in two world wars made their last, and unsuccessful, stand against the Gurkha invaders, and it is a matter of great regret to the people of Garhwal that their ancient city of Shreenagar, together with the palaces of their kings, was swept away, to the last stone, by the bursting of the Gohna Lake dam in 1894. This dam, caused by a landslide in the valley of the Birehi Ganga, a tributary of the Ganges, was 11,000 feet wide at the base, 2,000 feet wide at the summit and 900 feet high and when it burst, ten billion cubic feet of water were released in the short space of six hours. So, well was the bursting of the dam timed that though the flood devastated the valley of the Ganges right down to Hardwar and swept away every bridge, only one family was lost, the members of which had returned to the danger-zone after having been forcibly removed from it.

From Shreenagar you have to face a stiff climb to Chatikhal, which is compensated for by the magnificent views you will get of the Ganges valley and of the eternal snows above Kedarnath.

A day's march from Chatikhal, and you see in front of you Golabrai with its row of grass -thatched pilgrim shelters, a one roomed stone-built house and its drinking trough. This big and imposing drinking trough is fed by a tiny crystal-clear stream which in summer is sedately conducted down the mountainside by a series of channels rough-hewn from pine saplings. At other seasons of the year the water cascades unconfined and merrily over rocks draped with moss and maidenhair fern, through luxuriant beds of vivid green watercress and sky-blue strobilanthes.

A hundred yards beyond the pilgrim shelters, and on the right-hand side of the road, stands a mango tree. This tree and the two-storied house above it which is the home of the *pundit*, who owns the Golabrai pilgrim shelters are worthy of note, for they play an important part in the tale I have to tell.

Another two miles, along the last flat bit of ground you will see for many a day, and you have reached Rudraprayag, where you and I, my pilgrim friend, must part, for your way lies across the Alaknanda and up the left bank of the Mandakini to Kedarnath, while mine lies over the mountains to my home in Nainital.

The road in front of you, which has been trodden by the feet of millions of pilgrims like you, is excessively steep and incredibly rough and you, whose lungs have never breathed air above sea level, who have never climbed anything higher than the roof of your house and whose feet have never trodden anything harder than yielding sand, will suffer greatly. Times there will be a many, when, gasping for breath, you toil ..up the face of steep mountains on feet torn and bleeding by passage over rough rocks, sharp shale, and frozen ground, when you will question whether the prospective reward you seek is worth the present price you pay in suffering; but being a good Hindu you will toil on, comforting yourself with the thought that merit is not gained without suffering, and the greater the suffering in this world, the greater the reward in the next.

TERROR

The word 'terror' is so generally and universally used in connection with everyday trivial matters that it is apt to fail to convey, when intended to do so, its real meaning. I should like therefore to give you some idea of what terror, real terror meant to the fifty thousand inhabitants living in the five hundred square miles of Garhwal in which the man-eater was operating and to the sixty thousand pilgrims who annually passed through that area between the years 1918 and 1926. And I will give you a few instances to show you what grounds the inhabitants, and the pilgrims, had for that terror.

No curfew order has ever been more strictly enforced, and more implicitly obeyed, than the curfew imposed by the man-eating leopard of Rudraprayag.

During the hours of sunlight life in that area carried on in a normal way. Men went long distances to the bazaars to transact business or to outlying villages to visit relatives or friends; women went up the mountain-sides to cut grass for thatching or for cattle-fodder, children went to school or into the jungles to graze goats or to collect dry sticks and if it was summer, pilgrims, either singly or in large numbers, toiled along the pilgrim routes on their way to and from the sacred shrines of Kedarnath and Badrinath.

As the sun approached the western horizon and the shadows lengthened, the behaviour of the entire population of the area underwent a very sudden and a very noticeable change. Men who had sauntered to the bazaars or to outlying villages were hurrying home, women carrying great bundles of grass were stumbling down the steep mountainsides, children who had loitered on their way from school or who were late in bringing in their flocks of goats or the dry sticks they had been sent out to collect, were being called by anxious mothers and the weary pilgrims were being urged by any local inhabitant who passed them to hurry to shelter.

When night came, an ominous silence brooded over the whole area, no movement, and no sound anywhere. The entire local population was behind fast-closed doors and, in many cases, had sought further protection by building additional doors. Those of the pilgrims who had not been fortunate enough to find accommodation inside houses were huddled close together in pilgrim shelters. And all, whether in a house or shelter. Were silent for fear of attracting the dread man-eater.

This is what terror meant to the people of Garhwal, and to the pilgrims, for eight long years.

I will now give a few instances to show you what grounds there were for that terror.

A boy, an orphan aged fourteen, was employed to look after a flock of forty goats. He was of the depressed, untouchable class and each evening when he returned with his charges, he was given his food and then shut into a small room with the goats. The room was on the ground floor of a long row of double-storied buildings and was immediately below the room occupied by the boy's master, the owner of the goats. To prevent the goats crowding in on him as he slept, the boy had fenced off the far left- hand corner of the room.

This room had no windows and only one door and when the boy and the goats were safely inside, the boy's master pulled the door to, and fastened it by passing the hasp, which was attached by a short length of chain to the door, over the staple fixed in the lintel. A piece of wood was then inserted in the staple to keep the hasp in place, and on his side of the door the boy, for his better safety, rolled a stone against it.

On the night the orphan was gathered to his fathers, his master asserts the door was fastened as usual, and I have no reason to question the truth of his assertion. In support of it, the door showed many deep claw-marks, and it is possible that in his attempts to claw open the door the leopard displaced the piece of wood that was keeping the hasp in place, after which it would have been easy for him to push the stone aside and enter the room.

Forty goats packed into a small room, one corner of which was fenced off, could not have left the intruder much space to manoeuvre in and it is left to conjecture whether the leopard covered the distance from the door to the boy's corner of the room over the backs of the goats or under their bellies, for at this stage of the proceedings all the goats must have been on their feet.

It were best to assume that the boy slept through all the noise the leopard must have made when trying to force open the door and that the goats must have made when the leopard had entered the room and that he did not cry for help to deaf ears, only screened from him and the danger that menaced him by a thin plank.

After killing the boy in the fenced-off corner, the leopard carried him across the empty room, the goats had escaped into the night down a steep hillside and then over some terraced fields to a deep boulder-strewn ravine. It was here, after the sun had been up a few hours, that the master found all that the leopard had left of his servant.

Incredible as it may seem, not one of the forty goats had received so much as a scratch.

A neighbour had dropped in to spend the period of a long smoke with a friend. The room was L-shaped and the only door in it was not visible from where the two men sat on the floor with their backs to the wall, smoking. The door was shut but not fastened, for up to that night there had been no human kills in the village. The room was in darkness and the owner of it had just passed the hookah to his friend when it fell to the ground, scattering a shower of burning charcoal and tobacco. Telling his friend to be more careful or he would set the blanket on which they were sitting on fire, the man bent forward to gather up the embers and as he did so, the door came into view. A young moon was near setting and, silhouetted against it, the man saw a leopard carrying his friend through the door.

When recounting the incident to me a few days later the man said: I am speaking the truth, *sahib*, when I tell you I never heard even so much as the intake of a breath or any other sound from my friend who was sitting only an arm's-length from me, either when the leopard was killing him or when it was carrying him away. There was nothing I could do for my friend, so I waited until the leopard had been gone some little while and then I crept up to the door and hastily shut and secured it.'

The wife of the Headman of a village was ill from a fever, and two friends had been called in to nurse her.

✦✦✦

There were two rooms in the house. The outer room had two doors, one opening onto a small, flagged courtyard and the other leading into the inner room. This outer room also had a narrow slip of a window set some four feet above floor level and in this window, which was open, stood a large brass vessel containing drinking water for the sick woman.

Except for the one door giving access to the outer room, the inner room had no other opening in any of its four walls.

The door leading out on to the courtyard was shut and securely fastened, and the door between the two rooms was wide open.

The three women in the inner room were lying on the ground, the sick woman in the middle with a friend on either side of her. The husband in the outer room was on a bed on the side of the room nearest the window and on the floor beside his bed, where its light would shine into the inner room, was a lantern, turned down low to conserve oil.

Round about midnight, when the occupants of both the rooms were asleep, the leopard entered by way of the narrow slip of a window, avoiding in some miraculous way knocking over the brass vessel which nearly filled it, skirted round the man's low bed and, entering the inner room, killed the sick woman. It was only when the heavy brass vessel crashed to the floor as the leopard attempted to lift its victim through the window that the sleepers awoke.

When the lantern had been turned up the woman who had been sick was discovered lying huddled up under the window and in her throat were four great teeth-marks.

A neighbour, whose wife had been one of the nurses on that night, when relating the occurrence to me said, 'The woman was very ill from her fever and was likely to have died in any case, so it was fortunate that the leopard selected her.'

✦✦✦

Two Gujars were moving their herd of thirty buffaloes from one grazing-ground to another and accompanying them was the twelve-year-old daughter of the older of the two men, who were brothers.

They were strangers to the locality and either had not heard of the man-eater or which is more probable, thought the buffaloes would give them all the protection they needed.

Near the road and at an elevation of eight thousand feet was a narrow strip of flat ground below which was a sickle-shaped terraced field, some quarter of an acre in extent, which had long been out of cultivation. The men selected this site for their camp and having cut stakes from the jungle which surrounded them on all sides, they drove them deep into the field and tethered their buffaloes in a long row.

After the evening meal prepared by the girl had been eaten, the party of three laid their blankets on the narrow strip of ground between the road and the buffaloes and went to sleep.

It was a dark night, and some time towards the early hours of the morning the men were awakened by the booming of their buffalo-bells and by the snorting of the frightened animals. Knowing from long experience that these sounds indicated the presence of carnivora, the men lit a lantern and went among the buffaloes to quieten them, and to see that none had broken the ropes tethering them to the stakes.

The men were absent only a few minutes. When they returned to their sleeping-place they found that the girl whom they had left asleep was missing. On the blanket on which she had been lying were big splashes of blood.

When daylight came the father, and the uncle followed the blood trail. After skirting round the row of tethered buffaloes, it went across the narrow field and down the steep hillside for a few yards, to where the leopard had eaten his kill.

'My brother was born under an unlucky star, *sahib*, for he has no son, and he had only this one daughter who was to have been married shortly, and to whom he looked in the fullness of time to provide him with an heir, and now the leopard has come and eaten her.'

I could go on and on, for there were many kills, and each one has its own tragic story, but I think I have said enough to convince you that the people of Garhwal had ample reason to be terrified of the man-eating leopard of Rudraprayag, especially when it is remembered that Garhwalis are intensely superstitious and that, added to their fear of physical contact with the leopard, was their even greater fear of the supernatural of which I shall give you an example.

I set out from the small one-roomed Rudraprayag Inspection Bungalow one morning just as day was breaking, and as I stepped off the verandah I saw in the dust, where the ground had been worn away by human feet, the pugmarks of the man-eater.

The pugmarks were perfectly fresh and showed that the leopard had stepped out of the verandah only a few minutes in advance of me, and from the direction in which they were pointing it was evident that the leopard after his fruitless visit to the bungalow, was making for the pilgrim road some fifty yards away.

Tracking between the bungalow and the road was not possible owing to the hard surface of the ground, hut as I reached the gate, I saw the pugmarks were heading in the direction of Golabrai. A large flock of sheep and goats had gone down the road the previous evening, and in the dust, they had kicked up the leopard's tracks showed up as clearly as they would have on fresh-fallen snow.

I had by then, become quite familiar with the man-eater's pugmarks and could with little difficulty have distinguished them from the pugmarks of any hundred leopards.

A lot can be learnt from the pugmarks of carnivora, as for instance the sex, age, and size of the animal. I had examined the pugmarks of the man-eater very carefully the first time I had seen them, and I knew he was an out-sized male leopard, long past his prime.

As I followed the tracks of the man-eater on this morning, I could see that he was only a few minutes ahead of me, and that he was moving at a slow, even pace.

The road, which had no traffic on it at this early hour of the morning, wound in and out of a number of small ravines, and as it was possible that the leopard might on this occasion break his rule of never being out after daylight, I crept round each corner with the utmost care until I found, a mile farther on, where the leopard had left the road and gone up a great track into dense scrub and tree jungle.

A hundred yards from where the leopard left the road there was a small field in the centre of which was a thorn enclosure, erected by the owner of the field to encourage packmen to camp there and fertilize it. In this enclosure was the flock of sheep and goats that had come down the road the previous evening.

The owner of the flock, a rugged fellow who by the looks of him had been packing trade commodities up and down the pilgrim road for nigh on half a century, was just removing the thornbush closing the entrance to the enclosure when I came up. In reply to my inquiries, he informed me that he had seen nothing of the leopard but that, just as dawn was breaking, his two sheepdogs had given tongue and, a few minutes later, a *kakar* had barked in the jungle above the road.

When I asked the old packman if he would sell me one of his goats, he asked for what purpose it was wanted and when I told him it was to tie up for the man-eater, he walked through the opening in the fence replaced the bush, accepted one of my cigarettes and sat down on a rock by the side of the road.

We remained smoking for a while, with my question still unanswered, and then the man began to talk.

'You, *sahib*, are undoubtedly he whom I have heard tell of on my way down from my village near Badrinath, and it grieves me that you should' have come all this long way from your home on a fruitless errand. The evil spirit that is responsible for all the human deaths in this area is not an animal, as you think it is, that can be killed by ball or shot, or by any of the other means that you have tried and that others have tried before you; and in proof of what I say I will tell you a story while I smoke this second cigarette. The story was told to me by my father, who, as everyone knows, had never been heard to tell a lie.

'My father was a young man then, and I unborn, when an evil spirit, like the one that is now troubling this land, made its appearance in our village, and all said it was a leopard. Men, women, and children were killed in their homes and every effort was made, as has been made here, to kill the animal. Traps were set, and far-famed marksmen sat in trees and fired ball and shot at the leopard; and when all these attempts to kill it had failed, a great terror seized the people, and none dared leave the shelter of his home between the hours of sunset and sunrise.

'And then the headmen of my father's village and of the villages round about, bade all the men attend a *panchayat*, and when all were assembled the *panch* addressed the meeting and said they were assembled to devise some fresh means to rid themselves of this man-eating leopard. Then an old man, fresh back from the burning-ghat, whose grandson had been killed the previous night, arose and said it was no leopard that had entered his house and killed his grandson as he lay asleep by his side but one from among their own community who, when he craved for human flesh and blood, assumed the semblance of a leopard and that such a one could not be killed by the methods already tried, as had been amply proved, and could only be killed by fire. His suspicions, he said, fell on the fat *sadhu* who lived in the hut near the ruined temple.

'At this there was a great uproar, some exclaiming that the old man's sorrow at the loss of his grandson had demented him, others averring he was right. And these later recalled that the *sadhu* had arrived at the village at about the time the killings had started, and it was further recalled that on the day succeeding a killing the *sadhu* had been won't to sleep all day, stretched on his bed in the sun.

'When order had been restored the matter was long debated and the *panchayat* eventually decided that no immediate action would be taken, but that the *sadhu's* movements should in future be watched. The assembled men were then divided into three parties, the first party to start its watch from the night the next kill could be expected for the kills had taken place at more or less regular intervals.

'During the nights the first and the second parties were on watch, the *sadhu* did not leave his hut.

'My father was with the third party, and at nightfall he silently took up his position. Soon after, the door of the hut slowly opened, and the *sadhu* emerged and vanished into the night. Some hours later an agonized scream came floating down on the night air from the direction of a charcoal-burner's hut far up the mountainside, and thereafter there was silence.

'No man of my father's party closed an eye that night, and as the grey dawn was being born in the east, they saw the *sadhu* hurrying home and his hands and his mouth were dripping blood.

'When the *sadhu* had gone inside his hut and had closed the door, the watchers went up to it, and fastened it from the outside by passing the chain that was dangling from it over the staple in the lintel. Then they went each to his haystack and returned with a big bundle of straw and when the sun rose that morning there was nothing but smouldering ash where the hut had been. From that day the killing stopped.

'Suspicion has not yet fallen on any one of the many *sadhus* in these parts, but when it does the method employed in my father's time will be adopted in mine and until that day comes, the people of Garhwal must suffer.

'You have asked if I will sell you a goat. I will not sell you a goat, *sahib*, for I have none to spare. But if, after hearing my story, you still want an animal to tie up for what you think is a man-eating leopard, I will lend you one of my sheep. If it is killed, you shall pay me its price and if it is not killed no money shall pass between us. Today and tonight, I rest here, and tomorrow at the rising of the Bhootia star I must be on my way.'

Near sundown that evening I returned to the thorn enclosure and my packman friend very cheerfully let me select from his flock a fat sheep which I considered was heavy enough to give the leopard two nights' feed. This sheep I tied in the scrub jungle close to the path up which the leopard had gone some twelve hours earlier.

Next morning, I was up betimes. As I left the bungalow, I again saw the pugmarks of the man-eater where he had stepped off the verandah, and at the gate I found he had come up the road from the direction of Golabrai and after calling at the bungalow, had gone away towards the Rudraprayag bazaar.

The fact that the leopard was trying to secure a human kill was proof that he had no interest in the sheep I had provided for him, and I was therefore not surprised to find that he had not eaten any portion of the sheep which he had apparently killed shortly after I had tied it up.

'Go back to your home, *sahib*, and save your time and your money,' was the parting advice of the old packman as he whistled to his flock and headed down the road for Hardwar.

A parallel case, happily without as tragic an ending, occurred a few years previously near Rudraprayag.

Incensed at the killing of their relatives and friends and convinced that a human being was responsible for their deaths, an angry crowd of men seized an unfortunate sadhu of Kothgi village, Dasjulapatty but before they were able to wreak their vengeance on him, Philip Mason, then Deputy Commissioner of Garhwal, who was camping in the vicinity, arrived on the scene. Seeing the temper of the crowd, and being a man of great experience, Mason said he had no doubt that the real culprit had been apprehended but that before the *sadhu* was lynched justice demanded that his guilt should be established. To this end he suggested that the *sadhu* should be placed under arrest and closely guarded, night and day. To this suggestion the crowd agreed and for seven days and seven nights the *sadhu* was carefully guarded by the police, and as carefully watched by the populace. On the eighth morning, when the guard and the watchers were being changed, word was brought that a house in a village some miles away had been broken into the previous night, and a man carried off.

The populace raised no objection to the *sadhu* being released that day, contenting themselves by saying that on this occasion the wrong man had been apprehended, but that next time no mistake would be made.

In Garhwal all kills by man-eaters are attributed to sadhus and in Nainital and Almora districts all such kills are attributed to the Bokhsars, who dwell in the unhealthy belt of grass at the foot of the hills called the Terai, living chiefly on game. The *sadhus* are believed to kill for the lust of human flesh and blood and the Bokhsars are believed to kill for the jewellery their victims are wearing, or for other valuables they have on their person. More women than men have been killed by man-eaters in Nainital and Almora districts but for this there is a better reason than the one given.

✦✦✦

I have lived too long in silent places to be imaginative. Even so there were times a-many during the months I spent at Rudraprayag sitting night after night, on one occasion for twenty-eight nights in succession watching "bridges, or cross-roads or approaches to villages, or over animal or human kills, when I could imagine the man-eater as being a big, light-coloured animal, for so he had appeared to me the first time that I saw him with the body of a leopard and the head of a fiend.

A fiend who, while watching me through the long night hours, rocked and rolled with silent fiendish laughter at my vein attempts to outwit him, and licked his lips in anticipation of the time when, finding me off my guard for one brief moment, he would get the opportunity he was waiting for, of burying his teeth in my throat. It may be asked what the Government was doing all the years the Rudraprayag man-eater menaced the people of Garhwal. I hold no brief for the Government but after having spent ten weeks on the ground, during which time I walked many hundreds of miles and visited most of the villages in the affected area, I assert that the Government did everything in its power to remove the menace. Rewards were offered: the local population believed they amounted to ten thousand rupees in cash and the gift of two villages, sufficient inducement to make each one of the four thousand licensed gun-holders of Garhwal a prospective slayer of the man-eater. Picked *shikaris* were employed on liberal wages and were promised special rewards if their efforts were successful. More than three hundred special gun licenses over and above the four thousand in force were granted for the specific purpose of shooting the man-eater. Men of the Garhwal Regiments stationed in Lansdowne were permitted to take their rifles with them when going home on leave or were provided with sporting arms by their officers. Appeals were made through the press to sportsmen all over India to assist in the destruction of the leopard. Scores of traps of the drop-door type, with goats as bait, were erected on approaches to villages and on roads frequented by the man-eater. *Patwaris* and other Government officials were supplied with poison for the purpose of poisoning human kills and last but not least, Government servants often at great personal risk spent all the time they could spare from their official duties in pursuit of the man-eater.

The total results from all these many and combined efforts were a slight gunshot wound which creased the pad of the leopard's left hind foot and shot away a small piece of skin from one of its toes, and an entry in Government records by the Deputy Commissioner of Garhwal that so far from suffering any ill effects, the leopard appeared to thrive on and be stimulated by the poison he absorbed via human kills.

Three interesting incidents are recorded in a Government report, and I will summarize them here.

First: In response to the press appeal to sportsmen, two young British officers arrived at Rudraprayag in 1921 with the avowed object of shooting the man-eater. What reason they had for thinking that the leopard crossed from bank to bank of the Alaknanda river by the Rudraprayag suspension bridge I do not know anyway they decided to confine their efforts to this bridge and shoot the leopard as it was crossing at night. There are towers at each end of the bridge to carry the suspending cables, so one of the young sportsmen sat on the tower on the left bank of the river and his companion sat on the tower on the right bank.

After they had been sitting for two months on these towers, the man on the left bank saw the leopard walk out on to the bridge from the archway below him. Waiting until the leopard had got well on to the bridge, he fired, and as it dashed across, the man on the tower on the right bank emptied the six chambers of his revolver at it. Next morning blood was found on the bridge and on the hill up which the leopard had gone and as it was thought that the wound, or wounds, would be fatal, a search was kept up for many days. The report goes on to say that for six months after it was wounded the leopard did not kill any human beings.

I was told about this incident by men who had heard the seven shots and who had assisted in trying to recover the wounded animal. It was thought by the two sportsmen, and also by my informants, that the leopard had been hit in the back by the first bullet and possibly in the head by some of the subsequent bullets, and it was for this reason that a diligent and prolonged search had been made for it. From the particulars given me of the blood trail I was of the opinion that the sportsmen were wrong in thinking that they had inflicted a body and head wound on the leopard, for the blood trail as described to me could only have been made by a foot wound, and I was very gratified to find later that my deductions were correct and that the bullet fired by the man on the tower on the left bank had only creased the pad of the leopard's left hind foot and shot away a portion of one of its toes and that the man on the right bank had missed all his shots.

Second: After some twenty leopards had been caught and killed in traps of the drop-door type, a leopard which everyone thought was the man-eater was caught in one of these traps and as the Hindu population were unwilling to kill it for fear the spirits of the people whom the man-eater had killed would torment them, an Indian Christian was sent for. This Christian was living in a village thirty miles away and before he,' could arrive on the scene, the leopard had dug its way out of the trap and escaped.

Third: After killing a man the leopard layup with his kill in a small-isolated patch of jungle. Next morning, when search was being made for the victim, the leopard was detected leaving the jungle. After a short chase it was seen entering a cave, the mouth of which was promptly closed with thornbushes heaped over with big rocks. Every day a growing crowd of men visited the spot. On the fifth day, when some five hundred were assembled, a man whose name is not given but whom the report described as 'a man of influence' came, and, to quote the report, 'said scornfully "there is no leopard in this cave" and took the thorns off the cave. As he took the thorns up, the leopard suddenly rushed out of the cave and made his way safely through a crowd of some five hundred persons who had gathered there.'

These incidents took place shortly after the leopard had become a man-eater, and had the leopard been killed on the bridge, shot in the trap, or sealed up in the cave, several hundred people need not have died, and Garhwal would have been saved many years of suffering.

ARRIVAL

It was during one of the intervals of Gilbert and Sullivan's *Yeomen of the Guard*, which was showing at the Chalet Theatre in Nainital in 1925, that I first had any definite news of the Rudraprayag man-eater.

I had heard casually that there was a man-eating leopard in Garhwal and had read articles in the press about the animal but knowing that there were over four thousand licensed gun-holders in Garhwal, and a host of keen sportsmen in Lansdowne, only some seventy miles from Rudraprayag, I imagined that people were falling over each other in their eagerness to shoot the leopard and that a stranger under these circumstances would not be welcome.

It was with no little surprise therefore that, as I stood at the Chalet bar that night having a drink with a friend, I heard Michael Keene, then Chief Secretary to the Government of the United Provinces and later Governor of Assam telling a group of men about the man-eater and trying to persuade them to go after it. His appeal, judging from the remark of one of the groups and endorsed by the others, was not received with any enthusiasm. The remark was, 'Go after a man-eater that has killed a hundred people? Not on your life!'

Next morning, I paid Michael Keene a visit and got all the particulars I wanted. He was not able to tell me exactly where the man-eater was operating and suggested my going to Rudraprayag and getting in touch with Ibbotson. On my return home I found a letter from Ibbotson on my table.

Ibbotson, now Sir William Ibbotson and lately Adviser to the Governor of the United Provinces had very recently been posted to Garhwal as Deputy Commissioner and one of his first acts had been to try to rid his district of the man-eater. It was in this connection that he had written to me.

My preparations were soon made and by travelling via Ranikhet, Adbadri, and Karanprayag, I arrived on the evening of the tenth day at a Road Inspection Bungalow near Nagrasu. When leaving Nainital I did not know it was necessary to arm myself with a permit to occupy this bungalow, and as the caretaker had orders not to allow anyone to occupy it unless so armed, the six Garhwalis carrying my kit, my servant and I toiled on for another two miles down the Rudraprayag road until we found a suitable place on which to camp for the night.

While my men busied themselves getting water and dry sticks, and my servant collected stones for a cooking-place, I picked up an axe and went to cut down thornbushes to make an enclosure to protect us during the night, for we had been warned ten miles farther up the road that we had entered the man-eater's territory.

Shortly after the fires to cook our evening meal had been lit, a very agitated call came down to us from a village far up the mountainside, asking us what we were doing out in the open, and warning us that if we remained where we were one or more of us would surely be killed by the man-eater. When the good Samaritan had delivered his warning, to do which he had possibly taken a great risk for it was then dark Madho Singh, whom you have met elsewhere ('See 'The Chowgarh Tigers' in Man-eaters *ofKumaon.)*, expressed the wishes of all present when he said, 'We will stay here, *sahib*, for there is sufficient oil in the lantern to keep it alight all night, and you have your rifle.'

There was sufficient oil in the lantern to keep it alight all night, for I found it burning when I awoke in the morning, and my loaded rifle lay across my bed. But the thorn enclosure was very flimsy, and we were dead tired after our ten days' march, and if the leopard had paid us a visit that night, he would have secured a very easy victim.

Next day we arrived at Rudrapraya,g and were given a warm welcome by the men whom Ibbotson had instructed to meet us.

INVESTIGATION

I shall not attempt to give you a day-by-day account of my activities during the ten weeks I spent at Rudraprayag, for it would be difficult after this lapse of time to write such an account and, if written, it would be boring for you to read. I shall confine myself to relating a few of my experiences, sometimes while alone and at other times in company with Ibbotson. But before doing so I should like to give you some idea of the country over which the leopard ranged for eight years, and in which I hunted him for ten weeks.

If you were to climb the hill to the east of Rudraprayag you would be able to see the greater portion of the five hundred square miles of country that the Rudraprayag man-eater ranged over. This area is divided into two more or less equal parts by the Alaknanda river, which, after passing Karanprayag, flows south to Rudraprayag, where it is met by the Mandakini coming down from the northwest. The triangular bit of country between the two rivers is less steep than the country along the left bank of the Alaknanda and there are consequently more villages in the former area than in the latter.

From your elevated position, the cultivated land in the distance shows up as a series of lines drawn across the face of the steep mountains. These lines are terraced fields which vary in width from a yard to, in some cases, fifty or more yards. The village buildings, you will note, are invariably set at the upper end of the cultivated land; this is done with the object of overlooking and protecting the cultivation from stray cattle and wild animals for except in very rare cases there are no hedges or fences round the fields. The brown and the green patches that make up most of the landscape are, respectively, grassland and forests. Some of the villages, you will observe, are entirely surrounded by grasslands, while others are entirely surrounded by forests. The whole country, as you look down on it, is rugged and rough, and is cut up by innumerable deep ravines and rock cliffs. In this area there are only two roads, one starting from Rudraprayag and going up to Kedarnath, and the other the main pilgrim road to Badrinath. Both roads, up to the time I am writing about, were narrow and rough and had never had a wheel of any kind on them.

The number of human beings killed between 1918 and 1926 is shown below.

THE MAN-EATING LEOPARD OF RUDRAPRAYAG CASUALTY LIST

(by villages), 1918-1926

Six kills

CHOPRA

Five kills

KOTHKI, RATAURA

Four kills

BIJRAKOT

Three kills

NAKOT, GANDHARI, KOKHANDI, DADOLI, QUETHI, JHIRMOLI GOLABRAI, LAMERI

Two kills

BAJADU, RAMPUR, MAIKOTI, CHHATOLI, KOTI, MADOLA, RAUTA, KANDE (JOGI), BAWRUN, SARI, RANAU, PUNAR, TILANI, BAUNTHA, NAGRASU, GWAR, MARWARA

One kill

ASON, PILU, BHAUNSAL, MANGU, BAINJI, BHATWARI, KHAMOLI, SWANRI, PHALSI, KANDA DHARKOT, DANGI, GUNAUN, BHATGAON, BAWAL, BARSIL, BHAINSGAON, NARI, SANDAR, TAMEND, KHATYANA, SEOPURI, SAN, SYUND, KAMERA, DARMARI, DHAMKA BELA, BELA-KUND, SAUR, BHAINSARI, BAJNU, QUILI, DHARKOT, BHAINGAON, CHHINKA, DHUNG, KIURI, BAMAN KANDAI, POKHTA, THAPALGAON, BANSU, NAG, BAISANI, RUDRAPRAYAG, GWAR, KALNA, BHUNKA, KAMERA, SAIL, PABO, BHAINSWARA

ANNUAL TOTALS

1918	...	1
1919	...	3
1920	...	6
1921	...	23
1922	...	24
1923	...	26
1924	...	20
1923	....	8
1926	...	14
		125

It would be reasonable to assume that more human beings would have been killed in villages surrounded by forests than in villages surrounded by cultivated land. Had the man-eater been a tiger this would undoubtedly have been the case, but to a man-eating leopard, which only operates at night, the presence or absence of cover makes no difference and the only reason why there were more kills in one village than in another was due, in the one case, to lack of precautions, and in the other, to the observance of them.

I have mentioned that the man-eater was an out-sized male leopard long past his prime, but though he was old he was enormously strong. The ability of carnivora to carry their kills to a place where they can feed undisturbed determines, to a great extent, the place they choose to do their killing. To the Rudraprayag man-eater all places were alike, for he was capable of carrying the heaviest of his human victims for distances up to, on one occasion that I know of four miles. On the occasion I refer to the leopard killed a fully grown man in his own house and carried his victim for two miles up the steep slope of a well-wooded hill and down the far side for another two miles through dense scrub jungle. This was done for no apparent reason, for the kill had taken place in the early hours of the night and the leopard had not been followed up until noon of the next day.

✦✦✦

Leopards, other than man-eaters are the most easily killed of all animals in our jungles for they have no sense of smell.

More methods are employed in killing leopards than are employed in killing any other animal. These methods vary according to whether the leopard is being killed for sport or for profit. The most exciting, and the most interesting, method of killing leopards for sport is to track them down in the jungles and, when they are located, stalk and shoot them. The easiest and the cruelest, method of killing leopards for profit is to insert a small and very highly explosive bomb in the flesh of an animal which are been killed by a leopard. Many villagers have learnt to make these bombs, and when one of them comes in contact with the leopard's teeth, it explodes and blows the leopard's jaws off. Death is instantaneous in some cases but more often than not the unfortunate animal crawls away to die a lingering and very painful death, for the people who use the bombs have not the courage to follow the blood trail left by the leopard to dispatch it.

✦✦✦

The tracking, locating, and stalking of leopards, besides being exciting and interesting, is comparatively easy. For leopards have tender pads and keep to footpaths and game tracks as far as possible; they are not hard to locate for practically every bird and animal in the jungle assists the hunter and they are easy to stalk, for, though they are blessed with very keen sight and hearing, they are handicapped by having no sense of smell. The sportsman can therefore select the line of approach that best suits him, irrespective of the direction in which the wind is blowing.

Having tracked, located, and stalked a leopard, far more pleasure is got from pressing the button of a camera than is ever got from pressing the trigger of a rifle. In one case the leopard can be watched for hours and there is no more graceful and interesting animal in the jungles to watch. The button of the camera can be pressed as fancy dictates to make a record which never loses its interest. In the other case a fleeting glimpse, one press of the trigger and if the aim has been true, the acquisition of a trophy which soon loses both its beauty and its interest.

THE FIRST KILL

Shortly before my arrival at Rudraprayag, Ibbotson had organized a beat which if it had been successful would have saved the lives of fifteen human beings. The beat, and the circumstances leading up to it, are worthy of record.

Twenty pilgrims toiling up the road to Badrinath arrived towards evening at a small roadside shop. After the shopkeeper had met their wants, he urged them to be on their way, telling them there was only just sufficient daylight left for them to reach the pilgrim shelters four miles farther up the road, where they would get food and safe shelter. The pilgrims were unwilling to accept this advice; they said they had done a long march that day and were too tired to walk another four miles, and that all they wanted were facilities to prepare and cook their evening meal, and permission to sleep on the platform adjoining the shop. To this proposal the shopkeeper vigorously objected. He told the pilgrims that his house was frequently visited by the man-eater and that to sleep out in the open would be to court death.

While the argument was at its height a *sadhu* on his way from Mathura to Badrinath arrived on the scene and championed the cause of the pilgrims. He said that if the shopkeeper would give shelter to the women of the party he would sleep on the platform with the men and if any leopard, man-eater or otherwise dared to molest them he would take it by the mouth and tear it in half.

To this proposal the shopkeeper had perforce to agree. So, while the ten women of the party took shelter in the one-roomed shop behind a locked door, the ten men lay down in a row on the platform, with the *sadhu* in the middle.

> When the pilgrims on the platform awoke in the morning, they found the *sadhu* missing, the blanket on which he had slept rumpled, and the sheet he had used to cover himself with partly dragged off the platform and spotted with blood. At the sound of the men's excited chattering the shopkeeper opened the door and at a glance saw what had happened. When the sun had risen, the shopkeeper, accompanied by the men, followed the blood trail down the hill and across three terraced fields, to a low boundary wall; here, lying across the wall, with the lower portion of his body eaten away, they found the *sadhu*.

Ibbotson was staying at Rudraprayag at this time, trying to get in touch with the man-eater. There had been no kills during his stay, so he decided to beat, on spec, a very likely looking bit of cover, on the far side of the Alaknanda, which the locals suspected was used by the man-eater as a lying-up place during the hours of daylight. So, while the twenty pilgrims were toiling up the road towards the little shop, the *patwaris* and other members of Ibbotson's staff were going round the near-by villages warning men to be ready for the beat which was to take place on the morrow.

After an early breakfast next morning Ibbotson accompanied by his wife and a friend whose name I have forgotten and followed by some members of his staff and two hundred beaters, crossed the Alaknanda by the suspension bridge, went up the hill on the far side for a mile or so and took up positions for the beat.

While the beat was still in progress, word was brought by runner of the killing of the *sadhu*.

The beat, which proved to be a blank, was completed and a hurried council held, the upshot of which was that Ibbotson, his party, and the two hundred beaters set off up the right bank, to cross the river four miles farther up by a swing bridge, to make their way back along the left bank to the scene of the kill, while the staff dispersed over the countryside to collect as many men as possible and assemble them at the shop.

By late afternoon two thousand beaters and several additional guns had gathered, and the high rugged hill above the shop was beaten from top to bottom. If you know Ibbotson, there is no need for me to tell you that the beat was very efficiently organized, and as efficiently carried out and the only reason why it failed in its object was that the leopard was not in that area.

When a leopard or a tiger, leaves of his own accord a kill in the open, in an exposed spot, it is an indication that the animal has no further interest in the kill. After its feed it invariably removes itself to a distance, maybe only two or three miles, or in the case or man-eaters, maybe to a distance of ten or more miles. So, it is quite possible that, while the hill was being beaten, the man-eater was peacefully slumbering ten miles away.

LOCATING THE LEOPARD

Man-eating leopards are of rare occurrence, and for this reason very little is known about them.

My own experience of these animals was very limited, amounting to no more than a brief encounter with one many years previously, and though I suspected that the change-over from animal to human-and- animal diet would affect the habits of a leopard as much as it does those of a tiger, I did not know to what extent a leopard's habits would change, and meanwhile I decided to try to kill the man-eater by the methods usually employed for killing leopards.

The most common method of killing leopards is to sit up for them, either over a kill or over live bait in the form of a goat or a sheep. To carry out either one of these methods it is necessary in the one case to find a kill, and in the other to locate the quarry.

My object in going to Rudraprayag was to try to prevent further loss of human life, and I had no intention of waiting for another human kill to occur over which I could sit, therefore the obvious thing to do was to locate the man-eater and shoot it over live bait.

Here a formidable difficulty, which I hoped in time partly to overcome, presented itself. From the maps I had been supplied with I found that the man-eater was operating over an area of roughly five hundred square miles. Five hundred square miles of country anywhere would have been a considerable area in which to find and shoot any animal, and in this mountainous and rugged part of Garhwal the task of finding an animal that only operated at night appeared, at first glance, to be well-nigh impossible until I took the Alaknanda river, which divided the area into two more or less equal parts, into consideration.

It was generally believed that the Alaknanda offered no obstacle to the man-eater and that when he found it difficult to obtain a human kill on one bank, he crossed over to the other bank, by swimming the river.

I discounted this belief. No leopard in my opinion would under any circumstances voluntarily commit itself to the swift-flowing, ice-cold waters of the Alaknanda, and I was convinced that when the man-eater crossed from one bank to the other, he did so by one of the suspension bridges.

There were two suspension bridges in the area, one at Rudraprayag, and the other about twelve miles farther up the river, at Chatwapipal. Bfetween these two bridges there was a swing bridge, the one by which Ibbotson, his party and the two hundred men had crossed the river on the day of the beat. This swing bridge, which no animal excepting a rat could possibly have crossed, was the most fear-compelling structure of its kind that I have ever seen. The two hand-twisted grass cables, blackened by age and mouldy from the mists rising from the river, spanned some two hundred feet of foaming white water which, a hundred yards farther down, surged with a roar like thunder between two walls of rock, where a *kakar*, driven by wild dogs, is credited with having leapt across the Alaknanda. Between the cables, and forming the footway, were odd bits of sticks an inch and a half to two inches in diameter set about two feet apart and loosely tied to the cables with wisps of grass. To add to the difficulty in crossing this cobweb structure, one of the cables had sagged, with the result that the sticks on which one had to place one's feet were at an angle of forty-five degrees. The first time I met this fearsome *jhula*, I was foolish enough to ask the toll-collector, who for the payment of one piece permitted me to risk my life on it, whether the bridge was ever tested or repaired. His answer, given as he ran a speculative eye over me, that the bridge was never tested or repaired but was replaced when it broke under the weight of someone who was trying to cross it, gave me a cold feeling down my spine, a feeling that remained with me long after I had got safely to the other side.

This *jhula* being beyond the powers of the man-eater to cross, there remained the two suspension bridges, and I felt sure that if I could close them against the leopard, I should be able to confine him to one side of the Alaknanda and so reduce by half the area in which to look for him.

The first thing therefore was to try to find out on which bank of the river the leopard was. The last kill, of the *sadhu*, had taken place on the left bank of the river a few miles from the Chatwapipal suspension bridge and I felt sure that the leopard had crossed this bridge, after abandoning his kill, for no matter what precautions the locals and the pilgrims may have taken before a kill, their precautions were redoubled immediately after one, and made it almost impossible for the leopard to secure consecutive kills in the same area. Looking at the map you will ask why, if this was so, as many as six kills have been shown against a single village. I can only answer that an effort cannot be sustained indefinitely. The houses are small and without conveniences or means of sanitation and it would not be surprising if, hearing the man-eater was operating in a village ten, fifteen, or twenty miles away, some man, woman, or child should, at the urgent dictate of nature, open a door for a brief minute and so give the leopard the chance for which he had perhaps been waiting many nights.

THE SECOND KILL

No photographs or other means by which I could identify the man-eater by his pugmarks were available, so, until I had been given an opportunity of acquiring this information for myself, I decided to treat all leopards in the vicinity of Rudraprayag as suspect, and to shoot any that gave me a chance.

The day I arrived at Rudraprayag, I purchased two goats. One of these I tied up the following evening a mile along the pilgrim road; the other I took across the Alaknanda and tied up on a path running through some heavy scrub jungle where I found the old pugmarks of a big male leopard. On visiting the goats, the following morning, I found the one across the river had been killed and a small portion of it eaten. The goat had unquestionably been killed by a leopard but had been eaten by a small animal, possibly a pine-marten.

Having received no news about the man-eater during the day, I decided to sit up over the goat and at 3 p.m. took up my position in the branches of a small tree about fifty yards from the kill. During the three hours I sat in the tree I had no indication, from either animals or birds, that the leopard was anywhere in the vicinity, and as dusk was falling, I slipped off the tree, cut the cord tethering the goat which the leopard had made no attempt to break the previous night and set off for the bungalow.

I have already admitted that I had very little previous experience of man-eating leopards, but I had met a few man-eating tigers, and from the time I left the tree until I reached the bungalow, I took every precaution to guard against a sudden attack; and it was fortunate that I did so.

I made an early start next morning, and near the gate of the bungalow I picked up the tracks of a big male leopard. These tracks I followed back to a densely wooded ravine which crossed the path close to where the goat was lying. The goat had not been touched during the night.

The leopard that had followed me could only have been the man-eater, and for the rest of the day I walked as many miles as my legs would carry me, telling all the people in the villages I visited, and all whom I met on the roads, that the man-eater was on our side of the river, and warning them to be careful.

Nothing happened that day, but next day, just as I was finishing breakfast after a long morning spent in prospecting the jungles beyond Golabrai, a very agitated man dashed into the bungalow to tell me that a woman had been killed by the man-eater the previous night in a village on the hill above the bungalow, the same hill and almost at the exact spot from where you obtained your bird's-eye view of the five hundred square miles of country the man-eater was operating over.

Within a few minutes I collected all the things I needed a spare rifle and a shotgun, cartridges, rope, and a length of fishing-line and set off up the steep hill accompanied by the villager and two of my men. It was a sultry day, and though the distance was not great, three miles at the most, the climb of four thousand feet in the hot sun was very trying and I arrived at the village in a bath of sweat.

The story of the husband of the woman who had been killed was soon told. After their evening meal, which had been eaten by the light of the fire, the woman collected the metal pots and pans that had been used and carried them to the door to wash, while the man sat down to have a smoke. On reaching the door the woman sat down on the doorstep and as she did, so the utensils clattered to the ground. There was not sufficient light for the man to see what had happened, and when he received no answer to his urgent call he dashed forward and shut and barred the door. 'Of what use,' he said, 'would it have been for me to risk my life in trying to recover a dead body?' His logic was sound, though heartless; and I gathered that the grief he showed was occasioned not so much by the loss of his wife, as by the loss of that son and heir whom he had expected to see born within the next few days.

The door, where the woman had been seized, opened on to a four-foot-wide lane that ran for fifty yards between two rows of houses. On hearing the clatter of the falling pots and pans, followed by the urgent call of the man to his wife, every door in the lane had been instantaneously shut. The marks on the ground showed that the leopard had dragged the unfortunate woman the length of the lane, then killed her and carried her down the hill for a hundred yards into a small ravine that bordered some terraced fields. Here he ate his meal, and here he left the pitiful remains.

The body lay in the ravine at one end of a narrow-terraced field, at the other end of which, forty yards away was a leafless and stunted walnut tree in whose branches a hayrick had been built, four feet from the ground and six feet tall. In this hayrick I decided to sit.

Starting from near the body, a narrow path ran down into the ravine. On this path were the pugmarks of the leopard that had killed the woman, and they were identical with the pugmarks of the leopard that had followed me two nights previously from the killed goat to the Rudraprayag bungalow. The pugmarks were of an out-sized male leopard long past his prime, with a slight defect where a bullet fired four years previously had creased the pad of his left-hand paw.

I procured two stout eight-foot bamboos from the village and drove them into the ground close to the perpendicular bank that divided the field where the body was laying from the field below. To these bamboos I fixed my spare rifle and securely, tied lengths of dressed line to the triggers, looped the lines back over the trigger-guards and fastened them to two stakes driven into the hillside on the far side of and a little above, the path. If the leopard came along the path, he had used the previous night there was a reasonable chance of his pulling on the lines and shooting himself; on the other hand, if he avoided them, or came by any other way, and I fired at him while he was on the kill, he would be almost certain to run into the trap which lay on his most natural line of retreat. Both the leopard, because of its protective colouring and the body which had been stripped of all clothing, would be invisible in the dark so to give me an idea of the direction in which to fire, I took a slab of white rock from the ravine and put it on the edge of the field, about a foot from the near side of the body.

My ground arrangements completed to my satisfaction, I made myself a comfortable seat on the rick, throwing out some of the straw and heaping some behind me and up to my waist in front. As I was facing the kill and had my back to the tree, there was little chance of the leopard seeing me, no matter at what time he came; and that he would come during the night, in spite of his reputation of not returning to his kills, I was firmly convinced. My clothes were still wet after the stiff climb, but a comparatively dry jacket kept out the chill wind, so I settled down into my soft and comfortable seat and prepared for an all-night vigil. I sent my men away and told them to remain in the Headman's house until I came for them, or until the sun was well up next morning. (I had stepped from the bank on to the rick and there was nothing to prevent the man-eater from doing the same.)

The sun was near setting, and the view of the Ganges valley, with the snowy Himalayas in the background showing bluish pink under the level rays of the setting sun, was a feast for the eyes. Almost before I realized it, daylight had faded out of the sky and night had come.

Darkness, when used in connection with night, is a relative term and has no fixed standard; what to one man would be pitch dark, to another 'would be dark, and to a third moderately dark. To me, having spent so much of my life in the open, the night is never dark, unless the sky is overcast with heavy clouds. I do not wish to imply that I can see as well by night as by day, but I can see quite well enough to find my way through any jungle or for that matter, over any ground. I had placed the white stone near the body only as a precaution, for I hoped that the starlight, with the added reflection from the snowy range, would give me sufficient light to shoot by.

But my luck was out for night had hardly fallen when there was a flash of lightning, followed by distant thunder, and in a few minutes the sky was heavily overcast. Just as the first big drops of a deluge began to fall, I heard a stone roll into the ravine and a minute later the loose straw on the ground below me was being scratched up. The leopard had arrived; and while I sat in torrential rain with the icy-cold wind whistling through my wet clothes, he lay dry and snug in the straw below. The storm was one of the worst I have ever experienced, and while it was at its height, I saw a lantern being carried towards the village and marvelled at the courage of the man who carried it. It was not until some hours later that I learnt that the man who so gallantly braved both the leopard and the storm had done a forced march of over thirty miles from Pauri to bring me the electric night-shooting light the Government had promised me, the arrival of this light three short hours earlier *might*. But regrets are vain, and who can say that the fourteen people who died later would have had a longer span of life if the leopard had not buried his teeth in their throats? And again, even if the light had arrived in time there is no certainty that I should have killed the leopard that night.

The rain was soon over leaving me chilled to the bone and the clouds were breaking up when the white stone was suddenly obscured, and a little later I heard the leopard eating. The night before, he had lain in the ravine and eaten from that side; so, expecting him to do the same this night, I had placed the stone on the near side of the kill. Obviously, the rain had formed little pools in the ravine and to avoid them the leopard had taken up a new position and in doing so had obscured my mark. This was something I had not foreseen; however, knowing the habits of leopards, I knew I should not have to wait long before the stone showed up again. Ten minutes later the stone was visible and almost immediately thereafter I heard a sound below me and saw the leopard as a light-yellowish object disappearing under the rock. His light colour could be accounted for by old age but the sound he made when walking I could not then, nor can I now, account for it was like the soft rustle of a woman's silk dress and could not be explained by stubble in the field for there was none or by the loose straw lying about.

Waiting a suitable length of time, I raised the rifle and covered the stone, intending to fire the moment it was again obscured but there is a limit to the time a heavy rifle can be held to the shoulder, and when the limit had been reached, I lowered the rifle to ease my aching muscles. I had hardly done so when the stone for the second time disappeared from view. Three times within the next two hours the same thing happened, and in desperation, as I heard the leopard approaching the rick for the fourth time, I leant over and fired at the indistinct object below me.

The narrow terrace to which I have given the usual name of 'field' was only about two feet wide at this point, and when I examined the ground next morning I found my bullet-hole in the centre of the two-foot-wide space with a little hair, cut from the leopard's neck, scattered round it.

I saw no more of the leopard that night, and at sunrise I collected my men and set off down the steep hill to Rudraprayag, whilst the husband and his friends carried away the woman's remains for cremation.

PREPARATIONS

My thoughts as, cold, and stiff, I walked down the hill to Rudraprayag from the scene of my night's failure were very bitter, for, from whatever angle it was viewed, there was no question that the fickle jade chance had played both Garhwal and myself a scurvy trick which we did not deserve.

However, little I merit it, the people of our hills credit me with supernatural powers where man-eaters are concerned. News that I was on my way to try to rid Garhwal of the man-eater had preceded me, and while I was still many days' marches from Rudraprayag the men I met on the roads, and those who from their fields or village homes saw me passing, greeted me with a faith in the accomplishment of my mission that was as touching as it was embarrassing, and which increased in intensity the nearer I approached my destination. Had any been there to witness my entry into Rudraprayag, he would have found it hard to believe that the man whom the populace thronged round was no hero returning from the wars, but a man, very sensible of his limitations, who greatly feared that the task he had undertaken was beyond his powers of accomplishment.

Five hundred square miles, much of which was clothed with dense scrub jungle and all of which was rugged and mountainous, was an enormous area in which to find and shoot one particular leopard out of possibly fifty that inhabited it, and the more I saw of the grand and beautiful country the less I liked it from the viewpoint of the task I had undertaken. The populace quite naturally did not share my misgivings; to them I was one who had rid others of man-eaters and who had now come among them to rid them of the menace they had lived under for eight long years. And then with incredibly good luck, I had within a few hours of my arrival got the animal I was in pursuit of to kill one of my goats and, by staying out a little after dark, to follow me to that side of the Alaknanda where I believed it would be less difficult to deal with it than it would have been on the other side. Following on this initial success had been the kill of the unfortunate woman. I had tried to prevent the further loss of human life and had failed, and my failure had presented me with an opportunity of shooting the leopard which otherwise I might not have got for many months. As I had been toiling uphill behind my guide the previous day, I had weighed up my chances of killing the leopard and assessed them at two-to-one, despite the facts that the animal had in recent years earned the reputation of never returning to a kill, that it was a dark night and that I had no aid to night shooting. The day I visited Michael Keene and told him I would go to Garhwal he had asked me if I had everything I wanted; and hearing that I only lacked a night-shooting light and would telegraph to Calcutta for one, he said the least the Government could do for me was to provide me with a light and he promised to have the best one procurable waiting for me at Rudraprayag.

Though my disappointment was great when I found that the light had not arrived, it was mitigated by my ability to see in the dark, the ability on which I had assessed my chances at two-to-one. So much depended on the success of that night's venture, that I had armed myself with a spare rifle and shotgun, and when from my concealed position on the hayrick I viewed the scene, the short range at which I should get my shot, and the perfectly camouflaged gun-trap into which the leopard would of a certainty run if I missed or wounded him, my hopes rose high and I put my chances of success at ten-to-one. Then had come the storm. With visibility reduced to practically nil, and without the electric light, I had failed, and my failure would in a few hours be known throughout the stricken area.

Exercise, warm water, and food have a wonderfully soothing effect on bitter thoughts, and by the time I had picked my way down the steep hillside, had a hot bath, and breakfast, I had ceased to rail at fate and was able to take a more reasonable view of my night's failure. Regret over a bullet fired into the ground was as profitless as regret over milk spilt on sand and provided the leopard had not crossed the Alaknanda my chances of killing it had improved, for I now had the electric shooting light which the runner had braved both the leopard and the storm to bring me.

The first thing to do was to find out if the leopard had crossed the Alaknanda and as I was firm in my conviction that the only way it could do this was by way of the suspension bridges, I set out after breakfast to glean this information. I discounted the possibility of the leopard having crossed the Chatwapipal bridge, for no matter how great the shock he had received by the discharge of my heavy rifle a few feet from his head, it was not possible that he would have covered the fourteen miles that separated the kill from the bridge in the few hours that remained between the firing of my shot and daylight, so I decided to confine my search to the Rudraprayag bridge.

There were three approaches to the bridge one from the north, one from the south, and between these two a well-beaten footpath from the Rudraprayag bazaar. After examining these approaches very carefully I crossed the bridge and examined the Kedarnath pilgrim road for half a mile and then the footpath on which three nights previously my goat had been killed. Satisfied that the leopard had not crossed the river. I determined to put in operation my plan for closing the two bridges at night and thus confining the leopard to my side of the river, The plan was a simple one and, given the co- operation of the caretakers of the bridges, both of whom lived on the left bank and close to the bridge abutments, was certain of success.

To close the only means of communication between the two banks of the river over a stretch of some thirty miles would appear to be a very high-handed proceeding, but actually it was not so, for no human being dared to use the bridges between sunset and sunrise owing to the curfew imposed by the leopard.

The bridges were closed by wedging thornbushes in the four-foot-wide archway in the towers carrying the steel cables from which the plank footway was suspended, and during the whole period that the bridges were closed with thorn, or were guarded by me, no human being demanded passage across them.

I spent in all some twenty nights on the tower on the left bank of the Rudraprayag bridge, and those nights will never be forgotten. The tower was built out on a projecting rock and was twenty feet high and the platform on the top of it, which had been worn smooth by the wind, was about four feet wide and eight feet long. There were two means of reaching this platform, one by swarming along the cables, which ran through holes near the top of the tower and were anchored in the hillside some fifty feet from the tower, and the other by climbing up a very rickety bamboo ladder. I chose the latter way, for the cables were coated over with some black and very evil-smelling matter which clung to one's hands and permanently stained one's clothes.

The ladder, two uneven lengths of bamboo connected with thin sticks loosely held in position with string, only reached within four feet of the platform. Standing on the top rung of the ladder and dependent for a handhold on the friction of the palms of my hands on the smooth masonry, the safe gaining of the platform was an acrobatic feat that had less appeal the oftener it was tried.

All the rivers in this part of the Himalayas flow from north to south, and 'n the valleys through which they flow blows a wind which changes direction with the rising and the setting of the sun. During daylight hours the wind locally called dadu blows from the south and during the hours of night it blows from the north.

At the time when I used to take up my position on the platform there was usually a lull in the wind, but shortly thereafter it started blowing as a light zephyr gaining in strength as daylight faded and amounting by midnight to a raging gale. There was no handhold on the platform and even when lying flat on my stomach to increase friction and reduce wind-pressure, there was imminent risk of being blown off on to the rocks sixty feet below, off which one would have bounced into the ice-cold Alaknanda not that the temperature of the water would have been of any interest after a fall of sixty feet on to sharp and jagged rocks. Strangely enough, whenever I felt fear of falling it was always the water and never the rocks that I thought of. Added to the discomfort of the wind, I suffered torment from a multitude of small ants, which entered my clothes and ate away patches of skin. During the twenty nights I guarded the bridge, the thornbushes were not placed in position; and in all that long period the bridge was only crossed by one living thing, a Jackal.

MAGIC

Each evening when I went to the bridge, I was accompanied by two men who carried the ladder that enabled me to climb to the platform, and which they removed after handing me my rifle.

On the second day, as we arrived at the bridge, we saw a man dressed in flowing white robes with something glinting on his head and breast. He carried a six-foot silver cross and was approaching the bridge from the direction of Kedarnath. On reaching the bridge the man knelt down and, holding the cross in front of him, bowed his head. After remaining in this position for a little while he raised the cross high, rose to his feet, took a few steps forward, and again knelt down and bowed his head. This he continued to do at short intervals all the way across the long bridge.

As he passed me the man raised his hand in salutation, but since he appeared to be deep in prayer, I did not speak to him. The glints I had seen on his head-dress and breast were, I perceived, silver crosses.

My men had been as interested in this strange apparition as I had been and watching him climb the steep footpath to the Rudraprayag bazaar, they asked me what manner of man he was, and from what country he had come. That he was a Christian was apparent, and as I had not heard him speak, I assumed from his long hair, jet-black luxuriant beard, and what I could see of his features, that he was a man from Northern India.

The following morning, when with the help of the ladder I had climbed down from the tower and was proceeding to the Inspection Bungalow, where I passed that portion of the daylight hours that I did not spend in visiting near and distant villages in search of news of the man-eater, I saw the tall, white-robed figure standing on a great slab of rock near the road, surveying the river. At my approach he left the rock and greeted me, and when I asked him what had brought him to these part's he said he had come from a distant land to free the people of Garhwal from the evil spirit that was tormenting them. When I asked how he proposed accomplishing this feat, he said he would make an effigy of a tiger and after he had, by prayer, induced the evil spirit to enter it, he would set the effigy afloat on the Ganges and the river would convey it down to the sea from where it could not return and where it would do no farther harm to human beings.

However much I doubted the man's ability to accomplish the task he had set himself; I could not help admiring his faith and his industry. He arrived each morning before I left the tower and I found him still at work when I returned in the evening, labouring with split bamboos, string, paper, and cheap coloured cloth on his 'tiger'. When the effigy was nearing completion a heavy rainstorm one night made the whole structure come unstuck but nothing daunted, he cheerfully started on it again next morning, singing as he worked.

Came at last the great day when the 'tiger' about the size of a horse and resembling no known animal was fashioned to his satisfaction.

Who is there among our hill-folk who does not whole-heartedly enjoy taking part in a tamasha? When the effigy, tied to a long pole, was carried down a steep path to a small sandy beach, it had an escort of over a hundred men, many of whom were beating gongs and blowing long trumpets.

At the river's edge the effigy was unlashed from the pole. The white- robed man, with his silver crosses on headgear and breast and his six-foot cross in his hands, knelt on the sand and with earnest prayer induced the evil spirit to enter his handiwork and then the effigy, with a crash of gongs and blare of trumpets, was consigned to the Ganges and speeded on its way to the sea by a liberal offering of sweets and flowers.

Next morning the familiar figure was absent from the rock and when I asked some men who were on their way to have an early dip in the river where my friend of the flowing robes had come from, and where he had gone, they answered, 'Who can tell whence a holy man has come, and who dare question whether he has departed?'

These men with sandalwood-paste caste-marks on their foreheads, who spoke of the man as 'holy', and all those others who had taken part in the launching ceremony, were Hindus.

In India, where there are no passports or identity discs, and where religion counts for so much except among those few who have crossed the 'black water', I believe that a man wearing a saffron robe or carrying a beggar's bowl or with silver crosses on his headgear and chest, could walk from the Khyber Pass to Cape Comorin without once being questioned about his destination or the object of his journey.

A NEAR ESCAPE

While I was still guarding the bridge, Ibbotson and his wife Jean arrived from Pauri, and as the accommodation in the Inspection Bungalow was very limited, I moved out to make room for them, and set up my forty-pound tent on the hill on the far side of the pilgrim road.

A tent afforded little protection against an animal that had left his claw-marks on every door and window for miles round, so I helped my men to put a thorn fence round the ground we intended to camp on. Overhanging this plot of ground was a giant prickly-pear-tree, and as its branches interfered with the erection of the tent, I told the men to cut it down. When the tree had been partly cut through, I changed my mind, for I saw that I should be without shade during the heat of the day, so instead of felling the tree I told the men to lop the overhanging branches. This tree, which was leaning over the camp at an angle of forty-five degrees, was on the far side of the fence.

There were eight of us in the little camp and when we had eaten our evening meal, I wedged a thornbush securely into the opening in the fence we had entered by and as I did so I noticed that it would be very easy for the man-eater to climb the tree and drop down on our side of the fence. However, it was too late then to do anything about it and if the leopard left us alone for that one night, the tree could be cut down and removed in the morning.

I had no tents for my men and had intended that they should sleep with Ibbotson's men in the outbuildings of the Inspection Bungalow, but this they had refused to do, asserting that there was no more danger for them than there was for me in the open tent. My Cook who was, I discovered, a very noisy sleeper was lying next to and about a yard from me and beyond him, packed like sardines in the little enclosure, were the six Garhwalis, I had brought from Nainital.

The weak spot in our defence was the tree and I went to sleep thinking of it.

It was a brilliant moonlit night and round about midnight I was suddenly awakened by hearing the leopard climbing the tree. Picking up the riffle, which was lying ready loaded on the bed, I swung my legs off the bed and had just slipped my feet into my slippers to avoid the thorns which were scattered all round, when there was an ominous crack from the partly-cut-through tree, followed by a yell from the cook of 'Bagh! Baghl' In one jump I was outside the tent and, swinging round, was just too late to get the rifle to bear on the leopard as it sprang up the bank on to a terraced field. Pulling the bush out of the gap I dashed up to the field which was about forty yards in width and bare of crops, and as I stood scanning the hillside dotted over with thornbushes and a few big rocks, the alarm call of a jackal far up the hill informed me that the leopard had 'gone beyond my reach.

The cook informed me later that he had been lying on his back, a fact of which I had long been aware and hearing the tree crack he had opened his eyes and looked straight into the leopard's face just as it was preparing to jump down.

The tree was cut down next day and the fence strengthened, and though we stayed in that camp for several weeks our slumbers were not again disturbed.

THE GIN-TRAP

From reports received from nearby villages where unsuccessful attempts had been made to break into houses and from the pugmarks I had seen on the roads, I knew that the man-eater was still in the vicinity and a few days after the arrival of the Ibbotsons, news was brought that a cow had been killed in a village two miles from Rudraprayag and about half a mile from the village where I had sat on the hayrick in a walnut tree.

Arrived at the village we found that a leopard had broken down the door of a one-roomed house and had killed and dragged to the door one of the several cows that were in it, and not being able to drag it through the door, had left it on the threshold after eating a good meal.

The house was in the heart of the village, and on prospecting round, we found that by making a hole in the wall of a house a few yards away we could overlook the kill.

The owner of this house, who was also the owner of the dead cow, was only too willing to fall in with our plans and as evening closed in, we locked ourselves very securely into the room, and after eating our sandwiches and drinking the tea we had brought with us, we mounted guard in turns over the hole in the wall throughout the long night without either seeing or hearing anything of the leopard.

When we emerged in the morning the villagers took us round the village, which was of considerable size, and showed us the claw-marks on doors and windows made by the man-eater in the course of years, in his attempts to get at the inmates. One door in particular had more and deeper claw-marks than any other, it was the door the leopard had forced to enter the room in which the forty goats and the boy had been secured.

A day or two later another cow was reported to have been killed in a small village on the hill a few hundred yards from the bungalow. Here again we found that the cow had been killed inside a house, dragged as far as the door, and partly eaten. Facing the door, and distant from it about ten yards, was a newly built hayrick, sixteen feet tall and built on a wooden platform two feet above ground.

News of the kill was brought to us early in the morning, so we had the whole day before us, and the *machan* we built by evening was I am sure not only the most effective, but also the most artistic, that has ever been.' constructed for a similar purpose.

To start with the rick was dismantled and a scaffolding of poles was set round the platform. With these poles to support it, a second, and smaller, platform was built four feet above the lower one. Two-inch-mesh wire-netting was then wound round the whole structure, leaving only the space bare between the lower platform and the ground. Wisps of straw were then looped into the meshes of the netting, and a little straw was spread round the rick and under the platform, just as it had been before we started work. One of the joint owners of the hayrick, who had been absent from the village for a day or two and who returned just as we had finished our task, would not believe that the rick had been disturbed until he felt it all round, and had been shown the second rick we had built with the spare hay in an adjoining field.

As the sun was setting, we crawled through the hole we had left in the netting and entered the *machan*, securely closing the entrance behind us. Ibbotson is a little shorter than me, so he took the upper platform, and when we had made ourselves comfortable, we each made a small hole in the straw to shoot through. As it would not be possible for us to communicate with each other once the leopard arrived, we agreed that whoever saw it first was to fire. It was a bright moonlit night, so there was no need for either of us to use the electric light.

Sounds in the village quietened down after the evening meal had been eaten, and at about 10 p.m. I heard the leopard coming down the hill behind us. On arriving at the rock, it paused for a few minutes and then started to crawl under the platform I was sitting on. Immediately below me, and with only the thickness of a plank between my seat and his head, he paused for a long minute and then started to crawl forward and just as I was expecting him to emerge from under the platform and give me an easy shot at a range of three or four feet, there was a loud creak in the platform above me. The leopard dashed out to the right, where I could not see him and went up the hill. The creaking of the planks at the critical moment had resulted from Ibbotson changing his position to relieve a very painful cramp in both legs. After the fright he had got, the leopard abandoned the kill and did not return that night or the next night.

Two nights later another cow was killed a few hundred yards above the Rudraprayag bazaar.

The owner of this cow lived alone in an isolated house which contained only one room, a room which was divided by a rough partition made of odd bits of plank into a kitchen and living room. Sometime during the night, a noise in the kitchen, the door of which he had forgotten to shut awakened the man and a little later, in the dim moonlight which the open door was admitting, he saw the leopard through the wide chinks in the partition, trying to tear one of the planks out.

For a long time, the man lay and sweated, while the leopard tried plank after plank. Eventually, being unable to find a weak place in the partition, the leopard left the kitchen and killed the man's cow, which was tethered in a grass lean-to against the side of the house. After killing the Cow, the leopard broke the rope by which it was tethered, dragged it a short distance from the lean-to, and left it out in the open after partaking of a good meal.

On the very edge of the hill, and about twenty yards from where the dead cow was lying, there was a fair-sized tree, in the upper branches of which a hayrick had been built on this natural Mac-ban from which there was a sheer drop of several hundred feet into the valley below, Ibbotson and I decided to sit.

To assist in killing the man-eater, the Government a few days previously had sent us a gin-trap. This trap, which was five feet long and weighed eighty pounds, was the most fearsome thing of its kind I have ever seen. Its jaws, armed with sharp teeth three inches long, had a spread of twenty-four inches and were actuated by two powerful springs, which needed two men to compress.

When leaving the kill the leopard had followed a footpath across a field about forty yards wide, up a three-foot bank, and across another field bordered by a densely scrub-covered hill. At this three-foot step from the upper to the lower field, we set the trap, and to ensure the leopard stepping on to it we planted a few thorn twigs on either side of the path. To one of the traps was attached a short length of half-inch-thick chain, terminating in a ring three inches in diameter, through this ring we drove a stout peg, chaining the trap to the ground.

When these arrangements had been completed, Jean Ibbotson returned to the bungalow with our men and Ibbotson, and I climbed up to the hayrick. After tying a stick in front of us and looping a little hay over it, to act as a screen, we made ourselves comfortable, and waited for the leopard, which we felt sure would not escape us on this occasion.

As evening closed in heavy clouds spread over the sky, and as the moon was not due to rise until 9 p.m., we had of necessity to depend on the electric light for the accuracy of our shooting until then. This light was a heavy and cumbersome affair, and as Ibbotson insisted on my taking the shot, I attached it to my rifle with some little difficulty.

An hour after dark a succession of angry roars apprised us of the fact that the leopard was in the trap. Switching on the electric light, I saw the leopard rearing up with the trap dangling from his forelegs, and taking a hurried shot, my .450 bullet struck a link in the chain and severed it.

Freed from the peg the leopard went along the field in a series of great leaps, carrying the trap in front of him, followed up by the bullet from my left barrel and two lethal bullets from Ibbotson's shotgun, all of which missed him. In trying to reload my rifle I displaced some part of the light, after which it refused to function.

Hearing the roars of the leopard and our four shots, the people in Rudraprayag bazaar, and in nearby villages, swarmed out of their houses carrying lanterns and pine torches, and converged from all sides on the isolated house. Shouting to them to keep clear was of no avail, for they were making so much noise that they could not hear us so while I climbed down the tree, taking my rifle with me, a hazardous proceeding in the dark

Ibbotson lit and pumped up the petrol lamp we had taken into the *machan* with us. Letting the lamp down to me on the end of a length of rope, Ibbotson joined me on the ground and together we went in the direction the leopard had taken. Halfway along the field there was a hump caused by an outcrop of rock, this hump we approached with Ibbotson holding the heavy lamp high above his head, while I walked by his side with rifle to shoulder. Beyond the hump was a little depressed and crouching down in this depression and facing us and growling, was the leopard. Within a few minutes of my bullet crashing into his head, we were surrounded by an excited crowd, who literally danced with joy round their long-dreaded enemy.

The animal that lay dead before me was an out-sized male leopard, who the previous night had tried to tear down a partition to get at a human being, and who had been shot in an area in which dozens of human beings had been killed, all good and sufficient reasons for assuming that he was the man-eater. But I could not make myself believe that he was the same animal I had seen the night I sat over the body of the woman. True, it had been a dark night and I had only vaguely seen the outline of the leopard, even so, I was convinced that the animal that was now being lashed to a pole by willing hands was not the man-eater.

With the Ibbotsons leading the way, followed by the men carrying the leopard and a crowd of several hundred men, we set off via the bazaar for the bungalow.

As I stumbled down the hill in the wake of the procession, the only one in all that throng who did not believe that the man-eating leopard of Rudraprayag was dead, my thoughts went back to an occurrence that had taken place not far from our winter home when I was a small boy and which I saw recounted many years later in a book entitled Brave Deeds, or perhaps it was Bravest Deeds. The occurrence concerned two men: Smeaton of the Indian Civil Service and Braidwood of the Forest Department. One dark stormy night, in pre-railway days, these two men were travelling in a dak-gharry from Moradabad to Kaladhungi and ongoing round a bend in the road they ran into a rogue elephant. In killing the driver and the two horses, the elephant overturned the gharry. Braidwood had a rifle, and while he got it out of its case, put it together, and loaded it, Smeaton climbed on to the gharry and released the one unbroken lamp from its socket. Then Smeaton, holding the oil lamp which only gave a glimmer of light over his head, advanced up to the elephant and shone the light on his forehead to enable Braidwood to get in a killing shot. Admittedly there was a great difference between a rogue elephant and a leopard even so, there are few who would care to walk up to a pain-maddened leopard, which we later found had practically torn its paw free and was only held by a thin strip of skin holding a lamp above his head and depending for safety on a companion's bullet.

For the first night in many years every house in the bazaar was open, with women and children standing in the doorways. Progress was slow, for every few yards the leopard was put down to let the children cluster round and get a better view of it. At the farther end of the long street our escort left us, and the leopard was carried in triumph to the bungalow by our men.

Returning to the bungalow after a wash at my camp, the Ibbotsons and I, both during and long after it put forward our arguments for and against the dead leopard being the man-eater. Eventually, without either side convincing the other, we decided that as Ibbotson had to get back to his work at Pauri and I was tired out after my long stay at Rudraprayag, we would spend the next day in skinning the leopard and drying the skin and on the day after would break camp and make for Pauri.

From early morning to late evening, relays of men kept coming in from near and distant villages to see the leopard and as most of these men asserted that they recognized the animal as the man-eater, the conviction of the Ibbotsons, that they were right and I was wrong, grew. Two concessions at my request Ibbotson made: he added his warning to the people to mind, not to relax precautions against the man-eater, and he refrained from telegraphing to tell the Government that we had shot the man-eater.

We went to bed early that night because we were to start at daybreak the next morning. I was up while it was still dark and was having Chota hazri when I heard voices on the road. As this was very unusual, I called out to ask what men were doing on the road at that hour. On seeing me, four men climbed up the path to my camp, and informed me they had been sent by the *patwari* to tell me that a woman had been killed by the man-eater on the far side of the river, about a mile from the Chatwapipal bridge.

THE HUNTERS HUNTED

Ibbotson was just unbolting the door to admit his man with early tea when I arrived, and after he had countermanded his move to Pauri we sat on Jean's bed with a large-scale map between us, drinking tea and discussing our plans.

Ibbotson's work at his headquarters at Pauri was pressing, and at most he could only spare two more days and nights. I had telegraphed Nainital the previous day to say I was returning home via Pauri and Kotdwara; this telegram I decided to cancel and instead of going by rail, I would return on foot the way I had come. These details settled and the village where the woman had been killed found on the map, I returned to camp to tell my men of our change of plans, and to instruct them to pack up and follow us, accompanied by the four men who had brought news of the kill.

Jean was to remain at Rudraprayag, so after breakfast Ibbotson and I set off on two of his horses, a Gulf Arab, and an English mare, two of the most surefooted animals I have ever had the good fortune to ride.

We took our rifles, a blue-flame stove, a petrol-lamp, and some provisions with us, and were accompanied by one of Ibbotson's syces on a borrowed horse, carrying food for our horses.

We left the horses at the Chatwapipal bridge. This bridge had not been closed the night we shot the leopard, with the result that the man-eater had got across the river and secured a kill at the first village he visited.

A guide was waiting for us at the bridge, and he took us up a very steep ridge and along a grassy hillside, and then down into a deep and densely wooded ravine with a small stream flowing through it. Here we found the *patwari* and some twenty men guarding the kill.

The kill was a very robust and fair girl, some eighteen or twenty years of age. She was lying on her face with her hands by her sides. Every vestige of clothing had been stripped from her, and she had been licked by the leopard from the soles of her feet to her neck, in which were four great teeth-marks; only a few pounds of flesh had been eaten from the upper portion of her body, and a few pounds from the lower portion.

The drums we had heard as we came up the hill were being beaten by the men who were guarding the kill, and as it was then about 2 p.m. and there was no chance of the leopard being anywhere in the vicinity, we went up to the village to brew ourselves some tea, taking the *patwari* and the guard with us.

After tea we went and had a look at the house where the girl had been killed. It was a stone-built house, consisting of one room, situated in the midst of terraced fields some two or three acres in extent, and it was occupied by the girl, her husband, and their six-month-old child.

Two days previous to the kill, the husband had gone to Pauri to give evidence in a land dispute case and had left his father in charge of the house. On the night of the kill, after the girl and her father-in-law had partaken of their evening meal and it was getting near time to retire for the night, the girl, who had been nursing her child, handed it over to her father-in-law, unlatched the door and stepped outside to squat down, I have already mentioned that there are no sanitary conveniences in the houses of our hill-folk.

When the child was transferred from the mother to the grandfather, it started crying, so even if there had been any sound from outside and I am sure there was none, he would not have heard it. It was a dark night. After waiting for a few minutes, the man called to the girl; and receiving no answer he called again. Then he got up and hurriedly closed and latched the door.

Rain had fallen earlier in the evening, and it was easy to reconstruct the scene. Shortly after the rain had stopped, the leopard, coming from the direction of the village, had crouched down behind a rock in the field, about thirty yards to the left front of the door.

Here it had lain for some time possibly listening to the man and the girl talking. When the girl opened door she squatted down on its right-hand side, partly turning her back on the leopard, who had crept round the far side of the rock, covered the twenty yards separating him from the corner of the house with belly to ground and creeping along close to the wall of the house, had caught the girl from behind and dragged her to the rock. Here, when the girl was dead, or possibly when the man called out in alarm, the leopard had picked her up and holding her high, so that no mark of hand or foot showed on the soft newly ploughed ground, had carried her across one field, down a three-foot bank, and across another field which ended in a twelve-foot drop on to a well-used footpath. Down this drop the leopard had sprung with the girl, who weighed about eleven stone in his mouth and some idea of his strength will be realized from the fact that when he landed on the footpath, he did not let any portion of her body come in contact with the ground.

Crossing the footpath, he had gone straight down the hill for half a mile, to the spot where he had undressed the girl. After eating a little of her, he had left her lying in a little glade of emerald-green grass, under the shade of a tree roofed over with dense creepers.

At about four o'clock we went down to sit over the kill, taking the petrol-lamp and night-shooting light with us.

It was reasonable to assume that the leopard had heard the noise the villagers made when searching for the girl and later when guarding the body, and that if it returned to the kill, it would do so with great caution; so we decided not to sit near the kill, and selected a tree about sixty yards away on the hill overlooking the glade.

This tree, a stunted oak, was growing out of the hill at almost a right angle, and after we had hidden the petrol-lamp in a little hollow and covered it over with pine-needles, Ibbotson took his seat in a fork of the tree from where he had a clear view of the kill, while I sat on the trunk with my back to him and facing the hill; Ibbotson was to take the shot, while I saw to our safety. As the shooting light was not functioning, possibly because the battery had faded out, our plan was to sit up as long as Ibbotson could see to shoot and then, with the help of the petrol-lamp, get back to the village where we hoped to find that our men had arrived from Rudraprayag.

We had not had time to prospect the ground, but the villagers had informed us that there was heavy jungle to the east of the kill, to which they felt sure the leopard had retired when they drove it off. If the leopard came from this direction, Ibbotson would see it long before it got to the glade and would get an easy shot, for his rifle was fitted with a telescopic sight which not only made for accurate shooting, but which also gave us an extra half-hour, as we had found from tests. When a minute of daylight more or less may make the difference between success and failure, this modification of the light factor is very important.

The sun was setting behind the high hills to the west and we had been in shadow for some minutes when a *kakar* dashed down the hill, barking, from the direction in which we had been told there was heavy jungle. On the shoulder of the hill the animal pulled up, and after barking in one spot for some time went away on the far side, and the sound died away in the distance.

The *kakar* had undoubtedly been alarmed by a leopard, and though it was quite possible that there were other leopards in that area, my hopes had been raised, and when I looked round at Ibbotson, I saw that he too was keyed up and that he had both hands on his rifle.

Light was beginning to fade but was good enough to shoot by even without the aid of the telescopic sight, when a pinecone dislodged from behind some low bushes thirty yards above us came rolling down the hill and struck the tree close to my feet. The leopard had arrived and, possibly suspecting danger, had taken a line that would enable him to prospect from a safe place on the hill all the ground in the vicinity of his kill. Unfortunately, in so doing he had got our tree in a direct line with the kill, and though I, who was showing no outline, might escape observation, he would be certain to see Ibbotson, who was sitting in a fork of the tree.

When sufficient light for me to shoot by had long since gone and Ibbotson's telescopic sight was no longer of any use to him, we heard the leopard coming stealthily down towards the tree. It was then time to take action, so I asked Ibbotson to take my place, while I retrieved the lamp. This lamp was of German make and was called a petromax. It gave a brilliant light but, with its long body and longer handle, was not designed to be used as a lantern in a jungle.

I am a little taller than Ibbotson, and suggested that I should carry the lamp, but Ibbotson said he could manage all right, and, moreover, that he would rather depend on my rifle than his own. So, we set off, Ibbotson leading and I following with both hands on my rifle.

Fifty yards from the tree, while climbing over a rock, Ibbotson slipped, the base of the lamp came in violent contact with the rock, and the mantle fell in dust to the bottom of the lamp. The streak of blue flame directed from the nozzle on to the petrol reservoir gave sufficient light for us to see where to put our feet, but the question was how long we should have even this much light. Ibbotson was of the opinion that he could carry the lamp for three minutes before it burst. Three minutes, in which to do a stiff climb of half a mile, over ground on which it was necessary to change direction every few steps to avoid huge rocks and thornbushes, and possibly followed and actually followed as we found later by a man-eater, was a terrifying prospect.

There are events in one's life which, no matter how remote, never fade from memory; the climb up that hill in the dark was for me one of them. When we eventually reached the footpath, our troubles were not ended, for the path was a series of buffalo wallows, and we did not know where our men were. Alternately slipping on wet ground and stumbling over unseen rocks, we at last came to some stone steps which took off from the path and went up to the right. Climbing these steps we found a small courtyard, on the far side of which was a door. We had heard the gurgling of a hookah as we came up the steps, so I kicked the door and shouted to the inmates to open. As no answer came, I took out a box of matches and shook it, crying that if the door was not opened in a minute, I would set the thatch alight. On this an agitated voice came from inside the house, begging me not to set the house on fire, and saying that the door was being opened, a minute later first the inner door and then the outer door were opened, and in two strides Ibbotson and I were in the house, slamming the inner door, and putting our backs to it.

There were some twelve or fourteen men, women, and children of all ages in the room. When the men had regained their wits after the unceremonious entry, they begged us to forgive them for not having opened the doors sooner, adding that they and their families had lived so long in terror of the man-eater that their courage had gone. Not knowing what form the man-eater might take, they suspected every sound they heard at night. In their fear they had our full sympathy, for from the time Ibbotson had slipped and broken the mantle, and a few minutes later had extinguished the red-hot lamp to prevent it bursting, I had been convinced that one, and possibly both, of us would not live to reach the village.

We were told that our men had arrived about sundown, and that they had been housed in a block of buildings farther along the hill. The two able-bodied men in the room offered to show us the way, but as we knew it would be murder to let them return to their homes alone, we declined their offer which had been made with the full realization of the risk it would entail and asked if they could provide us with a light of some kind. After rummaging about in a corner of the room, an old and decrepit lantern with a cracked globe was produced, and when vigorous shaking had revealed that it contained a few drops of oil, it was lit and with the combined good wishes of the inmates we left the house, the two doors being shut and bolted on our heels.

More buffalo wallows and more sunken rocks but with the glimmer of light to help us we made good progress and, finding the second lot of steps we had been instructed to climb, we mounted them and found ourselves in a long courtyard facing a row of double-storied buildings extending to the right and to the left, every door of which was fast shut, and not a glimmer of light showing anywhere.

When we called a door was opened, and by climbing a short flight of.' stone steps we gained the verandah of the upper story and found the two adjoining rooms which had been placed at the disposal of our men and ourselves. While the men were relieving us of the lamp and our rifles, a dog arrived from nowhere. He was just a friendly village pye and after sniffing round our legs and wagging his tail, he went towards the steps up which we had just come. The next second, with a scream of fear followed by hysterical barking, he backed towards us with all his hair on end.

The lantern we had been lent had died on us as we reached the courtyard, but our men had procured its twin brother. Though Ibbotson held it at all angles while I hurriedly reloaded my rifle, he could not get its light to illuminate the ground eight feet below.

By watching the dog, it was possible to follow the movements of the leopard. When the leopard had crossed the yard and gone down the steps leading to the footpath, the dog gradually stopped barking and lay down intently watching in that direction and growling at intervals.

The room that had been vacated for us had no windows, and as the only way in which we could have occupied it in safety would have been by closing the solid door and excluding all air and light, we decided to spend the night on the verandah. The dog evidently belonged to the late occupant of the room and had been accustomed to sleeping there, for he lay contentedly at our feet and gave us a feeling of safety as we watched in turn through the long hours of the night.

RETREAT

At daybreak next morning we very carefully stalked the kill and were disappointed to find that the leopard had not returned to it, which we felt sure he would do after his failure to bag one of us the previous evening.

During the day, while Ibbotson dealt with some office work that had been sent out to him, I took a rifle and went off to see if I could get a shot at the leopard. Tracking on the hard and pine-needle-covered ground was not possible, so I made for the shoulder of the hill beyond which the villagers had told us there was heavy jungle. Here I found the ground very difficult to negotiate, for, in addition to dense scrub jungle through which it was not possible to penetrate, there was a series of rock cliffs on which it was impossible for a human being to find foothold. In this area there was a surprisingly large head of game, and on the paths that intersected it I found the tracks of *kakar*, ghooral, pig, and a solitary sarao. Of the leopard except for a few old scratch-marks, I found no trace.

The gin- trap that had been sent off from Rudraprayag the previous day arrived while we were having lunch, and in the early evening we took it down to the glade and, after setting it, poisoned the kill with cyanide. I had no experience of poisons, nor had Ibbotson, but in a conversation with a doctor friend before leaving Nainital I had mentioned that Government wanted me to try every means to kill the man-eater, and that there was little use in my trying poison, as the records showed that the leopard throve on it. I told him what poisons had hitherto been tried, and he then recommended my using cyanide, which was the best poison for the cat family. I had passed this information on to Ibbotson, and a few days previously a supply had arrived, with capsules with which to use it. We inserted a few of these capsules in the kill at the places where the leopard had eaten.

There was every hope of the leopard returning to the kill this second night and as he had seen us on the tree the previous evening we decided not to sit up, but to leave him to the gin-trap and to the poison.

In a big pine-tree near the footpath we built a *machan*, which we padded with hay and on which we took up our position after we had eaten the dinner which Ibbotson cooked on the blue-flame stove. Here on the comfortable *machan* we were able to lie at full stretch and talk and smoke, for our only reason for being there was to listen for sounds from the direction of the kill. We watched and slept by turns, hoping to hear the angry roar of the leopard if by accident it walked into the trap, for here there was no well-used track along which to direct the leopard to it.

Once during the night, a *kakar* barked, but in the opposite direction to that from which we expected the leopard to come.

At the first streak of dawn, we climbed out of the tree and after brewing ourselves a cup of tea, visited the kill, which we found lying just as we had left it.

Ibbotson left for Rudraprayag after an early breakfast, and I was packing my things and having a final word with the villagers before starting on my fifteen-day journey back to Nainital when a party of men arrived to give the news that a cow had been killed by a leopard in a village four miles away. They suspected that the cow had been killed by the man-eater, for the previous night, the night the leopard had followed Ibbotson and myself from the tree to the verandah and towards the small hours of the morning, the leopard had made a determined attempt to break down the door of the Headman's house; late the following evening, the cow had been killed in the jungle three hundred yards from this house. At the urgent request of these men, I postponed my departure to Nainital and accompanied them back to their village, taking the gin-trap and a supply of poison with me.

The Headman's house was on a little knoll surrounded by cultivated land and was approached by a footpath which for a short distance ran over soft and boggy ground; here I found the pugmarks of the man- eater.

The Headman had seen me approaching across the valley and had a steaming dish of tea brewed in fresh milk and sweetened with jaggery, waiting for me. While I drank this rich and over-sweetened liquid on the courtyard, sitting on a reed couch upholstered with ghooral skins, he drew my attention to the condition of the door which two nights previously the leopard had attempted to break down, in which attempt it would undoubtedly have succeeded if he had not fortunately had some sawn timber in the house, intended for repairing the roof which he had used to shore up the door from inside.

The Headman was old and crippled with rheumatism, so he sent his son to show me the kill while he made room in the house for myself and my men.

I found the kill, a young cow in grand condition lying on a flat bit of ground just above the cattle track, in an ideal position for setting up the gin-trap. Its back was against a tangle of wild rosebushes and its hooves were against a foot-high bank; while eating, the leopard had sat on the bank with its forepaws between the cow's legs.

Having dug away the ground between the cows' legs and removed it to a distance, I set the trap where the leopard had placed his paws and covered it over with big green leaves. Then, after sprinkling on a layer of earth, I replaced the deal leaves, bits of dry sticks, and splinters of bone in the exact position between the cow's legs in which I had found them. Not one of a hundred human beings going to the kill would have noticed that the ground had in any way been disturbed, and a deadly trap set.

My arrangements made to my satisfaction I retraced my steps and climbed a tree halfway between the kill and the Headman's house, where I would be handy if needed at the trap.

Near sundown a pair of *kalege* pheasants and their brood of five chicks, which I had been watching for some time, suddenly took alarm and went scuttling down the hill, and a few seconds later a *kakar* came dashing towards me and after barking under my tree for a little while, went off up the hill on tiptoe. Nothing happened after that, and when it was getting too dark under the shade of the trees for me to see the sights of my rifle, I slipped off the tree and myself tiptoed away on rubber-shod feet towards the village.

A hundred yards from the Headman's house the track ran across an open glade, some thirty yards long and twenty yards wide. On the upper hill side of the glade was a big rock. As I reached this open ground, I felt I was being followed and determined to exploit the situation, I left the track and, taking two long steps over soft and spongy ground, lay down behind the rock, with only one eye showing in the direction of the kill.

For ten minutes I lay on the wet ground. When daylight had all but gone, I regained the path and, taking every precaution, covered the remaining distance to the Headman's house.

Once during the night, the Headman roused me from a sound sleep to tell me he had heard the leopard scratching on the door and when I opened the door next morning, I saw the pugmarks of the man-eater in the dust in front of it. These pugmarks I followed back to the glade and found that the leopard had done just what I had done the previous evening. He had left the track where I had, had crossed the soft ground to the rock and, after regaining the track, had followed me to the house, round which he had walked several times.

On leaving the house the leopard had gone back along the track, and as I followed his pugmarks towards the kill my hopes rose high, for up to that time I had not fully realized the degree of cunning that a man-eating leopard can acquire after eight years of close association with human beings.

I left the track and approached from the high ground, and from a little distance away saw that the kill had gone, and that the ground where the trap had been buried was except for two pugmarks, undisturbed.

Sitting on the foot-high bank, as he had done the first night, the leopard had put both front paws between the cow's legs, but on this occasion, he had spread them wide apart and rested them on the buried levers of the trap which, released, would have closed the great jaws. Here, safe from the trap, he had eaten his meal, and when he had done, he skirted round the flat ground and getting hold of the cow by the head, had dragged it through the rose-thorns and rolled it down the hill, where fifty yards lower down it had fetched up against an oak sapling. Content with his nights work, the leopard had then gone along the cattle track, and after following him for a mile I lost his tracks on hard ground.

There was no hope of the leopard returning to the kill. However, to salve my conscience for not having done so the previous night, I put a liberal dose of cyanide in the carcass of the cow. Truth to tell I hated the very thought of using poison then, and I hate it no less now.

I visited the kill in the morning and found that a leopard had eaten all that portion of the cow that I had poisoned. So sure, was I that the poison had been eaten by a leopard that had accidentally come across the kill, and not by the man-eater, that on my return to the village I told the Headman that I would not stay to recover the leopard, though I would pay a hundred rupees to anyone who found it and took its skin to the pativari. A month later the reward was claimed, and the skin of a leopard which had been dead for many days was buried by the patwari.

It did not take my men long to pack up, and shortly after midday we started on our long journey back to Nainital. As we went down a narrow footpath to the Chatwapipal bridge a big rat snake leisurely crossed the path, and as I stood and watched it slip away Madho Singh, who was behind me, said, 'There goes the evil spirit that has been responsible for your failure.'

My action in leaving Garhwal to the tender mercies of the man-eater may appear heartless to you, it did so to me and was adversely criticized in the press, for the leopard at that time was daily mentioned in the Indian papers. Ip extenuation I would urge that an effort entailing great strain cannot be indefinitely sustained. There were twenty-four hours in every day of the many weeks I spent in Garhwal, and time and time again after sitting up all night, I walked endless miles next day, visiting distant villages from which reports had come of unsuccessful attacks by the man-eater. On many moonlit nights, when sitting in an uncomfortable position physical endurance had reached its limit, and when sitting where it would have been easy for the leopard to have got at me, I had no longer been able to keep my eyes open. I had for hours walked the roads which were alone open to me and to the leopard, trying every trick I knew of to outwit my adversary and the man-eater had with luck beyond his deserts or with devilish cunning, avoided the bullet that a press of my finger would have sent into him, for on retracing my steps in the morning after these night excursions I had found from the pugmarks on the road that I was right in assuming I had been closely followed. To know that one is being followed at night, no matter how bright the moon may be by a man-eater intent on securing a victim, gives one an inferiority complex that is very unnerving, and that is not mitigated by repetition.

Tired out in mind and in body, my longer stay at Rudraprayag would not have benefited the people of Garhwal and it might have cost me my own life. Knowing that the temporary abandonment of my self-imposed task would be severely criticized by the press, but that what I was now doing was right, I plodded on towards my distant home, having assured the people of Garhwal that I would return to help them as soon as it was possible for me to do so.

FISHING INTERLUDE

I left the scene of my failure, weary and dispirited, in the late autumn of 1925 and returned to continue my labour, refreshed and full of hope, in the early spring of 1926.

On this my second visit to Garhwal in pursuit of the man-eater, I travelled by train to Kotdwara and went from there by foot to Pauri, thus saving eight days on the journey. At Pauri, Ibbotson joined me and accompanied me to Rudraprayag.

During my three months' absence from Garhwal the man-eater had killed ten human beings, and during these three months no attempt had been made by the terror-stricken inhabitants to kill the leopard.

The last of these ten kills, the victim was a small boy, had taken place on the left bank of the Alaknanda, two days before our arrival at Rudraprayag. We had received telegraphic news of this kill at Pauri and though we had travelled as fast as it was possible for us to do, we were disappointed to learn from the *patwari*, who was awaiting our arrival at the Inspection Bungalow that the leopard disposed of the entire kill the previous night, leaving nothing of its small victim over which we could sit.

The boy had been killed at midnight in a village four miles from Rudraprayag, and as it was unlikely that the leopard had crossed the river after his undisturbed feed, we took steps immediately on our arrival to close the two suspension bridges.

During the winter Ibbotson had organized a very efficient intelligence service throughout the area in which the man-eater was operating. If in this area a dog, goat, cow, or human being was killed, or an attempt made to force open a door, news of the occurrence was conveyed to us by the service and in this way, we were able to keep in constant touch with the man-eater. Hundreds of false rumours of alleged attacks by the man-eater were brought to us, entailing endless miles of walking, but this was only to be expected for in an area in which an established man-eater is operating everyone suspects their own shadows and every sound heard at night is attributed to the man-eater.

One of these rumours concerned a man by the name of Galtu, a resident of Kunda, a village seven miles from Rudraprayag on the right bank of the Alaknanda. Galtu left the village in the evening to spend the night in his cattle shed a mile away from the village, and when his son went to the shed next morning, he found his father's blanket half in and half out of the door of the shed and in a patch of soft ground nearby he found what he thought was drag mark, and near it the pugmarks of the man-eater. Returning to the village he raised an alarm and while sixty men went off to search for the body, four men were dispatched to Rudraprayag to inform us. Ibbotson and I were beating a hillside on the left bank of the river for the man-eater when the men arrived and as I was convinced that the leopard was on our side of the river, and that there was no truth in the rumour that Galtu had been killed, Ibbotson sent a *patwari* back to Kunda with the four men, with instructions to make a personal search and report back to us. Next evening, we received thepatwari's report, with a sketch of the pugmarks in the soft earth near the door of the shed. The report stated that an all-day search of the surrounding country, with two hundred men, had not resulted in finding Galtu's remains, and that the search would be continued. The sketch showed six circles, the inner one as large as a plate, with five equally spaced circles round it, each the size of a teacup; all the circles had been made with a compass. Five days later, and just as Ibbotson and I were setting out to sit up on the tower of the bridge, a procession came up to the bungalow led by an irate man who was protesting loudly that he had committed no offence that justified his being arrested and brought to Rudraprayag. The irate man was Galtu. After we had pacified him, he gave us his story. It appeared that just as he was leaving his house on the night he was alleged to have been carried off by the man-eater, his son arrived and informed him that he had paid Rs 100 for a pair of bullocks which Galtu asserted were not worth more than Rs 70. The wanton waste of good money had angered him so much that, after sleeping the night in the cattle shed, he had got up early the next morning and gone to a village ten miles away, where a married daughter of his was living. On his return to his village that morning, he had been arrested by the *patwari*, and he wanted to know what crime he had committed that justified his arrest. It was some little time before he saw the humour of the situation but once having done so, he laughed as heartily as any of the assembled throng at the thought of an important person like a *patwari*, and two hundred of his friends, searching for five days for his remains, what time he was cooling off in a village ten miles away.

Ibbotson was averse to lying all night on the wind-swept tower of the Rudraprayag suspension bridge and as wood and carpenters were available, he had a platform built in the arch of the tower and on this platform, we sat for the five nights Ibbotson was able to spend at Rudraprayag.

After Ibbotson's departure the leopard killed one dog, four goats, and two cows. The dog and goats had been eaten out on the nights on which they had been killed, but I sat over each of the cows for two nights. On the second night on which I was sitting up over the first cow, the leopard came, but just as I was raising my rifle and preparing to switch on the torch, I had provided myself with, a woman in the house adjoining the one I was sitting in, thumped on the door preparatory to opening it and unfortunately frightened the leopard away.

No human beings had been killed during this period, but a woman and her baby had been badly mauled. The leopard had forced open the door of the room in which she was sleeping with her baby and seizing her arm had attempted to drag her out of the room. The woman fortunately was stout of heart and had not fainted or lost her wits and after the leopard dragging her along the floor had backed out of the room, she shut the door on it and escaped with a badly lacerated arm and several deep wounds on her breast, while the baby escaped with one head wound. I sat in this room for the following two nights, but the leopard did not return.

I was returning one day towards the latter end of March, after visiting a village on the Kedarnath pilgrim route, when, as I approached a spot where the road runs close alongside the Mandakini river, and where there is a waterfall ten to twelve feet high, I saw a number of men sitting on the rock at the head of the fall on the far side of the river, armed with a triangular net attached to a long bamboo pole. The roar of the water prevented conversation, so leaving the road I sat down on the rocks on my side of the fall, to have a rest and a smoke for I had walked for that day and to see what the men were doing.

Presently one of the men got to his feet and as he pointed down excitedly into the foaming white water at the foot of the fall, two of his companions manning the long pole held the triangular net close to the fall. A large shoal of *mahseer* fish, varying in size from five to fifty pounds, were attempting to leap the fall. One of these fish, about ten pounds in weight, leapt clear of the fall and when falling back was expertly caught in the net. After the fish had been extracted and placed in a basket, the net was again held out close to the fall. I watched the sport for about an hour,

during which time the men caught four fish, all about the same size, ten pounds.

On myis myrevious visit to Rudraprayag I had been informed by the *chowkidar* in charge of the Inspection Bungalow that there was good fishing in the spring before the snow-water came down in both the Alaknanda and Mandakini rivers, so I had come armed on this my second visit with a fourteen-foot split cane salmon rod, a silex reel with two hundred and fifty yards of line, a few stout traces, and an assortment of home-made brass spoons varying in size from one to two inches.

The following morning as no news had come in of the man-eater, I set off for the waterfall with my rod and tackle.

No fish were leaping the fall as they had been doing the previous day and the men on the far side of the river were sitting in a group round a small fire smoking a hookah which was passing from hand to hand. They watched me with interest.

Below the waterfall was a pool thirty to forty yards wide, flanked on both sides by a wall of rock and about two hundred yards long, one hundred yards of which was visible from where I stood at the head of the pool. The water in this beautiful and imposing pool was crystal-clear.

The rock face at the head of the pool rose sheer up out of the water to a height of twelve feet, and after keeping at this height for twenty yards, sloped gradually upwards to a height of a hundred feet. It was not possible to get down to water level anywhere on my side of the pool, nor would it be possible, or profitable, to follow a fish assuming that I hooked one, along the bank for at the top of the high ground there were trees and bushes, and at the tail of the pool the river cascaded down in a foaming torrent to its junction with the Alaknanda. To land a fish in this pool would be a difficult and a hazardous task but the crossing of that bridge could be deferred until the fish had been hooked and I had not yet put together my rod.

On my side of the pool the water shot through with millions of small bubbles was deep and from about halfway across a shingle bottom was showing, over which four to six feet of water was flowing. Above this shingle bottom, every stone and pebble of which was visible in the clear water, a number of fish, ranging in size from three to ten pounds, were slowly moving upstream. As I watched these fish, standing on the rocks twelve feet above the water with a two-inch spoon mounted with a single strong treble hook in my hand, a flight of fingerlings flashed out of the deep water and went skimming over the shingle bottom, hotly pursued by three big *mahseer*. Using the good salmon rod as friend Hardy had never intended that it should be used and as it had been used on many previous occasions. I slung the spoon out, and in my eagerness over-estimated the distance, with the result that the spoon struck the rock on the far side of the pool, about two feet above the water. The falling of the spoon into the water coincided with the arrival of the fingerlings at the rock, and the spoon had hardly touched the water, when it was taken by the leading *mahseer*.

Striking with a long line from an elevated position entails a very heavy strain, but my good rod stood the strain, and the strong treble hook was firmly fixed in the *mahseer's* mouth. For a moment or two the fish did not appear to realize what had happened as standing perpendicularly in the water with his white belly towards me, he shook his head from side to side, and then, possibly frightened by the dangling spoon striking against his head, he gave a mighty splash and went tearing downstream, scattering in all directions the smaller fish that were lying on the shingle bottom.

In his first run the mahseer ripped a hundred yards of line off the reel, and after a *moment's* check carried on for another fifty yards. There was plenty of line still on the reel, but the fish had now gone round the bend and was getting dangerously near the tail of the pool. Alternately easing and tightening the strain on the line, I eventually succeeded in turning his head upstream and having done so, very gently pulled him round the bend, into the hundred yards of water I was overlooking.

Just below me a projection of rock had formed a backwater, and into this backwater the fish, after half an hour's game fight, permitted himself to be drawn.

I had now very definitely reached my bridge and had just regretfully decided that, as there was no way of crossing it, the fish would have to be cut adrift, when a shadow fell across the rock beside me. Peering over the rock into the backwater, the new arrival remarked that it was a very big fish and in the same breath asked what I was going to do about it. When I told him that it would not be possible to draw the fish up the face of the rock, and that therefore the only thing to do was to cut it free, he said, 'Wait, *sahib*, I will fetch my brother.' His brother, a long and lanky stripling with dancing eyes had quite evidently been cleaning out a cow shed when summoned, so telling him to go upstream and wash himself lest he should slip on the smooth rock, I held council with the elder man.

Starting from where we were standing, a crack, a few inches wide, ran irregularly down the face of the rock, ending a foot above the water in a ledge some six inches wide. The plan we finally agreed on was that the stripling Adio presently returned with his arms and legs glistening with water, should go down to the ledge, while the elder brother went down the crack far enough to get hold of the stripling's left hand, while I lay on the rock holding the elder brother's other hand. Before embarking on the plan, I asked the brothers whether they knew how to handle a fish and whether they could swim and received the laughing answer that they had handled fish and swum in the river from childhood.

The snag in the plan was that I could not hold the rod and at the same time make a link in the chain. However, some risk had to be taken, so I put the rod down and held the line in my hand and when the brothers had taken up position I sprawled on the rock and reaching down, got hold of the elder brother's hand. Then very gently I drew the fish towards the rock, holding the line alternately with my left hand and with my teeth. There was no question that the stripling knew how to handle a fish, for before the fish had touched the rock, he had inserted his thumb into one side of the gills and his fingers into the other, getting a firm grip on the fish's throat. Up to this point the fish had been quite amenable but on having its throat seized, it lashed out and for seconds it appeared that the three of us would go headlong into the river.

Both brothers were bare-footed, and when I had been relieved of the necessity of holding the line and was able to help with both hands, they turned and, facing the rock, worked their way up with their toes, while I pulled lustily from on top.

When the fish at last had been safely landed, I asked the brothers if they ate fish, and on receiving their eager answer that they most certainly did, when they could get any, I told them I would give them the fish we had just landed, a *mahseer* in grand condition weighing a little over thirty pounds if they would help me to land another fish for my men. To this they very readily agreed.

The treble had bitten deep into the leathery underlip of the *mahseer*, and as I cut it out, the brothers watched interestedly. When the hook was free, they asked if they might have a look at it. Three hooks in one, such a thing had never been seen in their village. The bit of bent brass of course acted as a sinker. With what were the hooks baited? Why should fish want to eat brass? And was it really brass, or some kind of hardened bait? When the spoon, and the trace with its three swivels, had been commented on and marveled at, I made the brothers sit down and watch while I set about catching the second fish.

The biggest fish in the pool were at the foot of the fall, but here in the foaming white water? in addition to *mahseer* were some very big goonch, a fish that takes a spoon of dead bait very readily, and which is responsible for 90 per cent of the tackle lost in our hill rivers through its annoying habit of diving to the bottom of the pool when hooked and getting its head under a rock from where it is always difficult and often impossible to dislodge it.

No better spot than the place from where I had made my first cast was available, so here I again took up my position, with rod in hand and spoon held ready for casting.

The fish on the shingle bottom had been disturbed while I was playing the *mahseer* and by our subsequent movements on the face of the rock but were now beginning to return, and presently an exclamation from the brothers, and an excited pointing of fingers, drew my attention to a big fish downstream where the shingle bottom ended, and the deep water began. Before I was able to make a cast, the fish turned and disappeared in the deep water, but a little later it reappeared, and as it came into the shallow water, I made a cast but owing to the line being wet the cast fell short. The second cast was beautifully placed and beautifully timed, the spoon striking the water exactly where I wanted it to. Waiting for a second to give the spoon time to sink, I started to wind in the line, giving the spoon just the right amount of spin and as I drew it along in little jerks, the *mahseer* shot forward, and next moment, with the hook firmly fixed in his mouth, jumped clean out of the water, fell back with a great splash, and went madly downstream, much to the excitement of the spectators, for the men on the far bank had been watching the proceedings as intently as the brothers.

As the reel spun round and the line paid out, the brothers now standing one on either side of me, urged me not to let the fish go down the run at the trail of the pool. Easier said than done, for it is not possible to stop the first mad rush of a *mahseer* of any size with risking certain break or the tearing away of the hook-hold. Our luck was in, or else the fish feared the run, for when there was less than fifty yards of line on the reel he checked, and though he continued to fight gamely he was eventually drawn round the bend, and into the little backwater at the foot of the rock.

The landing of this second fish was not as difficult as the landing of the first had been, for we each knew our places on the rock and exactly what to do.

Both fish were the same length, but the second was a little heavier than the first and while the elder brother set off in triumph for his village with his fish carried over his shoulder threaded on a grass cable, he had made the stripling begged to be allowed to accompany me back to the Inspection Bungalow and to carry both my fish and my rod. Having in the days of long ago been a boy myself, and having had a brother who fished, there was no need for the stripling when making his request to have said, 'If you will let me carry both the fish and the rod and will walk a little distance behind me, *sahib*, all the people who see me on the road and in the bazaar, will think that I have caught this great fish, the like of which they have never seen.'

DEATH OF A GOAT

Ibbotson returned from Pauri on the last day of March and the following morning, while we were having breakfast, we received a report that a leopard had called very persistently the previous night near a village to the north-west of Rudraprayag, about a mile from the place where we had killed the leopard in the gin-trap.

Half a mile to the north of the village, and on the shoulder of the great mountain, there was a considerable area of rough and broken ground where there were enormous rocks and caves and deep holes in which the locals said their forefathers had quarried copper. Over the whole of this area there was scrub jungle, heavy in some places and light in others, extending down the hillside to within half a mile of the terraced fields above the village.

I had long suspected that the man-eater used this ground as a hideout when he was in the vicinity of Rudraprayag, and I had frequently climbed to a commanding position above the broken ground in the hope of finding him basking on the rocks in the early morning sun, for leopards are very fond of doing this in a cold climate, and it is a very common way of shooting them, for all that is needed is a little patience, and accuracy of aim.

After an early lunch Ibbotson and I set out armed with our .275 rifles and accompanied by one of Ibbotson s men carrying a short length of rope. At the village we purchased a young male goat, the leopard having killed all the goats that I had purchased from time to time.

From the village, a rough goat track ran straight up the hill to the edge of the broken ground, where it turned left and after running across the face of the hill for a hundred yards carried on round the shoulder of the mountain. The track where it ran across the hill was bordered on the upper side by scattered bushes and on the steep lower side by short grass.

Having tied the goat to a peg firmly driven into the ground at the bend in the track, about ten yards below the scrub jungle, we went down the hill for a hundred and fifty yards to where there were some big rocks, behind which we concealed ourselves. The goat was one of the best callers I have ever heard, and while his shrill and piercing bleat continued there was no necessity for us to watch him, for he had been very securely tied and there was no possibility of the leopard carrying him away.

The surf of a fiery red ball was a hand's breadth from the snow mountains above Kedarnath when we took up our position behind the rocks, and half an hour later, when we had been in shadow for a few minutes, the goat suddenly stopped calling. Creeping to the side of the rock and looking through a screen of grass, I saw the goat with ears cocked, looking up towards the bushes as I watched, the goat shook his head, and backed to the full length of the rope.

The leopard had undoubtedly come, attracted by the calling of the goat and that he had not pounced before the goat became aware of his presence was proof that he was suspicious. Ibbotson's aim would be more accurate than mine, for his rifle was fitted with a telescopic sight, so I made room for him, and as he lay down and raised his rifle I whispered to him to examine carefully the bushes in the direction in which the goat was looking, for I felt sure that if the goat could see the leopard and all the indications were that it could, Ibbotson should also be able to see it through his powerful telescope. For minutes Ibbotson kept his eye to the telescope and then shook his head, laid down the rifle, and made room for me.

The goat was standing in exactly the same position in which I had last seen it and taking direction from it I fixed the telescope on the same bush at which it was looking. The flicker of an eyelid or the very least movement of ear or even whiskers, would have been visible through the telescope but though I also watched for minutes I too could see nothing.

When I took my eye away from the telescope, I noted that the light was rapidly fading, and that the goat now showed a red and white blur on the hillside. We had a long way to go and waiting longer would be both useless and dangerous, so getting to my feet I told Ibbotson it was time for us to make a move.

Going up to the goat, who from the time he had stopped bleating had not made a sound, we freed it from the peg, and with the man leading it we set off for the village. The goat quite evidently had never had a rope round its neck before and objected violently to being led, so I told the man to take the rope off my experience being that when a goat is freed after having been tied up in the jungle, through fear or for want of companionship it follows at heel like a dog. This goat, however, had ideas of its own and no sooner had the man removed the rope from its neck, than it turned and ran up the track.

It was too good a calling goat to abandon, it had attracted the leopard once and might do so again. Moreover, we had only a few hours previously paid good money for it, so we in turn ran up the track in hot pursuit. At the bend, the goat turned to the left and we lost sight of it. Keeping to the track, as the goat had done, we went to the shoulder of the hill where a considerable extent of the hill, clothed in short grass, was visible, and as the goat was nowhere in sight, we decided it had taken a short cut back to the village, and started to retrace our steps. I was leading, and as we got halfway along the hundred yards of track, bordered on the upper side by scattered bushes and on the steep lower side by short grass, I saw something white on the track in front of me. The light had nearly gone, and on cautiously approaching the white object I found it was the goat laid head and tail on the narrow track in the only position in which it could have been laid to prevent it from rolling down the steep hillside. Blood was oozing from its throat and when I placed my hand on it the muscles were still twitching.

It was as though the man-eater for no other leopard would have killed the goat and laid it on the track had said, 'Here, if you want your goat so badly, take it; and as it is now dark and you have a long way to go, we will see which of you lives to reach the village.'

I do not think all three of us would have reached the village alive if I had not, very fortunately, had a full box of matches with me (Ibbotson at that time was a non-smoker). Striking a match and casting an anxious look all round and taking a few hurried steps, and then again striking another match, we stumbled down the rough track until we got to within calling distance of the village. Then, at our urgent summons, men with lanterns and pine torches came up to meet us.

We had left the goat lying where the leopard had placed it, and when I returned at daybreak next morning, I found the pugmarks of the man-eater where he had followed us down to the village and I found the goat untouched and lying just as we had left it.

CYANIDE POISONING

As I was returning to the Inspection Bungalow after visiting the goat that had been killed the previous night, I was informed in the village that my presence was urgently needed at Rudraprayag, for news had just been received that the man-eater had killed a human being the previous night. My informants were unable to give me any particulars as to where the kill had taken place, but as the pugmarks of the man -eater showed that, after following us to the village, it had gone back up the goat track and turned right at the bend, I assumed rightly, as I later found that the leopard, after failing to bag one of us, had secured a victim farther up the mountainside.

At the bungalow I found Ibbotson in conversation with a man by the name of Nand Ram. Nand Ram's village was about four miles from where we had sat the previous evening. Half a mile above this village and on the far side of a deep ravine, a man of the depressed class, named Gawiya, had cleared a small area of forest land and built himself a house in which he lived with his mother, wife and three children. At daybreak that morning, Nand Ram had heard the wailing of women from the direction of Gawiya's house and on his shouting out and asking what was wrong, he had been informed that 'the man of the house' had been carried off by the man-eater half an hour previously. With this information Nand Ram had come hot foot to the Inspection Bungalow.

Ibbotson had had the Arab and the English mare saddled, and after we had eaten a good meal, we set out, with Nand Ram to show us the way. There were no roads on the hill, only goat and cattle tracks, and as the big English mare found the hairpin bends on these tracks difficult to negotiate, we sent the horses back and did the rest of the hot and steep climb on foot.

Arrived at the little isolated clearing in the forest, the two distracted women who appeared to be nursing the hope that the 'man of the house' might still be alive showed us where Gawiya had been sitting near the door of the house when the leopard had seized him. The leopard had caught the unfortunate man by the throat, thus preventing him from making any sound and after dragging him for a hundred yards had killed him. Then he had carried him for four hundred yards to a little hollow surrounded by dense brushwood. The wailing of the women and the.' The shouting of Nand Ram had evidently disturbed the leopard at his meal, for he had only eaten the throat and jaw and a small portion of one shoulder and thigh.

There were no trees within sight of the kill on which we could sit, so we poisoned the kill with cyanide at the three places where the leopard had eaten, and as it was now getting towards evening, we took up position on a hill several hundred yards away from where we could overlook the hollow in which the kill was lying. The leopard was undoubtedly in the dense brushwood, but though we lay in our concealed position and watched for two hours, we saw nothing of him. At dusk we lit the lantern we had provided ourselves with and went back to the bungalow.

We were up very early next morning, and it was just getting light when we again sat down on the hill overlooking the hollow. We saw and heard nothing and when the sun had been up an hour, we went to the kill; the leopard had not touched the three places where we had buried the poison, but had eaten the other shoulder and leg, and had then carried the body away for a short distance and hidden it under some bushes.

Again there were no trees overlooking the kill on which we could sit, and after a prolonged discussion we eventually decided that while Ibbotson went down the hill for a mile to a village where there was a big mango-tree in which he could make himself a *machan* and spend the night, I would sit about four hundred yards from the kill, over a village path on which the previous day we had seen the pugmarks of the man-eater.

The tree I selected to sit in was a rhododendron which many years previously had been cut about fifteen feet above ground. Stout branches had grown out from the cut and sitting on the old stump surrounded by the branches I had a perfect seat and perfect concealment.

Facing me was a steep well-wooded hill with a dense undergrowth of bracken and dwarf bamboo. Running across the face of the hill east and west was a well-used footpath; the rhododendron tree was growing about ten feet below this footpath.

From my seat in the tree, I had an uninterrupted view of a length of about ten yards of the path, which to my left crossed a ravine and carried on at the same level on the far side, and to my right, and some three hundred yards farther on, passed a little below the bushes where the kill was lying. There was no water in the ravine where the path crossed it, but thirty yards lower down and immediately below, and three or four yards from, the root of my tree, there were several small pools, the start of a little spring which lower down became a stream providing drinking water to the villagers and irrigation for their crops.

The ten yards of path of which I had an uninterrupted view was joined at right-angles by a path coming down the hill from the house three hundred yards above me where Gawiya had been killed. Thirty yards up this path there was a bend, and from this point a small depression ran down to the lower path, the points where the depression started on the upper path and ended on the lower were not in my view.

There was no need for a torch, for it was a brilliant moonlit night, and if the leopard came along the level path or down the path from the house as its pugmarks showed it had done the previous day, I should get an easy shot at a range of from twenty to forty feet.

I had gone down the hill a short distance with Ibbotson, and then a little before sunset had taken up my position on the tree. A few minutes later three *kalege* pheasants, a cock and two hens came down the hill and after drinking at the spring went back the way they had come. On both occasions they had passed under my tree and that they had not seen me was proof that my hide was a good one.

The early part of the night was silent, but at eight o'clock a *kakar* started barking in the direction of the kill. The leopard had arrived, and I was convinced he had not gone to the kill along either of the paths I was watching. After barking for a few minutes, the *kakar* stopped, and thereafter the night was again silent up to ten o'clock, when the *kakar* again barked. The leopard had been at the kill for two hours sufficient time for him to have had a good meal, and for him to have poisoned himself several times over. And there was a good chance of his having done so, for on this second night the kill had been very effectively poisoned, the cyanide having been buried deep in the victim's flesh.

Without closing an eye, I sat watching the hill in front of me, where the moonlight was so brilliant that I could clearly see every blade of grass and at 2 a.m. I heard the leopard coming down the path from the direction of the house. I had scattered dry leaves on this path, and also on the lower path, with the object of getting some warning of the leopard's approach, and that he was now walking carelessly over these leaves, and not making any attempt at silence, filled me with hope though I expected within the next few seconds to put a bullet into him that all was not well with him.

At the bend in the path the leopard made a short pause and then leaving the path entered the little depression and followed it down to the lower path, reaching which he again paused.

I had sat without movement for hours with my hands on the rifle lying across my knees and as I was convinced that he would come along the path, I decided to let him pass in front of me, and when there was no longer any danger of his seeing the movement raise the rifle to my shoulder and hit him where I wanted to. For seconds I watched the path, expecting to see his head appear from behind the screen of branches, and then, when tension was becoming unbearable, I heard him jump down off the path and come diagonally across the hill towards my tree. For a moment I thought he had in some mysterious way become aware of my presence on the tree and, not liking the flavour of his last kill was intent on securing another human victim. His object, however, in leaving the path was not to try to get at me but to take a short cut down to the spring, for he passed the foot of the tree without a pause, and next second I heard him eagerly and noisily lapping water.

From the leopard's behaviour on the hill and from the way he was now drinking, I was convinced he had poisoned himself, but not having had any previous experience of the effect of cyanide, I did not know how long the poison would take to act. For ten minutes after the leopard had stopped drinking, and just as I was beginning to hope that he had died at the spring, I heard him going up the hill on the far side of the ravine, all sound ceasing when he regained the path which carried on round the shoulder of the hill.

At no time, either when the leopard was coming down the path, coming down the depression, coming across the hill to the foot of my tree, when drinking, or going up the hill on the far side of the ravine, had I seen him, for either by accident or intent he had kept under cover to which not a glint of moonlight had penetrated. There was now no hope of my getting a shot, but this was not much on account if the poison was as potent as the doctor in Nainital had claimed that it was.

I sat on it for the rest of the night, watching the path and listening for sounds. At daylight Ibbotson returned and while we brewed ourselves a very welcome cup of tea, I told him of the night's happenings.

On visiting the kill, we found that the leopard had eaten the leg from which he had taken a small portion two nights previously, and in which we had buried a full dose of poison and that he had in addition eaten two other doses of poison, one from the left shoulder and the other from the back.

It was now necessary to make a search for the leopard and for this purpose the *patwari*, who had returned with Ibbotson, set off to collect men. At about midday the *patwari* returned with two hundred men and with these we made a line and beat the whole side of the hill in the direction in which the leopard had gone.

Half a mile from where the leopard had quenched his thirst, and in the direct line in which I had heard him going away, there were some big rocks at the foot of which there was a cave extending far into the hill, with an opening large enough to admit a leopard. Near the mouth of this cave the leopard had scratched up the ground and rid himself of his victim's toes, which he had swallowed whole.

Willing hands brought loose stones from the hillside and when we left the cave, we had sealed it beyond all possibility of any leopard that might be lurking in it escaping.

Next morning, I returned with a roll of one-inch wire-netting and a number of iron tent-pegs and after removing the stones, very effectively wired up the mouth of the cave. Thereafter for the following ten days I visited the cave morning and evening and as during this period no news of the man-eater came in from any village on the left bank of the Alaknanda, my hopes each day grew stronger that on my next visit I would surely get some indication that the leopard had died in the cave.

On the tenth morning, when I returned from my visit to the cave where I had found the netting undisturbed Ibbotson greeted me with the news that a woman had been killed the previous night in a village five miles away and about a mile above the Rudraprayag-Badrinath pilgrim road.

Quite evidently cyanide was not the right poison for an animal that had the reputation of thriving on and being stimulated by arsenic and strychnine. That the leopard had eaten the cyanide there could be no doubt whatever, nor was there any doubt that he had entered the cave, for his hairs were adhering to the rock where his back had come in contact with it when entering the cave.

An overdose might account for the poison not having had the desired effect and a second opening somewhere farther up the hill might account for his escape from the cave. Even so, it was no longer any matter of surprise to me, who had only been acquainted with the leopard for a few short months that the people of Garhwal, who had lived in close and intimate association with him for eight long years, should credit him animal or spirit with supernatural powers and that they should cling to the belief that nothing, but fire would rid them of this evil spirit.

TOUCH AND GO

News that is of importance to every individual travels fast, and during the past ten days everyone in Garhwal had heard of the poisoning of the man-eater and of our hope that we had sealed it up in a cave. It was natural therefore for risks to have been taken, and quite evidently the leopard, having recovered from the effects of the poison and found a way out of the cave, had found the first person who was taking a risk.

We had the day before us, for I had returned early from my visit to the cave, and after breakfast, mounted on Ibbotson's surefooted horses and carrying our rifles, we set out for the village where the woman was reported to have been killed.

After a fast ride up the pilgrim road, we took a track that went diagonally across the hill, and a mile along this track, where the path from the village joined it, there were signs of a struggle and a big pool of blood.

The Headman and relatives of the victim were waiting for us at the village, and they showed us where the leopard had seized the woman as she was in the act of closing the door of her house behind her. From this point the leopard had dragged the woman along on her back for a hundred yards to the junction of the tracks, where he had released his hold, and after a violent struggle had killed her. The people in the village had heard the woman's screams as she was being dragged along the ground and as she was struggling for her life with the leopard but had been too frightened to render any help.

When the woman was dead, the leopard had picked her up and carried her over some waste land, across an open ravine a hundred yards wide, and up the hill on the far side for another two hundred yards. There were no drag marks, but the blood trail was easy to follow, and it led us to a flat bit of ground, four feet wide and twenty feet long. On the upper side of this narrow strip of ground there was a perpendicular bank eight feet high with a stunted medlar-tree growing on it and on the lower side of the narrow strip the hill fell steeply away and growing on it was a wild rosebush, which had reached up and smothered the medlar-tree. Lying huddled up between the steep bank and the rosebush, with her head against the bank, with every vestige of clothing stripped from her and with her naked body flecked with white rose-petals that had fallen from above was the kill was an old grey-haired lady, seventy years of age.

For this pitiful kill the leopard would have to pay with his life, and after a short council of war, Ibbotson, leading the spare horse, returned to Rudraprayag for the things we needed, while I set off with my rifle to see whether it was possible to make contact with the man-eater in daylight.

This part of the country was new to me, and the first thing to do was to reconnoiter the ground. I had already noted while at the village that the hill went steeply up from the ravine to a height of four to five thousand feet; that about two thousand feet of the top of the hill was clothed with dense oak and pine forest, below which was an open stretch of short grass about half a mile wide and that below the grass was scrub jungle.

Keeping now to the edge of the grass and scrub jungle I went round the shoulder of the hill and found in front of me a wide depression, extending for half a mile down to the pilgrim road and evidently caused in the days of long ago by a landslide. Beyond this depression, which was about a hundred yards wide at the upper end and about three hundred yards wide where it met the road, the ground was open. The ground in the depression was damp and growing on this damp ground were a number of big trees, and under the tree a dense growth of scrub jungle. At the upper end of the depression was a cliff of overhanging rock, varying in height from twenty to forty feet, and about a hundred yards long; halfway along the cliff was a deep cleft a few feet wide, down which a tiny stream was trickling. Above the rocks was a narrow belt of scrub jungle, and above that again, open grassland.

I had reconnoitered the ground with care, for I did not want the leopard which I was convinced was lying up in the depression to be aware of my presence before it suited me. It was now necessary to find approximately where the leopard was most likely to be lying up, and to gain this information I went back to the kill.

We had been told in the village that it had got light shortly after the woman had been killed, and as it must have taken the leopard some little time to affect the kill, carry his victim four hundred yards, and eat a portion of it, it was reasonable to assume that he had left the spot where he had hidden the kill when day was fully established.

The hill on which the kill was lying was in full view of the village, in which at this hour there must had been considerable movement, the leopard therefore on leaving the kill would very naturally have kept covering as far as was possible and working on this assumption and also because the ground was too hard to show pugmarks, I set out to follow him along the line I assumed he had taken.

When I 'had covered half a mile and was out of view of the village and was approaching the depression, I was gratified to find that I had followed on the leopard's tracks foot by foot for in the lee of a bush where there was some loose earth, I found where he had been lying for several hours. His pugmarks when leaving this spot showed that he had entered the depression about fifty yards below the cliff of rock.

For half an hour I lay where the leopard had lain, watching the small area of tree and scrub jungle in front of me in the hope that the leopard would make some slight movement and give away his position.

After I had been watching for a few minutes a movement among the dead leaves attracted my attention, and presently two scimitar babblers came into view industriously turning over the leaves, looking for grubs. Where carnivores are concerned, these birds are among the most reliable informants in the jungle, and I hoped later to make use of this pair to help in locating the leopard.

No movement had been visible, and no sound had come to indicate that the leopard was in the depression; but that he was there I was still convinced and having failed to get a shot in one way I decided to try another way.

Without coming out into the open, there were two natural lines of retreat for the leopard, one down the hill towards the pilgrim road, and the other up the hill. To move him down the hill would not profit me, but if I moved him up the hill, he would for a certainty go up the cleft in the rock cliff to gain the shelter of the bushes above the cliff, and while he was doing so, there was a reasonable chance of my getting a shot.

Entering the depression, a little below where I thought the leopard was, I started to zigzag very slowly across it, gaining a few feet in height at each turn. There was as yet no need for me to keep an eye on the cleft, for the babblers were on the ground a few feet below it, and they would let me know when the leopard was on the move. I had gained about forty yards in height in my movements forward and backwards across the depression and was about ten yards from, and a little to the left of the cleft, when the babblers rose in alarm and, flying into a small oak tree and hopping about excitedly on the branches, started to give their clear and ringing alarm call, which can in the hills be heard for a distance of half a mile. Holding the rifle ready to take a snapshot, I stood perfectly still for a minute, and then started slowly moving forward.

The ground here was wet and slippery and, with my eyes fixed on the cleft, I had only taken two steps when my rubber-soled shoes slipped on,' the wet surface and while I was endeavouring to regain my balance, the leopard sprang up the cleft and, in the bushes, above put up a covey of *kalege* pheasants, which came sailing down over my head.

My second attempt had failed, and though it would have been quite easy for me to have moved the leopard back to where he had started from, it would have been of no use for me to do so, for, from above, the cleft in the rock was not visible until one was right up to it, and long before I gained the position the leopard would have been far down the depression.

Ibbotson and I had arranged to meet in the open ravine at 2 p.m., and a little before that hour he returned from Rudraprayag, accompanied by several men carrying the things he had gone to fetch. These consisted of food, and drink in the way of tea, our old friend the petromax lamp which on this occasion I decided I would carry myself, if the necessity arose two spare rifles and ammunition, my fishing-reel, a liberal supply of cyanide, and the gin-trap.

Sitting in the ravine by a clear stream of water, we had our lunch and brewed ourselves cups of tea, and then went over to the kill.

I will give a description of the position of the kill, to enable you to follow our movements and the subsequent happenings.

The kill was lying about five feet from the near or ravine end of the flat strip of ground, which was four feet wide and about twenty feet long. The upper side of this strip of ground was protected by a high bank, and the lower side by a steep drop and a spreading rosebush. The stunted medlar tree on the bank was too small to allow a *machan* to be made in it, so we decided to depend entirely on a gun-trap, poison, and the gin-trap; having come to this decision we set about our preparations.

First we poisoned the kill, of which the leopard had for want of time only eaten a small portion; hoping that on this occasion he would only consume sufficient to poison himself effectively, '(hen, while I bent over the kill in the position we anticipated the leopard would assume when eating, Ibbotson sighted and securely lashed his .256 Mannlicher, which had a hair trigger and my .450 high-velocity rifle to two saplings, fifteen yards on our approach side of the kill.

There were no insuperable obstacles to the leopard getting at the kill from any side he might wish to, but his most natural line of approach from where I had left him was along the fifteen feet or so of flat ground, and on this strip of flat ground we proceeded to bury the huge gin-trap, first removing from the ground every dead leaf, bit of stick and blade of grass that were lying on it.

After we had dug a hole sufficiently long, wide, and deep removing the displaced earth to a distance, we put the gin-trap in it and when the powerful springs that closed the jaws had been depressed and the plate that constituted the trigger adjusted as delicately as we dared set it, we covered the whole trap with a layer of green leaves, over which we sprinkled earth, and blades of grass in the position we had found them. So tearfully had the trap been set in the ground that we who had set it found it difficult to determine its exact position.

My fishing-reel was now produced, and one end of the dressed silk line was tied to the trigger of one rifle, looped round the butt-end, and taken to within ten feet of the kill, from where it was taken back, looped round the butt end of the second rifle and tied to the trigger. The line was then cut, much to my regret, for it was a new and very good line and after the end had been tied round the woman's waist, the line was passed through the loop, the lines to the triggers pulled taut and a secure knot was tied. The line was then cut for the second time.

As we cast a final look over our handiwork which appeared to us very good, it struck us that if the leopard was to wander round and approach the kill from our side and not from the side we expected him to come, he might avoid both the guns and the gin-trap, and to prevent his doing so we sent to the village for a crowbar, while we cut five thornbushes from some little distance away. With the crowbar we made five holes a foot deep, on our side of the flat strip of ground and into these holes we planted the bushes, stamping the earth round them and making them almost as secure and quite as natural to look at as when they were growing on the hillside. We were now quite satisfied that no animal bigger than a rat could approach the kill and eat any portion of it without meeting death in one form or another, so throwing off the safety catches of the rifles, we returned to the village.

Fifty yards from the village, and close to where we had on our arrival found the pool of blood, there was a big wide-spreading mango tree. In this tree we made a *machan* from planks procured from the village, and on it we piled a lot of sweet-smelling rice straw for it was our intention to spend the night on it in anticipation of having to finish off the leopard if he was caught in the gin-trap.

Near sundown we took our position on the *machan*, which was long enough for us to lie on at length and wide enough for us to lie side by side. The distance from the *machan* to the kill across the ravine was two hundred yards, and the kill was on a higher level than the *machan* by about a hundred (eef.

Ibbotson feared that his aim with the telescopic sight fitted to his rifle would not be quite accurate, so while he took a pair of powerful field glasses from their case, I loaded my .275 rifle. Our plan was that while Ibbotson concentrated on the portion of the hill along which we expected the leopard to come, I would keep a general look-out all over the hill, and if we saw the leopard, I would risk taking a shot, even if the shot had to be taken at the extreme range to which my rifle was sighted, which was three hundred yards.

While Ibbotson dozed, I smoked and watched the shadows cast by the hills in the west slowly creep up the hill in front of us and when the rays from the setting sun were gilding the crest of the hill red, Ibbotson awoke and picked up his field glasses, and I picked up my rifle, for the time had now come when we could expect the leopard to make his appearance. There was still some forty-five minutes of daylight left and during the time we intently scanned, I with a pair of eyes that few are blessed with and Ibbotson with his field glasses every foot of the considerable expanse of hill visible from our *machan*, without seeing the movement of a bird or animal.

When there was no longer sufficient light to shoot by, I put down my rifle and a little later Ibbotson returned his field glasses to their case. One chance of killing the leopard had gone but there were still three chances left, so we were not unduly depressed.

Shortly after dark it came on to rain, and I whispered to Ibbotson that I feared it would prove our undoing, for if the additional weight of rainwater on the delicately set gin-trap did not set it off, the contracting of the fishing-line due to getting wet, no matter how slight it might be, would to a certainty fire off his hair-trigger rifle. Sometime later and while it was still raining, Ibbotson asked me what time it was. I had a luminous wristwatch, and I had just told him it was a quarter to eight when a succession of savage and angry roars came from the direction of the kill, the leopard, the much-famed man-eating leopard of Rudraprayag, was at long last in the gin-trap.

Ibbotson took a flying leap from the *machan* while I swung down from a branch, and that neither of us broke limbs in the descent can only be attributed to luck. The petromax lamp hidden in a nearby yam field was found and while Ibbotson proceeded to light it, I gave expression to my fears and doubts and admit I deserved Ibbotson's rejoinder, 'You are a rotten pessimist. First you think a few drops of rain are going to spring the trap tid fire off my rifle and now you think because the leopard is not making a noise that it has got out of the trap.' That was just what I was thinking, and fearing, for on that other occasion when we had trapped a leopard it had roared and growled continuously, whereas this one, after that one expression of rage which had brought us tumbling out of the *machan*, had been ominously silent.

Ibbotson is an expert with all makes of lamps and in a very short time he had the petromax lit and pumped up and throwing our doubts to the winds for even Ibbotson was by now beginning to suspect the silence, we set off over the rough ground as hard as we could go, circling wide to avoid the fishing-lines and a possible angry leopard, and approached the loll from above. When we got to the high bank and looked down, we saw the hole in the ground, but no gin-trap. Just as our hopes were bounding up, the brilliant light of the petromax revealed the trap; with its jaws closed and empty, ten yards down the hillside. The loll was no longer lying with its head against the bank and a glance revealed that a considerable portion of it had been eaten.

Our thoughts were too bitter to give expression to as we went back to the mango tree and climbed into the *machan*. There was no longer any need for us to keep awake, so heaping some of the straw over ourselves, for we had no bedding, and the night was cold, we went to sleep.

At the first streak of dawn a fire was built near the mango tree and water heated, and after we had drunk several cups of tea and warmed ourselves at the fire, we set off for the kill, accompanied by the *patwari* and several of Ibbotsons and my men, together with a number of men from the village.

I mention the fact that there were two of us, and that we had the *patwari* and a number of men with us, for had I been alone I would have hesitated to relate what I am now going to tell you.

Fiend or animal had the slayer of the old woman been present and watched our overnight preparations it would even then have been difficult to understand how it had, on a dark and rainy night, avoided capture of death in one form or another. The rain, though light, had been sufficient to soften the ground, and we were able to reconstruct and to follow his every movement of the previous night.

The leopard had come from the direction from which we had expected him to come, and on arrival at the flat strip of ground, had skirted round and below it, and had then approached the kill from the side where we had firmly planted the thornbushes. Three of these bushes he had pulled up, making a sufficiently wide gap to go through, and then, getting hold of the kill, he had drawn it a foot or so towards the rifles, thus slackening off the fishing-lines. Having done this he had started to eat, avoiding while doing so contact with the fishing -line that was tied round the woman's body. We had not thought it necessary to poison either the head or the neck. These he had eaten first and then very carefully he had eaten all that portion of the body between the many doses of poison we had inserted in different places.

After satisfying his hunger the leopard left the kill with the intention of seeking shelter from the rain and, while he was doing so, what I feared would happen actually happened. The weight of rainwater on the very finely set trap had depressed the plate that constituted the trigger and released the springs just as the leopard was stepping over the trap, and the great jaws had met on either side of the stifle, or knee-joint, of his hind leg. And here was the greatest tragedy of all, for when bringing the trap up from Rudraprayag the men carrying it had let it fall and one of the three-inch-long teeth had been broken off and the stifle of the leopard's left hind leg had been caught by the jaws exactly where this missing tooth formed a gap in the otherwise perfectly fitting set of teeth. But for this missing tooth the leopard would have been fixed to the trap without any possibility of getting free, for the grip on his leg had been sufficiently good for him to lift the eighty-pound trap out of the hole in which we had buried it and carry it ten yards down the hillside. And now, instead of the leopard, the jaws of the trap only held a tuft of hair and a small piece of skin, which we later, much later had the great satisfaction of fitting back into position.

However unbelievable the actions of the leopard may appear to have been, they were in fact just what one would have expected from an animal that had been a man-eater for eight years. Avoiding the open ground and approaching the kill under cover; removing the thorn obstruction we had erected across the blood trail he had left that morning; pulling the kill towards him into a convenient position for his meal and rejecting those portions of the kill that we had poisoned cyanide of which he now had experience, has a very strong smell were all quite normal and natural actions.

The explanation I have given for the springing of the trap is, I am convinced, correct. It was just a coincidence that the leopard happened to be directly over the trap the very moment that the additional weight of water set it off.

Having dismantled the gin-trap and waited until the relatives had removed what remained of the old woman for cremation, we set out to walk back to Rudraprayag, leaving our men to follow us. Sometime during the night the leopard had come to the mango tree, for we found his pugmarks near the tree where the pool of blood, now washed away by the rain had been and we followed these pugmarks down the track to the pilgrim road and four miles along the road to the gate of the Inspection Bungalow where, after scratching up the ground at the base of one of the pillars of the gate, he had gone on down the road for another mile to where my old friend the packman was camped, one of whose goats he had wantonly killed.

I need not tell those of you who have carried a sporting rifle in any part of the world that all these many repeated failures and disappointments so far from discouraging me, only strengthened my determination to carry on until that great day or night came when, having discarded poisons and traps, I would get an opportunity of using my rifle as rifles were intended to be used, to put a bullet truly and accurately into the man-eater's body.

A LESSON IN CAUTION

I have never agreed with those sportsmen who attribute all their failures in big-game hunting to their being Jonah's.

The thoughts of a sportsman, whether they be pessimistic or whether they be optimistic, sitting waiting for an animal, cannot in any conceivable way influence the actions of the animal he is endeavouring to shoot or maybe to photograph.

We are apt to forget that the hearing and sight of wild animals and especially of those animals that depend exclusively on these senses not only for food but also for self-preservation are on a plane far and away above that of civilized human beings and that there is no justification for us to assume that because we cannot hear or see the movements of our prospective quarry, our quarry cannot hear or see our movements. A wrong estimation of the intelligence of animals, and the inability to sit without making any sound or movement for the required length of time, is the cause of all failures when sitting up for animals. As an example of the acute sense of hearing of carnivores and the care it is necessary to exercise when contact with one of them is desired, I will relate one of my recent experiences.

On a day in March, when the carpet of dry leaves on the ground recorded the falling of every dead leaf and the movements of the smallest of the birds that feed on the ground, I located in some very heavy undergrowth the exact position of a tiger I had long wished to photograph, by moving a troop of *langurs* in the direction in which I suspected the tiger to be lying up. Seventy yards from the tiger there was an open glade, fifty yards long and thirty yards wide. On the edge of the glade, away from the tiger, there was a big tree overgrown with creepers that extended right up to the topmost branches; twenty feet from the ground the tree forked in two. I knew that the tiger would cross the glade in the late afternoon, for the glade lay directly between him and his sambhar kill which I had found early that morning. There was no suitable cover near the kill for the tiger to lie up in during the day, so he had gone to the heavy undergrowth where the langurs had *located* him for me.

It is often necessary, when shooting or photographing tigers and leopards on foot, to know the exact position of one's quarry, whether it be a wounded animal that one desires to put out of its misery or an animal that one wants to photograph, and the best way of doing this is by enlisting the help of birds or animals. With patience, and with a knowledge of the habit of the bird or animal the sportsman desires to use, it is not difficult to get a particular bird or animal to go in the required direction. The birds most suitable for this purpose are red jungle-fowl, peafowl, and white-capped babblers and of animals the most suitable are *kakars* and *langurs*.

The tiger I am telling you about was unwounded and it would have been quite easy for me to go into the undergrowth and find him myself, but in doing so I should have disturbed him and defeated my own purposes, whereas by using the troop of *langurs* and knowing what their reactions would be on sighting the tiger, if he happened to be in the undergrowth I was able to get the information I wanted without disturbing the tiger.

Very carefully I stalked the tree I have referred to and avoiding contact with the creepers, the upper tendrils, and leaves of which might have been visible from where the tiger was lying, I climbed to the fork, where I had a comfortable seat and perfect concealment. Getting out my 16-mm cinecamera, I made an opening in the screen of leaves in front of me just big enough to photograph through and having accomplished all this without having made a sound, I sat still. My field of vision was confined to the glade and to the jungle immediately beyond it.

After I had been sitting for an hour, a pair of bronzewing doves rose out of the jungle and went skimming over the low brushwood and a minute or two later, and a little closer to me, a small flight of upland pipits rose off the ground and, after daintily tripping along the branches of a leafless tree, rose above the tree-tops and went off. Neither of these two species of birds has any alarm call, but I knew from their behaviour that the tiger was afoot and that they had been disturbed by him. Minutes later I was slowly turning my eyes from left to right scanning every foot of ground visible to me, when my eyes came to rest on a small white object, possibly an inch or two squares, immediately in front of me and about ten feet from the edge of the glade. Focusing my eyes on this stationary object for a little while, I then continued to scan the bushes to the limit of my field of vision to the right and then back again to the white object.

I was now convinced that this object had not been where it was for more than a minute or two before I had first caught sight of it, and that it could not be anything other than a white mark on the tiger's face. Quite evidently the tiger had heard me when I was approaching or climbing the tree, though I had done this in thin rubber shoes without making as far as I was aware any sound, and when the time had come for him to go to his kill he had stalked, for a distance of seventy yards over dry leaves, the spot he had pin-pointed, as the source of some suspicious sound. After lying for half an hour without making any movement, he stood up, stretched himself, yawned and satisfied that he had nothing to fear, walked out into the glade. Here he stood, turning his headfirst to the right and then to the left, and then crossed the glade, passing right under my tree on his way to his kill.

When in my wanderings through the jungles I see the *machan* that have been put up for the purpose of shooting carnivores, and note the saplings that have been felled nearby to make the platform, the branches that have been cut to give a clear view, and see the litter and debris left lying about, and consider the talking and noise that must have accompanied these operations, I am not surprised when I hear people say they have sat up hundreds of times for tigers and leopards without ever having seen one of these animals and attribute their failures to their being Jonah's.

Our failure to bag the man-eater up to that date was not due to our having done anything we should not have done or left undone anything we should have done. It could only be attributed to sheer bad luck. Bad luck that had prevented my receiving the electric light in time; that had given Ibbotson cramps in both legs; that had made the leopard eat an overdose of cyanide; and, finally, that had made the men drop the gin-trap and break the one tooth that mattered. So, when Ibbotson returned to Pauri after our failure to kill the leopard over the body of his seventy-year-old victim, I was full of hope for I considered my chances of shooting the leopard as good as they were on the first day I arrived at Rudraprayag, and in fact better than they had then been, for I now knew the capabilities of the animal I had to deal with.

One thing was causing me a lot of uneasiness and much heart searching, and that was confining the man-eater to one bank of the river. However, I looked at it, it did not appear to be right that the people on the left bank of the Alaknanda should be exposed to attacks by the leopard, while the people on the right bank were free from the risk of such attacks. Including the boy killed two days before our arrival, three people had recently lost their lives on the left bank and others might meet with a like fate and yet to open the two bridges and let the leopard cross over to the right bank would add an hundredfold to my difficulties, which were already considerable, and would not benefit Garhwal as a whole, for the lives of the people on the right bank of the river were just as valuable as the lives of the people on the left bank; so, very reluctantly, I decided to keep the bridges closed. And here I should like to pay my tribute to the people numbering many thousands living on the left bank of the river who, knowing that the closing of the bridges was confining the activities of the dread man-eater to their area, never once, during the months f. closed the bridges, removed the barriers themselves, or asked me to do so.

Having decided to keep the bridges closed, I sent a man to warn the villagers of their danger and myself carried the warning to as many villages as time and my ability to walk permitted of my doing. No one whom I talked with on the roads and in the villages ever expressed one word of resentment at the leopard having been confined to their area and everywhere I went I was offered hospitality and speeded on my way with blessings and I was greatly encouraged by the assurances from both men and women, who did not know but what they might be the man-eater's next victim that it was no matter for regret that the leopard had not died yesterday, for surely it would die today or, maybe tomorrow.

A WILD BOAR HUNT

The old packman had arrived at the thorn enclosure late the previous evening. He was packing salt and gur from the bazaar at Hardwar to the villages beyond Badrinath and as his flock of sheep and goats was heavily laden and the last march had been a long one, he had arrived too late at the thorn enclosure to repair the weak places in it, with the result that several of the goats had strayed out of the enclosure and one of them the leopard had killed, close to the road, during the early hours of the morning. The barking of his dogs had awakened him, and when it got light, he saw his best goat, a beautiful steel-grey animal nearly as large as a Shetland pony lying dead near the road, want only killed by the man-eater.

The behaviour of the man-eater during the previous night showed the extent to which the habits of a leopard change when it has become a man-eater and has lived in close association with human beings over a long period of years.

It was reasonable to assume that the man-eater had received a great shock, and a great fright by being caught in the gin-trap; his having carried the heavy trap for ten yards and the angry way in which he had roared were in fact proof of this and one would have expected him, the moment he got out of the trap, to have retired to some secluded spot as far removed from human habitation as possible and to have remained there until he was again hungry, which he would not be for several days. But, so far from doing this, he had quite evidently remained in the vicinity of the kill, and after watching us climb into the *machan* and giving us time to go to sleep, had come to investigate; fortunately for us, Ibbotson had taken the precaution to protect the machan by putting wire-netting all round it, for it is not an unheard-of thing for man-eating leopards to kill people who are sitting up trying to shoot them. At the present time there is a man-eating leopard in the Central Provinces that has at different times killed and eaten four Indian sportsmen who were trying to shoot him up to the time I last heard of this animal he had killed forty human beings and owing to his habit of eating his would-be slayers, he was living a very peaceful and undisturbed life, varying his human diet with game and domestic animals.

After his visit to the mango tree, our man-eater went along the village path to it junction with the track. Here, where we had found the pool of blood, he had turned to the right and gone down the track for a mile, and then along the pilgrim road for another four miles and into the most densely populated part of the area in which he was operating. On arrival at Rudraprayag, he had gone through the main street of the bazaar, and half a mile farther on had scratched up the ground at the gate of the Inspection Bungalow. The rain of the previous night had softened the clay surface of the road, and on the soft clay the pugmarks of the leopard showed up clearly and from them it was possible to see that the leopard's encounter with the gin-trap had not resulted in injury to any of his limbs.

After breakfast I took up the tracks at the gate and followed them to the packman's camp. From a bend in the road, a hundred yards from the camp, the leopard had caught sight of the goats that had strayed from the enclosure and crossing from the outer to the inner edge of the road and creeping along under shelter of the hill he had stalked the grazing animals and, after killing the steel-grey goat but without even troubling to drink its blood, had returned to the road.

In the thorn enclosure, guarding the dead goat and the neatly stacked pile of packs, were the packman's two sheepdogs, tethered to stout pegs with short lengths of heavy chain. These big, black, and powerful dogs that are used by packmen throughout our hills are not accredited sheepdogs in the same sense that sheepdogs in Great Britain and in Europe are. On the march the dogs keep close to heel, and their duties which they perform very efficiently, start when camp is made. At night they guard the camp against wild animals, I have known two of them to kill a leopard and during the day and while the packmen are away grazing the flock, they guard the camp against all intruders. A case is on record of one of these dogs having killed a man who was attempting to remove a pack from the camp it had been left to guard.

I picked up the tracks of the leopard where he returned to the road after killing the goat and followed them through Golabrai and for a mile farther on, to where a deep ravine crosses the road, up which he had gone. The distance the leopard had covered from the mango tree to the ravine was about eight miles. This long and seemingly aimless walk away from a kill was in itself a thing no ordinary leopard would under any circumstances have undertaken, nor would an ordinary leopard have killed a goat when he was not hungry.

A quarter of a mile beyond the ravine the old packman was sitting on a rock by the side of the road, spinning wool and watching his flock, which Vere grazing on the open hillside. When he had dropped his spinning-stick and wool into the capacious pocket in his blanket robe and accepted a cigarette, he asked if I had come past his camp. When I told him I had done so and that I had seen what the evil spirit had done and added that it would be wise to sell his dogs to camel men on his next visit to Hardwar, for it was quite evident that they were lacking in courage, he nodded his head as one in agreement with what he heard. Then he said, '*Sahib*, even we old hands are apt at times to make mistakes, and suffer for them, even as I have this night suffered by losing my best goat. My dogs have the courage of tigers and are the best dogs in all Garhwal and it is an insult to them for you to say they are only fit to be sold to camel men. My camp as you doubtless observed, is very close to the road and I feared that if by chance anyone came along the road by night, my dogs might do him an injury, so I chained them up outside the thorn enclosure instead of leaving them loose, as is my wont. You have seen the result; but do not blame the dogs, *sahib*, for in their efforts to save my goat their collars have bitten deep into their necks and made wounds that will take many days to heal.'

While we were talking, an animal appeared on the crest of the hill on the far side of the Ganges. From its colour and size, I at first thought it was a Himalayan bear, but when it started to come down the hill towards the river, I saw it was a big wild boar. The pig was followed by a pack of village pye dogs, who in turn were followed by a rabble of boys and men, all armed with sticks of varying size. Last of all came a man carrying a gun. As this man crested the hill, he raised his piece and we saw a puff of smoke, and a little later heard the dull report of a muzzle-loading gun. The only living things within range of the gun were the boys and men but as none of them dropped out of the race, the sportsman appeared to have missed them.

The pig had a long grassy slope before him, with an odd bush dotted here and there, and below the grass slope was some broken ground, and below that again a dense belt of brushwood which extended right down to the river.

On the rough broken ground, the pig lost his lead, and pig and pye dogs disappeared into the brushwood together. Next minute all the dogs, with the exception of the big light-coloured animal that had been leading the pack, dashed back out of the brushwood. When the boys and men arrived, they appeared to urge the dogs to re-enter the cover, but this after apparently having recently seen what the pig could do with his tusks, they were unwilling to do. The man with the gun then arrived and was immediately surrounded by the boys and men.

To us sitting on our elevated grandstand with the river flowing between, the scene being enacted on the farther hill was a silent picture, for the noise of the water deadened sound and all we had heard was the dull report of the muzzle-loader.

The sportsman was apparently as reluctant to enter the cover as the dogs were, for presently he broke away from his companions and sat down on a rock, as if to say, 'I have done my bit, now you do yours.' Confronted with this double dilemma for the dogs, even after some of them had been beaten, stoutly refused to face the pig, first the boys and then the men started to throw stones into the brushwood.

While this was going on, we saw the pig emerge from the lower end of the brushwood on to a narrow strip of sand. With a few quick steps he came out into the open, stood perfectly still for a few seconds, took a few more steps, stopped again, and then with a little run plunged into the river. Pigs the wild variety are exceptionally good swimmers, and they do not cut their throats with their hooves while swimming, as is generally believed.

The current in the river was strong, but there is no bigger hearted animal than our wild pig, and when I last saw the old boar, he had been washed down the river a quarter of a mile but was swimming strongly and was nearing our bank, which I have no doubt he reached safely.

'Was the pig within range of your rifle, *sahib* asked the packman.

'Yes,' I replied, 'the pig was within range, but I have not brought a rifle to Garhwal to shoot pigs that are running for their lives but to shoot what you think is an evil spirit, and what I know is a leopard.' 'Have it your own way,' he rejoined; 'and now, as you are going and we may never meet again, take my blessings with you and time will prove whether you or I am right.'

I regret I never saw the packman again, for he was a grand old man, as proud as Lucifer, and as happy as the day was long, when leopards were not killing his best goats and when the courage of his dogs was not being questioned.

VIGIL ON A PINE TREE

Ibbotson returned to Pauri next day and the following morning, when I was visiting the villages on the hill to the east of Rudraprayag, I found the tracks of the man-eater on a path leading out of a village in which the previous night he had tried to break open the door of a house in which there was a child suffering from a bad cough. On following the tracks for a couple of miles they led me to the shoulder of the mountain where, some days previously, Ibbotson and I had sat up over the calling goat which the leopard had later killed.

It was still quite early, and as there was a chance of finding the leopard basking on one of the rocks in this considerable area of broken ground, I lay on a projecting rock that commanded an extensive view. It had rained the previous evening thus enabling me to track the leopard and washed the haze out of the atmosphere. Visibility was at its best and the view from the projecting rock was as good as could be seen in any part of the world where mountains rise to a height of twenty-three thousand feet. Immediately below me was the beautiful valley of the Alaknanda, with the river showing as a gleaming silver ribbon winding in and out of it. On the hill beyond the river, villages were dotted about, some with only a single thatched hut and others with long rows of slate-roofed houses. These row buildings are in fact individual homesteads, built one against the other to save expense and to economize space for the people are poor and every foot of workable land in Garhwal is needed for agriculture.

Beyond the hills were rugged rock cliffs, down which avalanches roar in winter and early spring, and beyond and above the cliffs were the eternal snows, showing up against the intense blue sky as clear as if cut out of white cardboard. No more beautiful or peaceful scene could be imagined, and yet when the sun, now shining on the back of my head, set on the far side of the snow mountains, terror, terror which it is not possible to imagine until experienced would grip, as it had done for eight long years, the area I was now overlooking.

I had been lying on the rock for an hour when two men came down the hill, on their way to the bazaar. They were from a village about a mile farther up the hill that I had visited the previous day, and they informed me that a little before sunrise they had heard a leopard calling in this direction. We discussed the possibilities of my getting a shot at the leopard over a goat and as at that time I had no goats of my own, they offered to bring me one from their village and promised to meet me where we were standing, two hours before sunset.

When the men had gone, I looked round for a place where I could sit. The only tree on the whole of this part of the mountain was a solitary pine. It was growing on the ridge close to the path down which the men had come, and from under it a second path took off and ran across the face of the mountain skirting the upper edge of the broken ground, where I had recently been looking for the leopard. The tree commanded an extensive view, but it could be difficult to climb, and would afford little cover. However, as it was the only tree in the area, I had no choice, so I decided I would try it.

The men were waiting for me with a goat when I returned at about 4 p.m., and when, in reply to their question where I intended sitting, I pointed to the pine, they started laughing. Without a rope ladder, they said, it would not be possible to climb the tree and further, if I succeeded in climbing the tree without a ladder and carried out my intention of remaining out all night, I should have no protection against the man-eater, to whom the tree would offer no obstacle. There were two white men in Garhwal Ibbotson was one of them who had collected birds' eggs when boys, and both of whom could climb the tree and as there is no exact equivalent in Hindustani for 'waiting until you come to a bridge before crossing it', I let the second part of the men's objection go unanswered, contenting myself by pointing to my rifle.

The pine was not easy to climb, for there were no branches for twenty feet, but once having reached the lowest branch, the rest was easy. I had provided myself with a long length of cotton cord, and when the men had tied my rifle to one end of it, I drew it up and climbed to the top of the tree, where the pine-needles afforded most cover.

The men had assured me that the goat was a good caller, and after they tied it to an exposed root of the tree, they set off for their village promising to return early next morning. The goat watched the men out of sight, and then started to nibble the short grass at the foot of the tree. The fact that it had not up to then called once did not worry me, for I felt sure that it would presently feel lonely and that it would then do its share of the business of the evening and if it did it while it was still night, from my elevated position I should be able to kill the leopard long before it got anywhere near the goat.

When I climbed the tree, the shadows cast by the snow mountains had reached the Alaknanda. Slowly these shadows crept up the hill and passed me, until only the top of the mountain glowed with red light. As this glow faded, long streamers of light shot up from the snow mountains where the rays of the setting sun were caught and held on a bank of clouds as soft and as light as thistledown. Everyone who has eyes to see a sunset and the number, as you might have observed is regrettably few thinks that the sunsets in his particular part of the world are the best ever. I am no exception, for I too think that there are no sunsets in all the world to "compare with ours and a good second are the sunsets in northern Tanganyika, where some quality in the atmosphere makes snow-capped Kilimanjaro and the clouds that are invariably above it, glow like molten gold in the rays of the setting sun. Our sunsets in the Himalayas are mostly red, pink, or gold. The one I was looking at the evening from my seat on the pine tree was rose pink, and the white shafts of light, starting as spear-points from valleys in the cardboard snows, shot through the pink clouds and broadening, faded out in the sky overhead.

The goat, like many human beings, had no interest in sunsets, and after nibbling the grass within reach, scratched a shallow hole for itself, lay down, curled up, and went to sleep. Here was a dilemma. I had counted on the animal now placidly sleeping below me to call up the leopard, and not once since I had first seen it had it opened its mouth, except to nibble grass and now having made itself comfortable, it would probably sleep throughout the night. To have left the tree at that hour in an attempt to return to the bungalow would have added one more to the number who deliberately commit suicide, and as I had to be doing something to kill the man-eater, and as in the absence of a kill, one place was as good as another, I decided to stay where I was, and try to call up the leopard myself.

If I were asked what had contributed most to my pleasure during all the years that I have spent in Indian jungles, I would unhesitatingly say that I had derived most pleasure from a knowledge of the language and the habits of the jungle folk. There is no universal language in the jungles; each species has its own language, and though the vocabulary of some is limited, as in the case of porcupines and vultures, the language of each species is understood by all the jungle folk. The vocal cords of human beings are more adaptable than the vocal cords of any of the jungle folk, with the one exception of the crested wire-tailed drongo and for this reason it is possible for human beings to hold commune with quite a big range of birds and animals. The ability to speak the language of the jungle folk, apart from adding hundredfold to one's pleasure in the jungle, can, if so, desired be put to great use. One example will suffice.

Lionel Fortescue up till recently a housemaster at Eton and I were on a photographing and fishing tour in the Himalayas shortly after 1918 and we arrived one evening at a Forest Bungalow at the foot of a great mountain, on the far side of which was our objective, the Vale of Kashmir. We had been marching over hard ground for many days and as the men carrying our luggage needed a rest, we decided to halt for a day at the bungalow. Next day, while Fortescue wrote up his notes, I set out to explore the mountain and try for a Kashmir stag. I had been informed by friends who had shot in Kashmir that it was not possible to shoot one of these stags without the help of an experienced *shikari* and this was confirmed by the *chowkidar* in charge of the Forest Bungalow. With the whole day before me I set out alone, after breakfast, without having the least idea at what elevation the red deer lived or the kind of ground on which they were likely to be found. The mountain, over which there is a pass into Kashmir, is about twelve thousand feet high and after I had climbed to a height of eight thousand a storm came on.

From the colour of the clouds I knew I was in for a hailstorm, so I selected with care a tree under which to shelter. I have seen both human beings and animals killed by hail and by the lightning that invariably accompanies hailstorms, so rejecting the big fir trees with tapering tops I selected a small tree with a rounded top and dense foliage and collecting a supply of dead wood and fir-cones, I built a fire and for the hour that the thunder roared overhead, and the hail lashed down, I sat at the foot of my tree safe and warm.

The moment the hail stopped the sun came out, and from the shelter of the tree I stepped into fairyland, for the hail that carpeted the ground gave off a million points of light to which every glistening leaf and blade of grass added its quota. Continuing up for another two or three thousand feet, I came on an outcrop of rock, at the foot of which was a bed of blue mountain poppies. The stalks of many of these, the most beautiful of all wildflowers in the Himalayas, were broken, even so these sky-blue flowers standing in a bed of spotless white were a never to be forgotten sight.

The rocks were too slippery to climb and there appeared to be no object in going to the top of the hill, so keeping to the con tours I went to the left, and after half a mile through a forest of giant fir trees I came to a grassy slope which, starting from the top of the hill, extended several thousand feet down into the forest. As I came through the trees towards this grassy slope, I saw on the far side of it an animal standing on a little knoll, with its tail towards me. From illustrations seen in game books I knew the animal was a red Kashmir deer and when it raised its head, I saw it was a hind.

On my side of the grassy slope, and about thirty yards from the edge of the forest, there was a big, isolated rock some four feet high; the distance between this rock and the knoll was about forty yards. Moving only when the deer was cropping the grass, and remaining still each time she raised her head, I crept up to the shelter of the rock. The hind was quite obviously a sentinel and from the way she looked to her right each time she raised her head, I knew she had companions, and the exact direction in which these companions were. To approach any nearer over the grass without being seen was not possible. To re-enter the forest and work down from above would not have been difficult but would have defeated my purpose, for the wind was blowing down the hill. There remained the alternative of re-entering the forest and skirting round the lower end of the grass slope, but this would take time and entail a stiff climb. I therefore finally decided to remain where I was and see if these deer which I was seeing for the first time would react in the same way as chital and sambhar do to the call of a leopard, of which I knew there was at least one on the mountain, for I had seen its scratch-marks earlier in the day. With only one eye showing, I waited until the hind was cropping the grass and then gave the call of a leopard.

At the first sound of my voice the hind swung round and facing me, started to strike the ground with her forefeet. This was a warning to her companions to be on the alert but those companions whom I wanted to see would not move until the hind called and this she would not do until she saw the leopard. I was wearing a brown tweed coat and projecting a few inches of my left shoulder beyond the rock I moved it up and down. The movement was immediately detected by the hind, who, taking a few quick steps forward, started to call the danger she had warned her companions of was in sight and it was now safe for them to join her. The first to come was a yearling, which, stepping daintily over the hail-covered ground, ranged itself alongside the hind; the yearling was followed by three stags, who in turn were followed by an old hind. The entire herd, numbering six in all, were now in full view at a range of thirty-five yards. The hind was still calling, while the others, with ears alternately held rigid or feeling forward and backward for sound and wind direction, were standing perfectly still, and gazing into the forest behind me. My seat on trammeling hail was uncomfortable and wet and to remain inactive longer would possibly result in a cold. I had seen a representative herd of the much-famed Kashmir deer and I had heard a hind call, but there was one thing more that I wanted. That was, to hear a stag call so, I again projected a few inches of my shoulder beyond the rock and had the satisfaction of hearing the stags, the hinds and the yearling calling in different pitched keys.

My pass permitted me to shoot one stag, and for all I knew one of the stags might have carried a record head, but though I had set out that morning to look for a stag, and procure meat for the camp, I now realized that I was in no urgent need of a trophy. In any case the stag's meat would probably be tough so, instead of using the rifle, I stood up, and six of the most surprised deer in Kashmir vanished out of sight, and a moment later I heard them crashing through the undergrowth on the far side of the knoll.

It was now time for me to retrace my steps to the bungalow and I decided to go down the grassy slope and work through the lighter forest at the foot of the mountain. The slope was at an angle that lent itself to an easy lope, provided care was taken to see that every step was correctly placed. I was running in the middle of the hundred-yard open ground and had gone about six hundred yards when I caught sight of a white object, standing on a rock at the edge of the forest on the left-hand side of the slope, and about three hundred yards below me. A hurried glance convinced me that the white object was a goat, that had probably been lost in the forest. We had been without meat for a fortnight, and I had promised Fortescue that I would bring something back with me, and there was my opportunity. The goat had seen me and if I could disarm suspicion would possibly let me pass close enough to catch it by the legs so as I loped along, I edged to the left, keeping the animal in sight out of the corner of my eyes. Provided the animal stayed where it was, no better place on all the mountains could have been found on which to catch it, for the flat rock, at the very edge of which it was standing, jutted out into the slope and was about five feet high. Without looking directly at it and keeping up a steady pace, I ran past the rock and, as I did so, made a sweep with my left hand for its forelegs. With a sneeze of alarm, the animal reared up, avoiding my grasp, and when I pulled up clear of the rock and turned round, I saw to my amazement that the animal I had mistaken for a white goat was an albino musk- deer. With only some ten feet between us the game little animal was standing its ground and sneezing defiance at me. Turning away I walked down the hill for fifty yards, and when I looked back, the deer was still standing on the rock, possibly congratulating itself on having frightened me away. When some weeks later I related the occurrence to the Game Warden of Kashmir he expressed great regret at my not having shot the deer and was very anxious to know the exact locality in which I had seen it, but as my memory for places, and my description of localities is regrettably faulty, I do not think that particular albino musk-deer is gracing any museum.

Male leopards are very resentful of intrusion of others of their kind in the area they consider to be their own. True, the man-eater's territory extended over an area of five hundred square miles in which there were possibly many other male leopards; still, he had been in this particular area for several weeks and might very reasonably consider it his own. And again, the mating season was only just over, and the leopard might mistake my call for the call of a female in search of a mate, so waiting until it was quite dark, I called and to my surprise and delight, was immediately answered by a leopard some four hundred yards below and a little to the right.

The ground between us was strewn with great rocks and overgrown with matted thornbushes and I knew the leopard would not come in a straight line towards me, and that he would probably skirt round the broken ground and come up a subsidiary ridge to the one my tree was on; this I found, when next he called, that he was doing. Five minutes later, I located his call as coming from the path that, starting from my tree, ran across the face of the hill, about two hundred yards away. This call I answered, to give the leopard direction. Three, or it may have been four, minutes later, he called again from a distance of a hundred yards.

It was a dark night, and I had an electric torch lashed to the side of my rifle, and my thumb on the push button. From the root of the tree the path ran in a straight line for fifty yards to where there was a sharp bend in it. It would not be possible for me to know when or where to direct the beam of the torch on this part of the path, so I should have to wait until the leopard was on the goat.

Just beyond the bend, and only sixty yards away, the leopard again called, and was answered by another leopard far up the mountainside. A complication as unexpected as it was unfortunate, for my leopard was too close now for me to call, and as he had last heard me from a distance of two hundred yards, he would naturally assume that the coy female had / removed herself farther up the hill and was calling to him to join her there. There was, however, just a possibility of his continuing along the path to its junction with the path coming down the hill, in which case he would be sure to kill the goat, even if he had no use for it. But the goat's luck was in and mine out for the leopard cut across the angle formed by the two paths and the next time he called he was a hundred yards farther from me and a hundred yards nearer his prospective coaxing mate. The calling of the two leopards drew nearer and nearer together, and finally stopped. After a long period of silence, the caterwauling of these two giant cats came floating down to me from where I judged the grassland ended and the dense forest began.

The leopard's luck was unfortunately in, in more ways than one, not least of all because it was dark, for leopards when courting are very easy to shoot. The same can be said of tigers, but the sportsman who goes on foot to look for courting tigers should be quite sure that he wants to see them, for a tigress never a tiger is very sensitive at these times and quite understandably so, for males of the cat tribe are rough in their courting and do not know how sharp their claws are.

The leopard had not died, nor would he die that night, but maybe he would die the next day, or the day after, for his sands were running out and so for a long moment I thought were mine for without any warning a sudden blast of wind struck the tree, and my heels and my head changed their relative position with the land of Garhwal. For seconds I thought it impossible for the tree to regain its upright position, or for me to retain contact with it. When the pressure eased, the tree and I got back to where we were before the wind struck us, and fearing that worse might follow, I hurriedly tied the rifle to a branch, to have the use of both hands. The pine had possibly withstood many windstorms equally bad, if not worse, but never with a human being on it to add weight and increase wind-pressure. When the rifle was safe, I climbed out on to one branch after another and broke off all the tassels of pine-needles that I could reach. It may only have been my imagination but after I had lightened the tree, it did not appear to heel over as dangerously as it had at first done. Fortunately, the pine was comparatively young and supple, and its roots firm set, for it was tossed about like a blade of grass for an hour and then, as suddenly as it had started, the wind died down. There was no possibility of the leopard returning so after I had smoked a cigarette, I followed the goat into the land of dreams.

As the sun was rising a cooee brought me back to within fifty feet of earth, and under the tree were my two companions of the previous evening, reinforced by two youths from their village. When they saw that I was awake they asked whether I had heard the leopards during the night, and what had happened to the tree, and were hugely amused when I told them I had had a friendly conversation with the leopards, and that having nothing else to do I had amused myself by breaking the branches of the tree. I then asked them if by chance they had noticed that there had been some, little wind during the night, on which one of the youths answered, 'A little wind, *sahib*! Such a big wind has never been known and it has blown away my hut!' To which his companion rejoined, 'That is no matter for regret, *sahib*, for Sher Singh has long been threatening to rebuild his hut and the wind has saved him the trouble of dismantling the old one.'

MY NIGHT OF TERROR

For several days after my experience on the pine tree I lost touch with the man-eater. He did not return to the broken ground, and I found no trace of him, or of the female who had saved his life, in the miles of forest. I searched on the high ground above the cultivated land. In these forests I was more at home and if the leopards had been anywhere in them, I should have been able to find them, for there were birds and animals in the forest that would have helped me.

The female, being restless, was quite evidently straying far from her home when she heard me call from the top of the pine tree, and on being joined by the male had gone back to her own area, accompanied by the mate I had helped her to find. The male would presently return alone and as the precautions now being taken by the people on the left bank were making it difficult for him to procure a human kill, he would probably try to cross over to the right bank of the Alaknanda, so for the next few nights I mounted guard on the Rudraprayag bridge.

Of the approaches to the bridge on the left bank, the one from the south passed close to the bridge *chowkidar's* house, and on the fourth night I heard the leopard killing the *chowkidar's* dog; a friendly nondescript little beast that used to run out and greet me every time I passed that way. The dog seldom barked, but that night it had been barking for five minutes when suddenly the bark ended in a yelp, followed by the shouting of the *chowkidar* from inside his house, after which there was silence. The thornbushes had been removed from the archway and the bridge was open, yet though I lay with finger on trigger for the rest of the night the leopard did not try to cross.

After killing the dog and leaving it lying on the road, the leopard, as I found from his tracks next morning, came to the tower. Five more steps in the direction in which he was going would have brought him out on the bridge but those five steps he did not take. Instead, he turned to the right and after going a short distance up the footpath towards the bazaar, he returned and went up the pilgrim road to the north. A mile up the road I lost his tracks.

Two days later I received a report that a cow had been killed the previous evening, seven miles up the pilgrim road. It was suspected that the cow had been killed by the man-eater, for the previous night, the night the dog had been killed, the leopard had tried to break open the door of a house close to where, the next evening, the cow had been killed.

On the road I found a number of men waiting for me who, knowing that the walk up from Rudraprayag would be a hot one, had very thoughtfully provided a dish of tea. While we sat in the shade of a mango-tree and smoked and I drank the dish of tea, they told me that the cow had not returned with the herd the previous evening, and that it had been found between the road and the river when a search had been made for it that morning. They also told me of the many hairbreadth escapes each of them had had from the man-eater during the past eight years. I was very interested to learn from them that the leopard had only adopted his present habit of trying and in many cases succeeding to break open the doors of houses three years previously and that before he had been content to take people who were outside their houses, or from houses the doors of which had been left open. 'Now,' they said, 'the shaitan has become so bold that sometimes when he has not been able to break down the door of a house, he has dug a hole through the mud wall, and got at his victims in the way.'

To those who do not know our hill-people, or understand their fear of the supernatural, it will seem incredible that a people renowned for their courage and who have won the highest awards on the field of battle, should permit a leopard to break open a door or to dig a hole in a wall of a house, in which in many cases there must have been men with axes, *kukris*, or, even in some cases, firearms at hand. I know of only one case in all those eight long years in which resistance was offered to the man-eater, and in that case the resister was a woman. She was sleeping alone in a house, the door of which she had left unfastened; this door, as in the case of the door of the house occupied by the woman who escaped with a lacerated arm, opened inwards. On entering the room, the leopard seized the woman's left leg, and as it dragged her across the room, the woman's hand came in contact with a *gandesa*, a tool used for chopping chaff for cattle and with this the woman dealt the leopard a blow. The leopard did not release his hold, but backed out of the room, and as it did so either the woman pushed the door or else this happened accidentally. Whichever it may have been, with the woman on one side of the door and the leopard on the other, the leopard exerted its great strength and tore the limb from the woman's body. Mukandi Lai, at that time Member for Garhwal in the United Provinces Legislative Council, who was on an electioneering tour, arrived in the village the following day and spent a night in the room but the leopard did not return. In a report to the Council, Mukandi Lai stated that seventy-five human beings had been killed by the leopard in the course of that one year and he asked the Government to launch a vigorous campaign against the man-eater.

Accompanied by one of the villagers to show me the way, and by Madho Singh, I went down to the kill. 'The cow had been killed in a deep ravine a quarter of a mile from the road and a hundred yards from the river. On one side of the ravine there were big rocks with dense brushwood between and on the other side of the ravine there were a few small trees, none of which was big enough to sit in. Under the trees, and about thirty yards from the kill, there was a rock with a little hollow at the base of it, so in the hollow I decided to sit.

Both Madho Singh and the villager objected very strongly to my sitting on the ground but as this was the first animal kill, I had got since my arrival at Rudraprayag in a place where it was reasonable to expect the leopard to come at an early hour about sundown, I overruled their objections and sent them back to the village.

My seat was dry and comfortable, and with my back to the rock and a small bush to conceal my legs I was confident the leopard would not see me, and that I should be able to kill it before it was aware of my presence. I had provided myself with a torch and a knife, and with my good rifle across my knees I felt that in this secluded spot my chances of killing the leopard were better than any I had yet had.

Without movement and with my eyes on the rocks in front of me I sat through the evening, each second bringing the time nearer when the undisturbed and unsuspecting leopard would for a certainty return to his kill. The time I had been waiting for had come and was passing. Objects near at hand were beginning to get blurred and indistinct. The leopard was a little later in coming than I had expected him to be, but that was not worrying me, for I had a torch, and the kill was only thirty yards from me, and I would be careful over my shot and make quite sure that I did not have a wounded animal to deal with.

In the deep ravine there was absolute silence. The hot sun of the past few days had made the dead leaves on the bank on which I was sitting as dry as tinder. This was very reassuring, for it was now dark and whereas previously I had depended on my eyes for protection I now had to depend on my ears and with thumb on the button of the torch and finger on trigger I was prepared to shoot in any direction in which I heard the slightest sound.

The non-appearance of the leopard was beginning to cause me uneasiness. Was it possible that from some concealed place among the rocks he had been watching me all these hours and was he now licking his lips in anticipation of burying his teeth in my throat? for he had long been deprived of human flesh. In no other way could I account for his not having come, and if I were to have the good fortune to leave the ravine on my feet, my ears would have to serve me now as they had never served me before.

For what seemed like hours I strained my ears and then, noticing it was getting darker than it should have been, I turned my eyes up to the sky and saw that a heavy bank of clouds was drifting across the sky, obscuring the stars one by one. Shortly thereafter big drops of rain started to fall, and where there had been absolute and complete silence there was now sound and movement all round, the opportunity the leopard had been waiting for had come. Hastily taking off my coat I wound it round my neck, fastening it securely in place with the sleeves. The rifle was now useless but might help to cause a diversion, so transferring it to my left hand I unsheathed my knife and got a good grip of it with my right hand. The knife was what is called an Afridi stabbing knife, and I devoutly hoped it would serve me as well as it had served its late owner, for when buying it from the Government store at Hangu on the North-west Frontier, the Deputy

Commissioner had drawn my attention to a label attached to it and to three notches on the handle and said it had figured in three murders. Admittedly a gruesome relic but I was glad to have it in my hand and I clutched it tight while the rain lashed down.

Leopards, that is ordinary forest leopards, do not like rain and invariably seek shelter, but the man-eater was not an ordinary leopard and there was no knowing what his likes or dislikes were, or what he might or might not do.

When Madho Singh was leaving he asked how long I intended sitting up, and I had answered, 'Until I have shot the leopard', so I could expect no help from him and of help I was at that time in urgent need. Should I go or should I remain were the questions that were troubling me, and one option was as unattractive as the other. If the leopard up to then had not seen me, it would be foolish to give my position away and possibly fall across him on the difficult ground I should have to negotiate on my way up to the pilgrim road. On the other hand, to remain where I was for another six hours momentarily expecting to have to fight for my life with an unfamiliar weapon would put a strain on my nerves which they were not capable of standing so getting to my feet and shouldering the rifle, I set off.

I had not far to go, only about five hundred yards, half of which was over wet clay and the other half over rocks worn smooth by bare feet and the hooves of cattle. Afraid to use the torch for fear of attracting the man-eater, and with one hand occupied with the rifle and the other with the knife, my body made as many contacts with the ground as my rubber-shod feet. When I eventually reached the road, I sent a full-throated cooee into the night and a moment later I saw a door in the village far up the hillside open and Madho Singh and his companion emerge, carrying a lantern.

When the two men joined me Madho Singh said he had had no uneasiness about me until the rain started, and that he had then lit the lantern, and sat with his ear against the door listening. Both men were willing to accompany me back to Rudraprayag, so we set out on our seven-mile walk, Bachi Singh leading, Madho Singh carrying the lantern following, and I bringing up the rear. When I returned next day, I found the kill had not been touched and, on the road, I found the tracks of the man-eater. What time had elapsed between our going down the road and the man-eater following us, it was not possible to say.

When I look back on that night, I look back on it as my night of terror. I have been frightened times without number, but never have I been frightened as I was that night when the unexpected rain came down and robbed me of all my defences and left me for protection a murderer's knife.

LEOPARD FIGHTS LEOPARD

After following us to Rudraprayag the leopard went down the pilgrim road through Golabrai, past the ravine up which he had gone a few days previously, and then up a rough track which the people living on the hills to the east of Rudraprayag use as a short cut on their way to and from Hardwar.

The pilgrimage to Kedarnath and Badrinath is seasonal, and the commencement of the pilgrimage and its duration depend in the one case on the melting and in the other on the falling of snow in the upper reaches of the high mountains in which these two shrines are situated. The High Priest of Badrinath temple had a few days previously sent the telegram that is eagerly awaited by good Hindus throughout the length and breadth of India, announcing that the road was open, and for the past few days pilgrims in small numbers had been passing through Rudraprayag.

During the past few years, the man-eater had killed several pilgrims on the road, and it appeared to be his more or less regular habit while the pilgrim season lasted to go down the road to the extent of his beat, and then circle round through the villages on the hills to the east of Rudraprayag and rejoin the road anything up to fifteen miles above Rudraprayag. The time taken for this round trip varied, but on an average, I had seen the leopard's tracks on the stretch of road between Rudraprayag and Golabrai once in every five days, so on my way back to the Inspection Bungalow I selected a place from where I could overlook the road and for the next two nights sat in great comfort on a hayrick, without however seeing anything of the leopard.

I received no news of the man-eater from outlying villages for two days and on the third morning I went down the pilgrim road for six miles to try to find out if he had recently visited any of the villages in the direction. From this twelve-mile walk I returned at midday and while I was having a late breakfast two men arrived and reported that a boy had been killed the previous evening at Bhainswara, a village eighteen miles south-east of Rudraprayag.

The intelligence system introduced by Ibbotson was working splendidly. Under this system cash rewards, on a graduated scale, were paid for information about all kills in the area in which the man-eater was "operating. These rewards, starting with two rupees for a goat and working up to twenty rupees for a human being, were keenly contested for, and so ensured our receiving information about all kills in the shortest time possible.

When I put ten rupees into the hands of each of the men who had brought me news about the boy, one of them offered to accompany me back to Bhainswara to show me the way, while the other said he would stay the night at Rudraprayag as he had recently had fever and could not do another eighteen miles that day. I finished breakfast while the men were telling me their tale, and a little before I p.m. I set off, taking only my rifle, a few cartridges, and a torch with me. As we crossed the road near the Inspection Bungalow and started up the steep hill on the far side of it, my companion informed me we had a very long way to go, adding that it would not be safe for us to be out after dark, so I told him to walk ahead and set the pace. I never, if I can help it, walk uphill immediately after a meal but here I had no option and for the first three miles, in which we climbed four thousand feet, I had great difficulty in keeping up with my guide. A short stretch of comparatively flat ground at the end of the three miles gave me back my wind, and after that I walked ahead and set the pace.

On their way to Rudraprayag the two men had told the people in the villages they had passed through about the kill and of their intention to try and persuade me to accompany them back to Bhainswara. I do not think that anyone doubted that I would answer to the call, for at every village the entire population were waiting for me and while some gave me their blessings, others begged me not to leave the district until I had killed their enemy.

My companion had assured me that we had eighteen miles to go, and as we crested hill after hill with deep valleys between, I realized I had undertaken to walk against time eighteen of the longest and hardest miles I had ever walked. The sun was near setting when, from the crest of one of these unending hills, I saw a number of men standing on a ridge a few hundred yards ahead of us. On catching sight of us some of the men disappeared over the ridge, while others came forward to meet us. The Headman of Bhainswara was among the latter and after he had greeted me, he cheered me by telling me that his village was just over the crest of the hill, and that he had sent his son back to get tea ready.

The 14th of April 1926 is a date that will long be remembered in Garhwal, for it was on that day that the man-eating leopard of Rudraprayag killed his last human victim. On the evening of that day a widow and her two children, a girl aged nine and a boy aged twelve, accompanied by a neighbour's son aged eight, went to a spring a few yards from Bhainswara village to draw water for the preparation of their evening meal.

The widow and her children occupied a house in the middle of a long row of homesteads. These homesteads were double-storied, the low-ceilinged ground floor being used for the storage of grain and fuel, and the first floor for residences. A verandah four feet wide ran the entire length of the building, and short flights of stone steps flanked by walls gave access to the verandah, each flight of steps being used by two families. A flagged courtyard, sixty feet wide and three hundred feet long, bordered by a low wall, extended along the whole length of the building.

The neighbour's son was leading as the party of four approached the steps used by the widow and her children, and as the boy started to mount the steps he saw an animal, which he mistook for a dog, lying in an open room on the ground floor adjoining the steps; he said nothing about the animal at the time, and the others apparently did not see it. The boy was followed by the girl, the widow came next, and her son brought up the rear. When she was halfway up the short flight of stone steps, the mother heard the heavy brass vessel her son was carrying a crash on the steps and rolling down them; reprimanding him for his carelessness, she set her own vessel down on the verandah and turned to see what damage her son had done. At the bottom of the steps, she saw the overturned vessel. She went down and picked it up and then looked round for her son. As he was nowhere in sight, she assumed he had got frightened and had run away, so she started calling to him.

Neighbours in adjoining houses had heard the noise made by the falling vessel and now, hearing the mother calling to her son, they came to their doors and asked what all the trouble was about. It was suggested that the boy might be hiding in one of the ground-floor rooms, so as it was now getting dark in these rooms, a man lit a lantern and came down the steps towards the woman and as he did, so he saw drops of blood on the flagstones where the woman was standing. At the sound of the man's horrified ejaculation other people descended into the courtyard, among whom was an old man who had accompanied his master on many shooting expeditions. Taking the lantern from the owner's hand, this old man followed the blood trail across the courtyard and over the low wall. Beyond the wall was a drop of eight feet into a yam field; here in the soft earth were the splayed-out pugmarks of a leopard. Up to that moment no one suspected that the boy had been carried off by a man-eater, for though everyone had heard about the leopard it had never previously been within ten miles of their village. As soon as they realized what had happened the women began screaming and while some men ran to their houses for drums, others ran for guns of which there were three in the village and in a few minutes, pandemonium broke out. Throughout the night drums were beaten and guns were fired. At daylight the boy's body was recovered and two men were dispatched to Rudraprayag to inform me.

As I approached the village in company with the Headman, I heard the wailing of a woman mourning her dead. It was the mother of the victim, and she was the first to greet me. Even to my unpracticed eye it was apparent that the bereaved mother had just weathered one hysterical storm and was heading for another, and as I lack the art of dealing with people in this condition I was anxious to spare the woman a recital of the events of the previous evening; but she appeared to be eager to give me her version of the story, so I let her have her way. As the story unfolded itself it was apparent that her object in telling it was to ventilate her grievance against the men of the village for not having run after the leopard and rescued her son 'as his father would have done had he been alive'. In her accusation against the men, I told her she was unjust and in her belief that her son could have been rescued alive, I told her she was wrong. For when the leopard clamped his teeth round the boy's throat, the canine teeth dislocated the head from the neck and the boy was already dead before the leopard carried him across the courtyard, and nothing the assembled men or anyone else could have done, would have been of any use.

Standing in the courtyard drinking the tea that had thoughtfully been provided for me and noting the hundred or more people who were gathered round, it was difficult to conceive how an animal the size of a leopard had crossed the courtyard in daylight without being seen by any of the people who must have been moving about at that time or how its presence had gone undetected by the dogs in the village.

I climbed down the eight-foot wall that the leopard carrying the boy had jumped down, and followed the drag across the yam field, down another wall twelve feet high, and across another field. At the edge of this second field there was a thick hedge of rambler roses, four feet high. Here the leopard had released his hold on the boy's throat, and after searching for an opening in the hedge and not finding one, he had picked the boy up by the small of the back and, leaping the hedge, gone down a wall ten feet high on the far side. There was a cattle track at the foot of this third wall and the leopard had only gone a short distance along it when the alarm was raised in the village. The leopard had then dropped the boy on the cattle track and gone down the hill. He was prevented from returning to his kill by the beating of drums and the firing of guns which had gone on all night in the village.

The obvious thing for me to have done would have been to carry the body of the boy back to where the leopard had left it and to have sat over it there. But here I was faced with two difficulties, the absence of a suitable place in which to sit and my aversion to sitting in an unsuitable place.

The nearest tree, a leafless walnut, was three hundred yards away, and was therefore out of the question and quite frankly I lacked the courage to sit on the ground. I had arrived at the village at sundown; it had taken a little time to drink the tea, hear the mothers story and trail the leopard and there was not sufficient daylight left for me to construct a shelter that would have given me even the semblance of protection; therefore if I sat on the ground I should have to sit just anywhere, not knowing from which direction the leopard would come, and knowing full well that if the leopard attacked me I should get no opportunity of using the one weapon with which I was familiar, my rifle, for when in actual contact with an unwounded leopard or tiger it is not possible to use firearms.

When after my tour of inspection, I returned to the courtyard, I asked the Headman for a crowbar, a stout wooden peg, a hammer, and a dog chain. With the crowbar I prised up one of the flagstones in the middle of the courtyard, drove the peg firmly into the ground and fastened one end of the chain to it. Then with the help of the Headman I carried the body of the boy to the peg and chained it there.

The working of the intangible force which sets a period to life, which one man calls Fate, and another calls kismet, is incomprehensible. During the past few days this force had set a period to the life of a breadwinner, leaving his family destitute; had ended in a very painful way the days of an old lady who after a lifetime of toil was looking forward to a few short years of comparative comfort and now, had cut short the life of this boy who, by the look of him, had been nurtured with care by his widowed mother. Small wonder then that the bereaved mother should, in between her hysterical crying, be repeating over and over and over again, 'What crime, Parmeshwar, has my son, who was loved by all, committed that on the threshold of life he has deserved death in this terrible way?'

Before prising up the flagstone, I had asked for the mother and her daughter to be taken to a room at the very end of the row of buildings. My preparations were completed, I washed at the spring and asked for a bundle of straw, which I laid on the verandah in front of the door of the house vacated by the mother.

Darkness had now fallen. Having asked the assembled people to be as silent during the night as it was possible for them to be and sent them to their respective homes, I took up my position on the verandah, whereby lying prone on my side and heaping a little straw in front, I could get a clear view of the kill without much chance of being seen myself.

In spite of all the noise that had been made the previous night, I had a feeling that the leopard would return, and that when he failed to find his kill where he had left it, he would come to the village to try to secure another victim. The ease with which he had got his first victim at Bhainswara would encourage him to try again, and I started my vigil with high hopes.

Heavy clouds had been gathering all the evening, and at 8 p.m., when all the village sound except the wailing of the woman were hushed, a flash of lightning followed by a distant roll of thunder heralded an approaching storm. For an hour the storm raged, the lightning being so continuous and brilliant that had a rat ventured into the courtyard I should have seen and probably been able to shoot it. The rain eventually stopped but the sky remained overcast, visibility was reduced to a few inches. The time had now come for the leopard to start from wherever he had been sheltering from the storm and the time of his arrival would depend on the distance of that place from the village.

The woman had now stopped wailing and in all the world there appeared to be no sound. This was as I had hoped, for all I had to warn me that the leopard had come were my ears and to help them I had used the dog chain instead of a rope.

The straw that had been provided for me was as dry as tinder and my ears, straining into the black darkness, first heard the sound when it was level with my feet something was creeping, very stealthily creeping, over the straw on which I was lying. I was wearing an article of clothing called shorts, which left my legs bare in the region of my knees. Presently, against this bare skin, I felt the hairy coat of an animal brushing. It could only be the man-eater, creeping up until he could lean over and get a grip of my throat. A little pressure now on my left shoulder to get a foothold and then, just as I was about to press the trigger of the rifle to cause a diversion, a small animal jumped down between my arms and my chest. It was a little kitten, soaking wet, that had been caught out in the storm and, finding every door shut, had come to me for warmth and protection.

The kitten had hardly made itself comfortable inside my coat, and I was just beginning to recover from the fright it had given me, when from beyond the terraced fields there was some low growling which gradually grew louder and then merged into the most savage fight I have ever heard. Quite evidently the man-eater had returned to the spot where the previous night he had left his kill and while he was searching for it, in not too good a temper, another male leopard who looked upon this particular area as his hunting-ground had accidentally come across him and set on him. Fights of the nature of the one that was taking place in my hearing are very unusual, for carnivores invariably keep to their own areas and if by chance two of a sex happen to meet, they size up each other's capabilities at a glance and the weaker gives way to the stronger.

The man-eater, though old, was a big and a very powerful male, and in the five hundred square miles he ranged over there was possibly no other male capable of disputing his rule, but here at Bhainswara he was a stranger and a trespasser and to get out of the trouble he had brought on himself he would have to fight for his life. And this he was undoubtedly doing.

My chance of getting a shot had now gone, for even if the man-eater succeeded in defeating his attacker, his injuries would probably prevent him from taking any interest in kills for some time to come. There was even a possibility of the fight ending fatally for him and here would indeed be an unexpected end to his career killed in an accidental encounter by one of his own kind, when the combined efforts of the Government and the public had failed, over a period of eight years, to accomplish this end.

The first round, lasting about five minutes, was fought with unabating savagery, and was inconclusive, for at the end of it I could still hear both animals. After an interval of ten or fifteen minutes the fight was resumed, but at a distance of two to three hundred yards from where it had originally started; quite evidently the local champion was getting the better of the fight and was gradually driving the intruder out of the ring. The third round was shorter than the two that had preceded it, but was no less savage, and when after another long period of silence, the fight was again resumed, the scene had receded to the shoulder of the hill, where after a few minutes it died out of hearing.

There were still six hours of darkness left; even so I knew my mission to Bhainswara had failed, and that my hope that the fight would be fought to a finish and would end in the death of the man-eater had been short lived. In the running fight into which the contest had now degenerated the man-eater would sustain injuries, but they were not likely to reduce his craving for human flesh or impair his ability to secure it.

The kitten slept peacefully throughout the night, and as the first streak of dawn showed in the east I descended into the courtyard and carried the boy to the shed from where we had removed him and covered him with the blanket which previously had been used for the purpose. The Headman was still asleep when I knocked on his door. I declined the tea, which I knew would take some time to make, and assured him that the man-eater would never again visit his village and when he had promised to make immediate arrangements to have the boy carried to the burning-ghat, I set off on my long walk back to Rudraprayag.

No matter how often we fail in any endeavour, we never get used to the feeling of depression that assails us after each successive failure. Day after day over a period of months, I had left the Inspection Bungalow full of hope that on this particular occasion I would meet with success and day after day I had returned disappointed and depressed. Had my failures only concerned myself they would not have mattered but, in the task, I had undertaken those failures concerned others more than they concerned me. Bad luck for to nothing else could I attribute my failures was being meted out to me in ever-increasing measure and the accumulated effect was beginning to depress me and give me the feeling that I was not destined to do what I had set out to do. What but bad luck had made the man-eater drop his kill where there were no trees? And what but bad luck had made a leopard who possibly had thirty square miles in which to wander, arrive at a particular spot in those thirty miles just as the man- eater, not finding his kill where he had left it, was quite conceivably on his way to the village where I was waiting for him?

The eighteen miles had been long yesterday, but they were longer today, and the hills were steeper. In the villages I passed through the people were eagerly awaiting me, and though I only had bad news they did not show their disappointment. Their boundless faith in their philosophy, a faith strong enough to move mountains and very soothing to depressed feelings, that no human beings and no animals can die before their appointed time, and that the man-eater's time had not yet come, called for no explanation, and admitted of no argument.

Ashamed of the depression and feeling of frustration that I had permitted to accompany me throughout the morning, I left the last f village where I had been made to halt and drink a cup of tea, greatly cheered and as I swung down the last four miles to Rudraprayag. I became aware that I was treading on the pugmarks of the man-eater. Strange how one's mental condition can dull, or sharpen, one's powers of observation. The man-eater had quite possibly joined the track many miles farther back and now after my conversation with the simple village-folk and a drink of tea. I was seeing his pugmarks for the first time that morning. The track here ran over red clay which the rain had softened, and the pug marks of the man-eater showed that he was walking at his accustomed pace. Half a mile farther on he started to quicken his pace and this pace he continued to maintain until he reached the head of the ravine above Golabrai, down this ravine the leopard had gone.

When a leopard or tiger is walking at its normal pace only the imprints of the hind feet are seen, but when the normal pace is for any reason exceeded, the hind feet are placed on the ground in advance of the forefeet, and thus the imprints of all four feet are seen. From the distance between the imprints of the fore and the hind feet it is possible to determine the speed at which an animal of the cat tribe was travelling. The coming of daylight would in this instance have been sufficient reason for the man-eater to have quickened his pace.

I had previously had experience of the man-eater's walking capabilities but only when ranging his beat in search of food. Here he had a better reason for the long walk he had undertaken, for he was anxious to put as great a distance as possible between himself and the leopard who had given him a lesson in the law of trespass; how severe that lesson had been will be apparent from a description given later.

A SHOT IN THE DARK

Mealtimes in India vary according to the season of the year and individual tastes. In most establishments the recognized times for the three principal meals are: breakfast 8 to 9; lunch 1 to 2 & dinner 8 to 9. During all the months I was at Rudraprayag my mealtimes were very erratic and contrary to the accepted belief that health depends on the composition and regularity of meals, my unorthodox and irregular meals kept me fighting fit. Porridge supped at 8 p.m., soup taken at 8 a.m., one combined meal in the day or no meal at all, appeared to have no injurious effect beyond taking a little flesh off my bones.

I had eaten nothing since my breakfast the previous day, so as I intended spending the night out, I had a nondescript meal on my return from Bhainswara and after an hour's sleep and a bath set off for Golabrai to warn the pundit who owned the pilgrim shelter of the presence in his vicinity of the man-eater.

I had made friends with the *pundit* on my first arrival at Rudraprayag and I never passed his house without having a few words with him, for in addition to the many interesting tales he had to tell about the man-eater and the pilgrims who passed through Golabrai, he was one of the only two people, the woman who escaped with the lacerated arm being the other whom I met during my stay in Garhwal who had survived an encounter with the man-eater.

One of his tales concerned a woman who had lived in a village further down the road, and with whom he had been acquainted. After a visit to the Rudraprayag bazaar one day this woman arrived at Golabrai late in the evening and fearing she would not be able to reach her home before dark she asked the *pundit* to let her spend the night in his shelter. This he permitted her to do advising her to sleep in front of the door of the storeroom in which he kept the articles of food purchased by the pilgrims for, he said, she would then be protected by the room on the one side, and by the fifty or more pilgrims who were spending the night in the shelter on the other.

The shelter was a grass shed open on the side nearest the road and boarded up on the side nearest the hill, the storeroom was midway along the shed but was recessed into the hill and did not obstruct the floor of the shed, so when the woman lay down at the door of the storeroom there were rows of pilgrims between her and the road. Sometime during the night one of the women pilgrims screamed out and said she had been stung by a scorpion. No lights were available, but with the help of matches the woman's foot was examined and a small scratch from which a little blood was flowing was found on her foot. Grumbling that the woman had made a lot of fuss about nothing, and that in any case blood did not flow from a scorpion sting the pilgrims soon composed themselves and resumed their sleep.

In the morning, when the *pundit* arrived from his house on the hill above the mango tree, he saw a sari worn by hill-women lying on the road in front of the shelter and on the sari, there was blood. The *pundit* had given his friend what he considered to be the safest place in the shelter, and with fifty or more pilgrims lying all round her the leopard had walked over the sleeping people, killed the woman, and accidentally scratched the sleeping pilgrim's foot when returning to the road. The explanation given by the *pundit* as to why the leopard had rejected the pilgrims and carried off the hill-woman was that she was the only person in the shelter that night who was wearing a coloured garment. This explanation is not convincing and but for the fact that leopards do not hunt by scent, my own explanation would have been that of all the people in the shelter the hill-woman was the only one who had a familiar smell. Was it just bad-luck or fate or being the only one of all the sleepers who realized the danger of sleeping in an open shed? Had the victim's fear in some inexplicable way conveyed itself to the man-eater, and attracted him to her?

It was not long after this occurrence that the *pundit* had his own encounter with the man-eater. The exact date which could if desired be ascertained from the hospital records at Rudraprayag is immaterial, and for the purpose of my story it will be sufficient to say that it took place during the hottest part of the summer of 1921, that is four years before I met the *pundit*. Late one evening of that summer ten pilgrims from Madras arrived weary and footsore at Golabrai and expressed their intention of spending the night in the pilgrim shelter. Fearing that if any more people were killed at Golabrai his shelter would get a bad reputation, the pundit tried to persuade them to continue on for another two miles to Rudraprayag, where they would be ensured of safe accommodation.

Finding that nothing he could say had any effect on the tired pilgrims, he finally consented to give them accommodation in his house, which was fifty yards above the mango-tree to which I have already drawn attention. The pundit's house was built on the same plan as the homesteads at Bhainswara, a low ground-floor room used for storage of fuel and a first- floor room used as a residence. A short flight of stone steps gave access to a narrow verandah, the door of the residential room being opposite to the landing at the top of the steps.

After the *pundit* and the ten guests that had been forced on him had eaten their evening meal, they locked themselves into the room, which was not provided with any means of ventilation. The heat in the room was stifling and fearing that he would be suffocated the *pundit* sometime during the night opened the door, stepped outside, and stretched his hands to the pillars on either side of the steps supporting the roof of the verandah. As he did so and filled his lungs with the night air, his throat was gripped as in a vice. Retaining his hold on the pillars, he got the soles of his feet against the body of his assailant and with a desperate kick tore the leopard's teeth from his throat and hurled it down the steps. Then, fearing that he was going to faint, he took a step sideways and supported himself by putting both hands on the railing of the verandah, and the moment he did so the leopard sprang up from below and buried its claws in his left forearm. The downward pull was counteracted by the railing on which the *pundit* had the palm of his hand, and the weight of the leopard caused its sharp claws to rip through the flesh of his arm until they tore free at his wrist. Before the leopard was able to spring a second time, the pilgrims, hearing the terrifying sounds the *pundit* was making in his attempts to breathe through the gap torn in his throat, dragged him into the room and bolted the door. For the rest of that long hot night the *pundit* lay gasping for breath and bleeding profusely, while the leopard growled and clawed at the frail door and the pilgrims screamed with terror.

At daylight the pilgrims carried the *pundit*, now mercifully unconscious, to a Kalakamli hospital at Rudraprayag, where for three months he was fed through a silver tube inserted in his throat. After an absence of over six months, he returned to his home in Golabrai, broken in health and with his hair turned grey. Photographs were taken five years later, and scarcely show the leopard's teeth-marks on the left side of the *pundit's* face and in his throat, and its claw-marks on his left arm, though they were still clearly visible.

In his conversations with me the *pundit* always referred to the man- eater as an evil spirit, and after the first day, when he had asked me what proof I could give him in face of his own experience that evil spirits could not assume material form, I also, to humour him, referred to the man-eater as 'the evil spirit'.

On arrival at Golabrai that evening I told the *pundit* of my fruitless visit to Bhainswara and warned him to take extra precautions for his safety and for the safety of any pilgrims who might be staying in his shelter; for the evil spirit, after its long excursion into the hills, had now returned to the vicinity.

That night and for the following three nights, I sat on the haystack, keeping a watch on the road and on the fourth day Ibbotson returned from Pauri.

Ibbotson always infused new life into me, for his creed, like that of the locals, was that no one was to blame if the man-eater had not died yesterday, for surely it would die today or maybe tomorrow. I had a lot to tell him, for though I had corresponded with him Regularly, extracts from my letters being embodied in his reports to the Government and by them made available to the press. I had not been able to give him all the details which he was now eager to hear. On his part Ibbotson also had a lot to tell me, this concerned the clamour being made in the press for the destruction of the man-eater, and the suggestion that sportsmen from all parts of India be encouraged to go to Garhwal to assist in killing the leopard. This press campaign had resulted in Ibbotson receiving only one inquiry and only one suggestion. The inquiry was from a sportsman who said that, if arrangements for his travel, accommodation, food, and so on, were made to his satisfaction, he would consider whether it was worth his while to come to Golabrai and the suggestion was from a sportsman in whose opinion the speediest and easiest way of killing the leopard was to paint a goat over with arsenic, sew up its mouth to prevent it licking itself, and then tie it up in a place where the leopard would find and eat it and so poison itself.

We talked long that day, reviewing my many failures in minutest detail, and by lunch-time, when I had told Ibbotson of the leopard's habit of going down the road between Rudraprayag and Golabrai on an average once in every five days, I convinced him that the only hope I now had of shooting the leopard was by sitting over the road for ten nights, for, as I pointed out to him, the leopard would be almost certain to use the road at least once during the period. Ibbotson consented to my plan very reluctantly, for I had already sat up many nights and he was afraid that another ten on end would be too much for me. However, I carried my point, and then told Ibbotson that if I did not succeed in killing the leopard within the stipulated time, I would return to Nainital and leave the field free for any newcomers who might consider it worth their while to take my place.

That evening Ibbotson accompanied me to Golabrai and helped me to put up a *machan* in the mango tree a hundred yards from the pilgrim shelter and fifty yards below the *pundit's* house. Immediately below the tree and in the middle of the road, we drove a stout wooden peg, and to this peg we tethered a goat with a small bell round its neck. The moon was nearly at its full, even so, the high hill to the east of Golabrai only admitted of the moon lighting up the deep Ganges valley for a few hours and if the leopard came while it was dark the goat would warn me of his approach.

When all our preparations had been made Ibbotson returned to the bungalow, promising to send two of my men for me early next morning. While I sat on a rock near the foot of the tree and smoked and waited for night to close in, the pundit came and sat down beside me; he was a bhakti and did not smoke. Earlier in the evening he had seen us building the *machan*, and he now tried to dissuade me from sitting all night in the tree when I could sleep comfortably in bed. Nevertheless, I assured him I would sit all that night in the tree, and for nine nights thereafter, for if I was not able to kill the evil spirit, I could at least guard his house and the pilgrim shelter from attack by all enemies. Once during the night, a *kakar* barked on the hill above me, but thereafter the night was silent. At sunrise next morning two of my men arrived and I set off for the Inspection Bungalow, examining the road as I went for pugmarks, and leaving the men to follow with my rug and rifle.

During the following nine days my programme did not vary. Leaving the bungalow accompanied by two men in the early evening, I took up my position in the *machan* and sent the men away in time for them to get back to the bungalow before dusk. The men had strict orders not to leave the bungalow before it was fully light, and they arrived each morning as the sun was rising on the hills on the far side of the river and accompanied me back to the bungalow.

During all those ten nights the barking of the *kakar* on the first night was all that I heard. That the man-eater was still in the vicinity we had ample proof, for twice within those ten nights it had broken into houses and carried off, on the first occasion, a goat and, on the second occasion, a sheep. I found both kills with some difficulty because they had been carried a long distance, but neither had been of any use to me as they had been eating out. Once also during those ten nights the leopard had broken down the door of a house which, fortunately for the inmates, had two rooms, the door of the inner room being sufficiently strong to withstand the leopard's onslaught.

On return to the bungalow after my tenth night in the mango tree, Ibbotson and I discussed our future plans. No further communications had been received from the sportsman, no one else had expressed a desire to accept the Government's invitation and no one had responded to the appeals made by the press. Neither Ibbotson nor I could afford to spend more time at Rudraprayag; Ibbotson because he had been away from his headquarters for ten days and it was necessary for him to return to Pauri to attend to urgent work, and I because I had work to do in Africa and had delayed my departure for three months and could not delay it any longer. Both of us were reluctant to leave Garhwal to the tender mercies of the man-eater and yet, situated as we were, it was hard to decide what to do. One solution was for Ibbotson to apply for leave, and for me to cancel my passage to Africa and cut my losses. We finally agreed to leave the decision over for that night, and to decide on our line of action the next morning. Having come to this decision I told Ibbotson I would spend my last night in Garhwal in the mango tree.

Ibbotson accompanied me on that eleventh, and last, evening, and as we approached Golabrai we saw a number of men standing on the side of the road, looking down into a field a little beyond the mango-tree, the men had not seen us and before we got up to them, they turned and moved off towards the pilgrim shelter. One of them, however looked back, and seeing me beckoning retraced his steps. In answer to our questions, he said he and his companions had for an hour been watching a great fight between two big snakes down in the field. No crops appeared to have been grown there for a year or more, and the snakes had last been seen near the big rock in the middle of the field. There were smears of blood on this rock, and the man said they had been made by the snakes, which had bitten each other and were bleeding in several places. Having broken a stick from a nearby bush, I jumped down into the field to see if there were any holes near the rock, and as I did so I caught sight of the snakes in a bush just below the road. Ibbotson had in the meantime armed himself with a stout stick and as one of the snakes tried to climb up on to the road, he killed it. The other one disappeared into a hole in the bank from where we were unable to dislodge it. The snake Ibbotson had killed was about seven feet long and of a uniform light straw colour and on its neck it had several bites. It was not a rat snake, and as it had very pronounced poison fangs, we concluded it was some variety of hoodless cobra. Cold-blooded creatures are not immune to snake poison, for I have seen a frog bitten by a cobra die in a few minutes, but I do not know if snakes of the same variety can poison each other and the one that escaped into the hole may have died in a few minutes or it may have lived to die of old age.

After Ibbotson left, the *pundit* passed under my tree on his way to the pilgrim shelter, carrying a pail of milk. He informed me that a hundred and fifty pilgrims, who had arrived during the day, were determined to spend the night in his shelter and that he was powerless to do anything about it. It was then too late for me to take any action, so I told him to warn the pilgrims to keep close together and not on any account to move about after dark. When he hurried back to his house a few minutes later, he said he had warned the pilgrims accordingly.

In a field adjoining the road, and about a hundred yards from my tree, there was a thorn enclosure in which a packman not my old friend earlier in the evening had penned his flock of goats and sheep. With the packman were two dogs who barked very fiercely at us as we came down the road and at Ibbotson after he left me to go back to the bungalow.

The moon was a few days past the full, and the valley was in darkness when, a little after 9 p.m., I saw a man carrying a lantern leave the pilgrim shelter and cross the road. A minute or two later, he recrossed the road and on gaining shelter, extinguished the lantern and at the same moment the packman's dogs started barking furiously. The dogs were unmistakably barking at a leopard, which quite possibly had seen the man with the lantern and was now coming down the road on its way to the shelter.

At first the dogs barked in the direction of the road but after a little while they turned and barked in my direction. The leopard had now quite evidently caught sight of the sleeping goat and lain down out of sight of the dogs which had stopped barking to consider his next move. I knew that the leopard had arrived, and I also knew that he was using my tree to stalk the goat and the question that was tormenting me as the long minutes dragged by was, whether he would skirt round the goat and kill one of the pilgrims or whether he would kill the goat and give me a shot.

During all the nights I had sat in the tree I adopted a position that would enable me to discharge my rifle with the minimum of movement and in the minimum of time. The distance between the goat and my *machan* was about twenty feet, but the night was so dark under the dense,' foliage of the tree that my straining eyes could not penetrate even this short distance, so I closed them and concentrated on my hearing.

My rifle, to which I had a small electric torch attached, was pointing in the direction of the goat, and I was just beginning to think that the leopard-assuming it was the man-eater had reached the shelter and was selecting a human victim, when there was a rush from the foot of the tree and the goat's bell tinkled sharply. Pressing the button of the torch I saw that the sights of the rifle were aligned on the shoulder of a leopard and without having to move the rifle a fraction of an inch I pressed the trigger and, as I did so the torch went out.

Torches in those days were not in as general use as they are now, and mine was the first I had ever possessed. I had carried it for several months and never had occasion to use it and I did not know the life of the battery or that it was necessary to test it. When I pressed the button on this occasion the torch gave only one dim flash and then went out and I was again in darkness without knowing what the result of my shot had been.

The echo of my shot was dying away in the valley when the *pundit* opened his door and called out to ask if I needed any help. I was at the time listening with all my ears for any sounds that might come from the leopard, so I did not answer him, and he hurriedly shut his door.

The leopard had been lying across the road with his head away from me when I fired, and I was vaguely aware of his having sprung over the goat and gone down the hillside, and just before the *pundit* had called, I thought I heard what may have been a gurgling sound, but of this I could not be sure. The pilgrims had been aroused by my shot but, after murmuring for a few minutes, they resumed their sleep. The goat appeared to be unhurt, for from the sound of his bell I could tell that he was moving about and apparently eating the grass of which he was given a liberal supply each night.

I fired my shot at 10 p.m. As the moon was not due to rise for several hours, and as there was nothing I could do in the meantime, I made myself comfortable, and listened and smoked.

Hours later the moon lit up the crest of the hills on the far side of the Ganges and slowly crept down into the valley, and a little later I saw it rise over the top of the hill behind me. As soon as it was overhead, I climbed to the top of the tree, but found that the spreading branches impeded my view. Descending again to the *machan*, I climbed out on the branches spreading over the road, but from here also I found it was not possible to see down the hillside in the direction in which I thought the leopard had.' gone. It was then 3 a.m. and two hours later the moon began to pale. When nearby objects became visible in the light of the day that was being born in the east, I descended from the tree and was greeted by a friendly bleat from the goat.

Beyond the goat and at the very edge of the road, there was a long low rock, and on this rock there was an inch-wide streak of blood; the leopard from which that blood had come could only have lived a minute or two, so dispensing with the precautions usually taken when following up the blood trail of carnivores, I scrambled down off the road and, taking up the trail on the far side of the rock, followed it for fifty yards, to where the leopard was lying dead. He had slid backwards into a hole in the ground, in which he was now lying crouched up, with his chin resting on the edge of the hole.

No marks by which I could identify the dead animal were visible, even so I never for one moment doubted that the leopard in the hole was the man-eater. But here was no fiend, who while watching me through the long night hours had rocked and rolled with silent fiendish laughter at my vein attempts to outwit him and licked his lips in anticipation of the time when, finding me off my guard for one brief moment, he would get the opportunity he was waiting for of burying his teeth in my throat. Here was only an old leopard, who differed from others of his kind in that his muzzle was grey and his lips lacked whiskers; the best-hated and the most feared animal in all India, whose only crime not against the laws of nature but against the laws of man was that he had shed human blood, with no object of terrorizing man but only in order that he might live and who now, with his chin resting on the rim of the hole and his eyes half-closed, was peacefully sleeping his long last sleep.

While I stood unloading my rifle, one bullet from which had more than cancelled my personal score against the sleeper, I heard a cough, and on looking up saw the *pundit* peering down at me from the edge of the road. I beckoned to him, and he came gingerly down the hill. On catching sight of the leopard s head he stopped and asked in a whisper whether it was dead, and what it was. When I told him it was dead, and that it was the evil spirit that had torn open his throat five years ago, and for fear of which he had hurriedly closed his door the previous night, he put his hands together and attempted to put his head on my feet. Next minute there was a call from the road above of, '*Sahib*, where are you?' It was one of my men calling in great agitation, and when I sent an answering call echoing over the Ganges, four heads appeared and catching sight of us, four men came helter-skelter down the hill, one of them swinging a lighted lantern which he had forgotten to extinguish.

The leopard had got stiff in the hole and was extracted with some little difficulty. While it was being tied to the stout bamboo pole the men had brought with them, they told me they had been unable to sleep that night and that as soon as Ibbotson's jemadar's watch showed them it was 4.30 a.m., they lit the lantern and arming themselves with a pole and a length of rope had come to look for me, for they felt that I was in urgent need of them. Not finding me in the machan and seeing the goat unhurt and the streak of blood on the rock, they concluded the man-eater had killed me, and not knowing what to do they had in desperation called to me.

Leaving the *pundit* to retrieve my rug from the *machan* and give the pilgrims who were now crowding round his version of the night's happenings, the four men and I, with the goat trotting alongside, set off for the Inspection Bungalow. The goat, who had escaped with very little injury owing to my having fired the moment the leopard caught him, little knew that his night's adventure was to make him a hero for the rest of his life, and that he was to wear a fine brass collar and be a source of income to the man from whom I had purchased him, and to whom I gave him back.

Ibbotson was still asleep when I knocked on the glazed door, and the moment he caught sight of me he jumped out of bed and dashing to the door flung it open, embraced me and next minute was dancing round the leopard which the men had deposited on the verandah. Shouting for tea and a hot bath for me, he called for his stenographer and dictated telegrams to the Government, the press, and my sister, and a cable to Jean. Not one question had he asked, for he knew that the leopard which I had brought home at that early hour was the man-eater, so what need was there for questions? On that previous occasion in spite of all the evidence that had been produced, I had maintained that the leopard killed in the gin-trap was not the man-eater and, on this occasion, I had said nothing.

Ibbotson had carried a heavy responsibility since October of the previous year, for to him was left the answering of questions of Councillors anxious to please their constituents of Government officials who were daily getting more alarmed at the mounting death-toll and of a press that was clamouring for results. His position had for a long time been like that of the head of a police force who, knowing the identity of a noted criminal, was unable to prevent his committing further crimes and for this was being badgered on all sides. Little wonder then that Ibbotson on that 2nd of May 1926 was the happiest man I had even seen, for not only was he now able to inform all concerned that the criminal had been executed, but he was also able to tell the people from the bazaars and from the surrounding villages and the pilgrims, all of whom were swarming into the compound of the Inspection Bungalow, that the evil spirit that had tormented them for eight long years was now dead.

After emptying a pot of tea and having a hot bath I tried to get a little sleep, but fear of a repetition of the cramps that twisted my feet and from which I was only relieved by the vigorous ministrations of Ibbotson, brought me out of bed. Then Ibbotson and I measured the leopard, and carefully examined it. The following are the results of our measurements and of our examination.

MEASUREMENTS

Length, between pegs 7 feet, 6 inches Length, over curves 7 feet, 10 inches [Note: these measurements were taken after the leopard had been dead twelve hours.]

DESCRIPTION

Colour: Light straw.

Hair: Short and brittle

Whiskers: None

Teeth: Worn and discoloured, one canine tooth broken.

Tongue and mouth: Black

Wounds: One fresh bullet-wound in right shoulder.

> One old bullet-wound in pad of left hind foot and part of one toe and one claw missing from same foot. Several deep and partly healed cuts on head. One deep and partly healed cut on right hind leg. Several partly healed cuts on tail. One partly healed wound on stifle of left hind leg.

I am unable to account for the leopard's tongue and mouth being black. It was suggested that this might have been caused by cyanide, but whether this was so or not I cannot say. Of the partly healed wounds, those on the head, right hind leg and tail were acquired in his fight at Bhainswara and the one on the stifle of his left hind leg was the result of his having been caught in the gin-trap, for the piece of skin and tuft of hair we found in the trap fitted into this wound. The injuries on the left hind foot were the result of the bullet fired on the bridge by the young army officer in 1921. When skinning the leopard later, I found a pellet of buckshot embedded in the skin of his chest which an Indian Christian years later claimed he had fired at the leopard the year it became a man-eater.

After Ibbotson and I had measured and examined the leopard it was laid in the shade of a tree, and throughout the day thousands of men, women, and children came to see it.

When the people of our hills visit an individual for any particular purpose, as for instance to show their gratitude or to express their thanks, it is customary for them not to go on their mission empty-handed. A rose, a marigold, or a few petals of either flower suffices, and the gift is proffered in hands cupped together. When the recipient has touched the gift with the tips of the fingers of his right hand, the person proffering the gift goes through the motion of pouring the gift on to the recipient's feet, in the same manner as if his cupped hands contained water.

I have on other occasions witnessed gratitude, but never as I witnessed it, that day at Rudraprayag, first at the Inspection Bungalow and later at a reception in the bazaar.

'He killed our only son, *sahib* and we being old, our house is now desolate.'

'He ate the mother of my five children, and the youngest is but a few months old and there is none in the home now to care for the children, or to cook the food.'

'My son was taken ill at night, and no one dared go to the hospital for medicine, and so he died.'

Tragedy upon pitiful tragedy and while I listened, the ground around my feet was strewn with flowers.

EPILOGUE

The events I have narrated took place between 1925 and 1926. Sixteen years later, in 1942, I was doing a war job in Meerut and my sister, and I were invited one day by Colonel Flye to help entertain wounded men at a garden party. The men, some fifty or sixty in number and from all parts of India, were sitting round a tennis-court just finishing a sumptuous tea and getting to the smoking stage, when we arrived. Taking opposite sides of the court, my sister and I started to go round the circle.

The men were all from the Middle East and after a rest, were to be sent to their homes, some on leave and some on discharge. Music, in the form of a gramophone with Indian records, had been provided by Mrs. Flye and as my sister and I had been requested to stay until the party gave over which would be in about two hours' time, we had ample time to make our circuit of the wounded men.

I had got about halfway round the circle when I came to a boy sitting in a low chair; he had been grievously wounded, and on the ground near his chair were two crutches. At my approach he very painfully slid off his chair and attempted to put his head on my feet. He was woefully light, for he had spent many months in hospital, and when I had picked him up and made him comfortable in his chair, he said; 'I have been talking with your lady sister and when I told her I was a Garhwali, she told me who you were. I was a small boy when you shot the man-eater, and as our village is far from Rudraprayag, I was not able to walk there and my father not being strong was unable to carry me, so I had to stay at home. When my father returned, he told me he had seen the man-eater and that with his own eyes he had seen the sahib who had shot it. He also told me of the sweets that had been distributed that day, his share of which he had brought back for me and of the great crowds he had seen. And now, sahib, I will go back to my home with great joy in my heart, for I shall be able to tell my father that with my own eyes I have seen you and, maybe, if I can get anyone to carry me to the fair that is held every year at Rudraprayag to commemorate the death of the man-eater, I shall tell all the people I meet there that I have seen and had speech with you.'

A cripple, on the threshold of manhood, returning from the wars with a broken body, with no thought of telling of brave deeds done, but only eager to tell his father that with his own eyes he had seen the man who years ago he had not had the opportunity of seeing, a man whose only claim to remembrance was that he had fired one accurate shot.

A typical son of Garhwal, of that simple and hardy hill-folk and of that greater India, whose sons only those few who live among them are privileged to know. It is these big-hearted sons of the soil, no matter what their caste or creed, who will one day weld the contending factions into a composite whole and make of India a great nation.

My India

INTRODUCTION

Having read my dedication you may ask: 'Who are these poor of India that you mention?' 'What do you mean by "My India"?' The questions are justified. The world has developed the habit of using the word 'Indian' to denote an inhabitant of the great peninsula that stretches upwards of two thousand miles from north to south, and as much from east to west. Geographically the term may pass muster, but when it comes to applying it to the people themselves one should not, without further explanation, use a description whose looseness has already led to infinite misunderstanding. The four hundred million people of India are divided horizontally by race, tribe and caste into a far greater diversity than exists in Europe, and they are cleft vertically by religious differences fully as deep as those which under any one nation from another. It was religion, not race that split the Indian Empire into Hindustan and Pakistan.

Let me therefore explain what I mean by the title of this book.

'My India', about which these sketches of village life and work are written, refers to those portions of a vast land which I have known from my earliest days and where I have worked; and the simple folk whose ways and characters I have tried to depict for you are those among whom I spent the greater part of seventy years. Look at a map of India. Pick

out Gape Comorin, the most southerly point of the peninsula, and run your eye straight up to where the Gangetic Plain slopes up into the foothills of the Himalayas in the north of the United Provinces. There you will find the hill station of Nainital, the summer seat of the Government of the United Provinces, packed from April to November with Europeans and wealthier

Indians seeking escape from the heat of the plains and occupied during the winter only by a few permanent residents, of whom most of my life I was one. Now leave this hill station and run your eyes down the Ganges River on its way to the sea, past Allahabad, Benares, and Patna, till you reach Mokameh Ghat, where I labored for twenty-one years. The scenes of my sketches Centre round these two points in India, Nainital and Mokameh Ghat.

In addition to many footpaths, Nainital is accessible by a motor road of which we are justly proud, for it has the reputation of being the best-aligned and the best-maintained hill road in India. Starting at the railway terminus of Kathgodam, the road in its course of twenty-two miles, passes through forests where occasionally Tiger and the dreaded hamadryad are to be seen and climbs 4,500 feet by easy gradients to Nainital. Nainital can best be described as an open valley running east and west, surrounded on three sides by hills, the highest of which, Gheena, rises to a height of 8,569 feet.

It is open at the end from which the motor road approaches it. Nestling in the valley is a lake a little more than two miles in circumference, fed at the upper end by a perennial spring and overflowing at the other end where the motor road terminates. At the upper and lower ends of the valley there are bazaars, and the surrounding wooded hills are dotted with residential houses, churches, schools, clubs, and hotels. Near the margin of the lake are boat houses, a picturesque Hindu temple and a very sacred rock shrine presided over by an old Brahmin priest who has been a lifelong friend of mine.

Geologists differ in their opinion as to the origin of the lake, some attributing it to glaciers and landslides, others to volcanic action. Hindu legends, however, give the credit for the lake to three ancient sages, Atri, Pulastyas and Pulaha. The sacred book Skanda-Puran tells how, while on a penitential pilgrimage, these three sages arrived at the crest of Cheena, and finding no water to quench their thirst, dug a hole at the foot of the hill and syphoned water into it from Manasarowar, the sacred lake in Tibet, After the departure of the sages the goddess Naini arrived and took up her abode in the waters of the lake. In course of time forests grew on the sides of the excavation and, attracted by the water and the vegetation, birds and animals in great numbers made their home in the valley. Within a radius of four miles of the goddess's temple I have, in addition to other animals, seen Tiger, leopard, bear, and sambhar and in the same area identified one hundred and twenty-eight varieties of birds. Rumours of the existence of the lake reached the early administrators of this part of India and as the hill people were unwilling to disclose the position of their sacred lake, one of these administrators, in the year 1839, hit on the ingenious plan of placing a large stone on the head of a hill man, telling him he would have to carry it until he arrived at goddess Naini's lake. After wandering over the hills for many days the man eventually got tired of carrying the stone and led the party who were following him to the lake. The stone alleged to have been carried by the man was shown to me when I was a small boy, and when I marked that it was a very big stone for a man to carry it weighed about six hundred pounds, the hill man who showed it to me said, 'Yes, it is a big stone, but you must remember that in those days our people were very strong'.

Provide yourself now with a good pair of field glasses and accompany me to the top of Cheena. From here you will get a bird's-eye view of the country surrounding Nainital. The road is steep, but if you are interested in birds, trees, and flowers you will not mind the three-mile climb and if you arrive at the top thirsty, as the three sages did, I will show you a crystal-clear spring of Coldwater to quench your thirst. Having rested and eaten your lunch, turn now to the north. Immediately below you is a deep well-wooded valley running down to the Kosi River. Beyond the river are a number of parallel ridges with villages dotted here and there; on one of these ridges is the town of Almora and on another, the cantonment of Ranikhet. Beyond these again are more ridges, the highest of which, Dungar Buqual, rises to a height of 14,200 feet and is dwarfed into insignificance by the mighty mass of the snowclad Himalayas.

Sixty miles due north of you, as the crow flies is Trisul and to the east and to the west of this imposing 23,406-foot peak the snow mountains stretch in an unbroken line for many hundreds of miles. Where the snow fades out of sight to the west of Trisul, are first the Gangotri group, then the glaciers and mountains above the sacred shrines of Kedarnath and Badrinath and then Kamet made famous by Smythe.

To the east of Trisul and set farther back, you can just see the top of Nanda Devi (25,689feet), the highest mountain in India. To your right front is

Nanda Kot, the spotless pillow of the goddess Parvati, and a little farther east are the beautiful peaks of Panch Chuli, the 'five cooking-places' used by the Pandavas while on their way to Kailas in Tibet. At the first approach of dawn, while Cheena and the intervening hills are still shrouded in the mantle of night the snowy range changes from indigo blue to rose pink and as the sun touches the peaks nearest to heaven the pink gradually changes to dazzling white. During the day the mountains show up cold and white, each crest trailing a feather of powdered snow, and in the setting sun the scene may be painted pink, gold, or red according to the fancy of heaven's artist.

Turn your back now on the snow, and face south. At the limit of your range of vision you will see three cities: Bareilly, Kashipur and Moradabad. These three cities, the nearest of which, Kashipur is some fifty miles as the crow flies are on the main railway that runs between Calcutta and the Punjab. There are three belts of country between the railway and the Foothills, first a cultivated belt some twenty miles wide, then a grass belt ten miles wide known as the Terai and third a tree belt ten miles wide known as the Bhabar. In the Bhabar belt, which extends right up to the foothills, clearings have been made and on this rich fertile soil, watered by many streams, villages of varying size have been established. The nearest group of villages, Kaladhungi, is fifteen miles from Nainital by road, and at the upper end of this group you will see our village, Choti Haldwani, surrounded by a three-mile-long stone wall. Only the roof of our cottage, which is at the junction of the road running down from Nainital with the road skirting the foothills is visible in a group of big trees. The foothills in this area are composed almost entirely of iron ore and it was at Kaladhungi that iron was first smelted in northern India. The fuel used was wood, and as the King of Kumaon, General Sir Henry Ramsay, feared that the furnaces would consume all the forests in the Bhabar, he closed down the foundries. Between Kaladhungi and your seat on Cheena the low hills are densely wooded with sal, the trees which supply our railways with ties or sleepers and in the nearest fold of the ridge nestles the little lake of Khurpa Tal, surrounded by fields on which the best potatoes in India are grown.

Away in the distance to the right, you can see the sun glinting on the Ganges, and to the left you can see it glinting on the Sarda, the distance between these two rivers where they leave the foothills is roughly two hundred miles.

Now turn to the east and before you in the near and middle distance you will see the country described in old gazetteers as 'the district of sixty lakes'. Many of these takes have silted up, some in my lifetime and the only ones of any size that now remain are Nainital, Sat Tal, Bhim Tal and Nakuchia Tal. Beyond Nakuchia Tal is the cone-shaped hill, Choti Kailas. The gods do not favour the killing of bird or beast on this sacred hill, and the last man who disregarded their wishes, a soldier on leave during the war unaccountably lost his footing alter killing a mountain goat and in full view of his two companions, fell a thousand feet into the valley below.

Beyond Choti Kailas is the Kala Agar ridge on which I hunted the Chowgarh man-eating tiger for two years and beyond this ridge the mountains of Nepal fade out of sight. Turn now to the west. But first it will be necessary for you to descend a few hundred feet and take up a new position on Deopatta, a rocky peak 7,991 feet high adjoining Cheena. Immediately below you is a deep, wide, and densely wooded valley which starts on the saddle between Cheena and Deopatta and extends through Dachouri to Kaladhungi. It is richer in flora and fauna than any other in the Himalayas and beyond this beautiful valley the hills extend in an unbroken line up to the Ganges, the waters of which you can see glinting m the sun over a hundred miles away. On the far side of the Ganges are the Siwalik range of hills, hills that were old before the mighty Himalayas were born.

I. THE QUEEN OF THE VILLAGE

Come with me now to one of the villages you saw in your bird's-eye view from the top of Cheena. The parallel lines you saw etched across the face of the hill are terraced fields. Some of these are no more than ten feet wide and the stone walls supporting them are in some cases thirty feet high. The ploughing of these narrow fields, with a steep hill on one side and a big drop on the other is a difficult and a dangerous job and is only made possible by the use of a plough with a short shaft and of cattle that have been bred on the hills and that are in consequence small and stocky and as sure-footed as goats. The stout-hearted people, who with infinite labour have made these terraced fields, live in a row of stone houses with slate roofs bordering the rough and narrow road that runs from the Bhabar and the plains beyond, to the inner Himalayas. The people in this village know me for in response to an urgent telegram, which the whole village subscribed to send me, and which was carried by runner to Nainital for transmission, I once came hot-foot from Mokameh Ghat, where I was working to rid them of a man-eating tiger.

The incident which necessitated the sending of the telegram took place at midday in a field just above the row of houses. A woman and her twelve-year-old daughter were reaping wheat when a tiger suddenly appeared. As the girl attempted to run to her mother for protection the tiger struck at her, severed her head from her body, and catching the body in mid-air bounded away into the jungle adjoining the field, leaving the head near the mother's feet. Telegrams, even urgent ones, take long in transmission, and as I had to do a journey of a thousand miles by rail and road and the last twenty miles on foot, a week elapsed between the sending of the telegram and my arrival at the village and in the meantime the tiger made another kill.

The victim on this occasion was a woman who with her husband and children had lived for years in the compound of the house adjoining our home in Nainital. This woman in company with several others was cutting grass on the hill above the village when she was attacked by the tiger killed and carried off in full view of her companions. The screams of the frightened women were heard in the village, and, while the women were running back to Nainital to report the tragedy, the men of the village assembled and with great gallantry drove away the tiger. Knowing, with an Indian's trust that I would respond to the telegram they had sent me, they wrapped the body in a blanket and tied it to the topmost branch of a thirty-foot rhododendron tree. From the tiger's subsequent action's, it was evident that he had been lying up close by and had watched these proceedings for if he had not seen the body being put up in a tree, he would never have found it as tigers have no sense of smell.

When the women made their report in Nainital the husband of the dead woman came to my sister Maggie and told her of the killing of his wife, and at crack of dawn next morning Maggie sent out some of our men to make a machan over the kill and to sit on the machan until I came for, I was expected to arrive that day. Materials for making the machan were procured at the village and accompanied by the villagers, my men proceeded to the rhododendron tree, where it was found that the tiger had climbed the tree, torn a hole in the blanket and carried away the body. Again, with commendable courage for they were unarmed, the villagers and my men followed up the drag for half a mile and on finding the partly eaten body they started to put up a machan in an oak tree immediately above it. Just as the machan was completed, a sportsman from Nainital, who was out on an all-day shoot, arrived quite by accident at the spot and, saying he was a friend of mine, he told my men to go away, as he would sit up for the tiger himself. So, while my men returned to Nainital to make their report to me, for I had arrived in the meantime the sportsman, his gun bearer and a man carrying his lunch basket and a lantern, took up their positions on the machan.

There was no moon, and an hour after dark the gun-bearer asked the sportsman why he had allowed the tiger to carry away the kill, without firing at it. Refusing to believe that the tiger had been anywhere near the kill, the sportsman lit the lantern and as he was letting it down on a length of string, to illuminate the ground, the string slipped through his fingers and the lantern crashed to the ground and caught fire. It was the month of May, when our forests are very dry and within a minute the dead grass and brushwood at the foot of the tree were burning fiercely. With great courage the sportsman shinned down the tree and attempted to beat out the flames with his tweed coat, until he suddenly remembered the man-eater and hurriedly climbed back to the machan. He left his coat, which was on fire, behind him.

The illumination from the fire revealed the fact that the Kill was indeed gone but the sportsman at this stage had lost all interest in kills and his anxiety now was for his own safety and for the damage the fire would do to the Government forest. Fanned by a strong wind the fire receded from the vicinity of the tree and eight hours later a heavy downpour of rain and hail extinguished it but not before it had burnt out several square miles of forest. It was the sportsman's first attempt to make contact with a man-eater and after his experience of first nearly having been roasted and later having been frozen, it was also his last. Next morning, while he was making his weary way back to Nainital by one road, I was on my way out to the village by another, in ignorance of what had happened the previous night.

At my request the villagers took me to the rhododendron tree, and I was amazed to see how determined the tiger had been to regain possession of his kill. The torn blanket was some twenty-five feet from the ground and the claw marks on the tree, the condition of the soft ground, and the broken brushwood at the foot of it, showed that the tiger had climbed and fallen off the tree at least twenty times before he eventually succeeded in tearing a hole in die blanket and removing the body.

From this spot the tiger had carried the body half a mile to the tree on which the machan had been built. Beyond this point the fire had obliterated all trace of a drag but, following on the line I thought the tiger would have taken a mile farther on I stumbled on the charred head of the woman. A hundred yards beyond this spot there was heavy cover which the fire had not reached and for hours I searched this cover, right down to the foot of the valley five miles away without however, finding any trace of the tiger.

(Five people lost their lives between the accidental arrivals of the sportsman at the machan and the shooting of the tiger.) I arrived back in the village, after my fruitless search of the cover, late in the evening and the wife of the headman prepared for me a meal which her daughters placed before me on brass plates. After a very generous, and a very welcome meal for I had eaten nothing that day, I picked up the plates with the intention of washing them in a nearby spring. Seeing my intention, the three girls ran forward and relieved me of the plates, saying, with a toss of their heads and a laugh, which it would not break their caste they were Brahmins, to wash the plates from which the White Sadhu had eaten.

The headman is dead now and his daughters have married and left the village, but his wife is alive and you, who are accompanying me to the village, after your bird's-eye view from Cheena, must be prepared to drink the tea, not made with water but with rich fresh milk sweetened with jaggery, which she will brew for us. Our approach down the steep hillside facing the village has been observed and a small square of frayed carpet and two wicker chairs, reinforced with Ghooral skins, have been set ready for us. Standing near these chairs to welcome us is the wife of the headman; there is no purdah here and she will not be embarrassed if you take a good look at her, and she is worth looking at. Her hair, snow-white now, was raven-black when I first knew her and her cheeks, which in those far-off days had a bloom on them, are now ivory-white, without a single crease or wrinkle. Daughter of a hundred generations of Brahmins, her blood is as pure as that of the ancestor who founded her line.

Pride of pure ancestry is inherent in all men, but nowhere is there greater respect for pure ancestry than there is in India. There are several different castes of people in the village this dear old lady administers, but her rule is never questioned, and her word is law, not because of the strong arm of retainers, for of these she has none, but because she is a Brahmin, the salt of India's earth.

The high prices paid in recent years for field produce have brought prosperity, as it is known in India to this hill village and of this prosperity our hostess has had her full share The string of fluted gold beads that she brought as part of her dowry are still round her neck, but the thin silver necklace has been deposited in the family bank, the hole in the ground under the cooking-place and her neck is now encircled by a solid gold band. In the far-off days her ears were unadorned but now she has number of thin gold rings in the upper cartilage and from her nose hangs a gold ring five inches in diameter, the weight of which is partly carried by a thin gold chain looped over her right ear. Her dress is the same as that worn by all high-caste hill women a shawl, a tight-fitting bodice of warm material and a voluminous sprint skirt. Her feet are bare, for even in these advanced days the wearing of shoes among our hill folk denotes that the wearer is unchaste.

The old lady has now retired to the inner recesses of her house to prepare tea, and while she is engaged on this pleasant task you can turn your attention to the bania's shop on the other side of the narrow road. The bania too, is an old friend. Having greeted us and presented us with a packet of cigarettes he went back to squat cross-legged on the wooden platform on which his wares are exposed. These wares consist of the few articles that the village folk and wayfarers need in the way of atta, rice, dal, ghee, salt, stale sweets purchased at a discount in the Nainital bazaar, hill potatoes fit for the table of a king, enormous turnips so fierce that when eaten in public they make the onlookers' eyes water, cigarettes and matches, a tin of kerosene oil and near the platform and within reach of his hand an iron pan in which milk is kept simmering throughout the day.

As the Bania takes his seat on the platform his few customers gather in front of him. First is a small boy, accompanied by an even smaller sister, who is the proud possessor of one Pice, all of which he is anxious to invest in sweets. Taking the Pice from the small grubby hand the Bania drops it into an open box. Then, waving his hand over the tray to drive away the wasps and flies, he picks up a square sweet made of sugar and curds, breaks it in half and puts a piece into each eager outstretched hand.

Next comes a woman of the depressed class who has two annas to spend on her shopping. One anna is invested in atta, the coarse ground wheat that is the staple food of our hill folk and two pice in the coarsest of the three qualities of dal exposed on the stall. With the remaining two pice she purchases a little salt and one of the fierce turnips and then, with a respectful salaam to the Bania, for he is a man who commands respect, she hurries off to prepare the midday meal for her family.

While the woman is being served the shrill whistles and shouts of men herald the approach of a string of pack mules, carrying cloth from the Moradabad hand looms to the markets in the interior of the hills. The sweating mules have had a stiff climb up the rough road from the foothills. A pice is worth about a farthing but is itself made up of three smaller coins called pies. Four pice make an anna, sixteen annas a rupee and while they are having a breather the four men in charge have sat down on the bench provided by the Bania for his customers and are treating themselves to a cigarette and a glass of milk. Milk is the strongest drink that has ever been served at this shop, or at any other of the hundreds of wayside shops throughout the hills, for, except for those few who have come in contact with what is called civilization our hill men do not drink.

Drinking among women, in my India, is unknown. No daily paper has ever found its way into this village, and the only news the inhabitants get of the outside world is from an occasional trip into Nainital and from wayfarers, the best-informed of whom are the packmen. On their way into the hills, they bring news of the distant plains of India and on their return journey a month or so later they have news from the trading centers where they sell their wares.

The tea the old lady has prepared for us is now ready. You must be careful how you handle the metal cup filled to the brim, for it is hot enough to take the skin off your hands. Interest has now shifted from the packmen to us and whether or not you like the sweet, hot liquid you must drink every drop of it, for the eyes of the entire village, whose guest you are, are on you and to leave any dregs in your cup would mean that you did not consider the drink good enough for you.

Others have attempted to offer recompense for hospitality, but we will not make this mistake, for these simple and hospitable people are intensely proud and it would be as great an insult to offer to pay the dear old lady for her cup of tea as it would have been to have offered to pay the bania for his packet of cigarettes. So, as we leave this village, which is only one of the many thousands of similar villages scattered over the vast area viewed through your good field glasses from the top of Cheena, where I have spent the best part of my life, you can be assured that the welcome we received on arrival, and the invitation to return soon are genuine expressions of the affection and goodwill of the people in my India for all who know and understand them.

II. KUNWAR SINGH

Kunwar Singh was by caste a Thakur and the headman of Chandni Chauk village. Whether he was a good or a bad headman I do not know. What endeared him to me was the fact that he was the best and the most successful poacher in Kaladhungi and a devoted admirer of my eldest brother Tom, my boyhood's hero.

Kunwar Singh had many tales to tell of Tom for he had accompanied him on many of his shikar expeditions and the tale I like best and that never lost anything in repetition, concerned an impromptus competition between brother Tom and a man by the name of Ellis, whom Tom had beaten by one point the previous year to win the B.P.R.A. gold medal for the best rifle-shot in India.

Tom and Ellis, unknown to each other, were shooting in the same jungle near Garuppu and early one morning, when the mist was just rising above the treetops, they met on the approach to some high ground overlooking a wide depression in which, at that hour of the morning, deer and pig were always to be found. Tom was accompanied by Kunwar Singh, while Ellis was accompanied by a shikari from Nainital named Budhoo, whom Kunwar Singh despised because of his low caste and his ignorance of all matters connected with the jungles.

After the usual greetings, Ellis said that, though Tom had beaten him by one miserable point on the rifle range, he would show Tom that he was a better game shot and he suggested that they should each fire two shots to prove the point. Lots were drawn and Ellis, winning, decided to fire first. A careful approach was then made to the low ground, Ellis carrying the -450 Martini-Henry rifle with which he had competed at the B.P.R.A. meeting, while Tom carried a -400 D.B. express by Westley-Richards of which he was justly proud, for few of these weapon shad up to that date arrived in India. The wind may have been wrong, or the approach careless. Anyway, when the competitors topped the high ground, no animals were in sight on the low ground.

On the near side of the low ground there was a strip of dry grass beyond which the grass had been burnt, and it was on this burnt ground now turning green with sprouting new shoots, that animals were to be seen both morning and evening. Kunwar Singh was of the opinion that some animals might be lurking in the strip of dry grass and at his suggestion he and Budhoo set fire to it.

When the grass was well alight and the drongos, rollers and starlings were collecting from the four corners of the heavens to feed on the swarms of grasshoppers that were taking flight to escape from the flames, a movement was observed at the farther edge of the grass, and presently two big board came out and went streaking across the burnt ground for the shelter of the tree jungle three hundred yards away. Very deliberately Ellis, who weighed fourteen stone, knelt down, raised his rifle, and sent a bullet after the hindmost pig, kicking up the dust between its hind legs. Lowering his rifle, Ellis adjusted the back sight to two hundred yards, ejected the spent cartridge, and rammed a fresh one into the breach. His second bullet sent up a cloud of dust immediately in front of the leading pig. This second bullet deflected the pigs to the right, bringing them broadside onto the guns and making them increase their speed.

It was now Tom's turn to shoot, and to shoot in a hurry, for the pigs were fast approaching the tree jungle and getting out of range. Standing four-square, Tom raised his rifle and as the two shots rang out the pigs, both shot through the head, went over like rabbits. Kunwar Singh's recital of this event invariably ended up with: 'And then I turned to Budhoo, that city-bred son of a low-caste man, the smell of whose oiled hair offended me and said, "Did you see that, you, who boasted that your sahib would teach mine how to shoot? Had my sahib wanted to blacken the face of yours he would not have used two bullets but would have killed both pigs with one".'

Just how this feat could have been accomplished, Kunwar Singh never told me, and I never asked for my faith in my hero was so great that I never for one moment doubted that, if he had wished, he could have killed both pigs with one bullet. Kunwar Singh was the first to visit me that day of days when I was given my first gun. He came early and as with great pride I put the old double-barreled muzzle-loader into his hands, he never even by the flicker of an eyelid, showed that he had seen the gaping split in the right barrel or the lapping's of brass wire that held the stock and the barrels together. Only the good qualities of the left barrel were commented on, and extolled; its length, thickness, and the years of service it would give. And then, laying the gun aside, he turned to me and gladdened my eight-year-old heart and made me doubly proud of my possession by saying: 'You are now no longer a boy but a man and with this good gun you can go anywhere you like in our jungles and never be afraid, provided you learn how to climb trees.

And I will now tell you a story to show how necessary it is for us men who shoot in the jungles to know how to do so. 'Har Singh and I went out to shoot one day last April and all would have been well if a fox had not crossed our path as we were leaving the village. Har Singh, as you know, is a poor shikari with little knowledge of the jungle folk and when after seeing the fox, I suggested we should turn round and go home he laughed at me and said, it was child's talk to say that a fox would bring us bad luck. So, we continued on our way. We had started when the stars were paling and near Garuppu, I fired at a chital stag and unaccountably missed it. Later Har Singh broke the wing of a pea fowl but though we chased the wounded bird as hard as we could it got away in the long grass, where we lost it. Thereafter, though we combed the jungles we saw nothing to shoot and towards the evening we turned our faces towards home.

'Having fired two shots and being afraid that the forest guards would be looking for us, we avoided the road and took a sandy nullah that ran through dense scrub and thorn-bamboo jungle. As we went along talking of our bad luck, suddenly a tiger came out into the nullah and stood looking at us. For a long minute the tiger stared and then it turned and went back the way it had come. 'After waiting a suitable time, we continued on our way, when the tiger again came out into the nullah and this time, as it stood and looked at us, it was growling and twitching its tail. We again stood quite still, and after a time the tiger quietened down and left the nullah. A little later a number of jungle fowl rose cackling out of the dense scrub, evidently disturbed by the tiger, and one of them came and sat on a haldu tree right in front of us. As the bird alighted on a branch in full view of us, Har Singh said he would shoot it and so avoid going home empty handed. He added that the shot would frighten away the tiger, and before I could stop him, he fired.

'Next second there was a terrifying roar as the tiger came crashing through the brushwood towards us. At this spot there were some runi trees growing on the edge of the nullah, and I dashed towards one while Har Singh dashed towards another. My tree was the nearer to the tiger, but before it arrived, I had climbed out of reach. Har Singh had not learnt to climb trees when a boy as I had, and he was still standing on the ground, reaching up and trying to grasp a branch, when the tiger after leaving me, sprang at him.

The tiger did not bite or scratch Har Singh but standing on its hind legs it clasped the tree, pinning Har Singh against it and then started to claw big bits of bark and wood off the far side of the tree. While it was so engaged Har Singh was screaming, and the tiger was roaring. I had taken my gun up into the tree with me so now, holding on with my bare feet, I cocked the hammer and fired the gun off into the air. On hearing the shot so close to it the tiger bounded away and Har Singh collapsed at the foot of the tree.'

When the tiger had been gone some time, I climbed down very silently and went to Har Singh. I found that one of the tiger's claws had entered his stomach and torn the lining from near his navel to within a few fingers' breadth of the backbone and that all his inside had fallen out. Here was great trouble for me. I could not run away and leave Har Singh and not having any experience in these matters, I did not know whether it would be best to try and put all that mass of inside back into Har Singh's stomach or cut it off. I talked in whispers on this matter with Har Singh, for we were afraid that if the tiger heard us, it would return and kill us and Har Singh was of the opinion that his inside should be put back into his stomach.

So, while he lay on his back on the ground, I stuffed it all back, including the dry leaves and grass and bits of sticks that were sticking to it. I then wound my pugree round him, knotting it tight to keep everything from falling out again and we set out on the seven-mile walk to our village, myself in front, carrying the two guns, while Har Singh walked behind. 'We had to go slowly, for Har Singh was holding the pugree in position and on the way, night came on and Har Singh said he thought it would be better to go to the hospital at Kaladhungi than to our village, so I hid the guns' and we went the extra three miles to the hospital.

The hospital was closed when we arrived, but the doctor babu who lives nearby was awake, and when he heard our story, he sent me to call Aladia the tobacco seller, who is also postmaster at Kaladhungi and who receives five rupees pay per month from Government, while he lit a lantern and went to the hospital hut with Har Singh. When I returned with Aladia, the doctor had laid Har Singh on a string bed and while Aladia held the lantern and I held the two pieces of flesh together, the doctor sewed up the hole in Har Singh's stomach. Thereafter the doctor, who is a very kind man of raw years and who refused to take the two rupees I offered him gave Har Singh a drink of very good medicine to make him forget the pain in his stomach and we went home and found our women folk crying for they thought we had been killed in the jungle by dacoits or by wild animals. So, you see Sahib, how necessary it is for us men who shoot in the jungles to know how to climb trees for if Har Singh had had someone to advise him when he was a boy, he would not have brought all that trouble on us.

I learnt many things from Kunwar Singh during the first few years that I carried the old muzzle-loader, one of them being the making of mental maps. The jungles we hunted in, sometimes together, but more often alone for Kunwar Singh had a horror of dacoits and there were times when for weeks on end he would not leave his village were many hundreds of miles square with only one road running through them. Times without number when returning from a shoot, I called in at Kunwar Singh's village, which was three miles nearer the forest than my house was, to tell him I had shot a chital or sambhar stag, or maybe a big pig and to ask him to retrieve the bag.

He never once failed to do so, no matter in how great a wilderness of tree or scrub or grass jungle I had carefully hidden the animal I had shot, to protect it from vultures. We had a name for every outstanding tree and for every water hole game track and nullah. All our distances were measured by imaginary flight of a bullet fired from a muzzle-loader, and all our directions fixed by' The runi tree against which the tigress, who evidently had just given birth to cubs in that area and who resented the presence of human beings pinned. Har Singh was about eighteen inches thick and in her rage the tigress tore away a third of it.

This tree became a landmark for all who shot or poached in the Garuppu jungles until, some twenty-five years later, it was destroyed by a forest fire. Har Singh in spite of the rough and ready treatment he received at the hands of his three friends and in spite of the vegetation that went inside him suffered no ill effects from his wound and lived to die of old age. The four points of the compass. When I had hidden an animal, or Kunwar Singh had seen vultures collected on a tree and suspected that a leopard or a tiger had made a kill, either he or I would set out with absolute, confidence that we would find the spot indicated, no matter what time of day or night it might be.

After I left school and started work in Bengal, I was only able to visit Kaladhungi for about three weeks each year and I was greatly distressed to find on one of these annual visits that my old friend Kunwar Singh had fallen a victim to the curse of our foothills, opium. With a constitution weakened by malaria the pernicious habit grew on him, and though he made me many promises he had not the moral strength to keep them. I was therefore not surprised on my visit to Kaladhungi one February to be told by the men in our village that Kunwar Singh was very seriously ill. News of my arrival spread through Kaladhungi that night and next day Kunwar Singh's youngest son, a lad of eighteen, came hot-foot to tell me that his father was at death's door and that he wished to see me before he died.

As headman of Chandni Chauk, paying Government land revenue of four thousand rupees, Kunwar Singh was an important person and lived in a big stone-built house with a slate roof in which I had often enjoyed his hospitality. Now as I approached the village in company with his son, I heard the wailing of women coming, not from the house but from a small one-roomed hut Kunwar Singh had built for one of his servants. As the son led me towards the hut, he said his father had been moved to it because the grandchildren disturbed his sleep. Seeing us coming, Kunwar Singh's eldest son stepped out of the hut and informed me that his father was unconscious and that he only had a few minutes to live. I stopped at the door of the hut and when my eyes had got accustomed to the dim light, made dimmer by a thick pall of smoke which filled the room, I saw Kunwar

Singh lying on the bare mud floor, naked, and partly covered with a sheet. His nerveless right arm was supported by an old man sitting on the floor near him and his fingers were being held round the tail of a cow. (This custom of a dying man being made to hold the tail of a cow preferably that of a black heifer has its origin in the Hindu belief that when the spirit leaves its earthly body it is confronted with a river of blood, on the far side of which sits the Judge before whom the spirit must appear to answer for its sins. The heifer's tail is the only way by which the departing spirit can cross the river and if the spirit is not provided with means of transit, it is condemned to remain on earth, to be a torment to those who failed to enable it to appear before the judgment seat.)

Near Kunwar Singh's head was a brazier with cow-dung cakes burning on it, and by the brazier a priest was sitting, intoning prayers, and ringing a bell. Every available inch of floor space was packed with men, and with women who were wailing and repeating over and over again, 'He has gone! He has gone!' I knew men died like this in India every day, but I was not going to let my friend be one of them. In fact, if I could help it he would not die at all and anyway not at present. Striding into the room, I picked up the iron brazier, which was hotter than I expected it to be, and burnt my hands. This I carried to the door and flung outside. Returning, I cut the bark rope by which the cow was tethered to a peg driven into the mud floor and led it outside.

As these acts, which I had performed in silence became evident to the people assembled in the room, the hubbub began to die down and it ceased altogether when I took the priest's arm and conducted him from the room. Then, standing at the door, I ordered everyone to go outside; the order was obeyed without a murmur or a single protest. The number of people, both old and young, who emerged from the hut was incredible. When the last of them had crossed the doorstep, I told Kunwar Singh's eldest son to warm two seers of fresh milk and to bring it to me with as little delay as possible. The man looked at me in blank surprise but when I repeated the order, he hurried off to execute it. I now re-entered the hut pulled forward a string bed which had been pushed against the wall, picked Kunwar Singh up and laid him on it.

Fresh air and plenty of it was urgently needed and as I looked round, I saw a small window which had been boarded up. It did not take long to tear down the boards and let a stream of sweet clean air blow directly from the jungles into the overheated room which reeked with the smell of human beings, cow dung, burnt ghee and acrid smoke. When I picked up Kunwar Singh's wasted frame, I knew there was a little life in it but only a very little. His eyes, which were sunk deep into his head, were closed, his lips were blue, and his breath was coming in short gasps.

Soon, however the fresh, clean air began to revive him and his breathing became less laboured and more regular and presently as I sat on his bed and watched through the door the commotion that was taking place among the mourners whom I had ejected from the death-chamber, I became aware that he had opened his eyes and was looking at me and without turning my head, I began to speak. 'Times have changed, Uncle and you with them. There was a day when no man would have dared to remove you from your own house and lay you on the ground in a servant's hut, to die like an outcaste and a beggar. You would not listen to my words of warning and now the accursed drug has brought you to this. Had I delayed but a few minutes in answering your summons this day, you know you would by now have been on your way to the burning-ghat. As headman of Chandni Chauk and the best shikari in Kaladhungi, all men respected you. But now you have lost that respect and you who were strong and who ate of the best are weak and empty of stomach, for as we came your son told me nothing has passed your lips for sixteen days. But you are not going to die, old friend, as they told you were. You will live for many more years and though we may never shoot together again in the Garuppu jungles, you will not want for game for I will share all I shoot with you, as I have always done. 'And now, here in this hut, with the sacred thread round your fingers and a pipal leaf in your hands, you must swear an oath on your eldest son's head that never again will you touch the foul drug. And this time you will, and you shall keep your oath. And now, while we wait for the milk your son is bringing, we will smoke.'

Kunwar Singh had not taken his eyes off me while I was speaking and now for the first time, he opened his lips and said, 'How can a man who is dying smoke?' 'On the subject of dying', I said, 'we will say no more, for as I have just told you, you are not going to die. And as to how we will smoke, I will show you.' Then, taking two cigarettes from my case, I lit one and placed it between his lips. Slowly he took a pull at it, coughed and with a very feeble hand removed the cigarette. But when the fit of coughing was over, he replaced it between his lips and continued to draw on it. Before we had finished our smoke, Kunwar Singh's son returned carrying a big brass vessel, which he would have dropped at the door if I had not hurriedly relieved him of it. His surprise was understandable, for the father whom he had last seen lying on the ground dying, was now lying on the bed, his head resting on my hat, smoking. There was nothing in the hut to drink from, so I sent the son back to the house for a cup and when he had brought it, I gave Kunwar Singh a drink of warm milk.

I stayed in the hut till late into the night, and when I left Kunwar Singh had drunk a seer of milk and was sleeping peacefully on a warm and comfortable bed. Before I left, I warned the son that he was on no account to allow anyone to come near the hut; that he was to sit by his father and give him a drink of milk every time he awoke; and that if on my return in the morning I found Kunwar Singh dead, I would burn down the village. The sun was just rising next morning when I returned to Chandni Chauk to find both Kunwar Singh and his son fast a-sleep and the brass vessel empty. Kunwar Singh kept his oath, and though he never regained sufficient strength to accompany me on my shikar expeditions, he visited me often and died peacefully four years later in his own house and on his own bed.

III. MOTHI

Mothi had the delicate, finely chiselled features that are the heritage of all high-caste people in India, but he was only a young stripling, all arms, and legs, when his father and mother died and left him with the responsibilities of the family. Fortunately, it was a small one, consisting only of his younger brother and sister. Mothi was at that time fourteen years of age and had been married for six years. One of his first acts on finding himself unexpectedly the head of the family was to fetch his twelve-year-old wife, whom he had not seen since the day of their wedding from her father's house in the Kota Dun, some dozen miles from Kaladhungi. As the cultivation of the six acres of land Mothi inherited entailed more work than the four young people could tackle, Mothi took on a partner, locally known as Agee, who in return for his day-and-night services received free board and lodging and half of the crops produced. The building of the communal hut with bamboos and grass procured from the jungles, under permit, and carried long distances on shoulder and on head, and the constant repairs to the hut necessitated by the violent storms that sweep the foothills, threw a heavy burden on Mothi and his helpers and to relieve them of this burden I built them a masonry house, with three rooms and a wide veranda, on a four-foot plinth. For with the exception of Mothi's wife who had come from a higher altitude, all of them were steeped in malaria.

To protect their crops the tenants used to erect a thorn fence round the entire village, but though it entailed weeks of hard labour, this flimsy fence afforded little protection against stray cattle and wild animals, and when the crops were on the ground the tenants or members of their families had to keep watch in the fields all night. Firearms were strictly rationed, and for our forty tenants the Government allowed us one single-barrelled muzzle-loading gun. This gun enables one tenant in turn to protect his crops with a lethal weapon, while the others had to rely on tin cans which they beat throughout the night. Though the gun accounted for a certain number of pigs and porcupines, which were the worst offenders, the nightly damage was considerable for the village was isolated and surrounded by forests. So, when my handling contract at Mokameh Ghat began paying dividends, I started building a masonry wall round the village. When completed, the wall was six feet high and three miles long. It took ten years to build, for my share of the dividends was small. If today you motor from Haldwani to Ramnagar, through Kaladhungi, you will skirt the upper end of the wall before you cross the Boar Bridge and enter the forest.

I was walking through the village one cold December morning, with Robin, my dog, running ahead and putting up covey after covey of grey partridge which no one but Robin ever disturbed for all who lived in the village loved to hear them calling at sunrise and at sunset, when in the soft ground at the edge of one of the irrigation channels I saw the tracks of a pig. This pig, with great, curved, wicked-looking tusks, was as big as a buffalo calf and was known to everyone in the village. As a squeaker he had wormed his way through the thorn fence and fattened on the crops the wall had worried him at first, but it had a rough face and, being a determined pig, he had in time learnt to climb it. Time and time again the watchers in the fields had fired at him and on several occasions, he had left a blood trail, but none of his wounds had proved fatal and the only effect they had had on him was to make him more wary.

On this December morning the pig's tracks led me towards Mothi's holding, and as I approached the house, I saw Mothi's wife standing in front of it, her hands on her hips, surveying the ruin of their potato patch. The pig had done a very thorough job, for the tubers were not mature and he had been hungry and while Robin cast round to see in which direction the marauder had gone the woman gave vent to her feelings. It is all Punwa's father's fault', she said. 'It was his turn for the gun last night, and instead of staying at home and looking after his own property he must need go and sit up in Kalu's wheat field because he thought there was a chance of shooting a sambhar there. And while he was away, this is what the shaitan has done.' No woman in our part of India ever refers to her husband, or addresses him, by name. Before children are born, he is referred to as the man of the house and after children come is spoken of and addressed as the father of the firstborn. Mothi now had three children, of whom the eldest was Punwa, so to his wife he was 'Punwa's father', and his wife to everyone in the village was 'Punwa's mother'.

Punwa's mother was not only the hardest-working woman in our village but she also had the sharpest tongue and after telling me in no uncertain terms what she thought of Punwa's father for having absented himself the previous night, she turned on me and said I had wasted my money in building a wall over which a pig could climb to eat her potatoes, and that if I could not shoot the pig myself it was my duty to raise the wall a few feet so that no pig could climb over it. Mothi, fortunately arrived while the storm was still breaking over my head, so whistling to Robin I beat a hasty retreat and left him to weather it.

That evening I picked up the tracks of the pig on the far side of the wall and followed them for two miles, at times along game paths and at times along the bank of the Boar River, until they led me to a dense patch of thorn bushes interlaced with lantana. At the edge of this cover, I took up position as there was a fifty-fifty chance of the pig leaving the cover while there was still sufficient light for me to shoot by. Shortly after I had taken up position behind a rock on the bank of the river, a sambhar hind started belling at the upper end of the jungle in which a few years later I was to shoot the Bachelor of Powalgarh. The hind was warning the jungle folk of the presence of a tiger. A fortnight previously a party of three guns, with eight elephants, had arrived in Kaladhungi with the express purpose of shooting a tiger which, at that time, had his headquarters in the forest block for which I had a shooting pass.

The Boar River formed the boundary between my block and the block taken by the party of three guns and they had enticed the tiger to kill in their block by tying up fourteen young buffaloes on their side of the river. Two of these buffaloes had been killed by the tiger, the other twelve had died of neglect, and at about nine o'clock the previous night I had heard the report of a heavy rifle. I sat behind the rock for two hours, listening to the belling sambhar but without seeing anything of the pig, and when there was no longer any light to shoot by, I crossed the river and gaining the Kota road, loped down it, easing up and moving cautiously when passing the caves in which a big python lived and where Bill Bailey of the Forest

Department a month previously had shot a twelve-foot hamadryad. At the village gate I stopped and shouted to Mothi to be ready to accompany me at crack of dawn next morning.

Mothi had been my constant companion in the Kaladhungi jungles for many years. He was keen and intelligent, gifted with good eyesight and hearing, could move through the jungles silently, and was as brave as man could be. He was never late for an appointment, and as we walked through the dew-drenched jungle that morning, listening to the multitude of sounds of the awakening jungle folk, I told him of the belling of the sambhar hind and of my suspicion that she had witnessed the killing of her young one by the tiger and that she had stayed to watch the tiger on his kill, a not uncommon occurrence for in no other way could I account for her sustained belling.

Mothi, was delighted at the prospect of our finding a fresh kill for his means only permitted of his buying meat for his family once a month and a sambhar, chital, or pig, freshly killed by a tiger or by a leopard was a godsend to him. I had located the belling sambhar as being due north and some fifteen hundred yards from me the previous evening and when we arrived at this spot and found no kill, we started looking on the ground for blood hair or a drag mark that would lead us to the kill, for I was still convinced that there was a kill to be found and that the killer was a tiger.

At this spot two shallow depressions, coming down from the foot of the hill a few hundred yards away met. The depressions ran more or less parallel to each other at a distance of about thirty yards and Mothi suggested that he should go up the right-hand depression while I went up the other. As there were only low bushes between and we should be close to and within sight of each other, I agreed to the suggestion.

We had proceeded a hundred yards examining every foot of the ground and going dead slow, when Mothi just as I turned my head to look at him started backwards, screaming as he did so. Then he whipped round and ran for dear life, beating the air with his hands as if warding off a swarm of bees and continuing to scream as he ran. The sudden and piercing scream of a human being in a jungle where a moment before all has been silent is terrifying to hear and quite impossible to describe. Instinctively I knew what had happened. With his eyes fixed on the ground, looking for blood or hair, Mothi had failed to see where he was going and had walked on to the tiger. Whether he had been badly mauled or not I could not see, for only his head and shoulders were visible above the bushes. I kept the sights of my rifle a foot behind him as he ran, intending to press the trigger if I saw any movement, but to my intense relief there was no movement as I swung round and after he had covered a hundred yards.

I considered him safe. I yelled to him to stop adding that I was coming to him, then backing away for a few yards for I did not know whether the tiger had changed his position, I hurried down the depression towards Mothi. He was standing with his back against a tree, and I was greatly relieved to see that there was no blood on him or on the ground on which he was standing. As I reached him, he asked what had happened and when I told him that nothing had happened, he expressed great surprise. He asked if the tiger had not sprung at him or followed him; and when I replied that he had done everything possible to make the tiger do so, he said, 'I know, Sahib. I know I should not have screamed and run, but I could not help' as his voice tailed away and his head came forward, I caught him by the throat, but he slipped through my hands and slumped to the ground. Every drop of blood had drained from his face and as he lay minute after long minute without any movement, I feared the shock had killed him.

There is little one can do in the jungles in an emergency of this kind, and that little I did. I stretched Mothi on his back, loosened his clothes, and massaged the region of his heart. Just as I was giving up hope and preparing to take him home, he opened his eyes.

When Mothi was comfortably seated on the ground with his back to the tree and a half-smoked cigarette between his lips I asked him to tell me exactly what had happened.

'I had gone a short distance up the depression after I left you', he said, 'closely examining the ground for traces of blood or hair, when I saw what looked like a spot of dry blood on a leaf. So, I stooped down to have a closer look and as I raised my head, I looked straight into the face of the tiger. The tiger was lying crouched down facing me at a distance of three or four paces. His head was a little raised off the ground; his mouth was wide open, and there was blood on his chin and on his chest. He looked as though he was on the point of springing at me, so I lost my head and screamed and ran away.

He had seen nothing of the sambhar kill. He said the ground was open and free of bushes and there was no kill where the tiger was lying.

Telling Mothi to stay where he was, I stubbed out my cigarette and set off to investigate for I could think of no reason why a tiger with its mouth open and blood on its chin and on its chest, should allow Mothi to approach within a few feet over open ground and not kill him when he screamed in its face. Going with the utmost caution to the spot where Mothi was standing when he screamed, I saw in front of me a bare patch of ground from which the tiger had swept the carpet of dead leaves as he had rolled from side to side at the nearer edge of this bare patch of ground there was a semicircle of clotted blood. Skirting round where the tiger had been lying, to avoid disturbing the ground, I picked up on the far side of it a light, and fresh blood trail, which for no apparent reason zigzagged towards the hill and then continued along the foot of the hill for a few hundred yards and entered a deep and narrow ravine in which there was a little stream. Up this ravine, which ran deep into the foothills, the tiger had gone. I made my way back to the bare patch of ground and examined the clotted blood. There were splinters of bone and teeth in it, and these splinters provided me with the explanation I was looking for. The rifle shot I had heard two nights previously had shattered the tiger's lower jaw, and he had made for the jungle in which he had his home. He had gone as far as his sufferings and loss of blood permitted and had then lain down on the spot where first the sambhar had seen him tossing about and where thirty hours later Mothi walked on to him.

The most painful wound that can be inflicted on an animal, the shattering of the lower jaw, had quite evidently induced high fever and the poor beast had perhaps only been semi-conscious when he heard Mothi screaming in his face. He had got up quietly and staggered away, in a last effort to reach the ravine in which he knew there was water.

To make quite sure that my deductions were correct Mothi, and I crossed the river into the adjoining shooting block to have a look at the ground where the fourteen buffaloes had been tied up. Here, high up in a tree, we found the machan the three guns had sat on, and the kill the tiger had been eating when fired at. From the kill a heavy blood trail led down to the river, with elephant tracks on each side of it. Leaving Mothi on the right bani, I recrossed the river into my block, picked up the blood trail and the elephant tracks and followed them for five or six hundred yards to where the blood trail led into heavy cover. At the edge of the cover the elephants had halted and, after standing about for some time, had turned to the right and gone away in the direction of Kaladhungi. I had met the returning elephants as I was starting out the previous evening to try and get a shot at the old pig, and one of the guns had asked me where I was going, and when I told him, had appeared to want to tell me something but was restrained from doing so by his companions. So, while the party of three guns went off on their elephants to the Forest Bungalow where they were staying, I had gone off on foot, without any warning, into the jungle in which they had left a wounded tiger.

The walk back to the village from where I had left Mothi was only about three miles, but it took us about as many hours to cover the distance, for Mothi was unaccountably weak and had to rest frequently. After leaving him at his house I went straight to the Forest Bungalow, where I found the party of three packed up and on the point of leaving to catch the evening train at Haldwani. We talked on the steps of the veranda for some little time, I doing most of the talking, and when I learnt that the only reason they could not spare the time to recover the tiger they had wounded was the keeping of a social engagement, I told them that if Mothi died as a result of shock or if the tiger killed any of my tenants, they would have to face a charge of manslaughter.

The party left after my talk with them, and next morning, armed with a heavy rifle, I entered the ravine up which the tiger had gone, not with the object of recovering a trophy for others, but with the object of putting the tiger out of his misery and burning his skin. The ravine, every foot of which I knew, was the last place I would have selected in which to look for a wounded tiger. However, I searched it from top to bottom, and also the hills on either side, for the whole of that day without finding any trace of the tiger, for the blood trail had stopped shortly after he entered the ravine.

Ten days later a forest guard on his rounds came on the remains of a tiger that had been eaten by vultures. In the summer of that year Government made a rule prohibiting sitting up for tigers between the hours of sunset and sunrise and making it incumbent on sportsmen wounding tigers to make every effort to bring the wounded animal to bag and to make an immediate report of the occurrence to the nearest Forest Officer and police outpost.

Mothi met with his experience in December, and when we left Kaladhungi in April he appeared to be little the worse for the shock. But his luck was out for a month later he was badly mauled by a leopard he wounded one night in his field and followed next morning into heavy covers, and he had hardly recovered from his wounds when he had the misfortune of being responsible for the death of a cow, the greatest crime a Hindu can commit.

The cow, an old and decrepit animal that had strayed in from an adjoining village, was grazing in Mothi's field and as he attempted to drive it out it put its hoof in a deep rat-hole and broke its leg. For weeks Mothi attended assiduously to the cow as it lay in his field, but it died eventually, and the matter being too serious for the village priest to deal with, he ordered Mothi to make a pilgrimage to Hardwar. So, having borrowed money for the journey to Hardwar Mothi went. Here to the head priest at the main temple Mothi confessed his crime and after that dignitary had given the offence due consideration, he ordered Mothi to make a donation to the temple this would absolve him of his crime but in order to show repentance he would have also to do penance. The priest then asked him from what acts he derived most pleasure and Mothi, being without guile, made answer that he derived most pleasure from shooting and from eating meat. Mothi was then told by the priest that in future he must refrain from these two pleasures.

Mothi returned from his pilgrimage cleared of his crime but burdened with a lifelong penance. His opportunities for shooting had been few for besides having to share the muzzle-loading gun with others he had had to confine his shooting to the village boundaries, as no man in his position was permitted to shoot in Government forests; even so, Mothi had derived great pleasure from the old gun, and from the occasional shots I had permitted him, against all rules to fire from my rifle. Hard as this half of his penance was the second half was even harder and moreover it adversely affected his health. Though his means had only allowed him to buy a small meat ration once a month, pigs and porcupines were plentiful and deer occasionally strayed into the fields at night. It was the custom in our village, a custom to which I also adhered, for an animal shot by one to be shared by all so Mothi had not, had to depend entirely on the meat he could buy.

It was during the winter following his pilgrimage to Hardwar that Mothi developed a hacking cough. As the remedies we tried failed to give relief, I got a doctor friend who was passing through Kaladhungi to examine him and was horrified to learn that he was suffering from tuberculosis.

On the doctor's recommendation I sent Mothi to the Bhowali Sanatorium thirty miles away Five days later he returned with a letter from the Superintendent of the Sanatorium saying that the case was hopeless, and that for this reason the Superintendent regretted he could not admit Mothi. A medical missionary who was staying with us at the time and who had worked for years in a sanatorium advised us to make Mothi sleep in the open and drink a quart of milk with a few drops of paraffin in it each morning.

So, for the rest of that winter Mothi slept in the open, and while sitting on our veranda, smoking a cigarette, and talking to me, each morning drank a quart of milk fresh from our cows.

The poor of India are fatalists and in addition have little stamina to fight disease. Deprived of our company, though not of our help, Mothi lost hope when we left for our summer home and died a month later.

The women of our foothills are the hardest workers in India, and the hardest working of them all was Mothi's widow, Punwa's mother. A small compact woman as hard as flint and a beaver for work, young enough to remarry but precluded from doing so by reasons of her caste, she bravely and resolutely faced the future and right gallantly she fulfilled her task, ably assisted by her young children, of her three children, Punwa, the eldest was now twelve and with the assistance of neighbors was able to do the ploughing and other field jobs.

Kunthi, a girl was ten and married and until she left the village five years later to join her husband, she assisted her mother in all her thousand and one tasks which included cooking the food and washing up the dishes, washing and mending the clothes for Punwa's mother was very particular about her own and her children's dress and no matter how old and patched the garments were, they always had to be clean, fetching water from the irrigation furrow or from the Boar river for domestic purposes; bringing firewood from the jungles and grass and tender young leaves for the milch, cows and their calves; weeding and cutting the crops; husking the paddy in a hole cut in a slab of rock, with an iron shod staff that was heavy enough to tire the muscles of any man; winnowing the wheat for Punwa to take to the watermill to be ground into atta; and making frequent visits to the bazaar two miles away to drive hard bargains for the few articles of food and clothing the family could afford to buy. Sher Singh, the youngest child, was eight, and from the moment he opened his eyes at the crack of dawn each morning until he closed them when the evening meal had been eaten, he did everything that a boy could do. He even gave Punwa a hand with the ploughing though he had to be helped at the end of each furrow as he was not strong enough to turn the plough.

Sher Singh, without a care in the world, was the happiest child in the village. When he could not be seen he could always be heard for he loved to sing. The cattle four bullocks, twelve cows, eight calves, and Lalu the bull were his special charge and each morning after milking the cows he released the herd from the stakes to which he had tethered them the evening before, drove them out of the shed and through a wicket in the boundary wall and then set to clean up the shed. It would now be time for the morning meal, and when he heard the call from his brother, or Kunthi, he would hurry home across the fields taking the milk can with him. The frugal morning meal consisted of fresh hot chapatis, and dal liberally seasoned with green chilies and salt and cooked in mustard oil. Having breakfasted and finished any chores about the house that he was called upon to do, Sher Singh would begin his day's real work. This was to graze the cattle in the jungle, prevent them from straying, and guard them against leopards and tigers. Having collected the four bullocks and twelve cows from the open ground beyond the boundary wall, where they would be lying basking in the sun and left Kunthi to keep an eye on the calves, this small tousle-headed boy, his axe over his shoulder and Lalu the bull following him, would drive his charges over the Boar Bridge and into the dense jungle beyond, calling to each by name.

Lalu was a young scrub bull destined to be a plough-bullock when he had run his course but who, at the time I am writing about, was free of foot and the pride of Sher Singh, his foster-brother for Lalu had shared his mother's milk with Sher Singh. Sher Singh had christened his foster-brother Lalu, which means red. But Lalu was not red. He was of a light dun colour, with stronger markings on the shoulders and a dark, almost black line running down the length of his back. His horns were short, sharp, and strong, with the light and dark colouring's associated with the shoehorns that adorned dressing tables of that period. When human beings and animals live in close association with each other under conditions in which they are daily subjected to common dangers, each infuses the other with a measure of courage and confidence which the one possesses and the other lacks. Sher Singh, whose father, and grandfather had been more at home in the jungles than in the walks of men, had no fear of anything that walked and Lalu, young and vigorous had unbounded confidence in himself. So, while Sher Singh infused Lalu with courage, Lalu in turn infused Sher Singh with confidence. In consequence Sher Singh's cattle grazed where others feared to go, and he was justly proud of the fact that they were in better condition than any others in the village and that no-leopard or tiger had ever taken toll of them.

Four miles from our village there is a valley about five miles in length, running north and south, which has no equal in beauty or richness of wildlife in the five thousand square miles of forest land in the United Provinces. At the upper end of the valley a clear stream, which grows in volume as it progresses, gushes from a cave in which a python lives, from under the roots of an old jamun tree. This crystal-clear stream with its pools and runs is alive with many kinds of small fish on which live no fewer than five varieties of kingfishers.

In the valley grow flowering and fruit-bearing trees and bushes that attract a multitude of nectar-drinking and fruit eating birds and animals, which in turn attract predatory birds and carnivorous animals which find ample cover in the dense undergrowth and matted canebrakes. In places the set of the stream has caused miniature landslides and on these grows a reedy kind of grass, with broad lush leaves, much fancied by sambhar and kakar.

The valley was a favourite haunt of mine. One winter evening, shortly after our descent to Kaladhungi from our summer home, I was standing at a point where there is a clear view into the valley when, in a clump of grass to the left, I saw a movement. After a long scrutiny the movement revealed itself as an animal feeding on the lush grass on a steep slope. The animal was too light for a sambhar and too big for a kakar, so I set out to stalk it, and as I did so a tiger started calling in the valley a few hundred yards lower down. My quarry also heard the tiger, and as it raised its head, I saw to my surprise that it was Lalu. With head poised he stood perfectly still listening to the tiger and when it stopped calling, he unconcernedly resumed cropping the grass. This was forbidden ground for Lalu, for cattle are not permitted to graze in Government Reserved Forests, and moreover Lalu was in danger from the tiger, so I called to him by name and after a little hesitation, he came up the steep bank and we returned to the village together. Sher Singh was tying up his cattle in the shed when we arrived, and when I told him where I had found Lalu he laughed and said, 'Don't fear for this one, Sahib. The forest guard is a friend of mine and would not impound my Lalu and as for the tiger, Lalu is well able to take care of himself.'

Not long after this incident, the Chief Conservator of Forests, Smythies and his wife arrived on tour in Kaladhungi and as the camels carrying their camp equipment were coming down the forest road towards the Boar Bridge, a tiger killed a cow on the road in front of them. On the approach of the camels, and the shouting of the men with them, the tiger left the cow on the road and bounded into the jungle. The Smythies were sitting on our veranda having morning coffee when the camel men brought word of the killing of the cow. Mrs. Smythies was keen to shoot the tiger, so I went off with two of her men to put up a machan for her and found that in the meantime the tiger had returned and dragged the cow twenty yards into the jungle. When the machan was ready I sent back for Mrs. Smythies and after putting her into the machan with a forest guard to keep her company, I climbed a tree on the edge of the road hoping to get a photograph of the tiger.

It was 4 p.m. We had been in position half an hour and a kakar had just started barking in the direction in which we knew the tiger was lying up, when down the road came Lalu. On reaching the spot where the cow had been killed, he very carefully smelt the ground and a big pool of blood then turned to the edge of the road and with head held high and nose stretched out started to follow the drag. When he saw the cow he circled round her, tearing up the ground with his hoofs and snorting with rage. After tying my camera to a branch, I slipped off the tree and conducted a very angry and protesting Lalu to the edge of the village. Hardly had I returned to my perch on the tree, however, when up the road came Lalu to do a second demonstration round the dead cow. Mrs. Smythies now sent the forest guard to drive Lalu away, and as the man passed me, I told him to take the bull across the Boar Bridge and to remain there with the elephant that was coming later for Mrs. Smythies.

The kakar had stopped barking some time previously and a covey of jungle fowl now started cackling a few yards behind the machan. Getting my camera ready I looked towards Mrs. Smythies and saw she had her rifle poised, and at that moment Lalu appeared for the third time. (We learnt later that after being taken across the bridge, he had circled round, crossed the riverbed lower down and disappeared into the jungle.) This time Lalu trotted up to the cow and, either seeing or smelling the tiger, lowered his head and charged into the bushes, bellowing loudly. Three times he did this, and after each charge he retreated backwards to his starting point, slashing upwards with his horns as he did so.

I have seen buffaloes driving tigers away from their kills and I have seen cattle doing the same with leopards but, with the exception of a Himalayan bear, I had never before seen a solitary animal and a scrub bull at that drive a tiger away from his kill. Courageous as Lalu was, he was no match for the tiger, who was now losing his temper and answering Lalu's bellows with angry growls. Remembering a small boy back in the village whose heart would break if anything happened to his beloved companion, I was on the point of going to Lalu's help when Mrs. Smythies very sportingly gave up her chance of shooting the tiger, so I shouted to the mahout to bring up the elephant. Lalu was very subdued as he followed me to the shed where Sher Singh was waiting to tie him up and I think he was as relieved as I was that the tiger had not accepted his challenge while he was defending the dead cow.

The tiger fed on the cow that night and next evening and while Mrs. Smythies was having another Unsuccessful try to get a shot at him, I took a cine picture which some who read this story may remember having seen.

In the picture the tiger is seen coming down a steep bank and drinking at a little pool.

The jungle was Sher Singh's playground, the only playground he ever knew, just as it had been my playground as a boy and of all whom I have known he alone enjoyed the jungles as much as I have done. Intelligent and observant his knowledge of jungle lore was incredible. Nothing escaped his attention, and he was as fearless as the animal whose name he bore. Our favourite evening walk was along one of the three roads which met on the far side of the Boar Bridge, the abandoned trunk road to Moradabad, the road to Kota and the forest road to Ramnagar. Most evenings at sundown we would hear Sher Singh before we saw him, for he sang with abandon in a clear treble voice that carried far as he drove his cattle home. Always he would greet us with a smile and a salaam and always he would have something interesting to tell us.

'The big tiger's tracks were on the road this morning coming from the direction of Kota and going towards Naya Gaon and at midday I heard him calling at the lower end of the Dhunigad cane-brake.' 'Near Saryapani I heard the clattering of horns, so I climbed a tree and saw two chital stags righting. One of them has very big horns, Sahib, and is very fat, and I have eaten no meat for many days.' '

What am I carrying?' He had something wrapped in big green leaves and tied round with bark balanced on his tousled head. 'I am carrying a pig's leg. I saw some vultures on a tree, so I went to have a look and under a bush I found a pig killed by a leopard last night and partly eaten. If you want to shoot the leopard, Sahib, I will take you to the kill.' 'Today I found a beehive in a hollow haldu tree', he said one day, proudly exhibiting a large platter of leaves held together with long thorns on which the snow-white comb was resting. 'I have brought the honey for you.' Then, glancing at the rifle in my hands, he added, 'I will bring the honey to the house when I have finished my work for perchance you may meet a pig or a kakar and with the honey in your hands you would not be able to shoot.' The cutting of the hive out of the haldu tree with his small axe had probably taken him two hours or more and he had got badly stung in the process, for his hands were swollen and one eye was nearly closed but he said nothing about this and to have commented on it would have embarrassed him.

Later that night, while we were having dinner, he slipped silently into the room and as he laid the brass tray, polished till it looked like gold, on our table, he touched the elbow of his right arm with the fingers of his left hand, an old hill custom denoting respect, which is fast dying out. After depositing such a gift on the table, leaving the tray for Kunthi to call for in the morning, Sher Singh would pause at the door and, looking down and scratching the carpet with his toes, would say, 'If you are going bird shooting tomorrow, I will send Kunthi out with the cattle and come with you for I know where there are a lot of birds'. He was always shy in a house and on these occasions spoke with a catch in his voice as though he had too many words in his mouth and was trying, with difficulty to swallow the ones that were getting in his way.

Sher Singh was in his element on these bird shoots, which the boys of the village enjoyed as much as he and I did for in addition to the excitement and the prospect of having a bird to take home at the end of the day, there was always a halt at midday at a prearranged spot to which the man sent out earlier would bring the fresh sweets and parched gram that would provide a meal for all.

When I had taken my position, Sher Singh would line up his companions and beat the selected cover towards me, shouting the loudest of them all and worming his way through the thickest cover. When a bird was put up, he would yell, 'it's coming, Sahib! It's coming!' Or when a heavy animal went crashing through the undergrowth, as very frequently happened, he would call to his companions not to run away, assuring them that it was only a sambhar or a chital, or maybe a sounder of pig. Ten to twelve patches of cover would be beaten in the course of the day, yielding as many pea fowl as possible and jungle fowl and two or three hares and possibly a small pig or a porcupine. At the end of the last beat the bag would be shared out among the beaters and the gun or if the bag was small only among the beaters and Sher Singh was never happier than when at the end of the day, he made for home with a peacock in full plumage proudly draped over his shoulders.

Punwa was now married, and the day was fast approaching when Sher Singh would have to leave the home for there was not sufficient room on the small holding of six acres for the two brothers. Knowing that it would break Sher Singh's heart to leave the village and his beloved jungles, I decided to apprentice him to a friend who had a garage at Kathgodam, and who ran a fleet of cars on the Nainital motor road. After his training it was my intention to employ Sher Singh to drive our car and accompany me on my shooting trips during the winter and to look after our cottage and garden at Kaladhungi while we were in Naini Tal during the summer. Sher Singh was speechless with delight when I told him of the plans, I had made for him, plans which ensured his continued residence in the village and within sight and calling distance of the home he had never left from the day of his birth. Plans a-many we make in life, and I am not sure there is cause for regret when some go wrong. Sher Singh was to have started his apprenticeship when we returned to Kaladhungi in November.

In October he contracted malignant malaria which led to pneumonia, and a few days before we arrived, he died. During his boyhood's years he had sung through life happy as the day was long and, had he lived, who can say that his life in a changing world would have been as happy, and as carefree, as those first few years?

Before leaving our home for a spell, to regain in new climes the health we lost in Hitler's war I called together our tenants and their families as I had done on two previous occasions, to tell them the time had come for them to take over their holdings and run the village for themselves. Punwa's mother was the spokesman for the tenants on this occasion and after I had had my say she got to her feet and, in her practical way, spoke as follows: 'You have called us away from our work to no purpose. We have told you before and we tell you again that we will not take your land from you, for to do so would imply that we were no longer your people. And now, Sahib, what about the pig, the son of the shaitan who climbed your wall and ate my potatoes? Punwa, and these others cannot shoot it and I am tired of sitting up all night and beating a tin can.'

Maggie and I were walking along the fire-track that skirts the foothills with David at our heels when the pig worthy son of the old shaitan who, full of years and pellets of buckshot had been killed in an all-night fight with a tiger trotted across the track.

The sun had set, and the range was long all of three hundred yards, but a shot was justifiable for the pig was quite evidently on his way to the village. I adjusted the sights and resting the rifle against a tree, waited until the pig paused at the edge of a deep depression. When I pressed the trigger, the pig jumped into the depression, scrambled out on the far side, and made off at top speed. 'Have you missed him?' asked Maggie and with his eyes David put the same question. There was no reason, except miscalculation of the range, why I should not have hit the pig, for my silver foresight had shown up clearly on his black skin and the tree had assisted me to take steady aim. Anyway, it was time to make for home, and as the cattle track down which the pig had been going would lead us to the Boar Bridge, we set off to see the result of my shot. The pig's feet had bitten deeply into the ground where he had taken off and on the far side of the depression, where he had scrambled out, there was blood. Two hundred yards in the direction in which the pig had gone there was a narrow strip of dense cover. I should probably find him dead in the morning in this cover for the blood trail was heavy but if he was not dead and there was trouble, Maggie would not be with me and there would be lighter to shoot by in the morning than there was now.

Punwa had heard my shot and was waiting on the bridge for us. 'Yes', I said, in reply to his eager inquiry, 'it was the old pig I fired at, and judging by the blood trail, he is hit hard.' I added that if he met me on the bridge next morning, I would show him where the pig was, so that later he could take out a party of men to bring it in. 'May I bring the old havildar too?' said Punwa and I agreed.

The havildar, a kindly old man who had won the respect and affection of all, was a Gurkha who on leaving the army had joined the police and having retired a year previously had settled down with his wife and two sons on a plot of land we had given him in our village. Like all Gurkhas the havildar had an insatiable appetite for pig's flesh and when a pig was shot by any of us it was an understood thing that, no matter who went short, the ex-soldier-policeman must have his share.

Punwa and the havildar were waiting for me at the bridge next morning. Following the cattle track, we soon reached the spot where, the previous evening, I had seen the blood. From here we followed the well-defined blood trail which led us, as I had expected, to the dense cover. I left my companions at the edge of the cover, for a wounded pig is a dangerous animal, and with one exception a bear is the only animal in our jungles that has the unpleasant habit of savaging any human being who has the misfortune to be attacked and knocked down by him. For this reason, wounded pigs, especially if they have big tusks, have to be treated with great respect. The pig had stopped where I had expected him to, but he had not died, and at daybreak he had got up from where he had been lying all night and left the cover. I whistled to Punwa and the havildar and when they rejoined me, we set off to trail the animal.

The trail led us across the fire-track and from the direction in which the wounded animal was going it was evident he was making for the heavy jungle on the far side of the hill from which I suspected he had come the previous evening. The morning blood trail was light and continued to get lighter the farther we went, until we lost it altogether in a belt of trees, the fallen leaves of which a gust of wind had disturbed. In front of us at this spot was a tinder-dry stretch of waist-high grass. Still under the conviction that the pig was heading for the heavy jungle on the far side of the hill, I entered the grass, hoping to pick up the tracks again on the far side.

The havildar had lagged some distance behind, but Punwa was immediately behind me when after we had gone a few yards into the grass, my woollen stockings caught on the thorns of a low bush. While I was stooping to free myself, Punwa, to avoid the thorns, moved a few paces to the right and I just got free and was straightening up when out of the grass shot the pig and with an angry grunt went straight for Punwa, who was wearing a white shirt. I then did what I have always asked companions who have accompanied me into the jungles after dangerous game to do if they saw me attacked by a wounded animal. I threw the muzzle of my rifle into the air and shouted at the top of my voice as I pressed the trigger.

If the thorns had not caught in my stockings and lost me a fraction of a second, all would have been well, for I should have killed the pig before it got to Punwa but once the pig had reached him the only thing, I could do to help him was to try to cause a diversion for to have fired in his direction would further have endangered his life. As the bullet was leaving my rifle to land in the jungle a mile away, Punwa, with adespairing scream of 'Sahib', was falling backwards into the grass with the pig right on top of him, but at my shout and the crack of the rifle the pig turned like a whiplash straight for me and before I was able to eject the spent cartridge and ram a fresh one into the chamber of the -275 rifle, he was at me. Taking my right hand from the rifle I stretched the arm out palm downwards, and as my hand came in contact with his forehead he stopped dead, for no other reason than that my time had not come, for he was big and angry enough to have knocked over and savaged a cart horse. The pig's body had stopped but his head was very active, and as he cut upwards with his great tusks, first on one side and then on the other, fortunately cutting only the air, he wore the skin off the palm of my hand with his rough forehead. Then, for no apparent reason, he turned away and as he made off, I put two bullets into him in quick succession and he pitched forward on his head. After that one despairing scream Punwa had made no sound or movement, and with the awful thought of what I would say to his mother and the still more awful thought of what she would say to me, I went with fear and trembling to where he was lying out of sight in the grass, expecting to find him ripped open from end to end. He was laying full stretch on his back and his eyes were closed but to my intense relief I saw no blood on his white clothes. I shook him by the shoulder and asked him how he was and where he had been hurt. In a very weak voice, he said he was dead and that his back was broken.

I straddled his body and gently raised him to a sitting position and was overjoyed to find that he was able to retain this position when I released my hold. Passing my hand down his back I assured him that it was not broken, and after he had verified this fact with his own hand, he turned his head and looked behind him to where a dry stump was projecting two or three inches above the ground. Evidently, he had fainted when the pig knocked him over and on coming to feeling the stump boring into his back, had jumped to the conclusion that it was broken.

And so, the old pig, son of the shaitan, died and in dying nearly frightened the lives out of two of us. But beyond rubbing a little skin off my hand he did us no harm for Punwa escaped without a scratch and with a grand story to tell. The havildar, like the wise old soldier he was, had remained in the background. None the less he claimed a lion's share of the pig, for had he not stood foursquare in reserve to render assistance if assistance had been called for? And further, was it not the custom for those present at a killing to receive a double share and what difference was there between seeing and hearing the shots that had killed the pig? So, a double share had not denied him and he too, in the course of time, had a grand story to tell of the part he took in that morning's exploit.

Punwa now reigns, and is raising a family, in the house I built for his father. Kunthi has left the village to join her husband, and Sher Singh waits in the Happy Hunting Grounds. Punwa's mother is still alive, and if you stop at the village gate and walk through the fields to Punwa's house you will find her keeping house for Punwa and his family and working as hard and as cheerfully at her thousand and one tasks as she worked when she first came to our village as Mothi's bride.

During the war years Maggie spent the winters alone in our cottage at Kaladhungi, without transport and fourteen miles from the nearest settlement. Her safety gave me no anxiety for I knew she was safe among my friends, the poor of India.

IV. PRE-RED-TAPE DAYS

I was camping with Anderson one winter in the Terai, the low-lying stretch of country at the foot of the Himalayas and having left Bindukhera after breakfast one morning in early January, we made a wide detour to Boksar our next camping place to give our servants time to pack up and pitch our tents before our arrival.

There were two small unbridged rivers to cross between Bindukhera and Boksar and at the second of these rivers one of the camels carrying our tents slipped on the clay bottom and deposited its load in the river. This accident resulted in a long delay, with the result that we arrived at Boksar after a very successful day's black partridge shooting, while our kit was still being unloaded from the camels.

The camp site was only a few hundred yards from Boksar village and as Anderson's arrival was a great event, the entire population had turned out to pay their respects to him and to render what assistance they could in setting up our camp.

Sir Frederick Anderson was at that time Superintendent of the Terai and Bhabar Government Estates and by reason of the large amount of the milk of human kindness that he was endowed with he had endeared himself to the large population, embracing all castes and creeds, living in the many thousands of square miles of country he ruled over. In addition to his kindly nature, Anderson was a great administrator and was gifted with a memory which I have only seen equalled in one other man, General Sir Henry Ramsay, who for twenty-eight years administered the same tract of country and who throughout his service was known as the Uncrowned King of Kumaon. Both Ramsay and Anderson were Scotsmen, and it was said of them that once having heard a name or seen a face they never forgot it. It is only those who have had dealings with simple uneducated people who can realize the value of a good memory, for nothing appeals so much to a humble man as the remembering of his name or the circumstances in which he has previously been met.

When the history of the rise and fall of British Imperialism is written, due consideration will have to be given to the important part red tape played in the fall of the British raj. Both Ramsay and Anderson served India at a time when red tape was unknown, and their popularity and the success of their administration was in great measure due to their hands' not being tied with it.

Ramsay, in addition to being Judge of Kumaon, was also magistrate, policeman, forest officer, and engineer, and as his duties were manifold and onerous, he performed many of them while walking from one camp to another. It was his custom while on these long walks and while accompanied by a crowd of people, to try all his civil and criminal cases. The complainant and his witnesses were first heard and then the defendant and his witnesses, and after due deliberation, Ramsay would pronounce judgment, which might be either a fine or a sentence to imprisonment. In no case was his judgment known to be questioned, nor did any man whom he had sentenced to a fine or imprisonment fail to pay the fine into the Government Treasury or fail to report himself at the nearest jail to carry out the term of simple or rigorous imprisonment to which Ramsay had sentenced him.

As Superintendent of the Terai and Bhabar, Anderson had only to perform a part of the duties that had been performed by his predecessor Ramsay, but he had wide administrative powers and that afternoon, while our tents were being pitched on the camping ground at Boksar, Anderson told the assembled people to sit down, adding that he would listen to any complaints they had to make and receive any petitions they wished to present.

The first petition came from the headman of a village adjoining Boksar. It appeared that this village and Boksar had a joint irrigation channel that served both villages and that ran through Boksar. Owing to the partial failure of the monsoon rains, the water in the channel had not been sufficient for both villages and Boksar village had used it all, with the result that the paddy crop of the lower village had been ruined. The headman of Boksar admitted that no water had been allowed to go down the channel to the lower village and justified his action by pointing out that, if the water had been shared, the paddy crops of both villages would have been ruined. The crop had been harvested and threshed a few days before our arrival and after Anderson had heard what the two headmen had to say, he ordered that the paddy should be divided up according to the acreage of the two villages. The people of Boksar acknowledged the justice of this decision but claimed they were entitled to payment of the labour that had been employed in harvesting and threshing the crop. To this claim the lower village objected on the ground that no request had been made to them for help while the Boksar crop was being harvested and threshed. Anderson upheld the objection and while the two headmen went off to divide the paddy the next petition was presented to him.

This was from Chadi, accusing Kalu of having abducted his wife Tilni. Chadi's complaint was that three weeks previously Kalu had made advances to Tilni that in spite of his protests Kalu had persisted in his advances; and that ultimately Tilni had left his hut and taken up residence with Kalu. When Anderson asked if Kalu was present, a man sitting at the edge of the semicircle in front of us stood up and said he was Kalu.

While the case of the paddy had been under discussion the assembled women and girls had shown little interest, for that was a matter to be decided by their menfolk. But this abduction case, judging from the expression on their faces and the sharp intakes of breath, was one in which they were all intensely interested.

When Anderson asked Kalu if he admitted the charge that Chadi had brought against him, he admitted that Tilni was living in the hut he had provided for her, but he stoutly denied that he had abducted her. When asked if he was prepared to return Tilni to her lawful husband, Kalu replied that Tilni had come to him of her own free will and that he was not prepared to force her to return to Chadi. 'Is Tilni present?' asked Anderson. A girl from among the group of women came forward and said, 'I am Tilni. What does Your Honour want with me?'

Tilni was a clean-limbed attractive young girl, some eighteen years of age. Her hair done in a foot-high cone in the traditional manner of the women of the Terai, was draped with a white-bordered black sari, her upper person was encased in a tight-fitting red bodice and a voluminous gaily coloured skirt completed her costume. When asked by Anderson why she had left her husband, she pointed to Chadi and said, 'Look at him. Not only is he dirty, as you can see, but he is also a miser; and during the two years I have been married to him he has not given me any clothes, nor has he given me any jewelry. "These clothes that you are looking at and this jewelry', she said, touching some silver bangles on her wrists, and several strings of glass beads round her neck,' were given to me by Kalu.' Asked if she was willing to go back to Chadi, Tilni tossed her head and said nothing would induce her to do so.

This aboriginal tribe, living in the unhealthy Terai, is renowned for two sterling qualities cleanliness and the independence of the women. In no other part of India are villages and the individual dwellings as spotlessly clean as they are in the Terai and in no other part of India would a young girl have dared or in fact been permitted, to stand before a mixed gathering including two white men to plead her own cause. Chadi was now asked by Anderson if he had any suggestions to make, to which he replied:

'You are my mother and my father. I came to you for justice, and if Your Honour is not prepared to compel my wife to return to me, I claim compensation for her.' 'To what extent do you claim compensation for her?' asked Anderson, to which Chadi replied, 'I claim one hundred and fifty rupees'. From all sides of the semicircle there were now exclamations of 'He claims too much', 'far too much', and 'She is not worth it'. On being asked by Anderson if he was willing to pay one hundred and fifty rupees for Tilni, Kalu said the price demanded was excessive and added that he knew as everyone in Boksar knew, that Chadi had only paid a hundred rupees for Tilni. This price, he argued, had been paid for Tilni when she was 'new' and as this was no longer the case the most, he was willing to pay was fifty rupees.

The assembled people now took sides; some maintaining that the sum demanded was too great, while others vigorously maintained that the sum offered was too small. Eventually, after giving due consideration to the arguments for and against, arguments that went into very minute and very personal details and to which Tilni listened with an amused smile on her pretty face. Anderson fixed the price of Tilni at seventy-five rupees and this sum Kalu was ordered to pay Chadi. Opening his waistband, Kalu produced a string purse, and emptied it on the carpet at Anderson's feet. The contents amounted to fifty-two silver rupees. When two of Kalu's friends had come to his assistance and added another twenty-three rupees, Chadi was told to count the money. When he had done so and stated that the sum was correct, a woman whom I had noticed coming very slowly and apparently very painfully from the direction of the village after all the others were seated and who had sat down a little apart from the rest, got with some difficulty to her feet and said, 'What about me, Your Honour?' 'Who are you?' asked Anderson. 'I am Kalu's wife', she replied.

She was a tall gaunt woman, every drop of blood drained from her ivory-white face, her bodyline distorted with an enormous spleen and her feet swollen the result of malaria, the scourge of the Terai.

In a tired, toneless voice the woman said that now that Kalu had purchased another wife she would be homeless; and as she had no relatives in the village, and was too ill to work, she would die of neglect and starvation. Then she covered her face with her sari and began to cry silently, great sobs shaking her wasted frame and tears splashing down on her distorted body.

Here was an unexpected and an unfortunate complication, and one that was for Anderson difficult of solution for while the case had been under discussion there had been no hint that Kalu already had a wife. The uncomfortable silence following on the woman's pitiful outburst had lasted some time when Tilni, who had remained standing, ran across to the poor weeping woman and flinging her strong young arms round her said, 'Don't cry, sister, don't cry and don't say you are homeless, for I will share the new hut Kalu has built for me with you and I will take care of you and nurse you and one half of all that Kalu gives me I will give you. So don't cry anymore sister and now come with me and I will take you to our hut.'

As Tilni and the sick woman moved off, Anderson stood up and, blowing his nose violently, said the wind coming down from the hills had given him a damned cold and that the proceedings were closed for the day. The wind coming down from the hills appeared to have affected others in the same way as it had affected Anderson, for his was not the only nose that was in urgent need of blowing. But the proceedings were not quite over, for Chadi now approached Anderson and asked for the return of his petition.

Having torn his petition into small bits, Chadi took the piece of cloth in which he had tied up the seventy-five rupees from his pocket, opened it and said: 'Kalu and I be men of the same village, and as he has now two mouths to feed, one of which requires special food, he will need all his money. So, permit me, Your Honour, to return this money to him.'

While touring his domain, Anderson and his predecessors in pre-red-tape days settled to the mutual satisfaction of all concerned hundreds, nay thousands, of cases similar to these, without the contestants being put to one pice of expense. Now, since the introduction of red tape, these cases are taken to courts of law where both the complainant and the defendant are bled white and where seeds of dissension are sown that inevitably lead to more and more court cases, to the enrichment of the legal profession and the ruin of the poor, simple, honest, hardworking peasantry.

V. THE LAW OF THE JUNGLES

Harkwar and Kunthi were married before their total ages had reached double figures. This was quite normal in the India of those days and would possibly still have been so had Mahatma Gandhi and Miss Mayo never lived. Harkwar and Kunthi lived in villages a few miles apart at the foot of the great Dunagiri Mountain and had never seen each other until the great day when, dressed in bright new clothes, they had for all too short a time been the Centre of attraction of a vast crowd of relatives and friends. That day lived long in their memories as the wonderful occasion when they had been able to fill their small bellies to bursting point with halwa and puris. The day also lived for long years in the memory of their respective fathers, for on it the village Bania, who was their 'father and mother', realizing their great necessity had provided the few rupees that had enabled them to retain the respect of their community by marrying their children at the age that which children should be married, and on the propitious date selected by the priest of the village and had made a fresh entry against their names in his register.

True, the fifty per cent interest demanded for the accommodation was excessive but God willing, a part of it would be paid for there were other children yet to be married and who but the good Bania was there to help them? Kunthi, returned to her father's home after her wedding and for the next few years performed all the duties that children are called upon to perform in the homes of the very poor. The only difference her married state made in her life was that she was no longer permitted to wear the one-piece dress that unmarried girls wear. Her new costume now consisted of three pieces, a chaddar a yard and a half long, one end of which was tucked into her skirt and the other draped over her head, a tiny sleeveless bodice, and a skirt a few inches long.

Several uneventful and carefree years went by for Kunthi until the day came when she was judged old enough to join her husband. Once again, the Bania came to the rescue and arrayed in her new clothes, a very tearful girl-bride set out for the home of her boy-husband. The change from one home to another only meant for Kunthi the performing of chores for her mother-in-law which she had previously performed for her mother. There are no drones in a poor man's household in India; young and old have their allotted work to do and they do it cheerfully. Kunthi was now old enough to help with the cooking and as soon as the morning meal had been eaten all who were capable of working for wages set out to perform their respective tasks, which, no matter how minor they were, brought grist to the family mill. Harkwar's father was a mason and was engaged on building a chapel at the American Mission School. I was Harkwar's ambition to follow in his father's profession and until he had the strength to do so, he helped the family exchequer by carrying the materials used by his father and the other masons, earning two annas a day for his ten hours' labour.

The crops on the low irrigated lands were ripening and after Kunthi had washed and polished the metal pots and pans used for the morning meal she accompanied her mother-in-law and her numerous sisters-in-law to the fields of the headman of the village, where with other women and girls she laboured as many hours as her husband for half the wage he received. When the day's work was done the family walked back in the twilight to the hut Harkwar's father had been permitted to build on the headman's land and with the dry sticks the younger children had collected during their elders' absence, the evening meal was cooked and eaten. Except for the fire, there had never been any other form of illumination in the hut, and when the pots and pans had been cleaned and put away, each member of the family retired to his or her allotted place, Harkwar and his brothers sleeping with their father and Kunthi sleeping with the other female members of the family.

When Harkwar was eighteen and Kunthi sixteen, they left and, carrying their few possessions, set up home in a hut placed at their disposal by an uncle of Harkwar's in a village three miles from the cantonment of Ranikhet. A number of barracks were under construction in the cantonment and

Harkwar had no difficulty in finding work as a mason; nor had Kunthi any difficulty in finding work as a labourer, carrying stones from a quarry to the site of the building.

For four years the young couple worked on the barracks at Ranikhet and during this period Kunthi had two children. In November of the fourth year the buildings were completed and Harkwar and Kunthi had to find new work because their savings were small and would only keep them in food for a few days.

Winter set in early that year and promised to be unusually severe. The family had no warm clothes and after a week's unsuccessful search for work, Harkwar suggested that they should migrate to the foothills where he heard a canal headworks was being constructed.

So, early in December, the family set out in high spirits on their long walk to the foothills. The distance between the village in which they had made their home for four years and the canal headworks at Kaladhungi, where they hoped to procure work, was roughly fifty miles.

Sleeping under trees at night, toiling up and down steep and rough roads during the day and carrying all their worldly possessions and the children by turns, Harkwar and Kunthi, tired and footsore, accomplished the journey to Kaladhungi in six days.

Other landless members of the depressed class had migrated earlier in the winter from the high hills to the foothills and built themselves communal huts capable of housing as many as thirty families. In these huts Harkwar and Kunthi were unable to find accommodation, so they had to build a hut for themselves. They chose a site at the edge of the forest where there was an abundant supply of fuel, within easy reach of the bazaar and laboured early and late on a small hut of branches and leaves, for their supply of hard cash had dwindled to a few rupees and there was no friendly Bania here to whom they could turn for help.

The forest at the edge of which Harkwar and Kunthi built their hut was a favourite hunting-ground of mine. I had first entered it carrying my old muzzle-loader to shoot red jungle fowl and pea fowl for the family larder and later I had penetrated every corner, armed with a modern rifle, in search of a big game. At the time Harkwar and Kunthi and their two children, Punwa, a boy aged three and Putali, a girl aged two, took up their residence in the hut, there were in that forest, to my certain knowledge, five tigers; eight leopards; a family of four sloth bears; two Himalayan black bears, which had come down from the high hills to feed on wild plums and honey; a number of hyenas who had their burrows in the grasslands five miles away and who visited the forest nightly to feed on the discarded portions of the tigers' and leopards' kills; a pair of wild dogs; numerous jackals and foxes and pine martens; and a variety of civet and other cats.

There were also two pythons, many kinds of snakes, crested and tawny eagles and hundreds of vultures in the forest. I have not mentioned animals such as deer, antelope, pigs, and monkeys, which are harmless to human beings, for they have no part in my story.

The day after the flimsy hut was completed, Harkwar found work as a qualified mason on a daily wage of eight annas with the contractor who was building the canal headworks and Kunthi purchased for two rupees a permit from the Forest Department which entitled her to cut grass on the foothills, which she sold as fodder for the cattle of the shopkeepers in the bazaar. For her bundle of green grass weighing anything up to eighty pounds and which necessitated a walk off from ten to fourteen miles, mostly up and down steep hills, Kunthi received four annas, one anna of which was taken by the man who held the Government contract for sale of grass in the bazaar. On the eight annas earned by Harkwar, plus the three annas earned by Kunthi, the family of four lived in comparative comfort, for food was plentiful and cheap and for the first time in their lives they were able to afford one meat meal a month.

Two of the three months that Harkwar and Kunthi intended to spend in Kaladhungi passed very peacefully. The hours of work were long, and admitted of no relaxation, but to that they had been accustomed from childhood. The weather was perfect, the children kept in good health, and except during the first few days while the hut was being built, they had never gone hungry. The children had in the beginning been anxious, for they were too young to accompany Harkwar to the canal headworks or Kunthi on her long journeys in search of grass. Then a kindly old, crippled woman living in the communal hut a few hundred yards away came to the rescue by offering to keep a general eye on the children while the parents were away at work. This arrangement worked satisfactorily for two months, and each evening when Harkwar returned from the canal headworks four miles away and Kunthi returned a little later after selling her grass in the bazaar, they found Punwa and Putali eagerly awaiting their return.

Friday was fair day in Kaladhungi and on that day everyone in the surrounding villages made it a point to visit the bazaar, where open booths were erected for the display of cheap food, fruit, and vegetables. On these fair days Harkwar and Kunthi returned from work half an hour before their usual time, for if any vegetables had been left over it was possible to buy them at a reduced price before the booths closed down for the night. One particular Friday, when Harkwar and Kunthi returned to the hut after making their modest purchases of vegetables and a pound of goat's meat, Punwa and Putali were not at the hut to welcome them. On making inquiries from the crippled woman at the communal hut, they learned that she had not seen the children since midday. The woman suggested that they had probably gone to the bazaar to see a merry-go-round that had attracted all the children from the communal hut and as this seemed a reasonable explanation Harkwar set off to search the bazaar while Kunthi returned to the hut to prepare the evening meal. An hour later Harkwar returned with several men who had assisted him in his search to report that no trace of the children could be found and that of all the people he had questioned, none admitted having seen them.

At that time a rumour was running through the length and breadth of India of the kidnapping of Hindu children by fakirs, for sale on the north-west frontier for immoral purposes. What truth there was in this rumour, I am unable to say but I had frequently read in the daily press of fakirs being man handled, and on several occasions being rescued by the police from crowds' intent on lynching them. It is safe to say that every parent in India had heard these rumours and when Harkwar and the friends who had helped him in his search returned to the hut, they communicated their fears to Kunthi that the children had been kidnapped by fakirs, who had probably come to the fair for that purpose.

At the lower end of the village there was a police station in charge of a head constable and two constables. To this police station Harkwar and Kunthi repaired, with a growing crowd of well-wishers. The head constable was a kindly old man who had children of his own and after lie had listened sympathetically to the distracted parents' story and recorded their statements in his diary, he said that nothing could be done that night but that next morning he would send the town crier round to all the fifteen villages in Kaladhungi to announce the loss of the children. He then suggested that if the town crier could announce a reward of fifty rupees, it would greatly assist in the safe return of the children. Fifty rupees! Harkwar and Kunthi were aghast at the suggestion, for they did not know there was so much money in all the world. However, when the town crier set out on his round the following morning, he was able to announce the reward for a man in Kaladhungi who had heard of the head constable's suggestion had offered the money.

The evening meal was eaten late that night. The childrens' portion was laid aside, and throughout the night a small fire was kept burning, for it was bitterly cold and at short intervals Harkwar and Kunthi went out into the night to call to their children, though they knew there was no hope of receiving an answer.

At Kaladhungi two roads cross each other at right angles, one running along the foot of the hills from Haldwani to Ramnagar and the other running from Naini Tal to Bazpur. During that Friday night, sitting close to the small fire to keep themselves warm, Harkwar and Kunthi decided that if the children did not turn up by morning, they would go along the former road and make inquiries, as this was the most likely route for the kidnappers to have taken.

At daybreak on Saturday morning, they went to the police station to tell the head constable of their decision and were instructed to lodge a report at the Haldwani and Ramnagar police stations. They were greatly heartened when the head constable told them that he was sending a letter by mail runner to no less a person than the Inspector of Police at Haldwani, requesting him to telegraph to all railway junctions to keep a look-out for the children, a description of whom he was sending with his letter.

Near sunset that evening Kunthi returned from her twenty-eight-mile walk to Haldwani and went straight to the police station to inquire about her children and to tell the head constable that, though her quest had been fruitless, she had lodged a report as instructed at the Haldwani police station. Shortly afterwards Harkwar returned from his thirty-six-mile walk to Ramnagar and he too went straight to the police station to make inquiries and to report that he had found no trace of the children but had carried out the head constable's instructions. Many friends, including a number of mothers who feared for the safety of their own children, were waiting at the hut to express their sympathy for Harkwar and for Punwa's mother for as is the custom in India, Kunthi when she married lost the name she had been given at birth and until Punwa was born had been addressed and referred to as 'Harkwar's wife' and after Punwa's birth as 'Punwa's mother.

Sunday was a repetition of Saturday, with the difference that instead of going east and west, Kunthi went north to Nainital while Harkwar went south to Bazpur. The former covered thirty miles, and the latter thirty-two. Starting early and returning at nightfall, the distracted parents traversed many miles of rough roads through dense forests, where people do not usually go except in large parties and where Harkwar and Kunthi would not have dreamed of going alone had not anxiety for their children overcome their fear of dacoits and of wild animals. On that Sunday evening, weary and hungry, they returned to their hut from their fruitless visit to Nainital and to Bazpur, to be met by the news that the town crier's visit to the villages and the police inquiries had failed to find any trace of the children. Then they lost heart and gave up all hope of ever seeing Punwa and Putali again. The anger of the gods, that had resulted in a fakir being able to steal their children in broad daylight, was not to be explained.

Before starting on their long walk from the hills-they had consulted the village priest and he had selected the propitious day for them to set out on their journey. At every shrine they had passed they had made the requisite offering; at one place, a dry bit of wood, in another a small strip of cloth torn from the hem of Kunthi's chaddar and in yet another a pice, which they could ill afford. And here, at Kaladhungi, every time they passed the temple that their low caste did not permit them to enter; they had never failed to raise their clasped hands in supplication. Why then had this great misfortune befallen them, who had done all that the gods demanded of them and who had never wronged any man?

Monday found the pair too dispirited and too tired to leave their hut. There was no food and would be none until they resumed work. But of what use was it to work now, when the children for whom they had ungrudgingly laboured from morn to night were gone? So, while friends came and went, offering what sympathy they could, Harkwar sat at the door of the hut staring into a bleak and hopeless future, while Kunthi, her tears all gone, sat in a corner, hour after hour, rocking herself to and from, to and from.

On that Monday a man of my acquaintance was herding buffaloes in the jungle in which lived the wild animals and birds I have mentioned. He was a simple soul who had spent the greater part of his life in the jungles herding the buffaloes of the headman at Patabpur village. He knew the danger from tigers and near sundown he collected the buffaloes and started to drive them to the village, along a cattle track that ran through the densest part of the jungle. Presently he noticed that as each buffalo got to a certain spot in the track it turned its head to the right and stopped, until urged on by the horns of the animal following. When he got to this spot, he also turned his head to the right and in a little depression a few feet from the track saw two small children lying.

Man had been in the jungle with his buffaloes when the town crier had made his round of the villages on Saturday but that night and the following night also, the kidnapping of Harkwar's children had been the topic of conversation round the village fire, as in fact it had been round every village fire in the whole of Kaladhungi. Here then were the missing children for whom a reward of fifty rupees had been offered.

But why had they been murdered and brought to this remote spot? The children were naked, and were clasped in each other's arms. The herdsman defended into the depression and squatted down on his hunkers to determine, if he could, how the children had met their death. That the children were dead he was convinced, yet now as he sat closely scrutinizing them, he suddenly saw that they were breathing, that in fact they were not dead, but sound asleep. He was a father himself and very gently he touched the children and roused

them. To touch them was a crime against his caste, for he was a Brahmin and they were low-caste children but what mattered caste in an emergency like this? So, leaving his buffaloes to find their own way home, he picked up the children, who were too weak to walk, and set out for the Kaladhungi bazaar with one on each shoulder. The man was not too strong himself for like all who live in the foothills, he had suffered much from malaria.

The children were an awkward load and had to be held in position. Moreover, as all the cattle tracks and game paths in this jungle ran from north to south and his way lay from east to west, he had to make frequent detours to avoid impenetrable thickets and deep ravines. But he carried on manfully, resting every now and then in the course of his six-mile walk. Putali was beyond speech, but Punwa was able to talk a little and all the explanation he could give for their being in the jungle was that they had been playing and had got lost.

Harkwar was sitting at the door of his hut staring into the darkening night, in which points of light were beginning to appear as a lantern or cooking-fire was lit here and there, when he saw a small crowd of people appearing from the direction of the bazaar. At the head of the procession a man was walking, carrying something on his shoulders. From all sides people were converging on the procession and he could hear an excited murmur of 'Harkwar's children'. Harkwar's children. He could not believe his ears and yet there appeared to be no mistake for the procession was coming straight towards his hut.

Kunthi, having reached the limit of her misery and of her physical endurance, had fallen asleep curled up in a corner of the hut. Harkwar shook her awake and got her to the door just as the herdsman carrying Punwa and Putali reached it.

When the tearful greetings and blessings and thanks for the rescuer and the congratulations of friends had partly subsided, the question of the reward the herdsman had earned was mooted. To a poor man fifty rupees was wealth, untold, and with it the herdsman could buy three buffaloes or ten cows and be independent for life. But the rescuer was a better man than the crowd gave him credit for. The blessings and thanks that had been showered on his head that night, he said, was reward enough for him and he stoutly refused to touch one pice of the fifty rupees. Nor would Harkwar or Kunthi accept the reward either as a gift or a loan. They had got back the children they had lost all hope of ever seeing again and would resume work as their strength returned. In the meantime, the milk, and sweets and puris that one and another of the assembled people, out of the goodness of their hearts, had run to the bazaar to fetch would be amply sufficient to sustain them.

Two-year-old Putali and three-year-old Punwa were lost at midday on Friday and were found by the herdsman at about 5 p.m. on Monday, a matter of seventy-seven hours. I have given a description of the wildlife which to my knowledge was in the forest in which the children spent those seventy-seven hours, and it would be unreasonable to assume that none of the animals or birds saw, heard, or smelt the children. And yet, when the herdsman put Putali and Punwa into their parents' arms, there was not a single mark of tooth or claw on them.

I once saw a tigress stalking a month-old kid. The ground was very open, and the kid saw the tigress while she was still some distance away and started bleating, where on the tigress gave up her stalk and walked straight up to it. When the tigress had approached within a few yards, the kid went forward to meet her and on reaching the tigress stretched out its neck and put up its head to smell her. For the duration of a few heartbeats the month-old kid and the Queen of the Forest stood nose to nose and 'then the queen turned and walked off in the direction from which she had come.

When Hitler's war was nearing its end, in one week I read extracts from speeches of three of the greatest men in the British Empire, condemning war atrocities, and accusing the enemy of attempting to introduce the 'law of the jungle' into the dealings of warring man and man. Had the Creator made the same law for man as He has made for the jungle folk, there would be no wars, for the strong in man would have the same consideration for the weak as is the established law of the jungles.

VI. THE BROTHERS

The long years of training boys for jungle warfare were over and we were sitting one morning after breakfast on the veranda of our cottage at Kaladhungi. My sister Maggie was knitting a khaki pullover for me, and I was putting the finishing touches to a favourite fly-rod that suffered from years of disuse, when a man wearing a clean but much-patched cotton suit walked up the steps of the veranda with a broad grin on his face, salaamed, and asked if we remembered him.

Many people, clean and not so clean, old, and young, rich and poor (but mostly poor), Hindus, Mohammedans, and Christians, walked up those steps, for our cottage was at a crossroads at the foot of the hills and on the border line between the cultivated land and the forest. All who were sick or sorry, in want of a helping hand or in need of a little human companionship and a cup of tea, whether living on the cultivated land or working in the forest or just passing on their way from one place to another, found their way to our cottage. Had a record been maintained over the years of only the sick and injured treated, it would have had thousands of names in it. And the cases dealt with would have covered every ailment that human flesh is heir to and subject to, when living in an unhealthy area, working in forests on dangerous jobs among animals who occasionally lose their tempers.

There was the case of the woman who came one morning and complained that her son had great difficulty in eating the linseed poultice that had been given to her the previous evening to apply on a boil as the poultice did not appear to have done the boy any good, she asked to have the medicine changed. And the case of the old Mohammedan woman who came late one evening, with tears streaming down her face and begged Maggie to save her husband who was dying of pneumonia. She looked a glance at the tablets of M. & B. 693 and asked if that was all that was to be given to a dying man to make him well; but next day she returned with a beaming countenance to report that her husband had recovered, and begged for the same kind of medicine for the four friends she had brought with her, each of whom had husbands as old as hers who might at any time get pneumonia. And there was the case of the girl about eight years old, who, after some difficulty in reaching the latch of the gate, marched up to the veranda firmly holding the hand of a boy some two years younger, and asked for medicine for the boy's sore eyes. She sat herself down on the ground, made the boy lie on his back, and having got his head between her knees said, 'Now, Miss Sahib, you can do anything you like to him.' This girl was the daughter of the headman of a village six miles away. Seeing her classmate suffering from sore eyes, she had taken it upon herself to bring him to Maggie for treatment and for a whole week, until his eyes were quite well, the young Samaritan brought the boy to the cottage, though in order to do so she had to walk an additional four miles each day.

Then there was the case of the lawyer from Delhi, who limped into the compound one day with his right leg ripped open by the tusk of a pig from his heel to the back of his knee. All the time his leg was being attended to him swore at the unclean beast that had done this terrible thing to him for he was a follower of the Prophet. His story was that when that morning he had approached the tree he had fallen on the previous day to saw it up, a pig which had been sheltering among the branches ran against him and cut his leg. When I suggested that it was his own fault for having got in the way of the pig, he indignantly exclaimed: 'With the whole jungle to run about in, what need was there for it to have run against me when I had done nothing, to offend it and in fact before I had even seen it?'

There was another lawyer too. While turning over a log he had been stung on the palm of his hand by a scorpion 'as big as this'. After treatment, he rolled on the ground loudly lamenting his fate and asserting that the medicine was doing him no good, but not long after he was observed to be holding his sides and choking with laughter. It was the day of the children's annual fete, and when the races had been run and the two hundred children and their mothers had been fed sweets and fruit, a circle had been formed. A blindfolded boy had been set to break a paper bag containing nuts of all kinds, which was slung between two bamboos held upright by two men and it was when the boy brought his stick down on the head of one of these men that the scorpion patient was found to be laughing the loudest of all the assembly. When asked how the pain now was, the man replied that it had gone, and that in any case he would not mind how many scorpions stung him provided he could take part in a tamasha like this.

The members of our family have been amateur physicians for more years than I can remember, and as Indians, especially the poorer ones, have long memories, and never forget a kindness no matter how trivial it may have been, not all the people who walked up the steps of our cottage at Kaladhungi were patients. Many there were who had marched for days over rough tracks in all weathers to thank us for the small kindnesses shown to them, maybe the previous year or maybe many years previously.

One of these was a sixteen-year-old boy who with his mother had been housed for some days in our village while Maggie treated his mother for influenza and badly inflamed eyes; now he had done a march of many days to bring Maggie his mother's thanks and a present of a few pomegranates which his mother had picked for her 'with her own hand '. And only that day, an hour before the man wearing the patched suit had arrived, an old man had walked up the steps and seated himself on the veranda with his back to one of the pillars and, after looking at me for some time, had shaken his head in a disapproving manner and said, 'You are looking much older, Sahib, than you were when I last saw you.' 'Yes', I replied, 'all of us are apt to look older after ten years.' 'Not all of us, Sahib,' he rejoined, 'for I look and feel no older than when I last sat in your veranda not ten, but twelve years ago. On that occasion I was returning on foot from a pilgrimage to Badrinath, and seeing your gate open, and being tired and in urgent need of ten rupees, I asked you to let me rest for a while and appealed to you for help. I am now returning from another pilgrimage, this time to the sacred city of Benares. I am in no need of money and have only come to thank you for the help you gave me before and to tell you that I got home safely. After this smoke, and a little rest, I shall return to rejoin my family, whom I left at Haldwani.' A fourteen-mile walk each way. And in spite of his assertion that twelve years had not made him look or feel any older, he was a frail old man.

Though the face of the man in the patched cotton suit who now stood before us on the veranda was vaguely familiar, we could not remember his name or the circumstances in which we had last seen him. Seeing that he was not recognized, the man removed his coat, opened his shirt, and exposed his chest and right shoulder. That shoulder brought him to instant memory. He was Narwa. Narwa the basket-maker, and there was some excuse for our not having recognized him, for when we had last seen him, six years previously, he was mere skin and bone; only with great difficulty had he been able to put one foot before another and he had needed a stick to support himself. Looking now at his misshapen shoulder, the crushed and broken bones of which had calloused without being set, the puckered and discoloured skin of his chest and back and his partially withered right arm, we who for three months had watched his gallant fight for life marvelled how well he had survived his ordeal. Moving his arm up and down, and closing and opening his hand, Narwa said that his arm was getting stronger every day. His fingers had not got stiff, as we feared they would, so he had been able to resume his trade. His object now, he said, was to show us that he was quite well and to thank Maggie which he proceeded to do by putting his head on her feet for having supplied all his wants, and the wants of his wife and child, during the months he had lain between life and death.

Narwa and Haria were not blood brothers though they so described themselves. They had been born and had grown up in the same village near Almora, and when old enough to work had adopted the same profession, basket-making which means that they were untouchables, for in the United Provinces baskets are only made by untouchables. During the summer months Narwa and Haria worked at their trade in their village near Almora, and in the winter months they came down to Kaladhungi where there was a great demand for the huge baskets, measuring up to fifteen feet in diameter, which they made for our villagers for the storage of grain. In their hill village near Almora they made their baskets of ringals thin bamboo an inch thick and up to twenty feet long, which grows at an altitude of four to ten thousand feet, and which incidentally makes the most perfect of fly-rods and in Kaladhungi, they made them of bamboos.

The bamboos in Kaladhungi grow in the Government Reserved Forests and we who cultivate land near the Reserved Forests are permitted to cut a certain number each year for our personal use. But people who use the bamboos for commercial purposes have to take out a license from the forest guard of the area, paying two annas per headload and a small consideration to the forest guard for his trouble in filling in the license. As the license is a personal one and covers an individual headload it is safe to assume that as many lengths of two-year-old bamboos, the age when a bamboo is best for basket-making were included in the load as a man could carry.

At daybreak on the morning of 26 December 1939 Narwa and Haria set out from their communal hut near the bazaar at Kaladhungi to walk eight miles to Nalni village, obtain a licence from the forest guard, cut two headloads of bamboos in the Nalni Reserved Forests, and return to Kaladhungi, the same evening. It was bitterly cold when they started, so the two men wrapped coarse cotton sheets round their shoulders to keep out the cold. For a mile their way ran along the canal bank. Then, after negotiating the series of high walls which form the headworks of the canal, they took a footpath which runs alternately through patches of dense scrub jungle and over long stretches of the boulder-strewn bank of the Boar river, stretches where a pair of otters are usually to be seen in the early morning, and where, when the sun is on the water, mahseer up to three or four pounds can be taken on a fly-rod. Two miles up they crossed by a shallow ford from the right to the left bank of the river and entered a tree and grass jungle, where morning and evening are to be seen several small herds of chital and sambhar and an occasional kakar, leopard, or tiger. A mile through this jungle, they came to where the hills converge, and where some years previously Robin picked up the tracks of the Bachelor of Powalgarh. From this point onwards the valley opens out and is known to all who graze cattle, or who poach or shoot in the area, as Samal Chour. In this valley one has to walk warily, for the footpath is used almost as much by tigers as it is by human beings.

At the upper end of the valley the footpath, before going steeply up the hill for two miles to Nalni village, passes through a strip of grass. This strip of eight-foot grass is thirty yards wide and extends for about fifty yards on either side of the path. In anticipation of the stiff climb up the Nalni hill, shortly before reaching the grass Narwa divested himself of his cotton sheet, folded it small and placed it on his right shoulder. Haria was leading with Narwa following a few steps behind, and he had only gone three or four yards into the grass when he heard the angry roar of a tiger and simultaneously a shriek from Narwa. Haria turned and dashed back and on the open ground at the edge of the grass he saw Narwa on his back with a tiger lying diagonally across him. Narwa's feet were nearest to him and grasping an ankle in each hand he started to pull him away from under the tiger. As he did this the tiger stood up, turned towards him, and started to growl. After dragging Narwa along on his back for a short distance Haria got his arms round him and set him on his feet. But Narwa was too badly injured and shaken to stand or walk so Haria put his arms round him and alternately dragged and carried him while the tiger continued to growl through the open ground skirting the grass, and so regained the path to Nalni village.

By superhuman efforts Haria eventually got Narwa to Nalni, where it was found that in spite of the folded sheet which he had been carrying on his right shoulder and which Haria had retrieved while pulling him away, the tiger had crushed the bones of the shoulder, lacerated the flesh, and exposed the bones on the right side of the chest and back. All four of the tiger's canine teeth had penetrated some eight folds of the sheet and but for this obstruction they would have met in Narwa's chest and inflicted a fatal wound.

The forest guard and the people of Nalni were unable to do anything for Narwa, so Haria hired a pack pony for two rupees, mounted Narwa on it, and set out for Kaladhungi. The distance, as I have already said, was eight miles but Haria was unwilling to face the tiger a second time, so he made a wide detour through Musabanga village, adding ten miles to Narwa's agonizing journey. There were no saddles at Nalni and he had been mounted on a hard pack used for carrying grain and the first nine miles of his ride was over incredibly steep and rough ground.

Maggie was having tea on the veranda of our cottage when Narwa, soaked in blood and being held on the pony by Haria, arrived at the steps. A glance was enough to show that the case was one she could not deal with, so she quickly gave Narwa a stiff dose of Sal volatile for he was on the point of fainting and made a sling for his arm. Then she tore up a bed sheet to be used for bandages and wrote a note to the Assistant Surgeon in charge of the Kaladhungi hospital, begging him to attend to Narwa immediately and do all he could for him. She gave the note to our head boy and sent him to the hospital with the two men.

I was out bird shooting that day with a party of friends who were spending their Christmas holiday at Kaladhungi and when I returned in the late evening Maggie told me about Narwa. Early next morning I was at the hospital, where I was informed by a very young and very inexperienced doctor that he had done all he could for Narwa but as he had little hope of his recovery and no arrangements for in-patients, he had sent Narwa home after treating him.

In the large communal hut, which housed about twenty families, each of which appeared to have a record number of small children, I found Narwa lying in a corner on a bed of straw and leaves. It was the last place for a man in his terrible condition to be in, for his wounds were showing signs of getting septic. For a week, Narwa lay in the corner of the noisy and insanitary hut at times raving in high fever, at times in a state of coma, watched over by his weeping wife, and his devoted 'brother' Haria, and by other friends.

It was now apparent, even to my inexperienced eyes, that if Narwa's septic wounds were not opened up, drained, and cleaned, there was a certainty of the doctor's predictions being fulfilled, so after making arrangements for his care while under treatment, I removed him to the hospital. To give the young doctor credit, when he undertook to do job, he did it thoroughly, and many of the long scars on his chest and back that Narwa will carry to the burning-ghat were made not by the tiger but by the doctor's lancet, which he used very freely.

With the exception of professional beggars, the poor in India can only eat when they work, and as Narwa's wife's days were fully occupied in visiting him at the hospital and later in nursing him when he returned to the communal hut and in caring for her three-year-old girl and her young baby, Maggie supplied all Narwa's wants, and the wants of his family (Small hospitals in India do not provide either attendants or food for patients.). Three months later, reduced to skin and bone and with a right arm that looked as though it could never be used again, Narwa crawled from the hut to our cottage to bid us goodbye and the next day he and Haria and their families set out for their village near Almora.

After visiting Narwa in the communal hut that first morning and getting a firsthand account of the incident from Haria, I was convinced that the tiger's encounter with Narwa was accidental. However, to satisfy myself that my reconstruction of the event was right and to shoot the tiger if I was wrong, I followed, foot by foot, the track the brothers had taken the previous day when on their way to Nalni village. For a few yards the track runs along the edge of the strip of high grass at the foot of the Nalni hill, before turning at right angles to cross the grass. Shortly before the two men arrived at this spot, the tiger had killed a sambhar stag and carried it into the grass close to the right-hand side of the track. When Haria entered the grass, the tiger heard the rustling and coming out, ran into Narwa, who was a few yards behind Haria and a yard or two from the turning. The encounter was accidental, for the grass was too thick and too high for the tiger to have seen Narwa before he bumped into him. Furthermore, it had made no attempt to savage Narwa and had even allowed Haria to drag the man on whom it was lying away from under it. So, the tiger was allowed to live and was later induced to join the party of tigers that are mentioned in the chapter 'Just Tigers' in *Man-eaters of Kumaon*.

Of all the brave deeds that I have witnessed, or that I have read or heard about, I count Haria's rescue of Narwa the greatest. Unarmed and alone in a great expanse of jungle, to respond to the cry of a companion in distress and to pull that companion away from an angry tiger that was lying on him and then to drag and carry that companion for two miles up a steep hill to a place of safety, not knowing but that the tiger was following, needed a degree of courage that is given to few, and that any man could envy. When I took down Haria's statement which was later corroborated in every detail by Narwa with the object, unknown to him of his act receiving recognition, so far from thinking that he had done anything deserving of commendation, after I had finished questioning him, he said: 'I have not done anything, Sahib, have I, that is likely to bring trouble on me or on my brother Narwa?'

And Narwa, a few days later, when I took down what I feared would be his dying declaration, said in avoice racked with pain and little above a whisper, 'Don't let my brother get into any trouble, Sahib for it was not his fault that the tiger attacked me, and he risked his life to save mine'.

I should have liked to have been able to end my story by telling you that Haria's brave act, and Narwa'sheroic fight for life against great odds, had been acknowledged by a certificate of merit, or some other small token of award, for both were poor men. Unfortunately, red tape proved too much for me for the Government was not willing to make any award in a case of which the truth could not be sworn to by independent and unbiased witnesses.

So, one of the bravest deeds ever performed has gone unrecognized because there were no 'Independent and unbiased witnesses' and of the brothers Haria is the poorer of the two, for he has nothing to show for the part he played, while Narwa has his scars and the sheet with many holes, stained with his blood.

For many days, I toyed with the idea of appealing to His Majesty the King, but with a world war starting and all it implied I very reluctantly abandoned the idea.

VII. SULTANA: INDIA'S ROBIN HOOD

In a country as vast as India, with its great areas of forest land and bad communications and with its teeming population chronically on the verge of starvation, it is easy to understand the temptations to embark on a life of crime, and the difficulty the Government have in rounding up criminals. In addition to the ordinary criminals to be found in all countries, there are in India whole tribes classed as criminals who are segregated in settlements set apart for them by the Government and subjected to a greater or lesser degree of restraint according to the crime's they specialize in.

While I was engaged on welfare work during a part of the last war, I frequently visited one of these criminal settlements. The inmates were not kept under close restraint, and I had many interesting talks with them and with the Government representative in charge of the settlement. In an effort to wean this tribe from a life of crime the Government had given them free of rent a large tract of alluvial land on the left bank of the Jumna river in the Meerut District. This rich land produced bumper crops of sugarcane, wheat, barley, rape seed, and other cereals, but crime persisted. The Government representative blamed the girls, who, he said, refused to marry any, but successful criminals. The tribe specialized in robbery and there were old men in the settlement who trained the younger generation on a profit-sharing basis.

Men were allowed to leave the settlement on ticket of leave for stated periods, but women were not permitted to leave. The elders of the tribe strictly enforced three rules:

First: that all robberies were to be carried out single-handed.

Second: that the scene of the crime was to be as distant from the settlement as possible and

Third: That violence while committing the crime was not to be resorted to in any circumstances.

The method invariably adopted by a young man, after he had completed his training, was to secure employment as a house servant with a rich man in Calcutta, Bombay, or some other distant city, and when opportunity offered to rob his master of articles which could be easily secreted, such as gold, jewelry or precious stones. On one occasion while I was paying a number of young men who had been driving black partridge out of a sugarcane field for me, the Government representative informed me that the young man into whose hands I had just dropped his wage of eight annas, plus two annas for a runner he had retrieved, had returned to the settlement a few days previously, after an absence of a year, with a diamond worth thirty thousand rupees.

After evaluation by the experts of the tribe the diamond had been hidden, and the most sought-after girl in the settlement had promised to marry the successful criminal during the next marriage season. Another of the men standing nearby, who had not taken part in the partridge drive, had conceived the novel plan of impressing the girl of his choice by driving up to the settlement, along a most appalling cart-track, in a new motorcar he had stolen in Calcutta. In order to carry out his plan he had first had to pay for driving lessons.

Some members of criminal tribes who are not subjected to strict control find employment as night watch men in private houses and I know of instances where it was a sufficient guarantee against theft for the watchman to place a pair of his shoes on the doorstep of the house in which he was employed. This may savour of blackmail, but it was cheap blackmail, for the wages paid varied from three to five rupees a month according to the standing of the criminal and the money was easily earned as all the watchmen had to do was to place his shoes in position at night and remove them again the next morning. Owing to their preference for violent crime the Bhantus were one of the criminal tribes in the United Provinces that were kept under strict restraint and Sultana, the famous dacoit who for three years defied all the Government's efforts to capture him, was a member of this tribe. It is about Sultana that this story is written.

When I first knew it, Naya Gaon was one of the most nourishing villages in the Terai and Bhabar, the tract of land running along the foothills of the Himalayas. Every yard of the rich soil, carved out of virgin forest, was under intensive cultivation and the hundred or more tenants were prosperous, contented, and happy. Sir Henry Ramsay, the King of Kumaon, had brought these hardy people down from the Himalayas, and for a generation they retained their vigour and flourished exceedingly.

Malaria at that time was known as 'Bhabar fever' and the few doctors, scattered over a wide area, who were responsible for the health of the people, had neither the ability nor the means to cope with this scourge of the foothills. Naya Gaon, situated in the heart of the forest, was one of the first villages in the Bhabar to be decimated by the disease. Field after field went out of cultivation as the tenants died, until only a handful of the sturdy pioneers were left and when these survivors were given land in our village Naya Gaon reverted to jungle.

Only once in later years was an attempt made to recultivate the land, the intrepid pioneer on this occasion being a doctor from the Punjab; but when first his daughter, then his wife and finally he himself died of malaria, Naya Gaon for the second time went back to the jungle.

On the land which had been cleared with great labour on which bumper crops of sugarcane, wheat, mustard, and rice had been grown, luxuriant grass sprang up. Attracted by this rich feed, the cattle from our village three miles away adopted the deserted fields of Naya Gaon as their regular feeding ground. When cattle graze for long periods over open ground surrounded by Jungle, they invariably attract carnivora and I was not surprised to hear one year, on our descent from our summer home in Nainital to our winter home in Kaladhungi that a leopard had taken up residence in the jungles adjoining the grazing-ground and that he was taking heavy toll of our cattle. There were no trees on the grassland in which I could sit over a kill, so I determined to shoot the leopard either in the early morning, when he was on his way to lie up in thick cover for the day or in the evening, when he was returning to a kill or intent on making a fresh one. For either of these plans to be effective it was necessary to discover in what part of the surrounding jungles the leopard had made his home, so early one morning Robin and I set out to glean this information.

Naya Gaon for though the land has been out of cultivation for many years it retains its name to this day is bounded on the north by the road known as the Kandi Sarak and on the east by the old Trunk Road which before the advent of railways connected the plains of the United Provinces with the interior of Kumaon.

To the south and west, Naya Gaon is bounded by dense jungle. Both the Kandi Sarak and the Trunk Road are little used in these days, and I decided to try them first before trying the more difficult ground to the south and west. At the junction of the roads, where in the days gone by a police guard was posted for the protection of wayfarers against dacoits, Robin and I found the tracks of a female leopard. This leopard was well known to Robin and me, for she had lived for several years in a heavy patch of lantana at the lower end of our village. Apart from never molesting our cattle, she had kept pigs and monkeys from damaging our crops, so we ignored her tracks and carried on along the Trunk Road in the direction of Garuppu. There had been no traffic on the road since the previous evening and the tracks of animals who had used or crossed it were registered on the dusty surface.

From the rifle in my hands Robin, who was a wise dog and my constant companion, knew we were not after birds, so he paid no attention to the pea fowl that occasionally scurried across the road or to the jungle fowl that were scratching up the dead leaves at the side of it but concentrated on the tracks of a tigress and her two half-grown cubs that had gone down the road an hour ahead of us. In places the wide road was overgrown with short dub grass. On this dew-drenched grass the cubs had rolled and tumbled, and Robin filled his nostrils to his heart's content with the sweet and terrifying smell of Tiger. The family had kept to the road for a mile and had then gone east along a game track. Three miles from the junction, and two miles above Garuppu, a well-used game track coming from the direction of Naya Gaon crosses the road diagonally and, on this track, we saw the fresh pug marks of a big male leopard.

We had found what we were looking for. This leopard had come from the grazing ground and crossed the road. It was capable of killing a full-grown cow and there were not likely to be two leopards of this size in the same area. Robin was keen on following up the tracks, but the dense scrub jungle the leopard was making for the same jungle in which Kunwar Singh and Har Singh had nearly lost their lives some years previously was not suitable for stalking an animal with the sight and hearing of a leopard. Moreover, I had a better and simpler plan of making contact with the leopard, so we turned about and made for home and breakfast.

After lunch Robin and I, accompanied by Maggie retraced our steps down the Garuppu road. The leopard had not killed any of our cattle the previous day, but he might have killed a chital or a pig which shared the grazing ground with the cattle; and even if he had no kill to return to there was a very good chance of his visiting his regular hunting ground. So, Maggie and I, with Robin lying between us took up position behind a bush on the side of the road, a hundred yards from the game track along which the leopard had gone that morning. We had been in position about an hour, listening to the multitude of bird calls, when a peacock in full plumage majestically crossed the road and went down the game path. A little later, ten or a dozen chital, in the direction of the heavy jungle in which we expected the leopard to be lying up, warned the jungle folk of the presence of a leopard. Ten minutes thereafter and a little nearer to us, a single chital repeated the warning. The leopard was on the move and coming in our direction, and as he was making no attempt to conceal himself, he was probably on his way to a kill.

Robin had lain with chin on outstretched paws without movement, listening as we were to what the jungle folk had to say, and when he saw me draw up my leg and rest the rifle on my knee, his body, which was against my left leg, started to tremble. The spotted killer, whom he feared more than any other beast in the jungle would presently put its head out of the bushes and after looking up and down the road, would come towards us. Whether it died in its tracks, or roared and tumbled about with a mortal wound, he would remain perfectly still and silent for he was taking part in a game with every move of which he was familiar, and which was as fascinating as it was terrifying.

After going a short distance down the game path, the peacock had climbed into the branches of a plum tree and was busily engaged in eating ripe fruit. Suddenly it sprang into the air with a harsh scream and alighted on the limb of a dead tree, adding its warning to that already given by the chital. A few minutes now, five at the most for the leopard would approach the road very cautiously and then out of the corner of my eye I caught sight of a movement far down the road. It was a man running, and every now and then, without slackening his pace, he looked over his shoulder behind him. To see a man on that road at this hour of the evening, the sun was near setting was very unusual and to see him alone was even more unusual. Every stride the man took lessened our chances of bagging the leopard. However, that could not be helped, for the runner was evidently in great distress and possibly in need of help. I recognized him while he was still some distance from us; he was a tenant in a village adjoining ours who during the winter months was engaged as herdsman at a cattle station three miles east of Garuppu.

On catching sight of us the runner started violently but when he recognized me, he came towards us and in a very agitated voice said, 'Run, Sahib, run for your life! Sultana's men are after me.'

He was winded and in great distress. Taking no notice of my invitation to sit down and rest, he turned his leg and said, 'See what they have done to me! If they catch me, they will surely kill me and you also, if you do not run.' The leg he turned for our inspection was slashed from the back of the knee to the heel, and dust-clotted blood was flowing from the ugly wound. Telling the man that if he would not rest there was at least no need for him to run any more, I moved out of the bushes to where I could get a clear view down the road, while the man limped off in the direction of his village. Neither the leopard nor Sultana's men showed up, and when there was no longer light for accurate shooting, Maggie, and I, with a very disgusted Robin at our heels, returned to our home at Kaladhungi.

Next morning, I got the man's story. He was grazing his buffaloes between Garuppu and the cattle station when he heard a gunshot. The nephew of the headman of his village had arrived at the cattle station at dawn that morning with the object of poaching a chital and while he had been sitting in the shade of a tree, speculating as to whether the shot had been effective or not and if effective, whether a portion of the venison would be left at the cattle station for his evening meal, he heard a rustle behind him. Looking round, he saw five men standing over him. He was told to get up and take the party to where the gun had been fired.

When he said he had been asleep and had not heard the shot he was ordered to lead the way to the cattle station, to which they thought the gunman would probably go. The party had no firearms but the man who appeared to be their leader had a naked sword in his hand and said he would cut the herdsman's head off with it if he attempted to run away or shout a warning.

As they made their way through the jungle the swordsman informed the herdsman that they were members of Sultana's gang and that Sultana was camped nearby. When he heard the shot Sultana had ordered them to bring him the gun. Therefore, if they met with any opposition at the cattle-station they would burn it down and kill their guide. This threat presented my friend with a dilemma. His companions at the cattle station were a tough lot and if they offered resistance he would undoubtedly be killed on the other hand, if they did not resist, his crime in leading the dread Sultana's men to the station would never be forgotten or forgiven. While these unpleasant thoughts were running through his head a chital stag pursued by a pack of wild dogs came dashing through the jungle and passed within a few yards of them. Seeing that his escort had stopped and were watching the chase the herdsman dived into the high grass on the side of the path and despite the wound he received on his leg as the swordsman tried to cut him down, he had managed to shake his pursuers off and gain the Trunk Road, where in due course he ran into us while we were waiting for the leopard.

Sultana was a member of the Bhantu criminal tribe. With the rights and wrongs of classing a tribe as' criminal' and confining it within the four walls of the Najibabad Fort, I am not concerned. It suffices to say that Sultana, with his young wife and infant son and some hundreds of other Bhantus, was confined in the fort under the charge of the Salvation Army. Chafing at his confinement, he scaled the mud walls of the fort one night and escaped, as any young and high-spirited man would have done. This escape had been affected a year previous to the opening of my story and during that year Sultana had collected a hundred kindred spirits, all armed with guns, around him. This imposing gang, whose declared object was dacoity, led a roving life in the jungles of the Terai and Bhabar, their activities extending from Gonda in the east to Saharanpur in the west, a distance of several hundred miles with occasional raids into the adjoining province of the Punjab.

There are many fat files in Government offices on the activities of Sultana and his gang of dacoits. I have not had access to these files and if my story, which only deals with events in which I took part or events which came to my personal notice, differs or conflicts in any respects with Government reports I can only express my regret. At the same time, I do not retract one word of my story.

I first heard of Sultana when he was camping in the Garuppu jungles a few miles from our winter home at Kaladhungi. Percy Wyndham was at that time Commissioner of Kumaon, and as the Terai and Bhabar forests in which Sultana had apparently established himself were in Wyndham's charge he asked Government for the services of Freddy Young, a keen young police officer with a few years' service in the United Provinces to his credit. The Government granted Wyndham's request and sanctioned the creation of a Special Dacoity Police Force of three hundred picked men. Freddy was put in supreme command of this force and given a free hand in the selection of his men. He earned a lot of unpopularity by building up his force with the best men from adjoining districts, for Sultana was a coveted prize and their own officers resented having to surrender men who might have helped them to acquire the prize.

While Freddy was mustering his force, Sultana was getting his hand in by raiding small townships in the Terai and Bhabar. Freddy's first attempt to capture Sultana was made in the forests west of Ramnagar. The Forest Department were felling a portion of these forests, employing a large labour force, and one of the contractors in charge of the labour was induced to invite Sultana, who was known to be camping in the vicinity, to a dance to be followed by a feast. Sultana and his merry men accepted the invitation, but just before the festivities began, they prevailed on their host to make a slight alteration in the programme and have the feast first and the dance later. Sultana said his men would enjoy the dance more on full stomachs than on empty ones.

Here it is necessary to interrupt my story to explain for the benefit of those who have never been in the East that guests at a dance or a 'nautch' as it is called here, do not take any part in the proceedings. The dancing is confined to a troop of professional dancing-girls and their male orchestra.

Funds in plenty were available on both sides and as money goes as far in the East towards buying information as it does in the West, one of the first moves of the two contestants in the game that was to be played was the organization of efficient secret services. Here Sultana had the advantage, for whereas Freddy could only reward for services rendered, Sultana could not only reward but could also punish for information withheld or for information about his movements to the police and when his method of dealing with offenders became known none were willing to court his displeasure.

Having known what, it was to be poor, really poor, during his long years of confinement in the Najibabad Fort, Sultana had a warm corner in his heart for all poor people. It was said of him that, throughout his career as a dacoit, he never robbed a pice from a poor man, never refused an appeal for charity and paid twice the price asked for all he purchased from small shopkeepers. Little wonder then that his intelligence staff numbered hundreds and that he knew the invitation he had received to the dance and feast had been issued at Freddy's instigation.

Meanwhile plans were on foot for the great night. The contractor, reputed to be a rich man, extended invitations to his friends in Ramnagar and in Kashipur; the best dancing girls and their orchestras were engaged, and large quantities of eatables and drink, the latter specially for the benefit of the dacoits were purchased and transported by bullock cart to the camp.

At the appointed time on the night that was to see the undoing of Sultana, the contractor's guests assembled, and the feast began. It is possible that the contractor's friends did not show who their fellow guests were for on these occasions the different castes sit in groups by themselves, and the illumination provided by firelight and a few lanterns was of the poorest. Sultana and his men ate and drank wisely and well and when the feast was nearing its end the dacoit leader led his host aside, thanked him for his hospitality, and said that as he and his men had a long away to go, he regretted they could not stay for the dance. Before leaving, however, he requested, and Sultana's requests were never disregarded that the festivities should continue as had been arranged.

The principal instrument of music at a nautch is a drum and the sound of the drums was to be Freddy's signal to leave the position he had taken up and deploy his force to surround the camp. One section of this force was led by a forest guard and the night being dark the forest guard lost his way. This section, which was to have blocked Sultana's line of retreat, remained lost for the remainder of the night. As a matter of fact, the forest guard, who had to live in the forest with Sultana and was a wise man, need not have given himself the trouble of getting lost, for by his request for a slight alteration in the programme Sultana had given himself ample time to get clear of the net before the signal was given. So, all that the attacking force found when they arrived at the camp, after a long and a difficult march through dense forest, was a troop of frightened girls, their even more frightened orchestra, and the mystified friends of the contractor.

After his escape from the Ramnagar forests Sultana paid a visit to the Punjab. Here, with no forests in which to shelter, he was out of his element and after a brief stay, which yielded a hundred thousand rupees' worth of gold ornaments, he returned to the dense jungles of the United Provinces. On his way back from the Punjab he had to cross the Ganges canal, the bridges over which are spaced at intervals of four miles, and as his movements were known, the bridges he was likely to cross were heavily guarded. Avoiding these, Sultana made for a bridge which his intelligence staff informed him was not guarded, and on his way passed close to a large village in which a band was playing Indian music. On learning from his guides that a rich man's son was being married, he ordered them to take him to the village.

The wedding party and some thousand guests were assembled on a wide-open space in the Centre of the village. As he entered the glare of the high-powered lamps Sultana's appearance caused a stir, but he requested the assembly to remain seated and added that if they complied with his request, they had nothing to fear. He then summoned the headman of the village and the father of the bridegroom and made it known that, as this was a propitious time for the giving and receiving of gifts, he would like the headman's recently purchased gun for himself and ten thousand rupees in cash for his men. The gun and the money were produced in the shortest time possible and having wished the assembly good night. Sultana led his men out of the village. Not till the following day did he learn that his lieutenant, Pailwan had abducted the bride. Sultana did not approve of women being molested by his gang, so Pailwan was severely reprimanded, and the girl was sent back with a suitable present to compensate her for the inconvenience to which she had been put.

After the incident of the herdsman's slashed leg Sultana remained in our vicinity for some time. He moved camp frequently and I came upon several old sites while out shooting. It was at this time that I had a very exciting experience.

One evening I shot a fine leopard on a fire-track five miles from home and as there was not sufficient time to collect carriers to bring it in, I skinned it on the spot and carried the skin home but on arrival I found that I had left my favourite hunting-knife behind.

Early next morning I set out to retrieve the knife and as I approached the spot where I had left it, I saw the glimmer of a fire through a forest glade some distance from the track. Reports of Sultana's presence in this forest had been coming in for some days, and on the spur of the moment I decided to investigate the fire. Heavy dew on the dead leaves made it possible to move without sound, so taking what cover was available I stalked the fire, which was burning in a little hollow, and found some twenty to twenty-five men sitting round it. Stacked upright against a nearby tree, the fire glinting on their barrels, were a number of guns. Sultana was not present for though I had not seen him up to that time, he had been described to me as a young man, small and trim, who invariably dressed in semi-military khaki uniform. This was evidently part of his gang, however and what was I going to do about it? The old head constable and his equally elderly force of two constables at Kaladhungi would be of little help and Haldwani, where there was a big concentration of police, was fifteen miles away.

While I was considering my next move, I heard one oi the men say it was time to be going. Fearing that if I now tried to retreat, I should be seen, and trouble might follow, I took a few rapid steps forward and got between the men and their guns. As I did so a ring of surprised faces looked up at me, for I was on slightly higher ground. When I asked them what they were doing here the men looked at each other and the first to recover from his surprise said, 'Nothing'. In reply to further questions, I was told that they were charcoal burners who had come from Bareilly and had lost their way. I then turned and looked towards the tree and found that what I had taken to be gun barrels were stacked axes, the handles of which, polished by long and hard use, had reflected the firelight. Telling the men that my feet were wet and cold I joined their circle and after we had smoked my cigarettes and talked of many things, I directed them to the charcoal-burners' camp they were looking for, recovered my knife and returned home.

In times of sustained excitement imagination is apt to play queer tricks. Sitting on the ground near a sambhar killed by a tiger I have heard the tiger coming and coming and getting no nearer and when the tension had become unbearable have turned round with finger on trigger to find a caterpillar biting minute bits out of a crisp leaf near my head. Again, when the light was fading and the time had come for the tiger to return to his kill, out of the corner of my eye I have seen a large animal appear; and as I was gripping my rifle and preparing for a shot an ant had crawled out on a dry twig a few inches from my face. With my thoughts on Sultana the glint of firelight on the polished axe-handles had converted them into gun barrels, and I never looked at them again until the men had convinced me they were charcoal burners.

With his efficient organization and better means of transport, Freddy was beginning to exert pressure on Sultana, and to ease the strain the dacoit leader took his gang, by this time considerably reduced by desertion and capture to Pilibhit on the eastern border of the district. Here he remained for a few months, raiding as far a-field as Gorakhpur, and building up his store of gold.

On his return to the forests in our vicinity he learned that a very rich dancing-girl from the State of Rampur had recently taken up residence with the headman of Lamachour, a village seven miles from our home. Anticipating a raid, the headman provided himself with a guard of thirty of his tenants. The guard was not armed and when Sultana arrived, before his men were able to surround the house the dancing-girl slipped through a back door and escaped into the night with all her jewelry. The headman and his tenants were rounded up in the courtyard, and when they denied all knowledge of the girl orders were given to tie them up and beat them to refresh their memories. To this order one of the tenants raised an objection. He said Sultana could do what he liked to him and his fellow tenants but that he had no right to disgrace the headman by having him tied up and beaten. He was ordered to keep his mouth shut but as one of the dacoits advanced towards the headman with a length of rope this intrepid man pulled a length of bamboo out of a lean-to and dashed at the dacoit. He was shot through the chest by one of the gangs but fearing the shot would arouse armed men in neighbouring villages Sultana beat a hasty retreat, taking with him a horse which the headman had recently purchased. I heard of the murder of the brave tenant next morning and sent one of my men to Lamachour to inquire what family the dead man had left, and I sent another man with an open letter to all the headmen of the surrounding villages to ask if they would join in raising a fund for the support of his family. The response to my appeal was as generous as I expected it to be, for the poor are always generous, but the fund was never raised, for the man who had given his life for his master came from Nepal twenty years previously and neither his friends nor the inquiries I made in Nepal revealed that he had a wife or children.

It was after the incident just related that I accepted Freddy's invitation to take a hand in rounding up Sultana, and a month later I joined him at his headquarters at Hardwar, During his eighteen years as Collector of Mirzapur Wyndham had employed ten Koles and ten Bhunyas from the tribes living in the Mirzapur forests to assist him in tiger shooting and the four best of these men, who were old friends of mine, were now placed by Wyndham at Freddy's disposal and I found them waiting for me at Hardwar.

Freddy's plan was for my four friends and myself to track down Sultana, and when we had done this, to lead his force to a convenient place from which to launch his attack. Both these operations for reasons already given were to be carried out at night. But Sultana was restless. Perhaps it was just nervousness, or he may have had forewarning of Freddy's plans anyway he never stayed for more than a day in anyone place and he moved his force long distances at night.

The weather was intensely hot and eventually, tired of inaction, the four men and I held a council of war the result of which was that after dinner that night, when Freddy was comfortably seated in a cool part of the veranda where there was no possibility of our being overheard, I put the following proposal before him. He was to let it be known that Wyndham had recalled his men for a tiger shoot, to which I had been invited, and was to have tickets to Haldwani purchased for us and see us off from the Hardwar station by the night train. At the first stop the train made however, the four men, armed with guns provided by Freddy and I with my own rifle were to leave the train. Thereafter we were to have a free hand to bring in Sultana, dead or alive, as opportunity offered.

Freddy sat for a long time with his eyes closed after hearing my proposal, he weighed 20 stone 4 pounds and was apt to doze after dinner, but he was not asleep for he suddenly sat up and in a very decided voice said, 'No. I am responsible for your lives, and I won't sanction this mad 'scheme'. Arguing with him was of no avail, so the next morning the four men and

I left for our respective homes. I was wrong to have made the proposal and Freddy was right in turning it down. The four men and I had no official standing, and had trouble resulted from our attempt to capture Sultana our action could not have been justified. For the rest, neither Sultana's life nor ours was in any danger for we had agreed that if Sultana could not be taken alive, he would not be taken at all, and we were quite capable of looking after ourselves.

Three months later, when the monsoon was in full blast, Freddy asked Herbert of the Forest Department, Fred Anderson, Superintendent of the Terai and Bhabar and myself to join him at Hardwar, On arrival we learnt that Freddy had located Sultana's permanent camp in the heart of the Najibabad jungles and he wanted us to assist him in surrounding the camp and to cut off Sultana's retreat if he slipped out of the ring.

Herbert, a famous polo player was to be put in command of the fifty mounted men who were to prevent Sultana's escape, while Anderson and I were to accompany Freddy and help him to form the ring. By this time Freddy had no illusions about the efficiency of Sultana's intelligence service, and with the exception of Freddy's two assistants, and the three of us no one knew of the contemplated raid. Each evening the police force, fully armed, were sent out on a long route march, while the four of us went out for an equally long walk, returning after dark to the Dam Bungalow in which we were staying. On the appointed night instead of marching over the level crossing as they had been wont to do, the route marchers went through the Hardwar goods yard to a siding in which a rake of wagons, with engine and brake-van attached, was standing with doors open on the side away from the station buildings. The last of the doors was being shut as we arrived and the moment, we had climbed into the guard's van the train, without any warning whistles, started. Everything that could be done to allay suspicion had been done, even to the cooking of the men's food in their lines and to the laying of our table for dinner. We had started an hour after dark. At 9 p.m. the train drew up between two stations in the heart of the jungle and the order was passed from wagon to wagon for the force to detrain and as soon as this order had been carried out the train steamed on.

Of Freddy's force of three hundred men, the fifty to be Led by Herbert, who served in France in the First World War with the Indian cavalry had been sent out the previous night with instructions to make a wide detour to where their mounts were waiting for them, while the main force of two hundred and fifty men with Freddy and Anderson in the lead and myself bringing up the rear, set off for a destination which was said to be some twenty miles away. Heavy clouds had been banking up all day and when we left the train it was raining in torrents.

Our direction was north for a mile, then east for two miles, again north for a mile, then west for two miles and finally again north. I knew the changes in direction were being made to avoid villages in which there were men in Sultana's pay, and the fact that not a village pye, the best watchdog in the world, barked at us testifies to the skill with which the manoeuvre was carried out. Hour after hour I plodded on, in drenching rain, in the wake of two hundred and fifty heavy men who had left potholes in the soft ground into which I floundered up to my knees at every second step. For miles we went through elephant grass higher than my head and balancing on the pitted and slippery ground became more difficult from the necessity of using one hand to shield my eyes from the stiff razor-edged grass. I had often marvelled at Freddy's 20 stone 4 pounds of energy but never as I did that night. True, he was walking on comparatively firm ground while I was walking in a bog; yet even so he was carrying nine stone more than I and the line moved on with never a halt.

We started at 9 p.m. At 2 a.m. I sent a verbal message up the line to ask Freddy if we were going in the right direction. I sent this message because for an hour we had left our original direction northwards and had been going east. After a long interval word came back that Captain Sahib said it was all right. After another two hours, through thick tree, and scrub jungle or across patches of high grass, I sent a second message to Freddy asking him to halt the line as I was coming up to speak to him. Silence had been enjoined before starting and as I made my way to the front, I passed a very quiet and weary line of men, some of them sitting on the wet ground and others leaning against trees.

I found Freddy and Anderson with their four guides at the head of the column. When Freddy asked if anything was wrong, this I knew referred to stragglers I said all was well with the men but otherwise everything was wrong, for we were walking in circles. Having lived so much of my life in jungles in which it is very easy to get lost I have acquired a sense of direction which functions as well by night as it does by day. Our change of direction when we first started had been as evident to me as it had been two hours back when we changed direction from north to east. In addition, an hour previously I had noted that we passed under a simul tree with a vulture's nest in it and when I sent my message to Freddy to halt the line I was again under the same tree.

Of the four guides, two were Bhantus of Sultana's gang who had been captured a few days previously in the Hardwar bazaar and on whose information the present raid had been organized. These two men had lived off and on for two years in Sultana's camp and had been promised their freedom for this night's work. The other two were cattle men who had grazed their cattle in these jungles all their lives, and who daily supplied Sultana with milk. All four men stoutly denied having lost their way, but on being pressed, they hesitated, and finally admitted that they would feel happier about the direction in which they were leading the force if they could see the hills. To see the hills, possibly thirty miles away, on a dark night with thick fog descending down to tree-top level, was impossible, so here was a check which threatened to ruin all Freddy's well-laid plans and, what was even worse to give Sultana the laugh on us. Our intention had been a surprise attack on the camp, and in order to accomplish this it was necessary to get within striking distance while it was still dark. The guides had informed us that it was not possible to approach the camp in daylight from the side we had chosen without being seen by two guards who were constantly on watch from a machan in a high tree which overlooked a wide stretch of grass to the south of the camp.

With our guides now freely admitting they had lost their way, only another hour of darkness left and worst of all without knowing how far we were from the camp or in which direction it lay, our chance of a surprise attack was receding with every minute that passed. Then a way out of the dilemma occurred to me. I asked the four men if there was any feature, such as a stream or a well-defined cattle-track, in the direction in which we had originally started, by which they could regain direction, and when they replied that there was an old and well-defined cart-track a mile to the south of the camp, I obtained Freddy's permission to take the lead. I set off at a fast pace in a direction which all who were following me were, I am sure, convinced would lead back to the railway line we had left seven hours earlier.

The rain had stopped, a fresh breeze had cleared the sky of clouds, and it was just getting light in the east when I stumbled into a deep cart-rut. Here was the disused track the guides had mentioned, and their joy on seeing it confirmed the opinion I had formed earlier, that losing themselves in the jungle had not been intentional. Taking over the lead again, the men led us along the track for a mile to where a well-used game-track crossed it. Half a mile up the game track we came to a deep and sluggish stream some thirty feet wide which I was glad to see the track did not cross, for I am terrified of these Terai streams on the banks and in the depths of which I have seen huge pythons lurking. The track skirted the right bank of the stream, through shoulder-high grass and after going along it for a few hundred yards the men slowed down. From the way they kept looking to the left I concluded we were getting within sight of the machan, for it was now full daylight with the sun touching the tops of the trees. Presently the leading man crouched down, and when his companions had done the same, he beckoned us to approach.

After signaling to the line to halt and sit down, Freddy, Anderson and I crept up to the leading guide. Lying beside him and looking through the grass in the direction in which he was pointing we saw a machan built in the upper branches of a big tree, between thirty and forty feet above ground. On the machan, with the level sun shining on them, were two men, one sitting with his right shoulder towards us smoking a hookah, and the other lying on his back with his knees drawn up. The tree in which the machan was built grew on the border of the tree and grass jungle and overlooked a wide expanse of open ground. Sultana's camp, the guides said, was three hundred yards inside the tree jungle.

A few feet from where we were lying was a strip of short grass twenty yards wide, running from the stream on our right far out onto the open ground. To retreat a little, cross the stream and recross it opposite Sultana's camp was the obvious thing to do but the guides said this would not be possible; not only was the stream too deep to wade but there was quicksand along the far bank. There remained the doubtful possibility of getting the whole force across the strip of short grass without being seen by the two guards, either of whom might at any moment look in our direction.

Freddy had a service revolver, Anderson was unarmed, and I was the only one in the whole force who was carrying a rifle, the police were armed with 12-bore muskets using buckshot, with an effective range of from sixty to eighty yards. I was therefore the only one of the parties who could deal with the two guards from our present position. The rifle shots would, of course, be heard in the camp but the two Bhantus with us were of the opinion that when the guards did not return to the camp to report, men would be sent out to make inquiries. They thought that while this was being done it would be possible for us to encircle the camp.

The two men on the machan were outlaws and quite possibly murderers to boot and with the rifle in my hands, I could have shot the hookah out of the smoker's hands and 'the heel off the other man's shoe without injury to either. But to shoot the men in cold, or in any other temperature of blood, was beyond my powers. So, I made the following alternative suggestion: that Freddy give me permission to stalk the men which would be quite easy, for the tall grass and tree jungle extended right up to the tree in which the machan was built and was soaking wet after the all-night rain and occupy the machan with them while Freddy and his men carried on with their job. At first Freddy demurred, for there were two guns on the machan within easy reach of the men's hands but eventually he consented and without further ado I slipped across the open ground and set off for the Bhantus said the time was approaching for the guards to be changed.

I had covered about a third of the way to the tree when I heard a noise behind and saw Anderson hurrying after me. What Anderson had said to Freddy, or Freddy had said to Anderson I do not know, both were my very good friends. Anyway, Anderson was determined to accompany me. He admitted he could not get through the jungle silently; that there was a good chance of the men on the machan hearing and seeing us; that we might run into the relief guard or find additional guards at the foot of the tree; that being unarmed he would not be able to defend himself, nevertheless and not-withstanding, *he was not going to let me go alone*. When a man from across the Clyde digs his toes in, he is more stubborn than a mule.

In desperation I started to retrace my steps to solicit Freddy's help. But Freddy in the meantime had had time to regret his sanction (I learnt later the Bhantus had informed him the men on the machan were very good shots), and when he saw us returning, he gave the signal for the line to advance.

Fifty or more men had crossed the open strip of ground and we who were in advance were within two hundred yards of the camp when a zealous young constable, catching sight of the machan, fired off his musket. The two men on the machan were down the ladder in a flash. They mounted the horses that were tethered at the foot of the tree and raced for the camp. There was now no longer any necessity for silence and in a voice that did not need the aid of a megaphone, Freddy gave the order to charge. In a solid line we swept down on the camp, to find it deserted.

The camp was on a little knoll and consisted of three tents and a grass hut used as a kitchen. One of the tents was a store and was stacked with sacks of atta, rice, dal, sugar, tins of ghee, two pyramids of boxes containing some thousands of rounds of 12-bore ammunition and eleven guns in gun cases. The other two tents were sleeping places and were strewn with blankets and a medley of articles of clothing. Hanging from branches near the kitchen were three flayed goats.

In the confusion following the arrival in camp of the two guards it was possible that some of the partly clothed gang had taken shelter in the high grass surrounding the camp, so orders were given to our men to make a long line, our intention being to beat a wide strip of jungle in the direction in which Herbert and his mounted men were on guard. While the line was being formed, I made a cast round the knoll. Having found the tracks of ten or a dozen barefooted men in a nullah close to the camp, I suggested to Freddy that we should follow them and see where they led to. The nullah was fifteen feet wide and five feet deep and Freddy, Anderson and I had proceeded along it for about two hundred yards when we came on an outcrop of gravel, where I lost the tracks. Beyond the gravel the nullah opened out and on the left bank, near where we were standing, was a giant banyan tree with multiple stems. With its forest of stems, and branches sweeping down to the ground, this tree appeared to me to be an ideal place for anyone to hide in, so going to the bank, which at this point was as high as my chin, I attempted to climb up. There was no handhold on the bank and each time I kicked a hole in the soft earth the foothold gave way, and I was just contemplating going forward and getting on to the bank where the nullah Rattened out, when a fusillade of shots followed by shouting broke out in the direction of the camp. We dashed back the way we had come and near the camp found a Havildar shot through the chest, and near him a dacoit, with a wisp of cloth round his loins, shot through both legs. The Havildar was sitting on the ground with his back to a tree, his shirt was open and on the nipple of his left breast there was a spot of blood. Freddy produced a flask and put it to the Havildar's lips, but the man shook his head and put the flask aside, saying, 'It is wine. I cannot drink it'. When pressed he added, 'All my life I have been an abstainer and I cannot go to my Creator with wine on my lips. I am thirsty and crave a little water'. His brother was standing nearby. Someone gave him a hat and he dashed off to the stream that had hampered our movements and returned in a few minutes with some dirty water which the wounded man drank eagerly. The wound had been made by a pellet of shot and when I could not feel it under the skin I said, 'Keep a strong heart, Havildar Sahib, and the doctor at Najibabad will make you well'. Smiling up at me he replied, 'I will keep a strong heart, Sahib but no doctor can make me well'.

The dacoit had no inhibitions about 'wine,' and in a few gulps he emptied the contents of the flask of which he was in great need for he had been shot with a 12-bore musket at very short range.

Two stretchers were improvised from material taken from Sultana's camp, and willing hands for no distinction was made between the high-caste member of the police force and the low-caste dacoit took them up. With spare runners running alongside, the stretchers set off through the jungle for the Najibabad hospital twelve miles away. The dacoit died of loss of blood and of shock on the way, and the Havildar died a few minutes after being admitted to the hospital.

The beat was abandoned. Herbert did not come into the picture, for Sultana had been warned of the concentration of horse and none of the dacoits tried to cross the line he was guarding. So, the sum total of our carefully planned raid, which had miscarried through no one's fault was Sultana's entire camp less a few guns, and two dead men One a poor man, who, chafing at confinement had sought liberty and adopted the only means of livelihood open to him and who would be mourned by a widow in the Najibabad fort. And the other a man respected by his superiors and loved by his men, whose widow would be cared for, and who had bravely died for a principle, for the 'wine' with which he refused to defile his lips would have sustained him until he had been laid on the operating table.

Three days after the raid Freddy received a letter from the dacoit leader in which Sultana regretted that a shortage of arms and ammunition in the police force had necessitated a raid on his camp and stating that if in future

Freddy would let him know his requirements, he, Sultana, would be very glad to supply him.

The supply of arms and ammunition to Sultana was a very sore point with Freddy. Stringent orders on the subject had been issued but it was not surprising that every licensed dealer and every licensed gun-holder in the area in which Sultana was operating was willing to risk the Government's displeasure when the alternative was the certainty of having his house raided, and the possibility of having his throat cut, if he refused Sultana's demands. So, the offer of arms and ammunition was no idle one and it was the unkindest cut the dacoit leader could have delivered to the head of the Special Dacoity Police Force.

With his hide-out gone, harried from end to end of the Terai and Bhabar and with his gang reduced to forty all well-armed for the dacoits had soon replaced the arms and ammunition taken from them Freddy thought the time had now come for Sultana to surrender. So, after obtaining Government sanction which was given on the understanding that he personally accepted full responsibility, he invited Sultana to a meeting, whenever and wherever convenient. Sultana accepted the invitation, named the time, date and place, and stipulated that both should attend the meeting alone and unarmed. On the appointed day, as Freddy stepped out on one side of a wide-open glade in the Centre of which a solitary tree was growing, Sultana stepped out on the other side. Their meeting was friendly as all who have lived in the East would have expected it to be and when they had seated themselves in the shade of the tree, one a mountain of energy and good humour with the authority of the Government behind him and the other a dapper little man with a price on his head Sultana produced a watermelon which he smilingly said Freddy could partake of without reservation. The meeting ended in a deadlock, however for Sultana refused to accept Freddy's terms of unconditional surrender. It was at this meeting that Sultana begged Freddy not to take undue risks. On the day of the raid, he said, he with ten of his men, all fully armed had taken cover under a banyan tree and had watched Freddy and two other sahibs coming down the nullah towards the tree. 'Had the sahib who was trying to climb the bank succeeded in doing so', Sultana added, 'it would have been necessary to shoot the three of you.'

The final round of the heavy-light-weight contest was now to be staged, and Freddy invited Wyndham and I myself to Hardwar to witness and take part in it. Sultana and the remnants of his gang, now weary of movement, had taken up residence at a cattle station in the heart of the Najibabad jungles and Freddy's plan was to convey his entire force down the Ganges in boats, land at a convenient spot and surround the cattle station. This raid, like the one already described, was to take place at night. But on this occasion the raid had been timed for the full moon.

On the day chosen, the entire force of three hundred men, with the addition of Freddy's cousin, Wyndham and myself, embarked as night was falling in ten country boats which had been assembled at a secluded spot on the right bank of the Ganges, a few miles below Hardwar. I was in the leading boat, and all went well until we crossed to the left bank and entered a side channel. The passage down this channel was one of the most terrifying experiences, off dry land, that I have ever had. For a few hundred yards the boat glided over a wide expanse of moonlit water without a ripple on its surface to distort the reflection of the trees on the margin. Gradually the channel narrowed, and the speed of the boat increased and at the same time we heard the distant sound of rushing water. I have often fished in these side channels of the Ganges, for they are preferred to the mainstream by fish, and I marvelled at the courage of the boatmen who were willing to risk their lives and their craft in the rapids we were fast approaching. The boat, like the other nine, was an open cargo freighter eminently suitable for work on the open Ganges but here in this narrow swift-flowing channel she was just an unmanageable hulk, which threatened to become a wreck every time her bottom planks came in violent contact with submerged boulders. The urgent call of the captain to his crew to fend the boat off the rocky banks and keep her in the middle of the stream, or she would founder, did nothing to allay my fears, for at the time the warning was given the boat was drifting sideways and threatening to break up or capsize every time she struck the bottom. But nightmares cannot last forever. Though the one that night was long-drawn-out, for we had twenty miles to go, mostly through broken water, it ended when one of the boatmen sprang ashore on the left bank with one end of a long rope and made it fast to a tree. Boat after boat passed us and tied up lower down, until all ten had been accounted for.

The force was disembarked on a sandy beach and when cuts and abrasions resulting from contact with the rough timbers of the boats had been attended to, and the boatmen had been instructed to take their craft five miles farther downstream and await orders, we set off in single file to battle our way through half a mile of the heaviest elephant grass I have ever tried to penetrate on foot. The grass was ten to twelve feet high and was weighed down with river fog and dew and before we had gone a hundred yards we were wet to the skin. When we eventually arrived on the far side, we were faced with a wide expanse of water which we took to be an old bed of the Ganges, and scouting parties were sent right and left to find the shortest way round the obstruction. The party that had gone to the right returned first and reported that a quarter of a mile from where we were standing the 'lake' narrowed, and that from this point to the junction of the channel down which we had come there was a swift-flowing river. Soon after the other party returned and reported that there was an unfordable river flowing into the upper end of the lake. It was now quite evident that our boatmen intentionally or accidentally had marooned us on an island.

With our boats gone and daylight not far off it was necessary to do something, so we moved down to the lower end of the wide expanse of water to see if we could affect a crossing between it and the junction of the two channels. Where the water narrowed and the toe or draw of the stream started, there appeared to be a possible crossing, above this point the water was twenty feet deep, and below it was a raging torrent. While the rest of us were looking at the fast-flowing water and speculating as to whether anyone would be able to cross it, Wyndham was divesting himself of his clothes. When I remarked that this was an unnecessary proceeding in view of the fact that he was already wet to the skin, he replied that he was not thinking of his clothes, but of his life. When he had taken off every stitch of clothing, he tied it into a bundle, using his shirt for the purpose, and placed the bundle firmly on his head, caught the arm of a strapping young constable standing nearby and said, 'Come with me'. The young man was so taken aback at being selected to have the honour of drowning with the Commissioner Sahib that he said nothing and together with linked arms, the two stepped into the water.

I do not think any of us breathed while we watched that crossing. With the water at times round their waists and at times up to their armpits, it seemed impossible for them to avoid being carried off their feet and swept into the raging torrent below where no man, no matter how good a swimmer he was, could have lived. Steadily the two brave men, one the oldest in the party and the other possibly the youngest fought their way on and when at last they struggled out on the far bank a sigh of relief went up from the spectators, which would have been a cheer audible in Hardwar, twenty miles away, had silence not been imposed on us.

Where two men could go three hundred could follow, so a chain was made and though individual links were at times swept off their feet, the chain held and the whole force landed safely on the far side. Here we were met by one of Freddy's most trusted informers who, pointing to the rising sun, said we had come too late, that it would not be possible for such a large force to cross the open ground between us and the forest without being seen by the herdsmen in the area, and that therefore the only thing for us to do was to go back to the island. So back to the island we went, the crossing from this side not being as bad as it had been from the other.

Back in the elephant grass our first concern was to dry our clothes. This was soon accomplished, for the sun was by now hot, and when we were once again dry and warm Freddy, from his capacious haversack, produced a chicken and a loaf of bread which were no less welcome for having been immersed in the cold waters of the Ganges. I have the ability to sleep anywhere and at any time, and, having found a sandy hollow, most of the day had passed when I was awakened by violent sneezing. On joining my companions, I found that all three of them were suffering from varying degrees of hay fever. The grass we were in was of the plumed variety and when we had passed through it in the early morning the plumes had been wet. But now, in the hot sun, the plumes had fluffed out and while moving about and trying to find cool places to rest in my companions had shaken the pollen down, with the result that they had given themselves hay fever.

Indians do not get hay fever and I myself have never had it. This was the first time I had ever seen anyone suffering from it, and what I saw alarmed me. Freddy's cousin, a planter on holiday from Bengal was the worst of the three, his eyes were streaming and swollen to the extent that he could not see, and his nose was running. Freddy could see a little, but he could not stop sneezing and when Freddy sneezed the earth shook. Wyndham, tough old campaigner that he was, while protesting that he was quite all right, was unable to keep his handkerchief away from his nose and eyes. It was bad enough being thrown about in an open boat, marooned on a desert island, and fording raging torrents but here was the climax. To lead three men who threatened to go blind back to Hardwar at the head of the three hundred policemen was a prospect that made me feel colder than I had felt when crossing the ice-cold waters of the Ganges. As evening closed in the condition of the sufferers improved, much to my relief, and by the time we had crossed the ford for the third time Freddy and Wyndham were all right and the cousin had regained his sight to the extent that it was no longer necessary to tell him when to raise his foot to avoid a stone.

Freddy's informer and a guide were waiting for us and led us over the open ground to the mouth of a dry watercourse about a hundred yards wide. The moon had just risen, and visibility was nearly as good as in sunlight when, rounding a bend, we came face to face with an elephant We had heard there was a rogue elephant in this area, and here he was, tusks flashing in the moonlight, ears spread out and emitting loud squeals. The guide did nothing to improve the situation by stating that the elephant was very bad tempered, that he had killed many people, and that he was sure to kill a number of us. At first it appeared that the rogue was going to make good the guide's predictions, for with trunk raised high he advanced a few yards. Then he swung round and dashed up the bank, trumpeting defiance as he gained the shelter of the jungle.

Another mile up the watercourse and we came on what the guide said was a fire-track. Here the going was very pleasant, for with short green grass underfoot and the moonlight glinting on every leaf and blade, it was possible to forget our errand and revel in the beauty of the jungle. As we approached a stretch of burnt grass where an old peacock, perched high on a leafless tree, was sending his warning cry into the night, two leopards stepped out on the track, saw us, and gracefully bounded away and faded out of sight in the shadows. I had been out of my element during the long passage down the side channel but now, what with the elephant who was, I knew, only curious and intended us no harm and then the peacock warning the jungle folk of the presence of danger and finally the leopards merging into the shadows, I was back on familiar ground, ground that I loved and understood.

Leaving the track, which ran from east to west, the guide led us north for a mile or more through scrub and tree jungle to the bank of a tiny stream overhung by a giant banyan tree. Here we were told to sit down and wait, while the guide went forward to confer with his brother at the cattle station. A long and weary wait it was, which was in no way relieved by pangs of hunger, for we had eaten nothing since our meal off the chicken and loaf of bread, and it was now past midnight; and to make matters worse I, the only one who smoked, had exhausted my supply of cigarettes. The guide returned towards the early hours of the morning and reported that Sultana and the remnants of his gang, now reduced to nine, had left the cattle station the previous evening to raid a village in the direction of Hardwar and that they were expected back that night or the following day. Before leaving to try to get us a little food which we were in urgent need, the guide and the informer warned us that we were in Sultana's territory and that it would be unwise for any of us to leave the shelter of the banyan tree.

Another weary day passed, the last Wyndham could spend with us, for in addition to being Commissioner of Kumaon, he was Political Agent of Tehri State and was due to meet the ruler at Narindra Nagar in two days' time.

After nightfall a cart loaded with grass arrived and when the grass had been removed a few sacks of parched gram and forty pounds of Gur were revealed. This scanty but welcome ration was distributed among the men. The guide had not forgotten the sahibs and before driving away he handed Freddy a few chapattis tied up in a piece of cloth that had seen hard times and better days. As we lay on our backs with all topics of conversation exhausted, thinking of hot meals and soft beds in far-off Hardwar, I heard the welcome sounds of a leopard killing a chital a few hundred yards from our tree. Here was an opportunity of getting a square meal, for my portion of chapatti, far from allaying my hunger, had only added to it so I jumped up and asked Freddy for his kukri. When he asked what on earth, I wanted it for I told him it was to cut off the hind legs of the chital the leopard had just killed. 'What leopard and what chital', he asked, 'are you talking about?' Yes, he could hear the chital calling, but how was he to know that they were not alarmed by some of Sultana's men who were scouting round to spy on us? And anyway, if I was right in thinking a leopard had made a kill, which he doubted, how was I going to take the chital away from it when I could not use a musket (I had not brought my rifle with me on this occasion for I did not know to what use I might be asked to put it) so close to the cattle station? No, he concluded, the whole idea was absurd. So very regretfully I again laydown with my hunger. How could I convince anyone who did not know the jungle folk and their language that I knew the deer had not been alarmed by human beings, that they were watching one of their number being killed by a leopard and that there was no danger in taking the kill or as much of it as I wanted away from the leopard?

The night passed without further incident and at the crack of dawn Wyndham and I set out on our long walk to Hardwar. We crossed the Ganges by the Bhimgoda Dam and after a quick meal at the Dam Bungalow had an evening's fishing on the wide expanse of water above the dam that will long be remembered.

Next morning, just as Wyndham was leaving to keep-his appointment at Narindra Nagar and I was collecting some eatables to take back to my hungry companions, word was brought to us by runner that Freddy had captured Sultana.

Sultana had returned to the cattle station the previous evening. After his men had surrounded the station, Freddy crept up to the large hut used by the cattle men and seeing a sheeted figure asleep on the only charpoy the hut contained, sat down on it. Pinned down by 20 stone 4 pounds, Sultana was not unable to offer any resistance, nor was he able to carry out his resolve of not being taken alive. Of the six dacoits in the hut at the time of the raid, four, including Sultana, were captured and the other two, Babu and Pailwan, Sultana's lieutenants, broke through, the police cordon and escaped, after being fired at.

I do not know how many murders Sultana was responsible for, but when brought to trial the main charge against him was the murder by one of his gangs of the tenant of the headman of Lamachour. While in the condemned cell Sultana sent Freddy and bequeathed to him his wife and son in the Najibabad Fort and his dog of whom he was very fond. Freddy adopted the dog, and those who know Freddy will not need to be told that he faithfully carried out his promise to care for Sultana's family.

Some months later Freddy, now promoted and the youngest man in the Indian Police service ever to be honoured by His Majesty the King with a C.I.E., was attending the annual Police Week at Moradabad. One of the functions at this week was a dinner to which all the police officers in the province were invited. During the dinner one of the waiters whispered to Freddy that his orderly wanted to speak to him. This orderly had been with Freddy during the years Freddy had been in pursuit of Sultana. Now, having an evening off, he had strolled down to Moradabad railway station. While he was there, a train came in and as he idly watched the passengers alighting two men came out of a compartment near him. One of these men spoke to the other, who hastily put a handkerchief up to his face but not before the orderly had seen that he had a piece of cotton wool sticking to his nose. The orderly kept his eye on the men, who had a considerable amount of luggage, and when they had made themselves comfortable in a corner of the waiting room, he commandeered an ekka and hastened to inform Freddy.

When Sultana's two lieutenants, Babu and Pailwan, broke through the cordon surrounding the cattle station, they had been fired at, and shortly thereafter a man had visited a small dispensary near Najibabad to have an injury to his nose, which he said had been caused by a dog bite, attended to. When reporting the case to the police, the compounder who dressed the wound said he suspected it had been caused by a pellet of buckshot. So, the entire police force of the province were on the lookout for a man with an injured nose, all the more so because Babu and Pailwan were credited with having committed most of the murders for which Sultana's gang were responsible.

When he heard the orderly's story Freddy jumped into his car and dashed to the station, dashed is the right word for when Freddy is in a hurry the road is before him and traffic and corners do not exist. At the station he placed guards at all the exits to the waiting room and then went up to the two men and asked them who they were. Merchants, they answered, on their way from Bareilly to the Punjab. Why then, asked Freddy, had they taken a train that terminated at Moradabad? He was told that there had been two trains at the Bareilly platform, and they had been directed to the wrong one. When Freddy learnt the men had not had any food, and that they would have to wait until next morning for a connecting train, he invited them to accompany him and be his guests. For a moment the men hesitated, and then said, 'As you wish, Sahib'.

With the two men in the back of the car Freddy drove slowly, closely questioning them, and to all his questions he received prompt answers. The men then asked Freddy if it was customary for sahibs to visit railway stations at night and carry off passengers, leaving their luggage to be plundered by any who cared to do so. Freddy knew that his action, without a duly executed warrant, could be described as high-handed and might land him in serious trouble if the members of Sultana's gang serving sentences In the Moradabad jail failed to identify their late companions. While these unpleasant thoughts were chasing each other through his mind, the car arrived at the bungalow in which he was putting up for the Police Week. All dogs love Freddy, and Sultana's dog was no exception. In the months that had passed this pye with a dash of terrier blood had given Freddy all his affection and now, when the car stopped and the three men got out, the dog came dashing out of the bungalow, stopped in surprise, and then hurled himself at the two travellers with every manifestation of delight that a dog can exhibit. For a tense minute Freddy and the two men looked at each other in silence and then Paitwan, who knew the fate that awaited him, stooped down and patting the dog's head said, 'In face of this honest witness what use is it, Young Sahib, for us to deny we are the men you think we are'.

Society demands protection against criminals and Sultana was a criminal. He was tried under the law of the land, found guilty and executed. Nevertheless, I cannot withhold a great measure of admiration for the little man who set at naught the might of the Government for three long years and who by his brave demeanor won the respect of those who guarded him in the condemned cell.

I could have wished that justice had not demanded that Sultana be exhibited in manacles and leg-irons and exposed to ridicule from those who trembled at the mere mention of his name while he was at liberty. I could also have wished that he had been given a more lenient sentence, for no other reasons than that he had been branded a criminal at birth and had not had a fair chance; that when power was in his hands, he had not oppressed the poor; that when I tracked him to the banyan tree, he spared my life and the lives of my friends. And finally, he went to his meeting with Freddy, not armed with a knife or a revolver but with a watermelon in his hands.

VIII. LOYALTY

The mail train was running at its maximum speed of thirty miles per hour through country that was familiar. For mile upon mile the newly risen sun had been shining on fields where people were reaping the golden wheat, for it was the month of April and the train was passing through the Gangetic valley, the most fertile land in India.

During the previous year India had witnessed one of her worst famines. I had seen whole villages existing on the bark of trees on minute grass seeds swept up with infinite labour from scorching plains and on the wild plums that grow on waste lands too poor for the raising of crops. Mercifully the weather had changed, good winter rains had brought back fertility to the land, and the people who had starved for a year were now eagerly reaping a good harvest. Early though the hour was, the scene was one of intense activity in which every individual of the community had his, or her, allotted part. The reaping was being done by women, most of them landless labourers who move from area to area, as the crop ripens and who for their labour which starts at dawn and ends when there is no longer light to work by receive one- twelfth to one-sixteenth of the crop they cut in the course of the day.

There were no hedges to obstruct the view and from the carriage window no mechanical device of any kind was to be seen. The ploughing had been done by oxen, two to a plough; the reaping was being done by sickles with a curved blade eighteen inches long; the sheaves, tied with twisted stalks of wheat straw, were being carted to the threshing floor on oxcarts with wooden wheels and on the threshing floor, plastered over with cow dung, oxen were treading out the corn; they were tied to a long rope, one end of which was made fast to a pole firmly fixed in the ground. As a field was cleared of the sheave's children drove cattle on to it to graze on the stubble and amongst the cattle old and infirm women were sweeping the ground to recover any seed that had fallen from the ears when the wheat was being cut. Half of what these toilets collected would be taken by the owner of the field and the other half, which might amount to as much as a pound or two, if the ground was not too sun cracked, they would be permitted to retain.

My journey was to last for thirty-six hours. I had the carriage to myself, and the train would stop for breakfast, lunch, and dinner. Every mile of the country through which the train was running was interesting and yet I was not happy for in the steel trunk under my seat was a string bag containing two hundred rupees which did not belong to me.

Eighteen months previously I had taken employment as a Fuel Inspector with the railway on which I was now travelling. I had gone straight from school to this job and for those eighteen months I had lived in the forest cutting five hundred thousand cubic feet of timber, to be used as fuel in locomotives. After the trees had been felled and billeted, each billet not more and not less than thirty-six inches long, the fuel was carted ten miles to the nearest point of the railway, where it was stacked and measured and then loaded into fuel trains and taken to the stations where it was needed. Those eighteen months alone in the forest had been strenuous but I had kept fit and enjoyed the work. There was plenty of game in the forest in the way of chital, four-horned antelope, pig, and pea fowl and in the river that formed one boundary of the forest there were several varieties of fish and many alligators and python. My work did not permit of my indulging in sport during daylight hours, so I had to do all my shooting for the pot, and fishing at night. Shooting by moonlight is very different from shooting in daylight for though it is easier to stalk a deer or a rooting pig at night it is difficult to shoot accurately unless the moon can be got to shine on the foresight. The pea fowl had to be shot while they were roosting, and I am not ashamed to say that I occasionally indulged in this form of murder, for the only meat I ate during that year and a half was what I shot on moonlight nights during the dark period of the moon, I had perforce to be a vegetarian.

The felling of the forest disarranged the normal life of the jungle folk and left me with the care of many waifs and orphans, all of whom had to share my small tent with me. It was when I was a bit crowded with two broods of partridges one black and the other grey, four pea fowl chicks, two leverets and two baby four-horned antelope that could only just stand upright on their spindle legs, that Rex the python took up his quarters in the tent. I returned an hour after nightfall that day, and while I was feeding the four-footed inmates with milk, I saw the lantern light glinting on something in a corner of the tent and on investigation found Rex coiled up on the straw used as a bed by the baby antelope. A hurried count revealed that none of the young inmates of the tent were missing, so I left Rex in the corner he had selected. For two months thereafter Rex left the tent each day to bask in the sun, returning to his corner at sundown, and during the whole of that period he never harmed any of the young life he shared the tent with.

Of all the waifs and orphans who were brought up in the tent, and who were returned to the forest as soon as they were able to fend for themselves, Tiddley-de-winks, a four-horned antelope was the only one who refused to leave me. She followed me when I moved camp to be nearer to the railway line to supervise the loading of the fuel and in doing so nearly lost her life. Having been brought up by hand she had no fear of human beings and the day after our move she approached a man who, thinking she was a wild animal, tried to kill her. When I returned to the tent that evening, I found her lying near my camp bed and on picking her up saw that both her forelegs had been broken, and that the broken ends of the bones had worked through the skin. While I was getting a little milk down her throat and trying to summon sufficient courage to do what I knew should be done, my servant came into the tent with a man who admitted to having tried to kill the poor beast. It appeared that this man had been working in his field when Tiddley-de-winks went up to him and thinking she had strayed in from the nearby forest, he struck her with a stick and then chased her and it was only when she entered my tent that he realized she was a tame animal. My servant had advised him to leave before I returned but this the man had refused to do. When he had told his story he said he would return early the next morning with a bonesetter from his village. There was nothing I could do for the injured animal, beyond making a soft bed for her and giving her milk at short intervals and at daybreak next morning the man returned with the bonesetter.

It is unwise in India to judge from appearances. The bonesetter was a feeble old man, exhibiting in his person and tattered dress every sign of poverty, but he was none the less a specialist and a man of few words. He asked me to lift up the injured animal, stood looking at her for a few minutes, and then turned and left the tent, saying over his shoulder that he would be back in two hours. I had worked week in week out for months on end, so I considered I was justified in taking a morning off and before the old man returned, I had cut a number of stakes in the nearby jungle and constructed a small pen in a corner of the tent. The man brought back with him a number of dry jute stalks from which the bark had been removed, a quantity of green paste, several young castor-oil plant leaves as big as plates and a roll of thin jute twine. When I had seated myself on the edge of the camp bed with Tiddley-de-winks across my knees, her weight partly supported by her hind legs and partly by my knees, the old man sat down on the ground in front of her with his materials within reach.

The bones of both forelegs had been splintered midway between the knees and the tiny hooves and the dangling portion of the legs had twisted round and round. Very gently the old man untwisted the legs, covered them from knee to hoof with a thick layer of green paste, laid strips of the castor-oil leaves over the paste to keep it in position and over the leaves laid the jute stalks, binding them to the legs with jute twine. Next morning, he returned with splints made of jute stalks strung together and when they had been fitted to her legs Tiddley-de-winks was able to bend her knees and place her hooves, which extended an inch beyond the splints on the ground.

The bone-setter's fee was one rupee, plus two annas for the ingredients he had put in the paste and the twine he had purchased in the bazaar and not until the splints had been removed and the little antelope was able to skip about again would he accept either his fee or the little present I gratefully offered him.

My work, every day of which I had enjoyed was over now and I was on my way to headquarters to render an account of the money I had spent, and I feared to look for another job for the locomotives had been converted to coal-burning and no more wood fuel would be needed. My books were all in perfect order and I had the feeling that I had rendered good service, for I had done in eighteen months what had been estimated to take two years.

Yet I was uneasy, and the reason for my being so was the bag of money in my steel trunk.

I reached my destination, Samastipur at 9 a.m. and after depositing my luggage in the waiting-room set out for the office of the head of the department I had been working for, with my account books and the bag containing the two hundred rupees. At the office I was told by a very imposing doorkeeper that the master was engaged and that I would have to wait. It was hot in the open veranda and as the minutes dragged by my nervousness increased, for an old railway hand who had helped me to make up my book shad warned me that to submit balanced accounts and then admit, as I had every intention of doing, that I had two hundred rupees in excess would land me in very great trouble. Eventually the door opened, and a very harassed looking man emerged and before the doorkeeper could close it, a voice from inside the room bellowed at me to come in.

Ryles, the head of the Locomotive Department of the Bengal and Northwestern Railway, was a man weighing sixteen stone, with a voice that struck terror into all who served under him, and with a heart of gold. Bidding me to sit down he drew my books towards him summoned a clerk and very carefully checked my figures with those received from the stations to which the fuel had been sent. Then he told me he regretted my services would no longer be needed, said that discharge orders would be sent to me later in the day, and indicated that the interview was over. Having picked my hat off the floor I started to leave but was called back and told I had forgotten to remove what appeared to be a bag of money that I had placed on the table. It was foolish of me to have thought I could just leave the two hundred rupees and walk away, but that was what I was trying to do when Ryles called me, so I went back to the table and told him that the money belonged to the Railway, and as I did not know how to account for it in my books, I had brought it to him. 'Your books are balanced', Ryles said, 'and if you have not faked your account's I should like an explanation. 'Tewari, the head clerk, had come into the room with a tray of papers and he stood behind Ryles's chair with encouragement in his kindly old eyes as I gave Ryles the following explanation.

When my work was nearing completion, fifteen cart-men, who had been engaged to cart fuel from the forest to the railway line came to me one night and stated they had received an urgent summons to return to their village, to harvest the crops. The fuel they had carted was scattered over a wide area, and as it would take several days to stack and measure it, they wanted me to make a rough calculation of the amount due to them, as it was essential for them to start on their journey that night. It was a dark night and quite impossible for me to calculate the cubic contents of the fuel, so I told them I would accept their figures. Two hours later they returned and within a few minutes of paying them, I heard their carts creaking away into the night. They left no address with me and several weeks later, when the fuel was stacked and measured, I found they had underestimated the amount due to them by two hundred rupees.

When I had told my story Ryles informed me that the Agent, Izat, was expected in Samastipur the next day and that he would leave him to deal with me. Izat, Agent of three of the most flourishing railways in India, arrived next morning and at midday I received a summons to attend Ryles's office. Izat, a small dapper man with piercing eyes was alone in the office when I entered it and after complimenting me on having finished my job six months ahead of time, he said Ryles had shown him my books and given him a report and that he wanted to ask one question. Why had I not pocketed the two hundred rupees and said nothing about it? My answer to this question was evidently satisfactory, for that evening, while waiting at the station in a state of uncertainty, I received two letters, one from Tewari thanking me for my contribution of two hundred rupees to the Railway men's Widows' and Orphans' Fund, of which he was Honorary Secretary and the other from Izat informing me that my services were being retained and instructing me to report to Ryles for duty.

For a year there after I worked up and down the railway on a variety of jobs, at times on the footplates of locomotives reporting on consumption of coal, a job I liked for I was permitted to drive the engines at times as guard of goods trains, a tedious job for the railway was short-handed and, on many occasions, I was on duty for forty-eight hours at a stretch; and at times as assistant storekeeper, or assistant stationmaster. And then one day I received orders to go to Mokameh Ghat and see Storrar, the Ferry Superintendent. The Bengal and Northwestern Railway runs through the Gangetic valley at varying distances from the Ganges river and at several places branch line stake off from the main line and run down to the river and by means of ferries, connect up with the broad-gauge railways on the right bank. Mokameh Ghat on the right bank of the Ganges is the most important of these connexions.

I left Samastipur in the early hours of the morning and at the branch-line terminus, Samaria Ghat, boarded the S.S.Gor akhpur. Storrar had been apprised of my visit, but no reason had been given and as I had not been told why I was to go to Mokameh Ghat, we spent the day partly in his house and partly walking about the extensive sheds in which there appeared to be a considerable congestion of goods. Two days later I was summoned to Gorakhpur, the headquarters of the railway, and informed that I had been posted to Mokameh Ghat as Trans-shipment Inspector, that my pay had been increased from one hundred to one hundred and fifty rupees per month, and that I was to take over the contract for handling goods a week later.

So back to Mokameh Ghat I went, arriving on this occasion at night, to take up a job about which I knew nothing, and to take on a contract without knowing where to get a single labourer and, most important of all, with a capital of only one hundred and fifty rupees, saved during my two and a half years' service.

Storrar was not expecting me on this occasion, but he gave me dinner, and when I told him why I had returned we took our chairs on to the veranda, where a cool wind was blowing off the river, and talked late into the night. Storrar was twice my age and had been at Mokameh Ghat for several years. He was employed as Ferry Superintendent by the Bengal and Northwestern (metre-gauge) Railway and was in charge of a fleet of steamers and barges that ferried passengers and metre-gauge wagons between Samaria Ghat and Mokameh Ghat. I learnt from him that eighty per cent of the long-distance traffic on the Bengal and Northwestern Railway passed through Mokameh Ghat and that each year, from March to September, congestion of goods traffic took place at Mokameh Ghat and caused serious loss to the Railway.

The transfer of goods between the two railways at Mokameh Ghat, necessitated by a break of gauge, was done by a Labour Company which held the contract for handling goods throughout the length of the broad-gauge railway. In Storrar's opinion the indifference of this company to the interests of the metre-gauge railway and the seasonal shortage of labour due to the harvesting of crops in the Gangetic valley, were the causes of the annual congestion. Having imparted this information, he very pertinently asked how I, a total stranger to the locality and without any capital, brushed aside my hard-earned savings proposed to accomplish what the Labour Company with all their resources had failed to do. The sheds at Mokameh Ghat, he added, were stacked to the roof with goods, there were four hundred wagons in the yard waiting to be unloaded and a thousand wagons on the far side of the river waiting to be ferried across. 'My advice to you', he concluded is to catch the early steamer to Samaria Ghat and to go straight back to Gorakhpur. Tell the Railway you will have nothing to do with the handling contract.'

I was up early next morning but I did not catch the steamer to Samaria Ghat. Instead, I went on a tour of inspection of the sheds and of the goods yard. Storrar had not overpainted the picture, in fact the conditions were even worse than he had said they were, for in addition to the four hundred metre-gauge wagons there were the same number of broad-gauge wagons waiting to be unloaded. At a rough calculation I put the goods at Mokameh Ghat waiting to be dealt with at fifteen thousand tons and I had been sent to clear up the mess. Well, I was not quite twenty-one years of age and summer was starting, a season when all of us are a little bit mad. By the time I met Ram Saran I had made up my mind that I would take on the job, no matter what the result might be. Ram Saran was stationmaster at Mokameh Ghat, a post he had held for two years. He was twenty years older than I was, had an enormous jet-black beard and was the father of five children. He had been advised by telegram of my arrival but had not been told that I was to take over the handling contract.

When I gave him this bit of news his face beamed all over and he said, 'Good, Sir. Very good. We will manage.' My heart warmed towards Ram Saran on hearing that 'we' and up to his death, thirty-five years later, it never cooled.

When I told Storrar over breakfast that morning that I had decided to take on the handling contract he remarked that fools never took good advice but added that he would do all he could to help me, a promise he faithfully kept. In the months that followed he kept his ferry running day and night to keep me supplied with wagons.

The journey from Gorakhpur had taken two days, so when I arrived at Mokameh Ghat I had five days in which to learn what my duties were, and to make arrangements for taking over the handling contract. The first two days I spent in getting acquainted with my staff which, in addition to Ram Saran, consisted of an assistant stationmaster, a grand old man by the name of Chatterji who was old enough to be my grandfather, sixty-five clerks and a hundred shunters, points men and watchmen. My duties extended across the river to Samaria Ghat where I had a clerical and menial staff a hundred strong. The supervising of these two staffs and the care of the goods in transit, was in itself a terrifying job and added to it was the responsibility of providing a labour force sufficient to keep the five hundred thousand tons of goods that passed through Mokameh Ghat annually flowing smoothly.

The men employed by the big Labour Company were on piece work, and as all work at Mokameh Ghat was practically at a standstill, there were several hundred very discontented men sitting about the sheds, many of whom offered me their services when they heard that I was going to do the handling for the metre-gauge railway. I was under no agreement not to employ the Labour Company's men but thought it prudent not to do so. However, I saw no reason why I should not employ their relatives, so on the first of the three days I had in hand I selected twelve men and appointed them headmen. Eleven of these headmen undertook to provide ten men each, to start with, for the handling of goods and the twelfth undertook to provide a mixed gang of sixty men and women for the handling of coal. The traffic to be dealt with consisted of a variety of commodities, and this meant employing different castes to deal with the different classes of goods. So, of the twelve headmen, eight were Hindus, two Mohammedans and two men of the depressed class and as only one of the twelve was literate I employed one Hindu and one Mohammedan clerk to keep their accounts.

While one Labour Company was doing the work of both railways the interchange of goods had taken place from wagon to wagon. Now each railway was to unload its goods in the sheds and reload from shed to wagon. For all classes of goods, excluding heavy machinery and coal, I was to be paid at the rate of Re 1-7-0 (equivalent to is. nd. at the rate of exchange then current) for every thousand maunds of goods unloaded from wagons to shed or loaded from shed to wagons. Heavy machinery and coal were one-way traffic and as these two commodities were to be trans-shipped from wagon to wagon and only one contractor could be employed for the purpose, the work was entrusted to me, and I was to receive Re 1-4- 0 {is. 8d.) for unloading and the same for loading, one thousand maunds.

There are eighty pounds in a maund and a thousand maunds therefore are equal to over thirty-five tons. These rates will appear incredible, but their accuracy can be verified by reference to the records of the two railways.

A call-over on the last evening revealed that I had eleven headmen, each with a gang of ten men, and one headman with a mixed gang of sixty men and women. This, together with the two clerks, completed my force. At daybreak next morning I telegraphed to Gorakhpur that I had assumed my duties as Trans-shipment Inspector and had taken over the handling contract.

Ram Saran's opposite number on the broad-gauge railway was an Irishman by the name of Tom Kelly. Kelly had been at Mokameh Ghat for some years and though he was very pessimistic of my success, he very sportingly offered to help me in every way he could. With the sheds congested with goods, and with four hundred wagons of each railway waiting to be unloaded, it was necessary to do something drastic to make room in the sheds and get the traffic moving, so I arranged with Kelly that I would take the risk of unloading a thousand tons of wheat on the ground outside the sheds and with the wagons so released clear a space in the sheds for Kelly to unload a thousand tons of salt and sugar. Kelly then with his empty wagons would clear a space in the sheds for me. This plan worked admirably. Fortunately for me it did not rain while my thousand tons of wheat were exposed to the weather and in ten days, we had not only cleared the accumulation in the sheds but also the accumulation of wagons. Kelly and I were then able to advise our respective headquarters to resume the booking of goods via Mokameh Ghat, which had been suspended for a fortnight.

I took over the contract at the beginning of the summer, the season when traffic on Indian railways is at its heaviest and as soon as booking was opened a steady stream of downwards traffic from the Bengal and Northwestern Railway and an equally heavy stream from the broad-gauge railway started pouring into Mokameh Ghat. The rates on which I had been given the contract were the lowest paid to any contractor in India, and the only way in which I could hope to keep my labour was by cutting it down to the absolute minimum and making it work harder in order that it would earn as much or possibly a little more, than other labour on similar work. All the labour at Mokameh Ghat was on piece work, and at the end of the first week my men and I were overjoyed to find that they had earned on paper fifty per cent, more than the Labour Company's men had earned. When entrusting me with the contract the Railway promised to pay me weekly and I on my part promised to pay my labour weekly. The Railway, however, when making their promise, failed to realize that by switching over from one handling contractor to another they would be raising complications for their Audit Department that would take time to resolve. For the Railway this was a small matter but for me it was very different. My total capital on arrival at Mokameh Ghat had been one hundred and fifty rupees and there was no one in all the world I could call on to help me with a loan, so until the Railway paid me, I could not pay my men.

I have entitled this story Loyalty and I do not think that anyone has ever received greater loyalty than I did, not only from my labour, but also from the railway staff, during those first three months that I was at Mokameh Ghat. Nor do I think that men have ever worked harder. The work started every morning, weekdays, and Sundays alike, at 4 a.m., and continued without interruption up to 8 p.m. The clerks whose duty it was to check and tally the goods took their meals at different hours to avoid a stoppage of work and my men ate their food, which was brought to them by wives, mothers, or daughters, in the sheds.

There were no trade unions or slaves and slavedrivers in those days and every individual was at liberty to work as many, or as few, hours as he or she wished to. And everyone worked cheerfully and happily, for no matter whether it was the procuring of more and better food and clothing for the family, the buying of a new ox to replace a worn-out one or the paying-off of a debt, the incentive, without which no man can work his best, was there. My work and Ram Saran's did not end when the men knocked off work, for there was correspondence to attend to, and the next day's work to be planned and arranged for and during those first three months neither of us spent more than four hours in bed each night. I was not twenty-one and as hard as nails, but Ram Saran was twenty years older and soft, and at the end of the three months he had lost a stone in weight but none of his cheerfulness.

Lack of money was now a constant worry to me, and as week succeeded week the worry became a hideous nightmare that never left me. First the headmen and then the labourers pledged their cheap and pitiful bits of jewelry and now all credit had gone and to make matters worse, the men of the Labour Company, who were jealous that my men had earned more than they did, were beginning to taunt my men. On several occasions ugly incidents were narrowly avoided, for semi-starvation had not impaired the loyalty of my men and they were willing to give battle to anyone who as much as hinted that I had tricked them into working for me and that they would never see a pice of the money they had earned.

The monsoon was late in coming that year and the red ball in the sky, fanned by a wind from an unseen furnace, was making life a burden. At the end of a long and a very trying day I received a telegram from Samaria Ghat informing me that an engine had been derailed on the slipway that fed the barges on which wagons were ferried across to Mokameh Ghat. A launch conveyed me across the river and twice within the next three hours the engine was replaced on the track, with the aid of hand jacks, only to be derailed again. It was not until the wind had died down and the powdery sand could be packed under the wooden sleepers that the engine was re-railed for the third time, and the slipway again brought into use. Tired and worn out, and with eyes swollen and sore from the wind and sand, I had just sat down to my first meal that day when my twelve headmen filed into the room and seeing my servant placing a plate in front of me with the innate courtesy of Indians, filed out again. I then, as I ate my dinner, heard the following conversation taking place in the veranda.

One of the headmen. What was on the plate you put in front of the sahib?

My servant. A chapati and a little dal.

One of the headmen. Why only one chapati and a little dal?

My servant. Because there is no money to buy more.

One of the headmen. What else does the sahib eat?

My servant. Nothing.

After a short silence I heard the oldest of the headmen, a Mohammedan with a great beard dyed with henna, say to his companions, 'Go home. I will stay and speak to the sahib.' When my servant had removed the empty plate, the old headman requested permission to enter the room and standing before me spoke as follows: 'We came to tell you that our stomachs have long been empty and that after tomorrow it would be no longer possible for us to work. But we have seen tonight that your case is as bad as ours and we will carry on as long as we have the strength to stand. I will, with your permission, go now, sahib, and, for the sake of Allah, I beg you will do something to help us.'

Every day for weeks I had been appealing to headquarters at Gorakhpur for funds and the only reply I could elicit was that steps were being taken to make early payment of my bills.

After the bearded headman left me that night I walked across to the Telegraph Office, where the telegraphist on duty was sending the report, I submitted each night of the work done during the day, took a form off his table and told him to clear the line for an urgent message to Gorakhpur. It was then a few minutes after midnight and the message I sent read: 'Work at Mokameh Ghat ceases at midday today unless I am assured that twelve thousand rupees has been dispatched by morning train.' The telegraphist read the message over and looking up at me said: 'If I have your permission I will tell my brother, who is on duty at this hour, to deliver the message at once and not wait until office hours in the morning.' Ten hours later, and with two hours of my ultimatum still to run, I saw a telegraph messenger hurrying towards me with a buff-coloured envelope in his hand. Each group of men he passed stopped work to stare after him, for everyone in Mokameh Ghat knew the purport of the telegram I had sent at midnight.

After I had read the telegram the messenger, who was the son of my office peon, asked if the news was good and when I told him it was good, he dashed off and his passage down the sheds was punctuated by shouts of delight. The money could not arrive until the following morning, but what did a few hours matter to those who had waited for long months?

The pay clerk who presented himself at my office next day, accompanied by some of my men carrying a cash chest slung on a bamboo pole and guarded by two policemen, was a jovial Hindu who was as broad as he was long and who exuded good humour and sweat in equal proportions. I never saw him without a pair of spectacles tied across his forehead with red tape. Having settled himself on the floor of my office he drew on a cord tied round his neck and from somewhere deep down in his person pulled up a key. He opened the cash chest and lifted out twelve string-bags each containing one thousand freshly minted silver rupees. He licked a stamp and stuck it to the receipt I had signed. Then, delving into a pocket that would comfortably have housed two rabbits, he produced an envelope containing banknotes to the value of four hundred and fifty rupees, my arrears of pay for three months.

I do not think anyone has ever had as great pleasure in paying out money as I had when I placed a bag containing a thousand rupees into the hands of each of the twelve headmen nor do I think men have ever received money with greater pleasure than they did. The advent of the fat pay clerk had relieved a tension that had become almost unbearable, and the occasion called for some form of celebration, so the remainder of the day was declared a holiday, the first my men and I had indulged in for ninety-five days. I do not know how the others spent their hours of relaxation. For myself, I am not ashamed to admit that I spent mine in sound and restful sleep.

For twenty-one years my men and I worked the handling contract at Mokameh Ghat and during the whole of that long period and even when I was absent in France and in Waziristan during the 1914-18 war, the traffic flowed smoothly through the main outlet of the Bengal and Northwestern Railway with never a hitch. When we took over the contract, between four and five hundred thousand tons of goods were passing through Mokameh Ghat and when I handed it over to Ram Saran the traffic had increased to a million tons.

IX. BUDHU

Budhu was a man of the Depressed Class, and during all the years I knew him I never saw him smile: his life had been too hard, and the iron had entered deep into his very soul. He was about thirty-five years of age, a tall gaunt man, with a wife and two young children, when he applied to me for work. At his request I put him on to trans-shipping coal from broad-gauge trucks to metre-gauge wagons at Mokameh Ghat, for in this task men and women could work together, and Budhu wanted his wife to work with him.

The broad-gauge trucks and metre-gauge wagons stood opposite each other with a four-foot-wide sloping platform between, and the coal had to be partly shoveled and partly carried in baskets from the trucks into the wagons.

The work was cruelly hard, for there was no covering to the platform. In winter the men and women worked in bitter cold often wet with rain for days on end and in summer the brick platform and the iron floors of the trucks and wagons blistered their bare feet. A shovel in the hands of a novice, working for his bread and the bread of his children, is a cruel tool. The first day's work leaves the hands red and sore and the back with an ache that is a torment. On the second day blisters form on the hands and the ache in the back becomes an even greater torment. On the third day the blisters break and become septic, and the back can with difficulty be straightened. Thereafter for a week or ten days only guts, and plenty of them, can keep the sufferer at work as I know from experience.

Budhu and his wife went through all these phases, and often, when they had done sixteen hours' piece work and were dragging themselves to the quarters, I had provided for them, I was tempted to tell them they had suffered enough and should look for other less strenuous work. But they were making good wages, better (Budhu said) than they had ever made before, so I let them carry on, and the day came when with hardened hands and backs that no longer ached, they left their work with as brisk and as light a step as they had approached it.

I had some two hundred men and women trans-shipping coal at that time, for the coal traffic was as heavy as it always was in the summer. India was an exporting country in those days and the wagons that took the grain, opium, indigo, hides, and bones to Calcutta returned from the collieries in Bengal loaded with coal, five hundred thousand tons of which passed through Mokameh Ghat.

One day Budhu and his wife were absent from work. Dhamari, the headman of the coal gang, informed me that Budhu had received a postcard the previous day and had left that morning with his family, saying he would return to work as soon as it was possible for him to do so. Two months later the family returned and reoccupied their quarters and Budhu and his wife worked as industriously as they had always done. At about the same time the following year Budhu, whose frame had now filled out and his wife, who had lost her haggard look again absented themselves from work. On this occasion they were absent three months and looked tired and worn out on their return.

Except when consulted, or when information was voluntarily given, I never inquired into the private affairs of my work people, for Indians are sensitive on this point so I did not know why Budhu periodically left his work which he invariably did after receiving a postcard. The post for the work people was delivered to the headmen and distributed by them to the men and women working under them, so I instructed Chamari to send Budhu to me the next time he received a card. Nine months later, when the coal traffic was unusually heavy and every man and woman in my employ was working to full capacity, Budhu, carrying a post card in his hand, presented himself at my office. The postcard was in a script that I could not read so I asked Budhu to read it to me. This he could not do, for he had not been taught to read and write, but he said Chamari had read it to him and that it was an order from his master to come at once as the crops were ready to harvest. The following was Budhu's story as he told it to me that day in my office, and his story is the story of millions of poor people in India.

'My grandfather, who was a field labourer, borrowed two rupees from the bania of the village in which he lived. The bania retained one of the rupees as advance interest for one year, and made my grandfather put his thumbmark to an entry in his *bhai khata* (*register of account*). When my grandfather was able to do so from time to time, he paid the bania a few annas by way of interest. On the death of my grandfather my father took over the debt, which then amounted to fifty rupees. During my father's lifetime the debt increased to one hundred and fifteen rupees. In the meantime, the old bania died and his son, who reigned in his place, sent for me when my father died and informed me that as the family debt now amounted to a considerable sum it would be necessary for me to give him a stamped and duly executed document. This I did and as I had no money to pay for the stamped paper and for the registration of the document the bania advanced the required amount and added it to the debt, which together with interest now amounted to one hundred and thirty rupees. As a special favour, the bania consented to reduce the interest to twenty-five per cent. This favour he granted me on condition that my wife and I helped him each year to harvest his crops, until the debt was paid in full. This agreement, for my wife and I to work for the bania without wages, was written on another piece of paper to which I put my thumbmark. For ten years my wife and I have helped to harvest the bania's crops and each year after the bania has made up the account and entered it on the back of the stamped paper he takes my thumb impression on the document. I do not know how much the debt has increased since I took it over. For years I was not able to pay anything towards it but since I have been working for you, I have paid five, seven and thirteen rupees, twenty-five rupees altogether.'

Budhu had never dreamed of repudiating the debt. To repudiate a debt was unthinkable: not only would it blacken his own face but what was far worse, it would blacken the reputation of his father and grandfather. So, he continued to pay what he could in cash and in labour and lived on without hope of ever liquidating the debt on his death, it would be passed on to his eldest son.

Having elicited from Budhu the information that there was a Vakil1 in the village in which the bania lived and taken his name and address, I told Budhu to return to work and said I would see what could be done with the bania. Thereafter followed a long correspondence with an advocate or lawyer. The Vakil, a stout-hearted Brahmin, who became a firm ally after the bania had insulted him by ordering him out of his house and telling him to mind his own business. From the Vakil I learnt that the *bhai khata* inherited by the bania from his father could not be produced in a court of law as evidence, for it bore the thumbmarks of men long since dead. The bania had tricked Budhu into executing a document which clearly stated that Budhu had *borrowed* one hundred and fifty rupees, at a rate of twenty-five per cent, interest. The Vakil advised me not to contest the case for the document Budhu had executed was valid and Budhu had admitted its validity by paying three installments as part interest and putting his thumbmark to these payments on the document. When I had sent the Vakil a money order in full satisfaction of the debt, plus interest at twenty-five per cent., the bania surrendered the legal document; but he refused to surrender the private agreement binding Budhu and his wife to work without wages on harvesting his crops. It was only when I threatened on Vakil's advice to prosecute for extortion that he handed the agreement over to the Vakil.

Budhu was very uneasy while these transactions were dragging on. He never spoke to me on the subject, but I could see from the way in which he looked at me whenever I passed him at work that he was speculating as to whether he had been wise in leaving me to deal with the all-powerful bania, and what his position would be if the bania suddenly appeared and demanded an explanation for his conduct. And then one day I received by registered post a heavily sealed letter containing a much thumb-marked legal document, an agreement also thumb-marked a stamped receipt for the Vakil's fees, and a letter informing me that Budhu was now a free man. The whole transaction had cost me two hundred and twenty-five rupees.

Budhu was leaving work that evening when I met him, took the documents out of the envelope, and told him to hold them while I set a match to them. 'No, Sahib, no', he said. 'You must not burn these papers for I am now your slave and God willing, I will one day pay off my debt to you.'

Not only did Budhu never smile but he was also a very silent man. When I told him that, as he would not let me burn the papers, he could keep them, he only put his hands together and touched my feet; but when he raised his head and turned to walk away, tears were ploughing furrows down his coal-grimed face.

Only one of millions freed of a debt that had oppressed three generations, but had the number been legion my pleasure could not have been greater, nor could any words have affected me more deeply than Budhu's mute gesture and the tears that blinded him as he stumbled away to tell his wife that the bania's debt had been paid and that they were free.

X. LALAJEE

The passenger steamer was late arriving from Samaria Ghat. I was standing on the landing stage, watching the passengers disembark and hurry up the ramp to the broad-gauge train, which I had arranged to detain a few minutes for them. Last to leave the steamer was a thin man with eyes sunk deep in their sockets, wearing a patched suit which in the days of long ago had been white, and carrying a small bundle tied up in a coloured handkerchief. By clutching the handrail of the gangway for support, he managed to gain the landing stage, but he turned off at the ramp, walked with slow and feeble steps to the edge of the river, and was violently and repeatedly sick. Having stooped to wash his face, he opened his bundle, took from it a sheet, spread it on the bank, and lay down with the Ganges water lapping the soles of his feet. Evidently, he had no intention of catching the train, for when the warning bell rang and the engine whistled, he made no movement. He was lying on his back, and when I told him he had missed his train he opened his sunken eyes to look up at me and said, 'I have no need of trains, Sahib, for I am dying'.

It was the mango season, the hottest time of the year, when cholera is always at its worst. When the man passed me at the foot of the gangway, I suspected he was suffering from cholera, and my suspicions were confirmed when I saw him being violently sick. In reply to my questions the man said he was travelling alone, and had no friends at Mokameh Ghat, so I helped him to his feet and led him the two hundred yards that separated my bungalow from the Ganges. Then I made him comfortable in my punkah coolie's house, which was empty, and detached from the servants' quarters.

I had been at Mokameh Ghat ten years, employing a large labour force. Some of the people lived under my supervision in houses provided by me, and the balance lived in surrounding villages. I had seen enough of cholera among my own people and also among the villagers to make me pray that if I ever contracted the hateful and foul disease some Good Samaritan would take pity on me and put a bullet through my head or give me an overdose of opium.

Few will agree with me that of the tens of thousands of people reported as having died of cholera each year at least half die not of cholera but of fear. We, who live in India, as distinct from those who visit the country for a longer or shorter period, are fatalists, believing that a man cannot die before his allotted time. This, however, does not mean that we are indifferent to epidemic diseases. Cholera is dreaded throughout the land and when it comes in epidemic form as many dies of stark fear as die of the actual disease.

There was no question that the man in my punkah coolie's house was suffering from a bad attack of cholera and if he was to survive, his faith and my crude treatment alone would pull him through, for the only medical aid within miles was a brute of a doctor as callous as he was inefficient, and whose fat oily throat I am convinced I should have one day had the pleasure of cutting had not a young probationer clerk, who had been sent to me to train, found a less messy way of removing this medico who was hated by the whole staff. This young hopeful gained the confidence of the doctor and of his wife, both of whom were thoroughly immoral and who confided to the clerk that they greatly missed the fleshpots of Egypt and the pleasures they had enjoyed before coming to Mokameh Ghat. This information set the clerk thinking and a few nights later and a little before the passenger steamer was due to leave for Samaria Ghat, a letter was delivered to the doctor, on reading which he told his wife that he had been summoned to Samaria Ghat to attend an urgent case and that he would be absent all night. He spruced himself up before leaving the house, was met outside by the clerk, and conducted in great secrecy to an empty room at the end of a block of buildings in which one of my pointsmen had died a few nights previously of coal-gas poisoning.

After the doctor had been waiting some time in the room, which had a single solid door and a small, grated window, the door opened to admit a heavily veiled figure and was then pulled to and locked on the outside.

I was returning late that night through the goods sheds and overheard part of a very animated conversation between the probationer clerk and a companion he was relieving on night duty. Next morning on my way to work I saw a crowd of men in front of the late points-man's quarters and was informed, by a most innocent looking spectator, that there appeared to be someone inside, though the door was padlocked on the outside. I told my informant to get a hammer and break the lock off and hurried away on my lawful occasions, for I had no desire to witness the discomfiture, richly as it was deserved, of the man and his wife when the door was broken open. Three entries appear in my diary for that date: '(1) Doctor and his wife left on urgent private affairs. (2) Shiv Deb probationer confirmed as a Tally Clerk on salary of twenty rupees per month. (3) Lock, points, alleged to have been run over by engine, replaced by new one.' And that was the last Mokameh Ghat ever saw of the man who was a disgrace to the honourable profession he claimed to belong to.

I could not spare much time to nurse the thin man for I already had three cholera patients on my hands. From my servants I could expect no help, for they were of a different caste to the sufferer, and further, there was no justification for exposing them to the risk of infection. However, this did not matter, provided I could instill sufficient confidence into the man that my treatment was going to make him well. To this end I made it very clear to him that I had not brought him into my compound to die and to give me the trouble of cremating him, but to make him well and that it was only with his co-operation that this could be affected. That first night I feared that in spite of our joint efforts he would die, but towards morning he rallied and from then on, his condition continued to improve and all that remained to be done was to build up his strength, which cholera drains out of the human body more quickly than any other disease. At the end of the week, he was able to give me his story.

He was a Lala, a merchant, and at one time possessed a flourishing grain business; then he made the mistake of taking as partner a man about whom he knew nothing. For a few years the business prospered, and all went well but one day when he returned from a long journey, he found the shop empty, and his partner was gone. The little money in his possession was only sufficient to meet his personal debts, and bereft of credit he had to seek employment. This he found with a merchant with whom he had traded, and for ten years he had worked on seven rupees a month, which was only sufficient to support himself and his son, his wife having died shortly after his partner robbed him. He was on his way from Muzaffarpur to Gaya, on his master's business, when he was taken ill in the train. As he got worse on board the ferry steamer, he crawled ashore to die on the banks of the sacred Ganges.

Lalajee, I never knew him by any other name, stayed with me for about a month and then one day he requested permission to continue his journey to Gaya. The request was made as we were walking through the sheds, for Lalajee was strong enough now to accompany me for a short distance each morning when I set out for work, and when I asked him what he would do if on arrival at Gaya he found his master had filled his place, he said he would try to find other employment. 'Why not try to get someone to help you to be a merchant again?' I asked; and he replied: 'The thought of being a merchant once again, and able to educate my son, is with me night and day, Sahib, but there is no one in all the world who would trust me, a servant on seven rupees a month and without any security to offer, with the five hundred rupees I should need to give me a new start.'

The train for Gaya left at 8 p.m. and when that evening I returned to the bungalow a little before that hour, I found Lalajee with freshly washed clothes and a bundle in his hand a little bigger than the one he had arrived with, waiting in the veranda to say goodbye to me. When I put a ticket for Gaya and five one-hundred-rupee notes into his hand he, like the man with the coal-grimed face, was tongue tied. All he could do was to keep glancing from the notes in his hand to my face, until the bell that warned passengers the train would leave in five minutes rang; then, putting his head on my feet, he said: 'Within one year your slave will return you this money.'

And so Lalajee left me, taking with him the greater part of my savings. That I would see him again I never doubted, for the poor of India never forget a kindness; but the promise Lalajee had made was, I felt sure, beyond his powers of accomplishment. In this I was wrong, for returning late one evening I saw a man dressed in spotless white standing in my veranda. The light from the room behind him was in my eyes, and I did not recognize him until he spoke. It was Lalajee, come a few days before the expiry of the time limit, he had set himself. That night as he sat on the floor near my chair he told me of his trading transactions, and the success that had attended them. Starting with a few bags of grain and being content with a profit of only four annas per bag he had gradually and steadily, built up his business until he was able to deal in consignments up to thirty tons in weight, on which he was making a profit of three rupees per ton. His son was in a good school and as he could now afford to keep a wife, he had married the daughter of a rich merchant of Patna; all this he had accomplished in a little under twelve months. As the time drew near for his train to leave, he laid five one-hundred-rupee notes on my knee. Then, he took a bag from his pocket, held it out to me and said, 'This is the interest, calculated at twenty-five per cent., that I owe you on the money you lent me'. I believe I deprived him of half the pleasure he had anticipated from his visit when I told him it was not our custom to accept interest from our friends.

Before leaving me Lalajee said, 'during the month I stayed with you I had talks with your servants, and with your workmen, and I learnt from them that there was a time when you were reduced to one chapati and a little dal. If such a time should ever come again, which Parmeshwar forbid, your slave will place all that he has at your feet.'

Until I left Mokameh Ghat, eleven years later, I received each year a big basket of the choicest mangoes from Lala-jee's garden, for he attained his ambition of becoming a merchant once again and returned to the home he had left when his partner robbed him.

XI. CHAMARI

Chamari, as his name implies, belonged to the lowest strata of India's sixty million Untouchables. Accompanied by his wife, an angular person whose face was stamped with years of suffering and whose two young children were clutching her torn skirts, he applied to me for work. Chamari was an undersized man with a poor physique and as he was not strong enough to work in the sheds, I put him and his wife on to trans-shipping coal. Next morning, I provided the pair of them with shovels and baskets, and they started work with courage and industry far beyond their strength. Towards evening I had to put others on to finishing their task, for the delay in unloading one of a rake of fifty wagons meant hanging up the work of several hundred labourers.

For two days Chamari and his wife laboured valiantly but ineffectively. On the third morning when, their blistered hands tied up in dirty rags, they were waiting for work to be allotted to them I asked Chamari if he could read and write. When he said that he knew a little Hindi, I instructed him to return the shovels and baskets to the store and to come to my office for orders. A few days previously I had discharged the headman of the coal gang for his inability to keep sober, the only man I ever discharged and as it was quite evident that neither Chamari nor his wife would be able to make a living at the job they were on, I decided to give Chamari a trial as a headman.

Chamari thought he had been summoned to the office to be sacked and was greatly relieved and very proud, when I handed him a new account book and a pencil and told him to take down the numbers of the rake of broad-gauge wagons from which coal was being unloaded, together with the names of the men and women who were engaged on each wagon. Half an hour later he returned with the information I had asked for, neatly entered in the book. When I had verified the correctness of these entries I handed the book back to Chamari, told him I had appointed him headman of the coal gang, at that time numbering two hundred men and women, and explained his duties to him in detail. A humble man who one short hour earlier had laboured under all the disqualifications of his lowly birth walked out of my office with a book tucked under his arm, a pencil behind his ear and for the first time in his life, his head in the air.

Chamari was one of the most conscientious and hardworking men I have ever employed. In the gang he commanded there were men and women of all castes including Brahmins, Chattris and Thakurs and never once did he offend by rendering less respect to these high-caste men and women than was theirs by birthright and never once was his authority questioned. He was responsible for keeping the individual accounts of everyone working under him and during the twenty years he worked for me the correctness of his accounts was never disputed.

On Sunday evenings Chamari and I would sit, he on a mat and I on a stool, with a great pile of copper pice between us and ringed round by coal-grimed men and women eagerly waiting for their week's wages. I enjoyed those Sunday evenings as much as did the simple hardworking people sitting round me, for my pleasure in giving them the wages they had earned with the sweat of their brows was as great as theirs in receiving them.

During the week they worked on a platform half a mile long and as some of them lived in the quarters I had built for them, while others lived in the surrounding villages, they had little opportunity for social intercourse. Sunday evenings gave them this opportunity, and they took full advantage of it. Hardworking people are always cheerful, for they have no time to manufacture imaginary troubles, which are always worse than real ones. My people were admittedly poor, and they had their full share of troubles; none the less they were full of good cheer and as I could understand and speak their language as well as they could, I was able to take part in their light-hearted banter and appreciate all their jokes.

The railway paid me by weight, and I paid my people, both those who worked in the sheds and those who worked on the coal platform at wagon rates. For work in the sheds, I paid the headmen, who in turn paid the gangs employed by them, but the men and women working on coal were paid individually by me. Chamari would change the currency notes I gave him for pice in the Mokameh bazaar and then on Sunday evenings, as we sat with the pile of pice between us he would read out the names of the men and women who had been engaged on unloading every individual wagon during the week, while I made a quick mental calculation and paid the amount due to each worker. I paid forty pice (ten annas) for the unloading of each wagon, and when the pice would not divide up equally among the number that had been engaged on unloading any particular wagon I gave the extra piece to one of their number, who would later purchase salt to be divided among them. This system of payment worked to the satisfaction of everyone, and though the work was hard, and the hours long, the wage earned was three times as much as could be earned on field work, and further, my work was permanent while field work was seasonal and temporary.

I started Chamari on a salary of fifteen rupees a month and gradually increased it to forty rupees, which was more than the majority of the clerks employed by the railway were getting, and in addition I allowed him to employ a gang of ten men to work in the sheds. In India a man's worth is assessed, to a great extent, by the money he is earning and the use he makes of it. Chamari was held in great respect by all sections of the community for the good wages he was earning, but he was held in even greater respect for the unobtrusive use he made of his money. Knowing hunger, he made it his business to see that no one whom he could succor suffered as he had suffered. All of his own lowly caste who passed his door were welcome to share his food, and those whose caste prohibited them from eating the food cooked by his wife were provided with material to enable them to prepare their own food. When at his wife's request I spoke to Chamari on the subject of keeping open house, his answer invariably was that he and his family had found the fifteen rupees per month, on which I had engaged him, sufficient for their personal requirements and that to allow his wife more than that sum now would only encourage her to be extravagant. When I asked what form her extravagance was likely to take, he said she was always nagging him about his clothes and telling him he should be better dressed than the men who were working under him, whereas he thought money spent on clothes could be better spent on feeding the poor. Then to clinch the argument he said: 'Look at yourself, Maharaj,' he had addressed me thus from the first day, and continued so to address me to the end 'you have been wearing that suit for years and if you can do that, why can't I?' As a matter of fact, he was wrong about the suit because I had two of the same material, one being cleaned of coal dust while the other was in use.

I had been at Mokameh Ghat sixteen years when Kaiser Wilhelm started his war. The railway opposed my joining up but gave their consent when I agreed to retain the contract. It was impossible to explain the implications of the war to my people at the conference to which I summoned them. However, each and every one of them was willing to carry on during my absence and it was entirely due to their loyalty and devotion that traffic through Mokameh Ghat flowed smoothly and without a single hitch during the years I was serving, first in France and later in Waziristan. Ram Saran acted as Trans-shipment Inspector during my absence and when I returned after four years, I resumed contact with my people with the pleasant feeling that I had only been away from them for a day. My safe return was attributed by them to the prayers they had offered up for me in temple and mosque and at private shrines.

The summer after my return from the war cholera was bad throughout Bengal, and at one time two women and a man of the coal gang were stricken down by the disease. Chamari and I nursed the sufferers by turns, instilling confidence into them and by sheer will power brought them through. Shortly thereafter I heard someone moving in my veranda one night, I had the bungalow to myself for Storrar had left on promotion and on my asking, who it was, a voice out of the darkness said, 'I am Chamari's wife. I have come to tell you that he has cholera'. Telling the woman to wait I hastily donned some clothes, lit a lantern and set off with her armed with a stick for Mokameh Ghat was infested with poisonous snakes.

Chamari had been at work all that day and in the afternoon had accompanied me to a nearby village in which a woman of his coal gang, by the name of Parbatti, was reported to be seriously ill. Parbatti, a widow with three children, was the first woman to volunteer to work for me when I arrived at Mokameh Ghat and for twenty years she had worked unflaggingly. Always cheerful and happy and willing to give a helping hand to any who needed it, she was the life and soul of the Sunday evening gatherings for being a widow, she could bandy words with all and sundry without offending India's very strict Mother Grundy.

The boy who brought me the news that she was ill did not know what ailed her, but was convinced that she was dying, so I armed myself with a few simple remedies and calling for Chamari on the way hurried to the village. We found Parbatti lying on the floor of her hut with her head in her grey-haired mother's lap. It was the first case of tetanus I had ever seen, and I hope the last I shall ever see. Parbatti's teeth, which would have made the fortune of a film star, had been broken in an attempt to lever them apart to give her water. She was conscious but unable to speak, and the torments she was enduring are beyond any words of mine to describe. There was nothing I could do to give her relief beyond massaging the tense muscles of her throat to try to ease her breathing, and while I was doing this, her body was convulsed as though she had received an electric shock. Mercifully her heart stopped beating and her sufferings ended. Chamari and I had no words to exchange as we walked away from the humble home in which preparations were already under way for the cremation ceremony, for though an ocean of prejudices had lain between the high-caste woman and us it had made no difference to our affection for her, and we both knew that we would miss the cheerful hardworking little woman more than either of us cared to admit. I had not seen Chamari again that evening for work had taken me to Samaria Ghat and now his wife had come to tell me he was suffering from cholera.

We in India loathe and dread cholera but we are not frightened of infection, possibly because we are fatalists, and I was not surprised therefore to find a number of men squatting on the floor round Chamari's string bed. The room was dark, but he recognized me in the light of the lantern I was carrying and said, 'Forgive the woman for having called you at this hour. 'it was 2 a.m. 'I ordered her not to disturb you until morning and she disobeyed me.' Chamari had left me, apparently in good health, ten hours previously and I was shocked to see the change those few hours had made in his appearance. Always a thin, lightly built man, he appeared to have shrunk to half his size, his eyes had sunk deep into their sockets, and his voice was weak and little more than a whisper. It was oppressively hot in the room, so I covered his partly naked body with a sheet and made the men carry the bed out into the open courtyard. It was a public place for a man suffering from cholera to be in but better a public place than a hot room in which there was not sufficient air for a man in his condition to breathe.

Chamari and I had fought many cases of cholera together and he knew, none better, the danger of panicking and the necessity for unbounded faith in the simple remedies at my command. Heroically he fought the foul disease, never losing hope and taking everything, I offered him to combat the cholera and sustain his strength. Hot as it was, he was cold, and the only way I was able to maintain any heat in his body was by placing a brazier with hot embers under his bed and getting helpers to rub powdered ginger into the palms of his hands and the soles of his feet. For forty-eight hours the battle lasted, every minute being desperately contested with death, and then the gallant little man fell into a coma, his pulse fading out and his breathing becoming hardly perceptible. From midnight to a little after 4 a.m. he lay in this condition, and I knew that my friend would never rally.

Hushed people who had watched with me during those long hours were either sitting on the ground or standing round when Chamari suddenly sat up and in an urgent and perfectly natural voice said, 'Maharaj, Maharaj! Where are you?' I was standing at the head of the bed, and when I leant forward and put my hand on his shoulder, he caught it in both of his and said, 'Maharaj, Parmeshwar is calling me, and I must go'. Then, putting his hands together and bowing his head, he said, 'Parmeshwar, I come'. He was dead when I laid him back on the bed.

Possibly a hundred people of all castes were present and heard Chamari's last words, and among them was a stranger, with sandalwood caste-marks on his forehead. When I laid the wasted frame down on the bed the stranger asked who the dead man was and, when told that he was Chamari, said: 'I have found what I have long been searching for, I am a priest of the great Vishnu temple at Kashi. My master the head priest, hearing of the good deeds of this man, sent me to find him and take him to the temple that he might have darshan of him. And now I will go back to my master and tell him Chamari is dead, and I will repeat to him the words I heard Chamari say.' Then, having laid the bundle he was carrying on the ground, and slipped off his sandals, this Brahmin priest approached the foot of the bed and made obeisance to the dead Untouchable.

There will never again be a funeral like Chamari's at Mokameh Ghat, for all sections of the community, high and low, rich, and poor, Hindu, Mohammedan, Untouchable and Christian, turned out to pay their last respects to one who had arrived friendless and weighed down with disqualifications and who left respected by all and loved by many. Chamari was a heathen, according to our Christian belief and the lowest of India's Untouchables but if I am privileged to go where he has gone, I shall be content.

XII. LIFE AT MOKAMEH GHAT

My men and I did not spend all our time at Mokameh Ghat working and sleeping. Work at the start had been very strenuous for all of us and continued to be so, but as time passed and hands hardened and back-muscles developed, we settled down in our collars, and as we were pulling in the same direction with a common object better conditions for those dependent on us, work moved smoothly and allowed of short periods for recreation. The reputation we had earned for ourselves by clearing the heavy accumulation of goods at Mokameh Ghat and thereafter keeping the traffic moving, was something that all of us had contributed towards, and all of us took a pride in having earned this reputation and were determined to retain it. When therefore an individual absented himself to attend to private affairs, his work was cheerfully performed by his companions.

One of my first undertakings, when I had a little time to myself and a few rupees in my pocket, was to start a school for the sons of my workmen, and for the sons of the lower paid railway staff. The idea originated with Ram Saran, who was a keen educationist, possibly because of the few opportunities he himself had had for education. Between us we rented a hut, installed a master and the school known ever afterwards as Ram Saran's School, started with a membership of twenty boys. Caste prejudices were the first snag we ran up against, but our master soon circum-navigated it by removing the sides of the hut. For whereas high and low-caste boys could not sit together in cold brittle air the same hut, there was no objection to their sitting in the same shed. From the very start the school was a great success, thanks entirely to Ram Saran's unflagging interest. When suitable buildings had been erected, an additional seven masters employed and the students increased to two hundred, the Government relieved us of our financial responsibilities. They raised the school to the status of a Middle School and rewarded Ram Saran, to the delight of all his friends, by conferring on him the title of Rai Sahib.

Tom Kelly, Ram Saran's opposite number on the broad-gauge railway, was a keen sportsman, and he and I started a recreation club. We cleared a plot of ground, marked out a football and a hockey ground, erected goalposts, purchased a football and hockey sticks and started to train each his own football and hockey team. The training for football was comparatively easy, but not so the training for hockey, for as our means did not run to the regulation hockey stick, we purchased what at that time was known as a Khalsa stick: this was made in the Punjab from a blackthorn or small oak tree, the root being bent to a suitable angle to form the crook. The casualties at the start were considerable, for 98 per cent of the players were bare footed, the sticks were heavy and devoid of lapping, and the ball used was made of wood. When our teams had learnt the rudiments of the two games, which amounted to no more than knowing in which direction to propel the ball, we started inter-railway matches.

The matches were enjoyed as much by the spectators as by us who took part in them. Kelly was stouter than he would have admitted to being and always played in goal for his side, or for our team when we combined to play out-station teams.

I was thin and light and played Centre forward and was greatly embarrassed when I was accidentally tripped up by foot or by hockey stick, for when this happened all the players, with the exception of Kelly, abandoned the game to set me on my feet and dust my clothes. On one occasion while I was receiving these attentions, one of the opposing team dribbled the ball down the field and was prevented from scoring a goal by the spectators, who impounded the ball and arrested the player!

Shortly after we started the recreation club the Bengal and Northwestern Railway built a club house and made a tennis court for their European staff which, including myself, numbered four. Kelly was made an honorary member of the club, and a very useful member he proved, for he was good at both billiards and tennis. Kelly and I were not able to indulge in tennis more than two or three times a month but when the day's work was done, we spent many pleasant evenings together playing billiards.

The goods sheds and sidings at Mokameh Ghat were over a mile and a half long, and to save Kelly unnecessary walking his railway provided him with a rail trolly and four men to push it. This trolley was a great joy to Kelly and myself for during the winter months, when the barheaded and greylag geese were in, and the moon was at or near the full, we trolled down the main line for nine miles to where there were a number of small tanks. These tanks, some of which were only a few yards across while others were an acre or more in extent, were surrounded by lentil crops which gave us ample cover. We timed ourselves to arrive at the tanks as the sun was setting and shortly after we had taken up our positions, Kelly at one of the tanks and I at another, we would see the geese coming.

The geese, literally tens of thousands of them, spent the day on the islands in the Ganges and in the evening left the islands to feed on the weeds in the tanks, or on the ripening wheat and grain crops beyond. After crossing the railway line, which was half-way between our positions and the Ganges, the geese would start losing height and they passed over our heads within easy range. Shooting by moonlight needs a little practice, for birds flighting overhead appear to be farther off than they actually are, and one is apt to fire too far ahead of them. When this happened, the birds, seeing the flash of the gun and hearing the report, sprang straight up in the air and before they flattened out again were out of range of the second barrel. Those winter evenings when the full moon was rising over the palm-trees that fringed the river, and the cold brittle air throbbed and reverberated with the honking of geese and the swish of their wings as they passed overhead in flights of from ten to a hundred, are among the happiest of my recollections of the years I spent at Mokameh Ghat.

My work was never dull, and time never hung heavy on my hands, for in addition to arranging for the crossing of the Ganges and the handling at Mokameh Ghat of a million tons of goods, I was responsible for the running of the steamers that ferried several hundred thousand passengers annually between the two banks of the river. The crossing of the river, which after heavy rains in the Himalayas was four to five miles wide, was always a pleasure to me, not only because it gave me time to rest my legs and have a quiet smoke but also because it gave me an opportunity of indulging in one of my hobbies, the study of human beings. The ferry was a link between two great systems of railways, one radiating north and the other radiating south, and among the seven hundred passengers who crossed at each trip were people from all parts of India, and from countries beyond her borders.

One morning I was leaning over the upper deck of the steamer watching the third-class passengers taking their seats on the lower deck. With me was a young man from England who had recently joined the railway, and who had been sent to me to study the system of work at Mokameh Ghat. He had spent a fortnight with me, and I was now accompanying him across the river to Samaria Ghat to see him off on his long railway journey to Gorakhpur. Sitting cross-legged or tailor wise on a bench next to me and also looking down on the lower deck was an Indian. Crosthwaite, my young companion was very enthusiastic about everything in the country in which he had come to serve, and as we watched the chattering crowds accommodating themselves on the open deck, he remarked that he would dearly love to know who these people were, and why they were travelling from one part of India to another. The crowd, packed like sardines, had now settled down so I said I would try to satisfy his curiosity. Let us start, I said, at the right and work round the deck, taking only the outer fringe of people who have their backs to the rail. The three men nearest to us are Brahmins, and the big copper vessels, sealed with wet clay, that they are so carefully guarding, contain Ganges water. The water on the right bank of the Ganges is considered to be more holy than the water on the left bank and these three Brahmins, servants of a well-known Maharaja, have filled the vessels on the right bank and are taking the water eighty miles by river and rail for the personal use of the Maharaja who, even when he is travelling, never uses any but Ganges water for domestic purposes. The man next to the Brahmins is a Mohammedan, a dhoonia by profession. He travels from station to station teasing the cotton in old and lumpy mattresses with the harp-like implement lying on the deck beside him. With this implement he teases old cotton until it resembles floss silk. Next to him are two Tibetan lamas who are returning from a pilgrimage to the sacred Buddhist shrine at Gaya, and who, even on this winter morning, are feeling hot, as you can see from the beads of sweat standing out on their foreheads. Next to the lamas are a group of four men returning from a pilgrimage to Benares, to their home on the foothills of Nepal. Each of the four men, as you can see, has two blown-glass jars, protected with wickerwork, slung to a short bamboo pole. These jars contain water which they have drawn from the Ganges at Benares and which they will sell drop by drop in their own and adjoining villages for religious ceremonies.

And so on round the deck until I came to the last man on the left. This man, I told Crosthwaite, was an old friend of mine, the father of one of my workmen, who was crossing the river to plough his field on the left bank.

Crosthwaite listened with great interest to all I had told him about the passengers on the lower deck, and he now asked me who the man was who was sitting on the bench near us. 'Oh', I said, 'he is a Mohammedan gentleman. A hide merchant on his way from Gaya to Muzaffarpur.' As I ceased speaking the man on the bench unfolded his legs, placed his feet on the deck and started laughing. Then turning home, he said in perfect English, 'I have been greatly entertained listening to the description you have given your friend of the men on the deck below us and also of your description of me. My tan hid my blushes for I had assumed that he did not know English. 'I believe that with one exception, myself, your descriptions were right in every case. I am a Mohammedan as you say and I am travelling from Gaya to Muzaffarpur, though how you know this I cannot think for I have not shown my railway ticket to anyone since I purchased it at Gaya. But you were wrong in describing me as a hide merchant. I do not deal in hides. I deal in tobacco.'

On occasions special trains were run for important people and in connection with these trains a special ferry steamer was run for the times of which I was responsible. I met one afternoon one of these special trains, which was conveying the Prime Minister of Nepal, twenty ladies of his household, a Secretary, and a large retinue of servants from Katmandu, the capital of Nepal, to Calcutta. As the train came to a standstill a blond-headed giant in Nepalese national dress jumped down from the train and went to the carriage in which the Prime Minister was travelling. Here the man opened a big umbrella, put his back to the door of the carriage, lifted his right arm and placed his hand on his hip. Presently the door behind him opened and the Prime Minister appeared, carrying a gold-headed cane in his hand. With practiced ease the Prime "Minister took his seat on the man's arm and when he had made himself comfortable the man raised the umbrella over the Prime Minister's head and set off. He carried his burden as effortlessly as another would have carried a celluloid doll on his 300-yard walk, over loose sand, to the steamer. When I remarked to the Secretary, with whom I was acquainted, that I had never seen a greater feat of strength, he informed me that the Prime Minister always used the blond giant in the way I had just seen him being used, when other means of transport were not available. I was told that the man was a Nepalese, but my guess was that he was a national of northern Europe who for reasons best known to himself or to his masters, had accepted service in an independent state on the borders of India.

While the Prime Minister was being conveyed to the steamer, four attendants produced a rectangular piece of black silk, some twelve feet long and eight feet wide, which they laid on the sand close to a carriage, which had all its windows closed. The rectangle was fitted with loops at the four corners, and when hooks at the ends of four eight-foot silver staves had been inserted into the loops, and the staves stood on end, the rectangle revealed itself as a box-like structure without a bottom. One end of this structure was now raised to the level of the door of the closed carriage, and out of the carriage and into the silk box stepped the twenty ladies of the Prime Minister's household. With the stave-bearers walking on the outside of the box and only the twinkling patent-leather-shod feet of the ladies showing, the procession set off for the steamer. On the lower deck of the steamer one end of the box was raised and the ladies, all of whom appeared to be between sixteen and eighteen years of age, ran lightly up the stairway on to the upper deck, where I was talking to the Prime Minister. On a previous occasion I had suggested leaving the upper deck when the ladies arrived and had been told there was no necessity for me to do so and that the silk box was only intended to prevent the common men from seeing the ladies of the household. It is not possible for me to describe in detail the dress of the ladies, and all I can say is that in their gaily coloured, tight-fitting bodices and wide-spreading trousers, in the making of each of which forty yards of fine silk had been used, they looked, as they flitted from side to side of the steamer in an effort to see all that was to be seen, like rare and gorgeous butterflies. At Mokameh Ghat the same procedure was adopted to convey the Prime Minister and his ladies from the steamer to their special train and when the whole party, and their mountain of luggage, were on board, the train steamed off on its way to Calcutta. Ten days later the party returned, and I saw them off at Samaria Ghat on their way to Katmandu.

A few days later I was working on a report that had to go in that night when my friend the Secretary walked into my office. With his clothes dirty and creased, and looking as though they had been slept in for many nights, he presented a very different appearance from the spruce and well- dressed official I had last seen in the company with the Prime Minister. He accepted the chair I offered him and said without any preamble, that he was in great trouble. The following is the story he told me.

'On the last day of our visit to Calcutta the Prime Minister took the ladies of his household to the shop of Hamilton and Co., the leading jewellers in the city and told them to select the jewels they fancied. The jewels were paid for in silver rupees for, as you know, we always take sufficient cash with us from Nepal to pay all our expenses and for everything we purchase. The selection of the jewels, the counting of the cash, the packing of the jewels into the suitcase I had taken to the shop for the purpose, and the sealing of the case by the jeweller, all took more time than we had anticipated. The result was that we had to dash back to our hotel, collect our luggage and retinue, and hurry to the station where our special train was waiting for us.

'We arrived back in Katmandu in the late evening, and the following morning the Prime Minister sent for me and asked for the suitcase containing the jewels. Every room in the palace was searched and everyone who had been on the trip to Calcutta was questioned, yet no trace of the suitcase was found, nor would anyone admit having seen it at any time. I remembered having taken it out of the motorcar that took me from the shop to the hotel, but thereafter I could not remember having seen it at any stage of the journey. I am personally responsible for the case and its contents and if it is not recovered, I may lose more than my job, for according to the laws of our land I have committed a great crime.

'There is in Nepal a hermit who is credited with second sight, and on the advice of my friends I went to him. I found the hermit, an old man in tattered clothing, living in a cave on the side of a great mountain, and to him I told my troubles. He listened to me in silence, asked no questions and told me to return the next morning. The following morning, I visited him again and he told me that as he was sleeping, the previous night he had a vision. In the vision he had seen the suitcase, with its seals intact, in a corner of a room hidden under boxes and bags of many kinds. The room was not far from a big river, had only one door leading into it, and this door was facing the east. This is all the hermits could tell me, so', the Secretary concluded, with tears in his eyes and a catch in his throat, 'I obtained permission to leave Nepal for a week and I have come to see if you can help me, for it is possible that the Ganges is the river the hermit saw in his vision.'

In the Himalayas no one doubts the ability of individuals alleged to be gifted with second sight to help in recovering property lost or mislaid. That the Secretary believed what the hermit had told him there was no question, and his anxiety now was to regain possession of the suitcase, containing jewellery valued at Rs.150,000 (£10,000), before others found and rifled it.

There were many rooms at Mokameh Ghat in which a miscellaneous assortment of goods was stored, but none of them answered the description given by the hermit. I did, however, know of one room that answered the description and this room was the parcel office at Mokameh Junction, two miles from Mokameh Ghat. Having borrowed Kelly's trolly, I sent the Secretary to the Junction with Ram Saran. At the parcel office the clerk in charge denied all knowledge of the suitcase but he raised no objection to the pile of luggage in the office being taken out on to the platform, and when this had been done, the suitcase was revealed with all its seals intact.

The question then arose as to how the case came to be in the office without the clerk's knowledge. The station master now came on the scene and his inquiries elicited the fact that the suitcase had been put in the office by a carriage sweeper, the lowest-paid man on the staff. This man had been ordered to sweep out the train in which the Prime Minister had travelled from Calcutta to Mokameh Ghat and tucked away under the seat in one of the carriages he had found the suitcase. When his task was finished, he carried the suitcase a distance of a quarter of a mile to the platform, and there being no one on the platform at the time to whom he could hand over the case he had put it in a corner of the parcel office. He expressed regret and asked for forgiveness if he had done anything wrong.

Bachelors and their servants, as a rule, get into more or less set habits and my servants and I were no exception to the rule. Except when work was heavy, I invariably returned to my house at 8 p.m. and when my house servant, waiting on the veranda, saw me coming he called to the waterman to lay my bath, for whether it was summer or winter I always had a hot bath. There were three rooms at the front of the house opening onto the veranda: a dining room, a sitting room, and a bedroom. Attached to the bedroom was a small bathroom, ten feet long and six wide's. This bathroom had two doors and one small window. One of the doors opened onto the veranda and the other led to the bedroom. The window was opposite the bedroom door and set high up in the outer wall of the house. The furniture of the bathroom consisted of an egg-shaped wooden bath, long enough to sit in, a wooden bathmat with holes in it and two earthen vessels containing cold water. After the waterman had laid the bath, my servant would bolt the outer door of the bathroom and on his way through the bedroom pick up the shoes I had discarded and take them to the kitchen to clean. There he would remain until I called for dinner.

One night after my servant had gone to the kitchen I took a small hand-lamp off the dressing table, went into the bathroom, and there placed it on a low wall, six inches high and nine inches wide, which ran half-way across- the width of the room. Then I turned and bolted the door, which like most doors in India sagged on its hinges and would not remain shut unless bolted. I had spent most of that day on the coal platform so did not spare the soap, and with a lather on my head and face that did credit to the manufacturers I opened my eyes to replace the soap on the bath-mat and, to my horror, saw the head of a snake projecting up over the end of the bath and within a few inches of my toes. My movements while soaping my head and splashing the water about had evidently annoyed the snake, a big cobra, for its hood was expanded and its long-forked tongue was flicking in and out of its wicked-looking mouth. The right thing for me to have done would have been to keep my hands moving, draw my feet away from the snake, and moving very slowly stand up and step backwards to the door behind me, keeping my eyes on the snake all the time. But what I very foolishly did was to grab the sides of the bath and stand up and step backwards, all in one movement, on to the low wall. On this cemented wall my foot slipped, and while trying to regain my balance a stream of water ran off my elbow onto the wick of the lamp and extinguished it, plunging the room in pitch darkness. So here I was shut in a small dark room with one of the deadliest snakes in India. One step to the left or one step to the rear would have taken me to either of the two doors, but not knowing where the snake was, I was frightened to move for fear of putting my bare foot on it. Moreover, both doors were bolted at the bottom, and even if I avoided stepping on the snake I should have felt about for the bolts where the snake, in his efforts to get out of the room, was most likely to be.

The servants' quarters were in a corner of the compound fifty yards away on the dining-room side of the house, so shouting to them would be of no avail, and my only hope of rescue was that my servant would get tired of waiting for me to call for dinner, or that a friend would come to see me, and I devoutly hoped this would happen before the cobra bit me. The fact that the cobra was as much trapped as I was in no way comforted me, for only a few days previously one of my men had had a similar experience. He had gone into his house in the early afternoon in order to put away the wages I had just paid him. While he was opening his box, he heard a hiss behind him and turning round saw a cobra advancing towards him from the direction of the open door. Backing against the wall behind him, for there was only one door to the room, the unfortunate man had tried to fend off the cobra with his hands, and while doing so was bitten twelve times on hands and on legs. Neighbours heard his cries and came to his rescue, but he died a few minutes later.

I learnt that night that small things can be more nerve-racking and terrifying than big happenings. Every drop of water that trickled down my legs was converted in my imagination into the long-forked tongue of the cobra licking my bare skin, a prelude to the burying of his fangs in my flesh.

How long I remained in the room with the cobra I cannot say. My servant said later that it was only half an hour, and no sound has ever been more welcome to me than the sounds I heard as my servant laid the table for dinner. I called him to the bathroom door, told him of my predicament, and instructed him to fetch a lantern and a ladder. After another long wait I heard a babel of voices, followed by the scraping of the ladder against the outer wall of the house. When the lantern had been lifted to the window ten feet above ground, it did not illuminate the room, so I told the man who was holding it to break a pane of glass and pass the lantern through the opening. The opening was too small for the lantern to be passed upright. However, after it had been relit three times it was finally inserted into the room and feeling that the cobra was behind me, I turned my head and saw it lying at the bottom of the bedroom door two feet away. Leaning forward very slowly, I picked up the heavy bathmat, raised it high and let it fall as the cobra was sliding over the floor towards me. Fortunately, I judged my aim accurately and the bathmat crashed down on the cobra's neck six inches from its head. As it bit at the wood and lashed about with its tail, I took a hasty stride to the veranda door and in a moment was outside among a crowd of men, armed with sticks and carrying lanterns, for word had got round to the railway quarters that I was having a life-and-death struggle with a big snake in a locked room.

The pinned-down snake was soon dispatched, and it was not until the last of the men had gone, leaving their congratulations, that I realized I had no clothes on and that my eyes were full of soap. How the snake came to be in the bathroom I never knew. It may have entered by one of the doors, or it may have fallen from the roof, which was made of thatch and full of rats and squirrels and tunneled with sparrows' nests. Anyway, the servants who had laid my bath and I had much to be thankful for, for we approached that night very near the gate of the Happy Hunting Grounds.

We at Mokameh Ghat observed no Hindu or Mohammedan holidays, for no matter what the day was work had to go on. There was, however, one day in the year that all of us looked forward to with anticipation and great pleasure, and that day was Christmas. On this day custom ordained that I should remain in my house until ten o'clock, and punctually at this hour Ram Saran dressed in his best clothes and wearing an enormous pink silk turban, specially kept for the occasion would present himself to conduct me to my office. Our funds did not run to bunting, but we had a large stock of red and green signal flags, and with these flags and strings of marigold and jasmine flowers, Ram Saran, and his band of willing helpers, working from early morning, had given the office and its surroundings a gay and festive appearance. Near the office door a table and a chair were set and, on the table, stood a metal pot containing a bunch of my best roses tied round with twine as tight as twine could be tied. Ranged in front of the table were the railway staff, my headmen and all my labourers. And all were dressed in clean clothes, for no matter how dirty we were during the rest of the year on Christmas Day we had to be clean.

After I had taken my seat on the chair and Ram Saran had put a garland of jasmine round my neck, the proceedings started with a long speech by Ram Saran, followed by a short one by me. Sweets were then distributed to the children, and after this messy proceeding was over to the satisfaction of all concerned the real business of the day started, the distribution of a cash bonus to Ram Saran, to the staff and to the labourers. The rates I received for my handling contract were woefully small, but even so, by the willing co-operation of all concerned, I did make a profit and eighty percent of this profit was distributed on Christmas Day. Small as this bonus was in the good years it amounted to no more than a month's pay or a month's earnings, it was greatly appreciated and the goodwill and willing co-operation it ensured enabled me to handle a million tons of goods a year for twenty-one years without one single unpleasant incident and without one single day's stoppage of work.

LIST OF TITLES WITH ISBN NO.

ISBN	TITLE
9788194914129	1984
9789390575220	1984 & Animal Farm (2In1)
9789390575572	1984 & Animal Farm (2In1): The International Best-Selling Classics
9789390575848	35 Sonnets
9789390575329	A Clergyman's Daughter
9789390575923	A Study In Scarlet
9789390896097	A Tale Of Two Cities
9789390896837	Abide in Christ
9789390896202	Abraham Lincoln
9789390896912	Absolute Surrender
9789390896608	African American Classic Collection
9789390575305	Aldous Huxley: The Collected Works
9789390896141	An Autobiography of M. K. Gandhi
9789390575886	Animal Farm
9789390575619	Animal Farm & The Great Gatsby (2In1)
9789390575626	Animal Farm & We
9789390896158	Anna Karenina
9789390575534	Antic Hay
9789390896165	Antony & Cleopatra
9789390896172	As I Lay Dying
9789390896226	As You like it
9789390575671	At Your Command
9789390575350	Awakened Imagination
9789390575114	Be What You Wish
9789390896233	Believe In yourself
9789390896998	Best of Charles Darwin: The Origin of Species & Autobiography
9789390896684	Best Of Horror : Dracula And Frankenstein
9789390575503	Best Of Mark Twain (The Adventures of Tom Sawyer AND The Adventures of Huckleberry Finn)
9789390896769	Black History Collection
9789390575756	Brave New World, Animal Farm & 1984 (3in1)
9789390896240	Brother Karamzov
9789390575053	Bulleh Shah Poetry
9789390575725	Burmese Days

9789390896257	Bushido
9789390896066	Can't Hurt Me
9788194914112	Chanakya Neeti: With The Complete Sutras
9789390896042	Crime and Punishment
9789390575527	Crome Yellow
9789390575046	Down and Out in Paris and London
9789390896844	Dracula
9789390575442	Emersons Essays: The Complete First & Second Series (Self-Reliance & Other Essays)
9789390575749	Emma
9789390575817	Essential Tozer Collection - The Pursuit of God & The Purpose of Man
9789390896578	Fascism What It Is and How to Fight It
9789390575688	Feeling is the Secret
9789390575190	Five Lessons
9789390575954	Frankenstein
9789390575237	Franz Kafka: Collected Works
9789390575282	Franz Kafka: Short Stories
9789390575060	George Orwell Collected Works
9789390575077	George Orwell Essays
9789390575213	George Orwell Poems
9788194914150	Greatest Poetry Ever Written Vol 1
9788194914143	Greatest Poetry Ever Written Vol 1
9789390896301	Gulliver's Travel
9789390575961	Gunaho Ka Devta
9789390575893	H. P. Lovecraft Selected Stories Vol 1
9789390575978	H. P. Lovecraft Selected Stories Vol 2
9789390896059	Hamlet
9789390575022	His Last Bow: Some Reminiscences of Sherlock Holmes
9789390896134	History of Western Philosophy
9789390575121	Homage To Catalonia
9789390896219	How to develop self-confidence and Improve public Speaking
9789390896295	How to enjoy your life and your Job
9789390575633	How to own your own mind
9789390896318	How to read Human Nature
9789390896325	How to sell your way through the life
9789390896370	How to use the laws of mind
9789390896387	How to use the power of prayer

9789390896028	How to win friends & Influence People
9788194824176	How To Win Friends and Influence People
9789390896103	Humility The Beauty of Holiness
9789390896653	Imperialism the Highest Stage of Capitalism
9789390575084	In Our Time
9789390575169	In Our Time & Three Stories and Ten poems
9789390575145	James Allen: The Collected Works
9789390896189	Jesus Himself
9789390575480	Jo's Boys
9789390896394	Julius Caesar
9789390575404	Keep the Aspidistra Flying
9789390896400	Kidnapped
9789390896424	King Lear
9789390575824	Lady Susan
9789390896455	Law of Success
9789390896264	Lincoln The Unknown
9789390575565	Little Men
9789390575640	Little Women
9788194914174	Lost Horizon
9789390896462	Macbeth
9789390896929	Man Eaters of Kumaon
9789390896523	Man The Dwelling Place of God
9789390896349	Man The Dwelling Place of God
9789390575909	Mansfield Park
9788194914136	Manto Ki 25 Sarvshreshth Kahaniya
9789390896509	Marxism, Anarchism, Communism
9789390575664	Mathematical Principles of Natural Philosophy
9788194914198	Meditations
9789390575800	Mein Kampf
9789390575794	Memory How To Develop, Train, And Use It
9789390896486	Mind Power
9789390896585	Money
9789390575039	Mortal Coils
9789390575770	My Life and Work
9789390896035	Narrative of the Life of Frederick Douglass
9789390575152	Neville Goddard: The Collected Works
9789390575985	Northanger Abbey
9789390896530	Notes From Underground

9789390896547	Oliver Twist
9789390575459	On War
9789390575541	One, None and a Hundred Thousand
9789390896554	Othelo
9789390575435	Out Of This World
9789390575015	Persuasion
9789390575510	Prayer The Art Of Believing
9789390575091	Pride and Prejudice
9789390896561	Psychic Perception
9789390575381	Rabindranath Tagore - 5 Best Short Stories Vol 2
9789390575367	Rabindranath Tagore - Short Stories (Masters Collections Including The Childs Return)
9789390575374	Rabindranath Tagore 5 Best Short Stories Vol 1 (Including The Childs Return
9789390896622	Romeo & Juliet
9789390896127	Sanatana Dharma
9789390575596	Seedtime & Harvest
9789390896639	Selected Stories of Guy De Maupassant
9789390575206	Self-Reliance & Other Essays
9789390575176	Sense and Sensibility
9789390575299	Shyamchi Aai
9789390896738	Socialism Utopian and Scientific
9789390896646	Success Through a Positive Mental Attitude
9789390575428	The Adventures of Huckleberry Finn
9789390575183	The Adventures of Sherlock Holmes
9789390575343	The Adventures of Tom Sawyer
9789390896691	The Alchemy Of Happiness
9789390575862	The Art Of Public Speaking
9789390896288	The Autobiography Of Charles Darwin
9788194914181	The Best of Franz Kafka: The Metamorphosis & The Trial
9789390575008	The Call Of Cthulhu and Other Weird Tales
9789390575107	The Case-Book of Sherlock Holmes
9789390896110	The Castle Of Otranto
9789390896745	The Communist Manifesto
9789390575589	The Complete Fiction of H. P. Lovecraft
9789390575497	The Complete Works of Florence Scovel Shinn
9789390896820	The Conquest of Breard
9789390896813	The Diary of a Young Girl

9789390896332	The Diary of a Young Girl The Definitive Edition of the Worlds Most Famous Diary
9789390575701	The Great Gatsby, Animal Farm & 1984 (3In1)
9789390575312	The Greatest Works Of George Orwell (5 Books) Including 1984 & Non-Fiction
9789390575992	The Hound of Baskervilles
9789390896707	The Idiot
9789390896714	The Invisible Man
9789390575657	The Knowledge of the holy
9789390575558	The Law & the Promise
9789390896721	The Law Of Attraction
9789390896776	The Leader in you
9789390896363	The Life of Christ
9789390896196	The Man-Eating Leopard of Rudraprayag
9789390896783	The Master Key to Riches
9789390575268	The Memoirs Of Sherlock Holmes
9789390896479	The Midsummer Night's Dream
9789390575466	The Mill On The Floss
9789390896790	The Miracles of your mind
9789390896660	The Mutual Aid A Factor in Evolution
9789390896448	The Origin of Species
9789390896905	The Peter Kropotkin Anthology The Conquest of Bread & Mutual Aid A Factor of Evolution
9789390896806	The Picture of Dorian Gray
9789390896271	The Picture of Dorian Gray
9789390575275	The Power Of Awareness
9789390896356	The Power of Concentration
9788194824169	The Power of Positive Thinking
9789390575411	The Power of the Spoken Word
9788194914105	The Power Of Your Subconscious Mind
9789390896899	The Power of Your Subconscious Mind
9789390896417	The Principles of Communism
9789390575787	The Psychology Of Mans Possible Evolution
9789390896615	The Psychology of Salesmanship
9789390575732	The Pursuit of God
9789390575398	The Pursuit of Happiness
9789390896851	The Quick and Easy Way to effective Speaking
9789390575947	The Return Of Sherlock Holmes

9789390575138	The Road To Wigan Pier
9789390896981	The Root of the Righteous
9789390575855	The Science Of Being Well
9788194914167	The Science Of Getting Rich, The Science Of Being Great & The Science Of Being Well (3In1)
9789390896011	The Screwtape Letters
9789390896073	The Screwtape Letters
9789390575336	The Secret Door to Success
9789390575695	The Secret Of Imagining
9789390896868	The Secret Of Success
9789390896431	The Seven Last Words
9789390575930	The Sign of the Four
9789390896004	The Sonnets
9789390896516	The Souls of Black Folk
9789390896875	The Sound and The Fury
9789390575244	The State and Revolution
9789390896882	The Story of My Life
9789390896936	The Story Of Oriental Philosophy
9789390896752	The Strange Case of Dr. Jekyll and Mr. Hyde
9789390896943	The Tempest
9789390575916	The Valley Of Fear
9789390575879	The Wind in the willows
9789390896080	The Wind in the willows
9789390575763	Their eyes were watching gofd
9789390575831	Three Stories
9789390896950	Twelfth Night
9789390896592	Twelve Years a Slave
9789390896677	Up from Slavery
9789390896974	Value Price and Profit
9789390896967	Wake Up and Live
9789390896493	With Christ in the School of Prayer
9789390575602	Your Faith is Your Fortune
9789390575473	Your Infinite Power To Be Rich
9789390575251	Your Word is Your Wand
9789390575718	Youth
9789391316099	A Christmas Carol
9789391316105	A Doll's House
9789391316501	A Passage to India

9789391316709	A Portrait of the Artist as a Young Man
9789391316112	A Tale of Two Cities
9789391316747	A Tear and a Smile
9789391316167	Agnes Gray
9789391316174	Alice's Adventures in Wonderland
9789391316136	Anandamath
9789391316181	Anne Of Green Gables
9789391316754	Anthem
9789391316198	Around The World in 80 Days
9789391316013	As A Man Thinketh
9789391316242	Autobiography of a Yogi
9789391316266	Beyond Good and Evil
9789391316761	Bleak House
9789391316778	Chitra, a Play in One Act
9789391316310	David Copperfield
9789391316075	Demian
9789391316785	Dubliners
9789391316051	Favourite Tales from the Arabian Nights
9789391316235	Gitanjali
9789391316068	Gravity
9789391316150	Great Speeches of Abraham Lincoln
9789391316662	Guerilla Warfare
9789391316839	Kim
9789391316822	Mother
9789391316211	My Childhood
9789391316846	Nationalism
9789391316327	Oliver Twist
9789391316853	Pygmalion
9789391316334	Relativity: The Special and the General Theory
9789391316389	Scientific Healing Affirmation
9789391316341	Sons and Lovers
9789391316587	Tales from India
9789391316372	Tess of The D'Urbervilles
9789391316396	The Awakening and Selected Stories
9789391316402	The Bhagvad Gita
9789391316303	The Book of Enoch
9789391316228	The Canterville Ghost
9789391316907	The Dynamic Laws of Prosperity

9789391316006	The Great Gatsby
9789391316860	The Hungry Stones and Other Stories
9789391316433	The Idiot
9789391316440	The Importance of Being Earnest
9789391316297	The Light of Asia
9789391316914	The Madman His Parables and Poems
9789391316457	The Odyssey
9789391316921	The Picture of Dorian Gray
9789391316464	The Prince
9789391316938	The Prophet
9789391316945	The Republic
9789391316518	The Scarlet Letter
9789391316143	The Seven Laws of Teaching
9789391316525	The Story of My Experiments with Truth
9789391316532	The Tales of the Mother Goose
9789391316549	The Thirty Nine Steps
9789391316594	The Time Machine
9789391316600	The Turn of the Screw
9789391316983	The Upanishads
9789391316617	The Yellow Wallpaper
9789391316426	The Yoga Sutras of Patanjali
9789391316990	Ulysses
9789391316624	Utopia
9789391316679	Vanity Fair
9789391316020	What Is To Be Done
9789391316686	Within A Budding Grove
9789391316693	Women in Love